MURDER OF Mercy

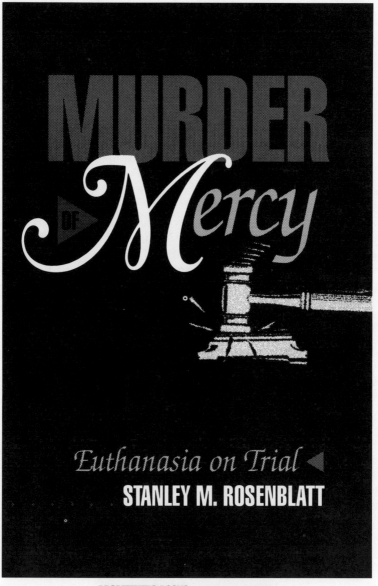

MURDER OF Mercy

Euthanasia on Trial ◀
STANLEY M. ROSENBLATT

PROMETHEUS BOOKS • BUFFALO, NEW YORK

For Susan,

without whose love, encouragement, and input
this book would have remained merely a concept.

Published 1992 by Prometheus Books

Murder of Mercy: Euthanasia on Trial. Copyright © 1992 by Stanley M. Rosenblatt.
All rights reserved. No part of this publication may be reproduced, stored in
a retrieval system, or transmitted in any form or by any means, electronic,
mechanical, photocopying, recording, or otherwise, without prior written permission of the publisher, except in the case of brief quotations embodied in critical
articles and reviews. Inquiries should be addressed to Prometheus Books, 59 John
Glenn Drive, Buffalo, New York 14228-2197, 716-837-2475/FAX: 716-835-6901.

96 95 94 93 92   5 4 3 2 1

Library of Congress Cataloging-in-Publication Data

Rosenblatt, Stanley M., 1936–
    Murder of mercy : euthanasia on trial / Stanley M. Rosenblatt.
        p.   cm.
    ISBN 0-87975-772-8
    1. Rosier, Peter—Trials, litigation, etc. 2. Trials (Murder)—Florida—
St. Petersburg. 3. Trials (Euthanasia)—Florida—St. Petersburg. I. Title.
KF224.R67R67   1992
345.759′6302523—dc20
[347.5963052523]   92-25910
                                                              CIP

Printed in the United States of America on acid-free paper.

Contents

1

Who Killed Patricia Rosier?

Patricia Rosier, a beautiful forty-three-year-old wife and mother of two, died at her home in Fort Myers, Florida, on January 15, 1986. Patricia had been diagnosed with lung cancer in April 1985, and by January 1986 the cancer had metastasized to her brain and adrenal glands. In November 1987, Dr. Peter Rosier, Patricia's husband and a prominent physician, was indicted by a Lee County grand jury and charged with the premeditated first degree murder of his wife. Under Florida law Peter faced death in the electric chair.

How could this happen? How does a loving husband and father get charged with first degree murder? Very easily, under the American legal system. Whether one calls it "mercy killing," "euthanasia," "assisting a suicide," or simply "hastening the death of a terminally ill patient"—the act is illegal in Florida and is against the laws of every other state as well.

It is certainly not unusual for physicians or loving family members to hasten the death of a terminally ill patient; the vast majority of perpetrators of these "crimes" are never prosecuted. Dr. Rosier was singled out because he granted an interview to the Fort Myers NBC affiliate, WBBH Channel 20, and openly admitted that he helped end his wife's life. That candid interview, which Peter naively thought would further the cause of euthanasia in this country, resulted in his prosecution for first degree murder.

Patricia Rosier's body had been cremated. Although many people suspected suicide or the administration of drugs by Dr. Rosier to end his wife's suffering, no one dreamed of reporting these actions to any legal authority. The Rosiers had been very open with relatives and friends about their joint suicide pact.

Peter knew as a board-certified pathologist, who had performed many autopsies, that doctors frequently hastened or caused death in order to end what they considered to be pointless suffering, often at the family's request, either express or implied. Several people, including physicians, knew of the details of Peter's direct involvement in his wife's death. Nonetheless, the odds were against any legal repercussions absent Peter voluntarily making a public confession. That is precisely what he did, not once but twice. He confessed in a manuscript he had written and he confessed again in the television interview with WBBH. According to the state attorney of Lee County, Joseph D'Alessandro, and the criminal statutes of the State of Florida, Dr. Peter Rosier confessed to murder.

Peter said on television: "I administered something to her to terminate her life. . . ."

In his manuscript, titled "The Lady," Peter was more explicit: "I gave her two injections of morphine. . . . I inserted four morphine suppositories into the rectum of my love."

Channel 20 displayed the most incriminating portions of the manuscript directly on the screen during Peter's interview. When the television interviewer asked Peter if he was aware of the criminal consequences of what he was saying, Peter responded—"I will challenge the law." Peter went further in his manuscript stating: "I fully understood the implications of what I was doing. I understood the legalities, but I did not care. I did not care if the world knew what I did."

The world was to learn of what he did soon enough since his television appearance received national and international media attention. Shortly after the television interview aired, Peter contacted Derek Humphry, the executive director of the National Hemlock Society. Humphry became intensely interested in Peter's case and attended the lengthy trial in Florida from beginning to end.

The day after Peter's television appearance the state attorney called a press conference and announced that he was commencing an investigation into the circumstances of Patricia Rosier's death. As an elected public official the chief prosecuting attorney for several counties in southwest Florida had few practical options; he had to react to Peter's "challenge of the law." And this was particularly so in a conservative area such as Fort Myers, where there was tremendous pressure against allowing "mercy killers" to go unpunished. This pressure was also national: in recent years there has been an upward trend in the prosecution of mercy killers in the United States.

That investigation led to a grand jury indictment charging Dr. Rosier with first degree murder and conspiracy to commit first degree murder, crimes punishable by death in Florida's electric chair. The state attorney had the option to charge Peter with far less serious crimes, such as assisting a self-murder (suicide), but he chose to go for the maximum. Invariably grand juries follow the recommendations of their legal advisor—in this case the state attorney or his assistants. It is a myth that grand juries function as independent bodies; in reality they are an instrument of the will of the presiding state attorney.

Although I was representing the Rosiers in a civil matter, I was not Peter's defense counsel until after his grand jury indictment. My first contact with Peter and Patricia Rosier was in early November 1985 when Peter called me in Miami, Florida. He stated he was the former chief of pathology at Lee Memorial Hospital and wanted to speak to me about a lawsuit against that very hospital and his wife's former internist, Dr. David Bernstein. Peter explained that there had been a six-month delay in diagnosing Patricia's lung cancer. According to Peter, Patricia should have had a chest X-ray in October 1984 when she was seen by Dr. Bernstein and complained of sudden weight loss, nausea, and excessive sweating.

When a sizeable lung tumor was diagnosed in late April 1985, Peter stated that the slides of the tumor were mishandled by employees of Lee Memorial Hospital and this delayed the proper treatment of Patricia's unusual cancer. Had Peter not been a physician, I would have immediately turned the case down. I was accepting very few medical malpractice actions; cancer cases are generally difficult to prove; and a six-month delay in diagnosing lung cancer would not make much difference with this deadly disease.

Lung cancer, even when diagnosed early and treated perfectly, has a poor prognosis. Patricia's lung tumor was extremely rare and Peter contended that the hospital was negligent in failing to properly preserve specimen tissue, thereby making accurate diagnosis and treatment far more difficult. Peter and Patricia traveled to America's leading medical centers during her illness trying to get a precise handle on the nature of the tumor and what to do to decrease the likelihood of its spread. They traveled to Sloan Kettering in New York, to the Yale Medical School, to M.D. Anderson Hospital in Houston, to the Mayo Clinic, and to Johns Hopkins. They received differing diagnoses and advice, and ultimately decided on a course of chemotherapy. In spite of the therapy the cancer spread to Patricia's brain by late October 1985. It may have actually spread far earlier, but by October it had finally reached a size at which the tumors could be viewed on a Computerized Axial Tomographer (CAT-scan), which is capable of precise visualization at any level of a bodily organ and is an extremely valuable tool in diagnosing cancer.

Radiotherapy was administered in the hope of eradicating the brain tumors. In spite of the horrors of this treatment, huge adrenal masses were discovered on January 10, 1986. The cancerous tumors were far larger than the adrenal glands themselves. Five days later Patricia Rosier was dead. Ten months following her death, Peter confessed on television.

The progress of Patricia's disease demonstrated that her original lung tumor was aggressive and would have inevitably metastasized in spite of early diagnosis and treatment. Of course, when Peter contacted me I had no way of knowing that, although metastasis is the usual scenario with lung cancer. I agreed to investigate the case because I was intrigued to meet the Rosiers and learn why a very successful physician would be willing to take on the medical community.

Patricia's condition continued to deteriorate so we arranged to have her testimony taken as a video deposition in late December 1985, only weeks before her death. In this way, her last words could be entered into evidence in open court.

I learned from the Rosiers how Patricia had been very upbeat and courageous during her battle against cancer. She had agreed to appear on local television, to shave her head and receive chemotherapy before the TV camera, and she spoke openly about all aspects of her disease. As her illness progressed, Patricia and Peter developed a close relationship with the local news reporter, Leisa Zigman, who conducted interviews with them. Patricia even agreed to an interview with Leisa on January 14, 1986, the day before she died.

I was not aware that during the fall of 1985 Peter and Patricia had formed a suicide pact; they had met with estate and tax lawyers to dispose of their sizeable holdings; and Peter had started receiving disability income. When I learned of Patricia's death on January 15, 1986, I wasn't aware that the immediate family had gathered at the Rosier home the day before for a final dinner at which they openly discussed Patricia's anticipated death later that night.

Peter not only incriminated himself during his TV confession, he also incriminated physician friends and family members who had provided support in Patricia's decision to take her life. By going public, Peter alienated most of Fort Myers as well as Patricia's extended family.

I had no fixed opinions on the practical aspects of mercy killing, but I did have both moral and religious objections in the abstract. I told Peter to hire a criminal attorney to advise him about the grand jury proceeding. I had a very busy trial schedule and anticipated that Peter would simply get a slap on the wrist; either no charges would be filed or only relatively minor ones. I was shocked to learn that the grand jury, after hearing seven days of testimony from numerous witnesses, including physicians who provided complex medical opinions, needed only five minutes of "deliberation" before deciding to put Peter on trial for his life. The members of the jury treated him like some serial murderer or a career criminal who robbed a supermarket and killed a clerk, rather than as a devoted husband of twenty-two years who was motivated by love and compassion.

I suppose I should not have been surprised since Florida law makes no distinction between killing for hire and terminating a loved one's life in order to end misery or to comply with the person's wishes. I was generally aware of the positions for and against the controversial act of euthanasia, but I certainly was not a student of the subject. I had never represented anyone who was even remotely involved in such a situation. Yet I knew it was somehow absurd to talk about Charles Manson, Ted Bundy, and Peter Rosier in the same breath.

Following his indictment for first degree murder Peter was arrested and incarcerated at the Lee County Jail: in their wisdom, the Lee County judiciary and passionate State Attorney's Office initially did not wish to permit bond, in the hope of keeping this "killer" in jail.

Peter called me several times from the Lee County Jail asking me to represent him. I had serious misgivings, both because of religious objections to his conduct and a burdensome trial schedule over the next several months. I understood Peter well enough to know the very broad implications that this case might have, the possible adverse consequences to Peter and his children, and that agreeing to represent him would be an all-consuming endeavor.

I recommended some outstanding criminal lawyers and he actually met with a few of them while still incarcerated. Peter had not been happy with the two experienced criminal defense attorneys who represented him at his bond hearing, and he was likewise uncomfortable with the lawyers he met in prison. They seemed to regard his situation as rather straight-forward, a business-as-usual murder case; they could not relate to the larger issues that Peter was interested in and were all anxious to avoid the philo-sophical and moral issues posed by euthanasia.

At the time Peter's case came to my attention, my wife and law partner, Susan, and I were the parents of six young children. We have been blessed with two more since the Rosier trial concluded. Accepting Peter's case would mean long absences from the children, in addition to which I hate to travel and try out-of-town cases since I do not handle change and new surroundings well.

Susan had an absolute veto power over my decision since she would be at counsel table with me throughout the trial. Susan had been an editor of law review while in law school; she is a legal scholar and appellate specialist. I am the fact part of the team; she is the law part. I question witnesses, cross examine, and make the final argument. When legal objections are made to admit or exclude evidence, Susan makes them; when legal arguments are made outside the presence of the jury Susan makes those as well. There was never a though in my mind of my going to Fort Myers without her.

Peter was very persistent. In listening to him I learned much about his and Patricia's background; I read his long manuscript and we developed a decent rapport. The personalities involved were intriguing; the facts were complex and fascinating; the legal, medical, and ethical issues were profound. We were in!

Peter was a superbly qualified pathologist, board certified in four subspecialty areas of this complex field of medicine. Pathologists are the men and women who perform autopsies and study tissues and organs removed by surgeons. Cancer is an everyday part of their lives. For him to face the prospect of death by execution made me shudder. Neither of us could relate to a legal system or a grand jury whose members could charge him with first degree murder.

I agreed to do everything within my power to turn this absurd situation around and win him his freedom. The state had a ten-month head start in its investigation. With much reluctance Susan agreed to join me, with the proviso that we would rent a private plane so we could leave the trial early enough on Fridays to be home for the Sabbath and spend the weekends with our children.

As Dr. Rosier's defense counsel I had to immerse myself in the literature and legal cases relating to euthanasia. I learned that there were no loopholes in the law. According to Florida statutes, it does not matter that a victim may be terminally ill with an extremely limited life expectancy; nor does it matter that the victim is in great pain and wants to die, and even expressly requests the assistance of a loved one. Consent by the victim is simply not a legal defense to ending a life.

Hastening death by any means whatsoever, even if only by minutes, is considered to be murder under Florida law, and the most loving and compassionate motives are not a legal defense. My son Joshua, who was then six years old, asked me whether it would be a crime to kill someone on death row as he was being strapped into Florida's electric chair. The answer clearly is yes, and the crime could well be first degree murder.

The criminal statutes that apply in a so-called mercy-killing case are a prosecutor's dream. Our trial judge, James R. Thompson, was a former prosecutor who had worked for this very same state attorney, Joseph D'Alessandro, for years. Hardly my idea of ideal casting. D'Alessandro was a very powerful figure in southwest Florida, virtually owning the public office he had served in for nearly twenty years and for which he usually ran unopposed.

Any defense lawyer worth his salt would want to argue to a jury that to follow the law in a rigid, technical sense would result in a profound injustice in this particular case. They could be putting in the electric chair a superbly trained physician, a productive member of society, who had never committed any other "crime" and who was in no way a threat to anyone. I assumed Peter would escape the death penalty, the other penalty for conviction of first degree murder in Florida being life imprisonment without the possibility of parole for twenty-five years. Peter much preferred the chair.

I would argue to the jury that that would be an insane result. Patricia Rosier was dying of cancer; she was intelligent and strong willed; she wanted to die at a moment of her own choosing; she did not wish to allow nature to take its cruel course. Instead, she wanted her husband of twenty-two years and the father of their two children to be with her and to assist her during her final leave-taking.

How could Peter Rosier refuse such a request from his beloved wife after chemotherapy and radiotherapy had failed, and after her lung cancer had spread to her brain and adrenal glands? She had valiantly battled the disease for more than eight months and she had lost. Patricia was in pain and was vomiting constantly. Was her husband to be punished for complying with her last request? Was their decision anything other than the personal exercise of a family's ultimate civil right?

Should Peter have abandoned his life's companion because legislators throughout our country have lacked the wisdom and strength to distinguish between the Ted Bundys of this world and the Peter Rosiers? Certainly not! When the law conflicts with common sense, common decency, and simple fairness and justice, it is the law that must yield. The jury should not get hung up on the nomenclature of obscure statutes; rather, they should deliberate and do the right thing, the decent thing—set Dr. Rosier free and restore him to his son and daughter who have already lost their beautiful and wonderful mother.

If we had had reachable people on the jury instead of a bunch of robots who viewed the judge as some kind of invincible oracle, the type of argument I just outlined, supported by underlying facts, might well result in an acquittal. The terrible problem was that Judge Thompson would not allow me to make that argument. He would not allow me to tell the jury that they had the power and right to ignore the law if they believed that strict application of the law on these facts would result in an injustice. The judge, the legal system, and the judicial system would not allow me to tell the jury the truth: that this group of men and women did in fact have that right and power, referred to as a "Jury Pardon."

If the jury chose to acquit the defendant of all charges, the state would have no right to inquire into their reasons and the state could not appeal the jury's verdict. Every juror could confess in an affidavit that they were swayed by emotion and sympathy and that they decided to disobey the court's clear instructions. This still could not change a verdict of "innocent"; the defendant simply could not be retried, because of the protection guaranteed to Americans against double jeopardy. Lawyers know that juries have the right to ignore the law, but attorneys don't have the right to tell jurors that they can do it.

Instead, the judge would repeat to the jury what the prosecutors would drive home over and over again in their four-hour final argument—"You must follow the law." The judge would give the following instruction to the jury after the closing arguments of both counsels, and immediately prior to the jurors beginning their deliberations: "Even if you do not like the laws that must be applied, you must still use them. No one of us has the right to violate the rules that we all share."

Judge Thompson felt very strongly that the jury "has no right to pardon anybody or to violate their oaths," meaning their oaths to follow the law.

Judge Thompson would give the jury this powerful instruction:

> There are some general rules that apply to your discussion. You must follow these rules in order to return a lawful verdict. Number one, you must follow the law as set out in these instructions. If you fail to follow the law, your verdict will be a miscarriage of justice. There is no reason for failing to follow the law in this case. All of us are depending upon you to make a wise and legal decision in this matter.

This instruction is damaging to the defendant because it is so intimidating. It tells the jury that even if they like the defendant, even if they feel sorry for him, even if they think he should not go to prison, their duty under the law is clear—convict!

The appeal of this kind of instruction to law-and-order types is overwhelming, and such individuals would form the basis of our jury pool in Fort Myers. These instructions deliberately telegraph to the jury what the system, what the establishment expects of them and it would take tremendous courage for any juror to disregard them.

I wanted to tell the jury in no uncertain terms to simply ignore the laws. I wanted to quote Shakespeare and Dickens about the law being an ass and worse. I wanted to remind the jury that laws were passed by politicians who lacked the foresight and the creativity to exclude acts such as Dr. Rosier's from the murder statutes. But I would need to fashion a defense out of other clay, for if I made the argument I wanted to make the Rosier trial would end this time in a mistrial and I would wind up in jail for contempt of court. For us to have any shot at a successful outcome, I would have to play the system's game, at least in part.

I would need to fashion a defense as if this were a routine first degree murder case. I would need to argue that the unindicted coconspirators—Patricia's brothers and stepfather—"killed" her, Peter didn't. I would need to argue that Peter never intended to kill Patricia and his criminal "intent" was a missing link in the State's case. I would also need to argue that the State's key witnesses, the Delmans, were disgusting, despicable liars who committed a fraud on the State of Florida in obtaining immunity. In other words, I would need to convince a jury that the State had failed to prove the essential elements of the crime of first degree murder.

The reason the Rosier case struck a particularly sensitive chord in Florida had to do with the first degree murder conviction of seventy-five-year-old Roswell Gilbert in Fort Lauderdale for the death of his wife. Because of the mandatory minimum sentence of twenty-five years, Gilbert would remain incarcerated until he reached the age of one hundred years before he would be eligible for release, absent a pardon. The harshness of this sentence for a person of Gilbert's age caused great controversy in Florida and elsewhere across the nation, and led to renewed and even more heated debate on the subject of euthanasia and the manner in which our criminal statutes attempt to deal with it. Only recently Roswell Gilbert received a pardon from the governor of Florida after serving several years of his sentence. Derek Humphry, who was to attend the entire Rosier trial, likewise attended the much briefer Gilbert trial.

The Gilberts, as the Rosiers, were a devoted and loving couple. Mr. and Mrs. Gilbert lived together in a Fort Lauderdale condominium. They had been married for fifty-one years. Emily Gilbert suffered from Alzheimer's disease and osteoporosis. Gilbert testified in his own defense.

> There she was in pain . . . I thought to myself I've got to end her suffering, this can't go on. I shot her in the head. I couldn't see any other end

than her dying. So if I put her in a nursing home and they won't let me stay there and she's separated from me. It would be a horrible death for her. She would die. The only solution to me was to terminate her suffering. Sure, I know I was breaking the law but there seems to be things more important than the law, at least to me in my private tragedy.

This kind of testimony can be very damaging when defending those who commit euthanasia. It plays into the prosecutor's hands of portraying the defendant as being arrogant, as one who is above the law, as one who thinks he or she has the right to take the law into his or her own hands. I would make sure that Peter exuded humility in the courtroom.

Gilbert's counsel, Joseph Varon, wanted the trial judge to instruct the jury on euthanasia as follows:

> The court instructs the jury of the definition of euthanasia to be: The act or practice of painlessly putting to death persons suffering from an incurable and distressing disease as an act of mercy.

The trial judge refused to give that instruction. On appeal the District Court of Appeal of Florida, Fourth District, on April 30, 1986, affirmed the conviction and said:

> In this case one of the principal defenses interposed by the Defendant, Roswell Gilbert, is for what he believed his wife wanted done under the circumstances and that he acted in good faith. *Euthanasia is not a defense to first degree murder in Florida and this Court has been furnished with no law or statute to the contrary.*

That was because no such law or statute existed. The appellate court went on to say: "Good faith is not a legal defense to first degree murder."

The court dismissed the unfairness argument as it dismissed the fact that Roswell Gilbert was not then and never had been a threat to society.

> Finally, this court notices that this aged Defendant has been a peaceful, law abiding and respected citizen up until this time. No one has suggested that he will again kill someone or enter upon a criminal career. However, the absolute rigidity of the statutory mandatory minimum sentences do not permit consideration of these factors or, for that matter, do not take into account any mitigating circumstances. Whether such sentences should somehow be moderated so as to allow a modicum of discretion and whether they should allow distinctions to be made in sentencing between different kinds of wrongdoers, for instance, between a hired

gangster killer and one, however misguided, who kills for love or mercy, are all questions which, under our system, must be decided by the legislature and not by the judicial branch. We leave it there.

This language is an absolute classic example of passing the buck to a legislature which has time and again skirted the issue. It is this kind of legislative do-nothingism that frequently leads appellate judges to become activists. Judges see an intolerable situation that they know will remain intolerable, so, through their opinions, they opt for change. Although the Fourth District Court of Appeals expressed some sympathy for Mr. Gilbert, they refused to "legislate." They reached the safe decision, a decision with which the vast majority of traditional lawyers would agree. They followed the law.

Judge Hugh Glickstein's opinion concurring with the appellate court decision scared the hell out of me. If his mentality was represented on our jury, we would have at least one juror who was unreachable. Glickstein made the standard argument of the prosecution in euthanasia cases.

> I have some concern about the hint in the main Opinion that trial courts should be enabled to vary minimum mandatory sentences according to the kind of wrongdoer; e.g., hired killer versus misguided mercy killer. I do not favor opening the door to such distinctions. My thoughts lie with the victim, who was silenced forever by her husband's criminal act. She would be no more dead if a hired gangland killer had pulled the trigger. The Decalogue states categorically, thou shalt not murder. It draws no distinction between murder by members of the middle class and murder by members of an under class. It draws no distinction between murder by a family member and murder by a stranger. It draws no distinction between murder out of a misguided notion of compassion and murder for hire. The victims in all such cases are equally dead. If the act was deliberate, the minimum penalty should not vary with the actor's purported motivation.

Another event that intensified the controversy surrounding euthanasia was an extraordinary letter written by an anonymous physician to the *Journal of the American Medical Association* on January 8, 1988. The letter was unique because a physician publically admitted that he killed a patient in a large, private hospital; and he further admitted that this patient was a total stranger to him. A legal system that allows the letter writer to go unprosecuted and Dr. Rosier to stand trial for first degree murder is both perverse and laughable.

The letter writer described himself as a gynecology resident who received a telephone call in the middle of the night to see an unknown patient. The doctor discovered from a glance at the chart that the patient was a twenty-year-old woman with ovarian cancer. Without consulting the patient, family members, or her attending physician, the letter writer asked the nurse to draw morphine into a syringe. Within five minutes or so the patient's breathing became irregular, and then ceased. The doctor writes: "It's Over, Debbie." Presumably he then went back to sleep.

Instead of ending with a name or signature, the letter ends: "Name Withheld by Request." Even Derek Humphry disapproved of this doctor's actions. In one of an avalanche of letters to the *Journal,* Mr. Humphry stated:

> If the physician who helped Debbie to die had acted as he did in Holland now, or in America in the future when the Humane and Dignified Death Act is passed, he would be prosecuted. Dutch rules, and the proposed act in the United States, are clear that a request to be helped to die must be in writing and must have been carefully considered. Also, two physicians must agree that the patient is dying. The family must be informed but cannot veto the patient's wishes.

The *Journal's* editor, Dr. George Lundberg, justified publication of the "Debbie letter" in a lengthy editorial.

> The essay was offered for our consideration with the proviso that the identity of the author be withheld. Thus, it was published unsigned, and we consider the author's identity to be privileged. As we do with authors of all articles and essays we receive, we trusted the author of "It's Over, Debbie" to be telling the truth, and we made no independent investigation of the facts. . . .
>
> Euthanasia may become one of the predominant medical and ethical debates for the rest of this century. While our early mail was heavily in opposition, our recent letters have run strongly in favor of the act described by the physician and of the *Journal's* courage in publishing about euthanasia. If physicians' letters are any indication, mainstream physician involvement in active euthanasia is unlikely in the near future in this country.

All his medical life Peter had heard the "whispers in doctors dressing rooms and hallways" about patients who were deliberately terminated— sometimes with their consent, though just as often without it, because it seemed the pragmatic course to follow. He knew doctors deliberately hastened death all the time; he hastened death at the specific request of his beloved wife; the anonymous letter writer did it at no one's request to a total stranger, yet only Peter's future was on the line. Call it what you will, but it isn't justice.

Susan, Peter, and I figured that when the time came for the presentation of our case, we would be able to make the jury understand that euthanasia is an everyday fact of life and death. We would also be able to make them understand (if they were reachable) that although the victim was just as dead, the acts of physicians and family members were of a totally different nature than criminal conduct carried out for profit or hatred. To lump both groups together as murderers, as the law did, was a vile absurdity.

I lined up medical evidence from impressive witnesses to demonstrate that terminally ill people frequently commit suicide with the assistance of loved ones, and their physicians; yet these deaths, which clearly violate criminal statutes, are generally not investigated or prosecuted. Certain unlucky mercy killers are periodically and systematically prosecuted throughout the United States. In Peter's case, the whole community of Fort Myers turned on him for opening his mouth. In other instances, a jealous neighbor, a fanatically religious acquaintance, a bitter sister-in-law, or an enemy can get the wheels of "justice" turning and murder charges brought against a loving spouse or grieving relative. Similarly, the laws vary from state to state and it may be advantageous for a terminally ill patient to end her life in a state with favorable laws.

Suicide is not a crime in Florida but assisting a self-murder (suicide) is illegal. Joseph D'Alessandro and the grand jury chose to ignore the self-murder statute and instead opted for murder one.

We would also be able to demonstrate the hypocrisy of pretending that morphine and other respiratory depressants are given only to reduce pain and keep the patient comfortable. We had doctors who were willing to expose the reality that when people are terminally ill and placed on morphine drips through an intravenous needle, overdoses are frequently given, which result in death or at the very least the hastening of death. In terminal patients who may be semiconscious, it does not take much of an overdose to end their lives.

This practice is that part of the iceberg which is under water as far as doctors and nurses are concerned. Morphine drips are constantly varied as to dosage depending upon pain and other factors, and absent an admission of guilt it would be just about impossible to prove any criminal intent. No one said a word about the death of "Debbie" until the unknown doctor wrote his famous letter.

Peter felt very strongly that the laws against euthanasia were hypocritical and unjust, and he felt that way long before Pat's lung cancer was first diagnosed. It was the opportunity to deal with such significant issues that played a major role and was a strong motivating factor in my decision to undertake Peter's defense.

Dr. Rosier was a prosecutor's dream in terms of publicity and career advancement. The great majority of criminal defendants are poor and uneducated and are subsequently processed by the criminal justice system in an unimaginative, bureaucratic fashion. The system is an assembly line whose primary objective is the speedy resolution of huge volumes of cases. That is accomplished by the great majority of defendants pleading guilty to one charge or another. Very few criminal cases actually go to trial.

Truth, justice, and even-handed treatment of persons who commit similar crimes all get lost in the shuffle. It becomes one huge crap shoot. Who gets the best lawyer from the public defender's office and who gets the lazy one? Who has the lawyer who gets along with or is connected to that particular prosecutor? Which prosecutor is leaving to join what criminal defense firm? The average tenure of assistants in a prosecutor's office is very short—usually two or three years. They learn the system and tricks at taxpayer expense and then use that knowledge to put real criminals on the street.

To use Tom Wolfe's great phrase from *Bonfire of the Vanities,* Dr. Rosier was truly "The Great White Defendant." He was intelligent, rich, arrogant, and opinionated. And best of all (in Fort Myers) he was a liberal New York Jew.

Peter was born on Long Island, his father was a physician and his mother a famous interior designer in New York City. He attended Dartmouth and received his medical degree from the State University of New York, Downstate Medical Center in Brooklyn. He did his residency in pathology at Duke University. He and Patricia first met when they were thirteen. They married young and moved to Fort Myers in 1973 where Peter became a hugely successful pathologist. Peter was Chief of Pathology at Lee Memorial Hospital in Fort Meyers and maintained a private medical office that was extremely profitable. Dr. Rosier and his staff worked primarily for fellow physicians, conducting laboratory tests and diagnosing diseases, including cancers.

Peter and Pat were leading the television version of the "American Dream," the so-called good life. They worked hard and they played hard. They jogged, they played tennis. Patricia was into gourmet cooking, and they dined magnificently at home. Both collected objects of art and rare butterflies. The couple and their children played various musical instruments; the family took seven-week annual vacations in locations as diverse as Manhattan, Aspen, Jackson Hole, and all of America's national parks. When traveling abroad they visited every country in South America and had explored both the Andes Mountains and the Amazon River extensively.

This is how Peter described Patricia and their relationship in "The Lady."

> She was a talented swimmer and runner, a strong hiker, a good volleyball player, and a euphoric roller skater. She was a genius in the kitchen, an avid student of biology, and had great knowledge of medicine. She loved poetry, the theater; she loved Mozart, Schubert, Vivaldi, the Beatles, and Stevie Wonder. She collected butterflies and gardened; she mothered her family, and she ran a busy doctor's [Peter's] billing office. She collected gemstones in South America and gave money to the poor in the United States. She taught Sunday School and was a Cub Scout and Brownie leader. She read Plato, Winston Churchill, Somerset Maugham, and Gertrude Stein. And she loved many works of Pablo Picasso, Paul Klee, and Leonardo da Vinci.
>
> We agreed on everything. We even liked the same colors. Our politics were identical. Our desires in life were the same. When I played tennis, Pat played tennis, and when she went shopping, I went shopping. We did almost everything together. We held hands and kissed and laughed wherever we went. Alone, each of us was less than one adult person, and, together, the two of us were more than two adult people. We enjoyed the same theater, the same books, and the same music. I did not watch football games on Sundays, nor did she talk to women about babies. She and I talked together about the sports that held my interests; we talked about the style of dresses she liked and about the table settings she preferred.

The State would be able to blow some of this sweetness and light away with other material in the manuscript as well as Peter's behavior after his wife's death.

Patricia's mother, Lorraine, had married Vincent Delman when Patricia was eight years old. The two children from that marriage were Farrell and Russell. Vincent Delman practiced dentistry in Brooklyn for forty years, even after he moved to Long Island about a year after the birth of Farrell. Vincent and Lorraine were divorced shortly after Patricia and Peter were married. Patricia's mother had died before Patricia contracted cancer. Farrell, age thirty-eight at the time of the trial, was president of the Tobacco Merchant's Association of the United States. Russell, eighteen months younger than Farrell and ten years younger than Patricia, lived in California where he was a Feldenkrais practitioner, allegedly teaching people self-awareness in terms of their body movements and sitting arrangements. The Delmans were to play a key role in the murder trial.

Not only did Peter do an incredibly stupid and self-destructive thing in confessing on television and in his book, he needlessly invited the Delmans to become eyewitnesses to Patricia's death.

What was it about Peter's character that required him to involve others in his dangerous and sensitive activities? Why did he have to talk about everything he did? Why the hell couldn't he just act? In the hours of Patricia's unconsciousness, Peter involved three physicians, the three Delmans, as well as two office employees. He was responsible for the Delmans becoming the State's star witnesses against him.

Since there had been no autopsy and since Patricia's body had been cremated, under Florida law, without the testimony of the Delmans there would have been no mercy-killing trial involving Dr. Peter Rosier. Without the testimony of the Delmans the State of Florida could not have prosecuted even if Peter wrote ten books and appeared on television every week for a year. Unfortunately, Peter handled his in-laws as poorly as he did his manuscript and television interview. More about that later.

A jury would ultimately decide who killed Patricia Rosier. Was it suicide? Was it Peter? Was it the Delmans? Was it a conspiracy? Or was it simply a terrible form of cancer?

2

Let's Get the Hell Out of Fort Myers

Criminal cases often turn on the location of the trial. The trial judge's decision *not* to transfer the case of Dr. Sam Shepard, another physician on trial for murder, clearly resulted in a conviction. Dr. Shepard had similarly been charged with the murder of his wife and, like Dr. Rosier, he was tried and convicted in the local media. There had been an incredible media circus in Cleveland, the location of Mrs. Shepard's murder, and the Ohio Supreme Court affirmed the lower court's decision to keep the case in that city. Only after Dr. Shepard had spent many years in prison and ruined his life did the United States Supreme Court finally rule that there should have been a change of venue because of the impossibility of a fair trial in that atmosphere. Dr. Shepard was released and never retried.

It would be impossible for Peter to get a fair trial in Fort Myers. Likewise, it was a given fact that in Fort Myers Peter would be convicted of murder in the first degree. A trial jury in Fort Myers would follow the example of the Lee County Grand Jury which had indicted Peter. Fort Myers is a company town, a town with the mentality of "we must stick together"; it's us against them, a town that does what is expected of it by the pace setters of the community.

As if the law were not favorable enough to the prosecution, they also had the benefit of county-wide hatred against Peter. This outsider had dared to challenge the customs, mores, and laws of dear old Fort Myers, Florida.

The negative publicity, particularly in the very dominant Fort Myers *News-Press,* had been devastating. The *News-Press* is part of the Gannett chain, which publishes *USA Today.* Nearly every description of Peter in the media ran against the grain of the basic makeup of the majority of citizens in Fort Myers. Most people who were not native to the west coast of Florida came there from the Midwest (particularly Ohio) after retirement. Peter was portrayed as rich, arrogant, opinionated, and rude; his lifestyle and sex life were painted as lavish, kinky, exotic, and flamboyant.

I came to know Fort Myers people well. They played the game of being ever so low key and private. Their most admired virtue appeared to be that of quiet composure; the worst sin was to raise one's voice and get excited about anything.

Such people are unreachable as jurors. They accept without question the fiction that "the law is the law." They are not into subtle distinctions. A Fort Myers jury would be only too happy to follow the law in Dr. Rosier's case. To arrive at an acquittal Peter would need a jury with the courage to conclude that strict application of the law to his situation would result in a grave injustice.

My temperament and style were such that I was always raising my voice and getting excited or indignant or angry. My wife and I knew perfectly well that the aggressive Jewish lawyer representing the rich Jewish doctor definitely would not play in Fort Myers. I try a case differently if my jury is made up of elderly southern ladies as opposed to, let's say, construction workers, cab drivers, bartenders, or secretaries. The facts would be the same but my presentation of those facts would be entirely different. I could adapt my style somewhat, but never enough to satisfy Fort Myers. Miami is a two-and-a-half-hour drive from Fort Myers, but it is a different world. Although Peter had lived and practiced his profession in Fort Myers since 1973, we would both be viewed as foreigners.

Peter Rosier was probably the most hated guy in town. We conducted interviews and talked to hundreds of people and that was the consensus. He was pretty much despised across the board but particularly so within the medical community. Apparently when doctors turn on one of their own it is with a vengeance. The doctors hated him for making public sensitive issues surrounding euthanasia and making the profession acutely aware of its hypocrisy in dealing with terminal patients. Peter talked directly about the vast gap that existed between the reality of treatment and nontreatment, and the platitudes mouthed about respect for the law.

While there was no true respect for the law, there was respect for keeping one's mouth shut and doing what had to be done in terms of ending pain and hastening death. The medical profession hates malpractice cases more than it hates serial killers and child abusers. They despised Peter for suing Lee Memorial Hospital and a fellow physician. Such a lawsuit by a doctor in Fort Myers was the equivalent of committing professional suicide.

The Fort Myers *News-Press* and, to a lesser degree, the local television stations did their best to characterize Peter Rosier as a despicable human being. The all-powerful *News-Press,* with an approximate circulation of 135,000, consistently and repeatedly reported that Peter Rosier "killed his wife," that he confessed to "killing his wife." In view of the murder statutes and the Roswell Gilbert precedent, the *News-Press* felt very confident in concluding that Peter's words on television amounted to a confession of murder.

The management of this newspaper made an early decision that the Rosier case was a major story of great significance, as exemplified by their "Sunday Special," which appeared November 23, 1986—less than two weeks after Dr. Rosier's television appearance. Three reporters were assigned to write these articles and they interviewed nearly a hundred people.

The *News-Press* asserted as fact that the reason Peter went on television was to "drum up publicity" for his manuscript in the hope that it could become a best-selling book. Was it any wonder that people hated him for going on television if he was willing to endanger friends and fellow doctors simply to create controversy and to promote his manuscript?

One *News-Press* story carried this headline:

"FRIEND: ROSIER DREAMED OF BILLIONS FROM STORY"

The article said:

Peter Rosier, a millionaire Fort Myers doctor . . . hoped to make a billion dollars on the story of her death. . . . Peter said he would like to make a billion dollars from the book or the movie or both, buy a bunch of Rolls Royces and drive around Fort Myers and poop on everyone. . . .

The *News-Press* saw fit to mention an affair Peter had had, though it was history long before Patricia became ill—an affair that the paper said "began on a dirt road in the back seat of a Mercedes."

In addition to painting Peter as arrogant, weird, scheming, and ostentatious the *News-Press* said he was fabulously wealthy, earning $800,000 the year before Pat contracted cancer. The paper referred to him as "a retired pathologist worth an estimated four million dollars." The newspaper revelled in anything juicy: such as how Peter and Patricia "made love for the last time," and the "nude photos of Pat," displayed on walls throughout the Rosier home.

The *News-Press* attacked Peter from every conceivable angle. If he had wanted to, State Attorney Joseph D'Alessandro could not have orchestrated a more favorable pro-prosecution atmosphere.

> Peter Rosier, who admitted killing his terminally ill wife, receives $15,000 a month in disability payments because he is too emotionally scarred to practice medicine. Rosier filed a disability claim two days after he killed his wife. . . . Rosier's medical practice brought him $66,000 a month for the six months before her death. . . . The Dartmouth-educated Peter is worth about four million dollars. His insurance policy was for another two million dollars.

The *News-Press* advised its readers that Dr. Rosier had paid $40,000 to have a movie script made of his manuscript, "The Lady"; that Peter had a fancy Park Avenue apartment in Manhattan; that the Rosiers had had his-and-hers matching Rolls Royces; and other such juicy tidbits. Regardless of the truth of these articles, they were clearly not legally relevant and would be highly prejudicial to a defendant on trial for his life.

We were hopeful that Judge Thompson would keep out much of this "evidence" that the State wished to present to the jury. It would matter little, though, in Fort Myers, where Dr. Rosier's fate was discussed anywhere and everywhere and with everyone. My wife, Susan, always made a point of asking taxi drivers, bellhops, waitresses, or sales clerks in Fort Myers, during our many hearings and depositions, what they had heard about the mercy-killing case involving a local physician. Invariably, and without exception, we heard comments such as, "I hope he gets the electric chair" or "He's brought disgrace on our town." Rarely did we let on that we were representing Dr. Rosier.

I knew the situation was utterly hopeless in Fort Myers when Susan and I went to dinner with some old friends who had recently moved to Fort Myers to escape the crime in Miami. We assumed that the couple, a well-seasoned attorney and his realtor wife, would be kindred spirits on all issues. While the attorney was quiet, his wife couldn't control herself and expressed her contempt for Dr. Rosier. She thought it was disgusting that he boasted of his affair in his manuscript. I have always had the philosophy that the fate of a client may hinge upon his or her likeability; juries would rarely convict a man or woman they truly admired and liked. In Peter Rosier's case, the opposite was true.

Even if we could get jurors who did not know Peter, had not followed media reports about his case, and were unconnected with the medical profession, it would not matter. The trickle-down effect in a place like Fort Myers is all-pervasive; during a lengthy trial all the jurors would fully understand that the community demanded punishment. Fort Myers doctors had contact with nearly everyone, were highly respected, and, other than perhaps golf and the stock market, Dr. Rosier was their favorite subject. They would talk to their patients, who in turn would talk to their families and friends. The Fort Myers *News-Press* and all the television stations would repeat and embellish all the old gossip.

The single most important thing we needed to accomplish prior to the actual trial was getting the case out of Fort Myers! We wanted a diverse jury of different ethnic groups; in Fort Myers we would get a homogenous jury of polite zombies who would convict Peter of first degree murder in a flash, and then tell him to "have a nice day." We wanted a jury that would not be offended by tough, straight talk. We wanted people who would not be offended by vigorous cross examination of prominent citizens. In Fort Myers I would have to walk on eggs when questioning any one of the great and holy representatives of the medical profession.

The State wanted a jury that would simply add the Seconal and the morphine to Peter's actions and match them with slide-rule precision to the abstract principles of law that the judge would give them. In other words, the State wanted a jury that would conclude: "Hey, it all fits. We may not be happy with the result since Dr. Rosier is a well-qualified physician who poses no threat to society. But our duty is very clear, we took an oath to uphold the law; punishment is for the judge to decide. As for Dr. Rosier, we didn't tell him to go on television or write a manuscript or involve his in-laws. GUILTY! HAVE A NICE DAY!"

The defense needed a jury that could go beyond naked facts and law, a jury motivated to grope for understanding and compassion. We needed people who were unwilling to act as robots and surrender their souls; we needed people who could make allowances for human failings, who could distinguish between poor judgment and evil intent. Fundamentally we needed a jury that believed in fairness, one that could appreciate the big picture and had the courage to do the right thing in spite of the law.

Peter's daughter, Elizabeth, was going to get a bumper sticker saying ABFM (Anywhere But Fort Myers). Susan dissuaded her. We would have been satisfied with a change of venue to Fort Lauderdale, West Palm Beach, Tampa, or Jacksonville. I am a realist. I knew there was no chance of Judge Thompson transferring the trial to our number one choice — Miami. Outside of Florida's major population centers the rest of the state is very similar to small-town Georgia or Alabama.

Through pretrial discovery we were able to uncover some of the prejudice against Peter in Fort Myers. Florida is one of very few states that permits pretrial depositions of witnesses in criminal proceedings. Depositions are not permitted in criminal actions in the federal judicial system. Without the ability to subpoena and question witnesses prior to trial, I would not have uncovered valuable evidence demonstrating the prejudice against Peter. Many key witnesses refused to speak with me, absent a subpoena.

The deposition of a close friend of the Rosiers, Landis Faye McMahon, was critical on the issue of transferring the trial from Fort Myers to another location.

Landis had become one of Peter's bitterest critics; she was also an expert on the mores and manners of Fort Myers. Landis was thirty-six years of age when her deposition was taken on June 2, 1988, at the Lee County Justice Center, the courthouse where State Attorney Joseph D'Alessandro's office was located and where the case would be tried if we were unsuccessful in getting it moved. Landis was a lifelong resident of Fort Myers and her father had gone to grade school there. Landis educated us about Fort Myers during her deposition.

> This is a small town still, though we're growing. You talk about a Peyton Place, this is the town. You can't slip off with Jane without everybody knowing about it. Everybody loves to talk. It's mean. And we're all guilty of it, and I'm number one. I'm right up there with them all.

That was precisely why I knew that everyone on a Fort Myers jury would learn about all the hearsay gossip relating to Peter and Patricia.

> I lived here all my life. You only have a few real true friends in Fort Myers because it's real small and everybody knows your business. There is just no way you can practically go to the bathroom without somebody knowing it.
>   He [Peter] doesn't even care about our town and the people in it. And we're all real clicky people, you know, the Junior League and the Community Club stuff. We're all real clicky and we all care, you know, about our town. It's just going to be one big mess and it's just another scandal in Fort Myers that nobody needs.

Nearly all the long-time residents of Fort Myers had a Chamber of Commerce mentality. Anyone who tarnished the image of their community was regarded as an enemy.

I was certainly willing to take the Rosier trial and scandal on the road. My observations of Fort Myers coincided perfectly with Landis's deposition. Landis McMahon had grown up with Joseph D'Alessandro and several of his assistant state attorneys and their wives. Their children went to school together, lawyers in the state attorney's office purchased Pontiacs from Landis's father's dealership. Her child had played soccer and little league with assistant prosecutor Edward Volz's children for several years. Their kids attended the same birthday parties.

> Q: So it was obvious both to you and your husband, this was it, this was the night Patricia was going to commit suicide?
> A: Sure, oh yeah, no doubt about it.

This question and answer refers to January 14, 1986, the day and night before Patricia's death. On that day Patricia said goodbye to her friends and relatives and gave them expensive going-away gifts. Peter told many of the visitors that, "Pat would not be around tomorrow."

Patricia's intentions were hardly a mystery. Not one of these law-and-order citizens of Fort Myers dreamed of trying to prevent a suicide, and in the ten months between Pat's death and Peter's television confession, no one considered reporting anything to the authorities. People in Fort Myers hated Peter Rosier, not for what he did in connection with his wife's death, but for talking about it on television and for writing a book about it. They were not angry because Peter administered morphine to his wife; they were angry because he went public.

Landis was a superb example of why the trial had to be moved from Fort Myers. She had spent much time with Patricia during her illness and was a great admirer of hers, describing Patricia as someone "I really adored being with; she was amazing to be with; she had nothing bad to say about anyone; she knew a lot; she was a very smart woman."

In spite of this relationship, Landis wanted Peter to burn. This type of testimony became a common phenomenon; people who despised Peter and wanted him in jail had only positive things to say about Patricia. Landis seemed to take pleasure in Peter's anguish; during her deposition he was sitting next to me hanging on her every word. It was impossible for me to keep Peter away from the numerous pretrial depositions; the case had become his life. I tried to make Landis concede that going on television was not a capital crime; I was not successful.

Q: The man is charged with first degree murder.
A: Well, that's his problem.
Q: You don't care that he's charged with first degree murder?
A: He brought it on himself.
Q: And you hope he gets convicted?
A: He didn't do it? Did it bother him when he was shitting on everyone?

This was the prevailing Fort Myers attitude: Peter had dumped on them by airing his dirty linen in public and by endangering doctor friends and others who were only trying to help him. At another point in the deposition Landis said, "Shit, the whole world hates him." Maybe not the whole world, but certainly the whole of Fort Myers.

One of Landis McMahon's favorite little old southern-girl expressions was "If you lay down with dogs, you come up with fleas." And to her everything associated with Peter was in the dog category. It was clear from her testimony that rumors were circulating all over town about the content of "The Lady." Peter had voluntarily given the manuscript to several friends. He gave it to Leisa Zigman the interviewer for Channel 20, and the state attorney's office had it. The rumor mill said that Peter trashed Fort Myers in the manuscript and showed disdain for its people. That was basically true. All the more reason to get even with him.

The most amazing part of Landis's psyche was yet to come. I wanted to know how much she had heard about the circumstances leading up to Patricia's death, and we got into the area of Peter asking doctors to provide him with morphine.

Q: Which doctor, do you know?
A: You know this is like when the niggers all line up and they all look alike and you think you know which one it is, but they say you have to be 100 percent sure and you're only 99 percent sure.

She said referring to Peter:

He would tell us, I am the richest eligible bachelor in Lee County and I can't get anybody to screw me. It wasn't screw, it was the other word. He said I can't even get a nigger, or he would even screw a nigger, or something like that.

I certainly expected and wanted blacks to serve on Peter's jury. If a black person believed that Peter made that remark, that in and of itself could prevent us from gaining an acquittal. Would Judge Thompson allow the jury to hear this testimony? It was clear to Susan and me that the supposed statement was clearly inadmissible, but at trial you must be prepared for every eventuality. Such a statement had no relevance but it could inflame a jury to Peter's detriment. Yet if that were held admissible, it was our position that Landis McMahon could be exhaustively cross examined as to her regular use of "niggers," "jigaboos," and other similar expressions.

I was not about to exclude black jurors because of this potential risk. I believed Peter completely when he said that offensive word was not in his vocabulary, and the statement Landis attributed to him was absolutely untrue. I asked Landis:

Q: When you are talking privately among friends and you're referring to someone that's black, it's common for you to use the word nigger, isn't that correct?
A: Probably. Not all the time.
Q: Well? How often?
A: The majority of times, yes.
Q: Because as you grew up in the South, that was the accepted expression.
A: Yeah.
Q: Not black people?
A: Jigaboos, niggies, whatever.

I could not believe that I was hearing this in the late 1980s. I didn't kid myself about what people said privately, but how could Mrs. McMahon not understand that such offensive terms were simply not socially acceptable?

Q: Landis, I simply want to understand that even today if you're talking with a close friend, that's how you will refer to black people.
A: I would say the stupid nigger pulled out in front of me on Highway 41.

This deposition testimony from Landis McMahon would provide me with the necessary ammunition for a very tough cross examination at trial, if the judge admitted into evidence the comments Peter allegedly uttered at the McMahon party. The prosecution would have a difficult time getting a jury to believe her testimony if that jury was composed of any blacks or even fair-minded whites. Realizing my reaction to her testimony, Landis said, "We're not poor white trash, I'm not a bad person you know."

Once again she gratuitously expressed some strong feelings: "We hate

Ohio people." I guess she was trying to demonstrate that she had prejudices that were not based on race.

Q: You hate Ohioans?
A: Yes.
Q: Why?
A: Because they are slow and they drive ten miles an hour down High-way 41.
Q: They are the opposite of New York aggressive?
A: They don't have any culture and they live over there in Cape Coral and, I mean forget it, don't even start me on Ohio people. No, Ohio is the biggest joke in Fort Myers.

During his deposition, Landis's husband, Robert, a stockbroker, confirmed that in the view of those who live in Fort Myers Peter's crime was spilling the beans on television, not in participating in his wife's death.

Q: You have told me it was very common knowledge, everybody knew or everybody assumed that Patricia had committed suicide?
A: Yes.
Q: And certainly no one cared from the standpoint of hey, we should notify the State Attorney's Office or the police department; you never heard anyone suggest that, did you?
A: No.
Q: And even to this day, whatever anger or resentment there may be, it has nothing to do with the circumstances of Patricia's death, it all has to do with Peter going on television; wouldn't you agree that's true?
A: To my knowledge it is, yes.

All the law-and-order people seemed to have very much of a double standard. As long as the deed was kept private, everything was cool. I asked Robert McMahon,

Q: What was the reaction of the group at the Park Meadow Tennis Club to Peter's appearance on television?

Peter and most of his friends had been members of this private tennis club for years.

A: Most of what had occurred with Pat taking her own life was common knowledge. Everybody knew it. When the program was aired, the general consensus in the room was, what the hell is this guy doing? He's dragging all of this laundry out of the closet. For what reason?

Q: Did anyone ever advance a plausible explanation as to what motivated him to go on television?

A: I think most people felt that Pete was having trouble getting the book published, and his reason for going on television was to promote the book.

That was certainly the State's theory and it would haunt us throughout the trial, for even to fair-minded people that was not an unreasonable conclusion to reach. My honest response was, so what? What if Peter didn't give a damn about euthanasia and simply wanted to pump his ego and have a best seller and that's why he confessed on television. What does that really have to do with first degree murder? As a realist and a pragmatist, though, I was only too aware that if the jury perceived Dr. Rosier as a selfish SOB who wanted fame and glory and used his fellow physicians and friends in the process, it would be only too easy to "follow the law" and convict him. This was particularly so in Fort Myers, where politeness, etiquette getting along, and avoiding controversy are elevated far above principle.

Cindy Carlino's husband, a physician specializing in X-ray interpretation (radiologist), was probably Peter's best friend at the time of Patricia's death. Yet Cindy could not find it in her heart to forgive Peter for involving her husband and for making public the circumstances of Patricia's death. She could not forgive him for making it necessary for her to give a deposition. Her deposition was taken some two and a half years after Patricia died. Her husband had been granted full immunity from prosecution. He had suffered no practical consequences from his involvement and yet Cindy was still angry.

Cindy had spent a tremendous amount of time with Patricia during the eight and a half months of her illness. She, like many others, was invited to the Rosier home on January 14, and like them she received expensive gifts from Patricia. While Pat lay unconscious Peter came to the Carlino home at about 3:30 A.M. on January 15. Later on that morning, Dr. Carlino came to the Rosier home to discuss what constituted a lethal dose of Seconal. What led to the use of morphine was the fact that Peter concluded he had underestimated the amount of Seconal required to cause death. In her suicide attempt Patricia had been provided with only twenty Seconal capsules of 100 mgs each.

Dr. Carlino put himself on the line for a close friend in need and he felt betrayed when Peter confessed on television. Peter never mentioned Carlino's name on television but he did talk about him in his manuscript. I understood how Carlino felt and didn't blame him in the slightest for being very angry at Peter. But I expected some kind of balance now that Peter faced the prospect of many years in jail or possibly the electric chair. I asked Cindy in her deposition.

Q: Did you ever get over your anger, or are you still angry?

A: I'm still very angry.

Q: Why are you still very angry?

A: Because Michael and I gave him a lot of emotional support and feelings and he destroyed that. And I'm very angry with him because he doesn't know what he did to my family during that time that he did all this. He put my husband through such stress that it just tore us apart. And there was a time in this that I didn't think my marriage was going to survive it, all right? Plus, my children were all affected by it because of the mood swings of their father and because of me being upset. My husband is a very, very private person and he doesn't give himself to people very often, and he gave a lot to this friendship.

Q: Are you so angry that you want him to be convicted?

A: I want him to be punished for this yeah, in some way. I think it was a very selfish thing that he did.

Q: But obviously you want him to be punished for going on television. You don't want him to be punished for anything that he may have done in connection with Patricia's death because you have already told me that if you knew everything that he did you would not have gone to the authorities, so Peter wouldn't have been punished and the facts would be the same. What you want him to be punished for is going on television?

A: Well, you're basically right on that. You know, I guess, if he didn't want to be punished for it, he wouldn't have done it.

I was unable to convince any of Peter's former friends that behaving stupidly on television was not a capital offense. The unforgiving attitude of the Carlinos remained steadfast right through the trial. Although Dr. Carlino had several private meetings with representatives from the state attorney's office, he always refused to meet with me.

Dr. Carlino had become Peter's best friend in Fort Myers; the Rosiers had attended parties and functions given by the Carlinos, and the Carlinos had attended various Rosier celebrations. Their children were friends. They were all tennis buddies. Peter could go to prison for life, and yet

Carlino would do nothing to help. When the Rosiers' children, Elizabeth and Jacob, tried to speak with him about at least meeting with Peter or me, he refused to see them.

It is very difficult to persuade a judge to transfer a case to another city. It is a very disruptive process both personally and professionally. Judges become very comfortable in familiar surroundings and with court personnel whom they know: clerks, bailiffs, secretaries, and court reporters. And as the law views it, decisions on motions to change venue are held to be within the very broad discretion of trial judges. A judge will rarely be reversed by an appellate court for denying such a motion.

If a judge transfers a case to another city, he goes with it as do the prosecutors. Judge James Thompson had graduated from the University of Florida School of Law in 1971. He had been an assistant county attorney and then an assistant state attorney working for this same Joseph D'Alessandro. Trial lawyers by their natures and through their experiences become the most suspicious people on the planet; yet strangely enough I trusted Thompson's basic integrity and was not worried that he would be having private conversations with D'Alessandro or anyone from his office.

Thompson was elected a county judge in 1976, serving until September, 1981, at which time he was appointed to the circuit bench of the Twentieth Judicial Circuit, which includes Lee and several other counties. The circuit bench is the highest trial court in Florida.

Judge Thompson's professional history represented an absolutely classic route for an aspiring lawyer to become a circuit court judge. Considering the fact that Thompson had served four years in the United States Marine Corps, his demeanor was extraordinarily low key and mild. He almost never raised his voice. He was cordial and had a very even temperament. Susan and I were convinced that he had a heart.

I had tried one case before Judge Thompson about a year before my involvement with the Rosiers. It was a civil medical malpractice case against Lee Memorial Hospital involving the birth of a boy who turned out to be seriously and permanently brain damaged. We contended that nursing mismanagement and a delay in delivering the baby, who was suffering from fetal distress, caused the brain damage. How could I dream that I would be representing the chief pathologist of that very hospital in a fight for his life?

After a two-week trial, a Fort Myers jury awarded the highest verdict in the history of Lee and several surrounding counties in southwest Florida. The trial judge in a civil trial, unlike a criminal case, has a veto power: Judge Thompson threw the verdict out and ordered a new trial.

He said that I had been too tough and unfair in cross examining a treating physician, a doctor whom the judge knew very well.

I could never forgive Judge Thompson for what he did. I am convinced that had the judge not been a part of the establishment in Fort Myers he would have let the verdict stand. Yet having said all that, and in terms of the other judges available in Lee County, Thompson was still our clear first choice. We knew that he at least would allow us to have a fair trial by as impartial a jury as we could obtain. We believed that Thompson would be his fairest in a city other than Fort Myers.

In a criminal case, if the defendant is acquitted it's all over. The State does not have the right to appeal. The judge has no veto power over the verdict, nor does he have the power to alter the jury's verdict in any way. The fat lady has truly sung!

Edward Volz and Stephen Russell had both worked for Joseph D'Alessandro for many years; they were career prosecutors who looked the part. We could not imagine them ever representing a person charged with a crime. They were straight-arrow, tough, and solid. Both were physically imposing, and one would guess they had been linebackers in college.

Volz and Russell knew southwest Florida and its people like the back of their hands. They were D'Alessandro's top guns and along with James Fitzpatrick, who had retired after some twenty-five years of active police work in the Washington, D.C., area, they were a formidable team. Volz and Russell would divide the trial responsibilities—one would handle jury selection, the other would make the opening statement; they would split up witnesses both on direct and cross examination, and they would share the State's final argument.

We had our battles and arguments, but to their credit neither of them engaged in the petty maneuvering and deceit that have become the trademark of so many civil lawyers. I knew where they stood, and they knew where I stood; we didn't lie to each other. Although unsmiling and totally professional and absorbed when working, they had personalities plus an occasional sense of humor.

I suppose because of all the publicity and pressure, they became emotionally involved to the extent of really despising Peter. Volz and Russell would deny that, because lawyers are trained to pretend that they are detached, but their animosity toward Peter was not disguisable. Both were a lot nastier than they had to be. In all the hours and days we were in each other's presence during depositions, hearings, and the trial itself I never saw any member of the prosecution team directly exchange anything on a human level with Peter. They treated him like a leper.

I felt that the deposition testimony of Landis McMahon and Cindy

Carlino laid a very strong foundation for the granting of our motion to change the trial location. Yet Susan and I knew that we would need more, much more, to convince Judge Thompson who had already expressed his intention to keep the trial in Fort Myers.

Ultimately we would have to rely on Judge Thompson's sense of fairness. We put Peter and Elizabeth and Jacob to work calling friends, acquaintances, and even enemies to beg, plead, and cajole them to say the obvious: that Peter could not get a fair trial by an impartial jury in Lee County or any other location in southwest Florida. Two associates from my office worked almost nonstop for three weeks nailing down the necessary people.

Eventually we gathered an incredible ninety-one affidavits from a cross section of the community including teachers, accountants, hospital employees, business people of all sorts, the president of Edison Community College, musicians, an architect, a retired engineer, and an automobile mechanic. People signing the affidavits said some startling things: they personally heard prominent and highly educated members of the Fort Myers area calling Peter "a murderer" and a "wife killer"; saying that he was "guilty of murder." Many of these people thought the appropriate punishment for my client was death in the electric chair. Peter started referring to himself as "Killer Doc."

Several affidavits said that when these inflammatory statements were made, frequently in the presence of relatively large groups of people, no one came to Peter's defense. No one mentioned that Peter was entitled to a presumption of innocence; no one made the point that even the worst low-life career criminal was entitled to have a fair trial by an impartial jury. When it came to Peter Rosier these otherwise laid back, emotionally placid people became livid with rage. Some of the affiants said in referring to conversation they had heard: "I never saw this person express anger, but when the discussion turned to Dr. Rosier, he became passionate and emotional and could hardly control himself."

In the lengthy hearing on our motion for change of venue, I told Judge Thompson about Derek Humphry, who had then been the executive director of the National Hemlock Society for eight years. The Hemlock Society is a right-to-die organization founded in 1980 with 57,000 members and eighty-six chapters across the country. Mr. Humphry had spent most of his career as a journalist: twelve years with the *Times* of London, and he had also worked for the *Los Angeles Times*. He is the author of at least eight books. He became obsessed with euthanasia when his first wife, Jean, was suffering from terminal cancer, and he recounted in one of his books how he assisted in ending her life. The public prose-

cutor in England exercised sound judgment in deciding not to file criminal charges against Mr. Humphry.

Since Derek had also written a book about his wife, I thought he
felt a special kinship to Peter. He had traveled to Miami to meet with
Peter and me well in advance of the trial and he was unfailingly sympathetic and supportive. He became the most quoted person during the trial
since Peter and I refused interview requests. We would not allow Peter
or his children to speak with the media; they didn't need much convincing
since they fully understood it was Peter's television interview with Channel 20 that led directly to the grand jury indictment for first degree murder. I had an affidavit from Mr. Humphry, who described his experiences
while addressing the membership and supporters of the Hemlock Society
of Lee County. Mr. Humphry said:

> The negative comments and attitudes toward Dr. Rosier were based
> on newspaper and television stories that had appeared in the local media.
> This shocked me because this should have been the most supportive
> and sympathetic audience one could imagine for what Dr. Rosier is
> alleged to have done. There was widespread antagonism toward Dr.
> Rosier's supposed life style, personality, and views. In spite of my very
> best efforts the general feelings of prejudice toward Dr. Rosier persisted,
> and these people were pro-right-to-die and pro-euthanasia.

The hearing on our motion for change of venue was held August
3, 1988. I told Judge Thompson that as recently as June 16, 1988, the
Fort Myers *News-Press* saw fit to announce in one of its many nonstories
that Dr. Rosier and his attorney and several of his witnesses are Jewish.
This Jewishness was combined with arrogance in the opening sentence
of an article that carried this headline: "JEWISH HOLIDAYS MAY
DELAY START OF ROSIER MURDER TRIAL."

> Dr. Peter Rosier, his attorney, and several important witnesses will not
> attend the start of Rosier's first degree murder trial if the trial date
> is not changed from September 12th.

Of course, if Judge Thompson were to grant our motion for change
of venue, the case could not have started on September 12, because detailed arrangements would have had to be made in some other city. Susan
and I were totally unavailable during many days in September because
of the major Jewish holidays of Rosh Hashana, Yom Kippur, and Sukkot.
The first day of Rosh Hashana fell on September 12, 1988, the very day

the trial was to begin. Yom Kippur, a day of total fasting and prayer, fell on September 21.

As an Orthodox Jew I am not permitted to work on those days; I am required to be in synagogue and that's where I would be come hell or high water. Jewish holidays are determined by the Hebrew calendar so that, unlike Christmas for example, a particular holiday does not fall on the same American date every year. One year Yom Kippur may occur in September and the next year it may occur in October. Judge Thompson was a reasonable and fair-minded man, so I was not in the least worried that he would force us to trial during the High Holy days.

I told the court that no one in southwest Florida cared whether this trial began in September or October. In spite of the fact that there were plenty of Jewish doctors and lawyers in Fort Myers I sensed and heard about an abundance of anti-Semitism. Undoubtedly, part of the reason for that was the presence of so many northern, Jewish professionals who were making a ton of money. In one of our affidavits, from a faculty member at Edison Community College—an institution named after the famous inventor, Thomas Edison, who had had a magnificent home in Fort Myers, which was now a leading tourist attraction—it read:

> I have specifically heard anti-Semitic remarks against Dr. Rosier. . . .
> There has been a great deal of anti-Semitism spoken regarding Peter Rosier, in reference to his earnings and possessions, and many other negative comments.

The affidavit of a landscaper read in part: "One of my customers stated that Dr. Rosier was a rich, spoiled Jew who wanted to show his ass in public." And another affidavit said:

> One of the gentlemen I was with who is a socially prominent member of the Naples Community (very near Fort Myers) said that Dr. Rosier was a murderer. This prompted someone else in my company to say—that little Jew bastard put her away. . . . The Fort Myers *News-Press* has vilified Dr. Rosier personally, professionally, and has conjured up an image of him as some effete, Jewish, New York, intellectual physician.

I pointed out how very unbalanced the *News-Press* had been in its coverage of the case. The many excellent qualities and deeds of the Rosiers were ignored: such as their charitable contributions to the blind and homeless, their deliveries of meals on wheels to the poor and disabled,

the fact that every Christmas and every Thanksgiving they invited homeless and lonely strangers into their home as guests. No mention was made
of the fact that Peter Rosier and his wife donated butterflies collected
by them in the jungles of South America over a period of years to the
University of Florida and the Florida State Museum in Gainesville. No
mention was made by the *News-Press* of the fact that Dr. Rosier was
the first chairman of the board of the Nature Center and Planetarium
of Fort Myers. He was likewise on the board of the Fort Myers Symphony
for which he played the flute for several years.

In my argument I asked: "Why had the Fort Myers *News-Press* never
told the people of southwest Florida that Peter Rosier was on the executive committee of Lee Memorial Hospital (*which is the committee that
makes policy for and runs the hospital*) for eleven consecutive years or
that he had served on the board of governors of the Medical Society
of Lee County? And why didn't the newspaper point out that Dr. Rosier
was so interested in advancing his medical knowledge and skills that he
became board certified in four subspecialty areas of pathology: (1) anatomic, (2) clinical, (3) dermato, and (4) radioisotopic?"

Although Peter's parents were financially successful and his circumstances were very comfortable, he had not been at all close to them or
to his two older sisters. He made this painfully clear in his manuscript.
Gertrude and Fred Ahlbrecht, his parents' housekeeper and handyman
couple, had saved Peter's emotional life by their tenderness toward him,
and he loved them for it. He had told them since he was eight years
old that he would always take care of them.

I wanted Judge Thompson and the world to know that Peter kept
his word in every respect, buying the Ahlbrechts a home in Durham, North
Carolina, when he was doing his pathology residency at Duke University
and buying them another home when his career took him to Birmingham,
Alabama, for about a year and a half. In terms of evaluating Peter as
a person, I was most impressed by his relationship with the Ahlbrechts
and the fact that after Fred died, Gertrude continued to live with Peter
and Patricia as a member of the household. She would eat with them
and was treated in every respect as a loving grandmother, not as an employee. Patricia and the children happily went along with this arrangement; that is the kind of private and continuing act which is an index
of a person's true character. Gertrude was one of our true aces because
her love for Peter knew no bounds, and the jury would readily observe
that Dr. Rosier could not possibly be the monster that the State wished
to portray.

I was using this public hearing as a forum to enumerate some of

Peter's good qualities in an attempt to balance the overall perception of him. The arguments on the motion for change of venue were front-page news throughout Florida. I pointed out to Judge Thompson that if the *News-Press* had given the Rosier case such intense and massive coverage up until now, he could imagine what they would do once the trial began.

There would be major and sensational headlines and front-page stories every day, television crews would be on the sidewalk outside the courthouse, and jurors could not escape being influenced even if they were sequestered in a hotel. There would be representatives from the national and international media present at the trial: the Associated Press, *People* magazine, the *New York Times, Newsweek, Time, USA Today,* as well as all the major television networks. The interest in euthanasia and the manner in which individual countries deal with it in terms of crime and punishment is worldwide.

So if Peter went on television to elevate the public's consciousness regarding euthanasia he was eminently successful. If he went on television to promote his still unpublished manuscript, as both the State attorney and the *News-Press* contended, then he failed dismally.

The State thought our motion to change the location of the trial was much ado about nothing. Ed Volz argued that the community in general could care less about Dr. Rosier; he said that I was greatly exaggerating the hostility against Peter even within the medical community.

The State had done its homework, obtaining sixty-two affidavits from citizens who said in effect that they didn't know of any reason why Peter couldn't get a fair trial in Lee County, and they asserted that they knew next to nothing about his case. I told Judge Thompson that I wasn't aware of the existence of a hermit sect in Fort Myers. No literate person could have been unaware of the Peter Rosier case. Our affidavits made it clear that the "Peter and Patricia Rosier show" was gossiped about in supermarkets, at cocktail parties, at little league games, wherever two or more doctors got together, at tennis courts—literally everywhere.

The State's affidavits were essentially forms, all saying pretty much the same thing and giving no specifics; we felt that our mountain of affidavits was far more impressive in that we recited facts. I saved one of our best affidavits for near the end of my argument. I pointed out that in spite of the tragic history of Patricia's battle with lung cancer, brain tumors, and adrenal masses, the prevailing mentality at Lee Memorial Hospital saw fit to ridicule the subject of Patricia's death during a Christmas skit in 1986, which surely had to take first prize for the "Worst Taste Demonstration of the Year" award. There was one person in that audience who had the courage to sign an affidavit:

The most popular and well-attended event during the year at Lee Memorial Hospital is the annual Christmas skit. Portions of one skit involved two actors; one of these actors was a vice president from the hospital and another was a physician. One of the actors asked the other the nature of the bottle on stage, and the other actor responded by turning the bottle around, and it had in large writing the word "morphine"—and the actor said this was a little Christmas gift he had picked up to bring home to his wife. It appeared that the audience in very many hundreds completely understood this sick and perverse joke since they all had a great laugh. The Christmas program is exhibited two or three times during the day and is probably attended by close to two thousand employees of the hospital, staff and others.

The hostility toward Peter had reached such a level of pathology that one restaurant owner said in his affidavit that doctors had stopped coming into his restaurant because on the rare occasions when Peter would frequent his establishment, the affiant had been polite to him. The doctors nearly all snubbed Peter, and they expected the rest of the citizens to do likewise.

Judge Thompson didn't say very much during the lengthy hearing but listened very carefully to the recitation of facts in the affidavits we presented. On August 10, 1988, Judge Thompson entered an order changing venue to St. Petersburg, Florida, approximately one hundred miles north of Fort Myers, and likewise on Florida's west and Gulf coast.

St. Petersburg had an elderly and conservative population, but it was next door to Tampa and far more metropolitan than Fort Myers. It sure wasn't our first choice or even our fifth, but it was a lot better than Fort Myers. We would have a decent shot at getting some jurors from states like New York or New Jersey as well as some Italians or Jews. We were elated! We would at least have a fighting chance!

The trial would commence on Monday, October 31, 1988, at 9:00 A.M. Since this was a capital case where the defendant could receive the death penalty, a jury of twelve rather than six jurors was empaneled. The first week of trial consisted of jury selection (*voir dire*) and opening statements. The state's first witness was called on Monday, November 7, 1988.

3

Dr. Rosier Confesses, Again and Again

Whenever I started feeling great about my cross examination of the Delmans or some dynamite medical testimony on the issue of euthanasia, Susan would turn on the VCR back at the hotel and play Peter's confession. Then she would show me chapter 34 of "The Lady." Invariably my heart would sink. The man said "I helped my wife end her life and I knew it was against the law—and I will change the law." The gruesome details of Patricia's death were quoted on television as excerpts from "The Lady," and of course were also detailed in the manuscript. Sometimes I truly believed that Peter was on a suicide mission: such irrational behavior in a conservative southern community must have some underlying psychological basis. We even discussed presenting a plea of insanity, but always half heartedly.

Peter simply could not grasp the basic fact that under Florida law helping his terminally ill wife end her life was the equivalent of walking into a school yard and gunning down an innocent child. Peter didn't consider his acknowledgments of assistance in Patricia's suicide to be murder confessions. A classic example occurred at Yale University. One of the top pathologists in the United States, Dr. Raymond Yesner, who had been at Yale for half a century, had reviewed Patricia's tumor slides during her illness. Dr. Yesner had advised against chemotherapy since he recognized that the cancer cells were extremely aggressive and not controllable. I contacted Dr. Yesner after Peter had been charged with murder and he readily agreed to be an expert for the defense. Dr. Yesner's pretrial deposition was scheduled by Edward Volz at Yesner's office in New Haven. Since Peter's flight arrived several hours before ours, we arranged to all

43

meet at Dr. Yesner's office. Peter arrived early. Volz asked Dr. Yesner a few basic preliminary questions about any conversations the doctor had had with Peter, and Dr. Yesner detailed Peter's description that morning of how he administered morphine to end Patricia's life. Volz displayed an extremely rare grin, and Susan and I looked at each other, thinking "Peter is truly a moron!" Peter couldn't help himself and just kept on confessing to murder every opportunity he had.

As anticipated, a focal point of the State's case against Dr. Rosier was his many confessions. Under Florida law the confessions alone were insufficient to convict Peter since the evidence (Patricia's body) had been cremated. The Delmans as well as Peter's former friends and colleagues provided the required corroborating evidence. It was our job to raise some questions as to the circumstances surrounding these confessions. I knew as the trial commenced that I had to avoid the subject of mercy killing or euthanasia since I couldn't flat-out ask the jury to change or ignore the law; I also had to build some type of smoke screen around the confessions.

Undoubtedly, any juror would want to know why Peter Rosier confessed to murder on television. What possessed Peter to write a manuscript that detailed his role in his wife's death? Why would he voluntarily place himself in a position to be charged with first degree murder? The State of Florida wanted to convince a jury that Peter went on television to obtain a publisher for his manuscript, to make it a best seller, and to become a national celebrity on the subject of euthanasia. The State also sought to introduce evidence on subjects that were not even remotely related to the crime with which Peter was charged. This was designed to make him an object of hatred and derision in the eyes of a jury. How much of this extraneous material would the judge allow the jury to hear? The answer to that question would play a significant role in determining defense strategy.

Those who are strongly anti-euthanasia repeat again and again the theme song of prosecutors: "the law is the law." What the law is depends greatly upon the temperament and philosophy of the trial judge and this is particularly so in the highly discretionary area of the admissibility or inadmissibility of evidence. For many years the law said that separate but so-called equal facilities did not violate the United States Constitution; the Constitution didn't change but the makeup of the U.S. Supreme Court did, and "separate but equal" suddenly became a violation of the law.

Even though a jury would make the ultimate decision on guilt or innocence, the manner in which the trial would be conducted would depend upon the rulings of the trial judge. Judge Thompson would decide what the jury would see and hear. He would decide the all-important question of whether the jury would get to read Peter's entire manuscript or only a part of it.

A case before a judge with a very narrow view of the admissibility of evidence, as opposed to a liberal, loose judge, can become two totally different trials even though the facts are precisely the same. Some judges rule on objections in a flash, whereas others entertain lengthy legal arguments every time an objection is made. The latter kind of judge encourages objections because the objecting lawyer thereby destroys the tempo and chronology of his opponent, irrespective of the final ruling on the objection.

Although the State's attorneys had an incredibly strong legal case against Peter, that apparently was not good enough for them. If the jury were to believe only 50 percent of all the State's claims and innuendos against Peter, they would send him to prison or even the electric chair on general principles. Simply put, the prosecutors tried to paint Peter Rosier as a despicable human being. Even though their endless barrage of what I characterized as cheap shots usually had nothing whatsoever to do with the elements of the crimes with which the defendant was charged, the State of Florida was relentless in its fury to bury Dr. Rosier.

The prosecutors wanted to dredge up the one affair Peter had had during his twenty-two-year marriage, an affair that ended well before Patricia became ill. Of course, the ever-talkative and ever-blunt Dr. Rosier had hand-delivered this ammunition to the State in his manuscript. According to the prosecutors, Peter never had a decent motive for doing anything, including his confessions of murder.

The State portrayed him as money hungry. They wanted the jury to know he paid $40,000 to have a movie script made of the manuscript. To my mind that made him an incredible sucker, hardly money hungry. They wanted the jury to know that he told a friend he hoped to make a billion dollars on the book and movie so that he could drive all around Fort Myers in his Rolls Royce and shit on everyone.

There would be no best seller if Patricia merely died from cancer; there would be no drama in that. A very significant part of the prosecution was that Peter allegedly convinced Patricia that she would die a gruesome death vomiting up all her blood if she allowed nature to take its course. They claimed that he manipulated Patricia into suicide by pretending that he would commit suicide alongside her, since he could not bear the thought of living without her. He also led her to believe that her life expectancy was much shorter than it was.

The State wanted the jury to believe that Peter was a Jewish Machiavelli. Not only did he manipulate Patricia but he manipulated the Delmans and his doctor friends into doing his dirty work. He manipulated the medical examiner's office into not performing an autopsy and he cleverly arranged to have Patricia's body cremated. As a former assistant medical examiner himself Peter knew the value of an autopsy in a criminal prosecution. According to the State, his confessions to murder on television and in "The Lady" were merely publicity stunts to generate a market for his manuscript and movie script.

The State contended that Peter was a financial manipulator and schemer as well. He didn't stop practicing medicine so that he could be with Patricia every moment of her ordeal; rather he stopped to lay the foundation for collecting on disability insurance policies worth $15,000 per month. He engaged in phony estate planning in order to cheat the government out of tax revenues.

The supposed love affair of the century was a fiction. Peter allegedly was trying to get friends to fix him up with women only a week or so after Patricia's death. The State twisted and distorted nearly every fact in its effort to have the jury detest my client. The prosecutors would try to have admitted as evidence nude photographs of the Rosiers and erotic movie making the couple had engaged in, even while Patricia was battling cancer. They wanted the jury to know how the Rosiers made love on the last night of Patricia's life.

The State's attorneys tried to present Peter as the medical profession's version of Rockefeller. They wanted the jury to know that Peter had earned $800,000 the year before Patricia contracted cancer. They wanted the jury to know about the couple's his-and-hers Rolls Royces and Peter's expensive apartment in New York. They wanted to put in evidence Peter's entire 641-page manuscript, "The Lady."

Susan and I strongly believed that if members of any jury read the entire manuscript, Peter could not avoid being convicted. He had opinions about everything and was not the least bit hesitant to express unorthodox views on controversial subjects. Worse still, he expressed these opinions oftentimes with brutal force and moral certainty. No topic or relationship was taboo. There was something in his manuscript to offend everyone, including Peter's fellow Jews and fellow physicians. To him the world, and particularly the medical profession, was corrupt; most people lied most of the time and most people were weak and shallow, living their lives from moment to moment without a bedrock of fundamental principles to guide them. Peter had a knack for offending people and this is a particularly dangerous trait for a defendant to have.

Writing "The Lady" was a form of therapy for Peter and he desperately wanted the world to know about and remember Patricia. But the world wasn't interested; submission of the manuscript to various publishers resulted in one rejection after another. The State wanted to put into evidence Peter's letters to various publishers as well as the rejection letters. The screenplay as well came to nothing and the State had listed as a witness the Hollywood screenwriter.

Susan was very offended by photographs mounted on the walls throughout the Rosier home. During our first visit to the home it was a bit distracting to discuss the murder charges while facing nude photographs of Patricia, including one where she was squatting on the floor. Susan told Peter in no uncertain terms that if he expected her to continue working on the case he should remove the photographs and place them in a closet before our visits.

Peter did not return to the practice of medicine after Patricia's death; he had nothing but time on his hands and he got involved with many shallow people. Peter went from being a busy, productive, well-respected physician with huge earnings to a guy who got up in the morning wondering what to do with himself.

All he wanted to do was talk about Patricia and he was becoming a terrible bore, even to people who liked him. The fundamental thing that Peter could not handle was the fact that life was going on as if Patricia had never existed, and no one seemed interested in their great love.

Volz and Russell were successful in large part in introducing into evidence many irrelevant matters.

Lawyers try to convince a judge, in a self-righteous manner, that clearly irrelevant and prejudicial evidence is somehow probative of an issue. What lawyers say about evidence is almost always phony. Who really cared if Dr. Rosier said at a cocktail party the week after Patricia died that he wanted to get laid? The State argued that the "door was opened" since I had said in my opening statement that Peter loved Patricia. The bottom line is, trial lawyers want to place in evidence anything that will help them, and they want to keep out any evidence that could hurt. Just as the State wanted to depict Dr. Rosier as some skirt chaser, we wanted to convince the jury that he was a kind and gentle man who supported his parents' former housekeeper, Gertrude, all of her life and made her a part of his family. None of this evidence was legally relevant but that is part of the great legal fiction.

The State's line of attack was: (1) the confession that aired on television, (2) the confession to Leisa Zigman, (3) the confession in the manuscript "The Lady," (4) incriminating testimony from former friends and colleagues, (5) a lot of collateral dirt on Peter Rosier, and (6) the key testimony of the unindicted coconspirators [the Delmans] who witnessed the act of "murder." The State led off the trial with Channel 20's interviewer, Leisa Zigman. Through her the State was to introduce the television confession along with the incriminating portions of Peter's manuscript.

Leisa had established a trusting relationship with the Rosiers well before Patricia's death. Patricia even granted Leisa an interview on January 14, 1986, one day before her death. This interview was shown on the 6:00 P.M. news on the very day that Patricia died. That is the kind of exclusive that can result in promotions and raises and it is the kind of exclusive that news directors lust for.

Patricia had agreed to allow the filming of her chemotherapy treatments. When her hair started to fall out, she agreed to be shaved totally bald on camera. Her message was: "Even though you have cancer, you are still a person of value and life still has meaning and you should still try and be positive and look your best."

Peter actually did two lengthy interviews with Leisa in October, but the first interview was never aired. Channel 20's then news director, David Cromwell, realized that this was a bombshell confession to murder by a very prominent member of the community.

Every television station in Florida had covered intensely the trial and conviction for first degree murder of Roswell Gilbert. With this precedent staring him in the face, Cromwell knew it was unthinkable for Channel 20 to air the interview without Peter signing a release absolving the station of all liability. Leisa's instructions were to get the release signed and do a second interview; Peter had been too emotional in the first one, according to Channel 20 representatives.

Without consulting a lawyer, Peter obligingly signed the release on October 31 and agreed to be interviewed a second time. The interview wasn't actually aired until November 12, so Peter had plenty of time to cancel it. Naturally he didn't, for that would have been intelligent and Peter was not functioning in a rational manner during that time frame.

I used to scold Peter for trusting people and for shooting off his big mouth; I told him that I would be happy to plead him guilty to being a gullible fool. To his credit Peter agreed. Like paying $40,000 to a so-called screenwriter who did not have a single movie to his credit. When I made that offer to the State nobody laughed. A sense of humor does not appear to be one of the strong suits of those sworn to bring dangerous criminals to justice.

From the time I agreed to accept the Rosier case until the time the trial began I talked to Peter every day (with the exception of the Sabbath) at his insistence. That was a lot of talking for a guy who hates to talk on the telephone. Susan screens all my calls, not because I am such a big shot but because she wants to spare me the stress of doing something I hate. Besides, she is very good on the telephone and I am awful.

With the exception of family, I got to know Peter better than I knew anyone. I recognized his strengths and his weaknesses; when he would go off on a tangent, which was often, or when he would get on his soap box or get mired down in petty irrelevancies I could always bring him back on course by simply saying, "Just cut the shit Peter, we have work to do and you need to keep your eye on the target; I have neither the time nor the inclination for these abstract discussions which don't go anywhere."

In truth the time never arrived when I looked forward to his daily phone calls. There was much repetition in them, which, of course, was understandable; he needed to be reassured constantly and I did my best, but that is certainly not my strong suit. Peter understood that if he were convicted, Susan and I would be devastated; we would not just accept it as a professional loss in a very tough case. Peter felt (correctly) that all his prior lawyers who represented him wanted to have a cordial relationship with the prosecutors and the judge after the trial was over, irrespective of the outcome. They wanted to be respected as professionals for a job well done. Peter knew I cared about one thing only, a not guilty verdict! And that was enough for him.

If Peter had had the sense to talk to me before signing Channel 20's release, the interview would never have aired.

At trial Stephen Russell questioned Ms. Zigman for the State:

Q: Did you have occasion to interview Patricia Rosier on January 14, 1986?
A: Yes, sir.
Q: And how did that interview come about?
A: Dr. Rosier called me.
Q: What did he say?
A: Dr. Rosier said that you have done a number of interviews with my wife and Patty is going to die. After she's gone will you do a follow-up?

The State was trying to show that Peter was always thinking about publicity and ways to promote his manuscript and screenplay.

Q: What did you say to Dr. Rosier?
A: I said yes.
Q: Did you suggest a particular time to do the interview?
A: Yes sir.
Q: What did you suggest?
A: I asked him if I could do an interview with his wife the following day.
Q: What was his response?
A: Dr. Rosier said, "Patty won't be here tomorrow."

According to Zigman, this statement did not trigger in her mind the likelihood or even the possibility that Mrs. Rosier would be committing suicide before tomorrow.

Q: Now, after that day what was the nature of your next contact with Dr. Rosier?
A: Dr. Rosier called me a few weeks after Patricia's death.
Q: For what general purpose?
A: He said he was distraught, he was very upset, he needed someone to talk to, would I have lunch with him.
Q: What was your response?
A: I said no.

The State was trying to show that Peter had a romantic interest in Leisa. This would in part bolster their contention that he initiated the contact in October rather than the other way around, as Peter would assert. Peter was ready to refute Leisa as to nearly every aspect of her testimony.

Q: Now your next contact after that phone conversation with Dr. Rosier would have been when, approximately?
A: October of 1986.
Q: Who initiated the contact?
A: Dr. Rosier called me at work.
Q: And what did he tell you at that time?
A: He said that he had been writing a book about Patricia's death, about their life together, and there was a screenplay writer in California who was interested in it, would I be interested in doing a story on the book?

Q: And how did you respond to his inquiry?
A: I said yes.

Peter, his children, and his secretary were ready to testify that Leisa hounded Peter for follow-up stories.

Q: Did you have occasion to read parts of the book?
A: Yes sir.
Q: And how did you get the book?
A: Dr. Rosier handed it to me.

During Zigman's direct testimony the jury saw Peter's television confession and they saw Patricia's last interview of January 14, 1986. The State wanted the jury to see how good Patricia looked (relatively speaking) on the day before her death. Stephen Russell very skillfully tried to anticipate and defuse my cross examination on the subject of the disappearance of all portions of the interviews which were not publicly aired. From a journalistic standpoint, the loss of film and sound relating to a confession to murder was both embarrassing and inexplicable. Russell's direct examination continued:

Q: Now, at the time you made these two trips to the Rosier residence, was there other film that was shot that was not in fact aired or used in your story?
A: Yes sir.

Prosecutors always tell their witnesses to be very polite and courteous. Although I knew Zigman hated my guts she nonetheless exhibited a plastic kind of politeness to me as well.

[MR. RUSSELL]: Is that a normal course of events in your business?
A: Yes sir.
Q: And in this case do you know what would have happened to the other portions that you chose not to use in the story?
A: I gave the raw video to my news director.
Q: And is it common practice in your market at your station to recycle film that is shot but not used in a particular story?
A: Yes.

It sure as hell isn't normal or common practice when a prominent doctor confesses to murder. Steve Russell had a far greater familiarity with the inner workings of a television station than would the average lawyer. He was divorced from Chere Avery, Channel 20's current news director. I was not about to let that fact go unnoticed.

> [MR. RUSSELL]: Now, in the course of your talking to Dr. Rosier did you ask him if he knew what he was doing and what he was saying in terms of legal liability?
> A: Yes sir.

The station did not want to appear to be in the position of exploiting Dr. Rosier and his family.

> Q: What did you ask him and what did he respond?
> A: On the taped interview I asked him, why are you doing this? Are you trying to lead a crusade? And Dr. Rosier said that he wasn't a fanatic, but he believed that the laws needed to be changed. He felt there was a great lag between medical technology's ability to keep a person alive and the laws that deal with death. And he said that he would hire the best attorneys to try and fight those laws.

Stephen Russell ended his direct examination of Zigman with the obligatory questions relating to the identity of the defendant. Every witness was asked these same questions even though the jury knew the identity of Dr. Rosier better than anyone outside their immediate families.

> Q: Ms. Zigman, do you see Dr. Rosier, who you referred to, in the courtroom today?
> A: Yes sir.
> Q: Would you please point to him, describe what he's wearing? (*Only in the movies does the witness sometimes point to the wrong person.*)
> A: He's sitting next to Mr. Rosenblatt in an olive green suit.
> MR. RUSSELL: Your Honor, I ask the court to allow the record to reflect the witness referred to the defendant in this case, Robert Peter Rosier.
> THE COURT: May so reflect.

I knew the jury would require a reasonable explanation as to why Peter agreed to go on television, for if they believed he did it to hustle his manuscript we would be in deep trouble. Peter had difficulty articulating his reasons for appearing on television. He wanted to talk about Patricia and that was an available forum. Leisa Zigman had kept in touch with Peter following Patricia's death and when she learned that Peter was writing a book about his life with Patricia, she begged him to give her an exclusive interview. They talked of the good Peter could do by bringing into the open the plight of terminally ill patients.

Peter indicated there were two lengthy emotion-filled interviews and both he and Leisa cried during the first one. Peter also felt that he was self-destructive since he was aware of the potential consequences of his conduct. Basically, he denied trying to be a media star or to plug his manuscript or screenplay.

We believed Peter and hoped the jury would as well. I wanted the jury to understand very early in my cross examination of Leisa Zigman that Channel 20 had a commercial motive for going after this interview. I wanted the jury to believe that Channel 20's News Department was primarily interested in ratings and pizzazz, not in educating the public about cancer.

[MR. ROSENBLATT]: Television is very interested in ratings, isn't it?

A: Yes sir.

Q: That's the name of the game on television, isn't it?

A: In television, I would question news though.

Q: You would question what?

A: That it would be with news. I don't think that's the name of the game with news.

Q: You don't think that local newsmen and local news directors get hired and fired and get increases in salary based on whether they are number one in a given market or last in a given market?

THE LAWYER FOR MS. ZIGMAN AND CHANNEL 20: Your Honor, I'm going to object.

Judge Thompson allowed the lawyer for Zigman and Channel 20 to make objections. On the one hand it aggravated me to no end that this person was permitted to interrupt the flow and crescendo of my questioning, and particularly when as in this instance the State had not objected. On the other hand I saw it as a plus since his objections were academic nonsense in the context of a first degree murder trial, and his vigorous participation made it appear that Channel 20 felt vulnerable in some way. They were not on trial. They had not been charged with anything. What did they need a lawyer for? Normal jurors would think this way even though the legal profession loves to say that everyone is entitled to a lawyer during every waking moment.

A bench conference followed. As usual, Susan did nearly all the arguing at bench conferences that took place outside the presence of the jury. The jury usually remained in their seats but they were unable to hear what was said. Zigman's lawyer said my questions about ratings and promotions, as well as my repeated questions about the lost tapes, were not relevant and they went beyond the scope of anything covered on direct examination.

> MRS. ROSENBLATT: Your Honor, it's highly relevant as to the motivation to seek out further stories, and there's an issue as to how those stories came about and whether or not they were solicited. Maybe the jury will choose not to believe her based upon her motivation to get a story and her desire to get promoted, which in fact she did. (*Zigman was nonchalantly leaning in the witness chair trying to hear every word.*) Also, I don't appreciate the witness listening so that she can be coached as to how she should answer the questions.
>
> The sentence preceding what was quoted could have been, "Well you called me fifty times, Leisa, and that's why I'm doing this interview." That could have been the sentence that was edited out immediately preceding what he said on the air, so certainly that goes to her motivation and credibility.
>
> THE COURT: The questions bear arguably, on perhaps how the story was edited, about why certain matters might have been excluded if there is a desire for ratings and sensationalism. I'm going to allow Mr. Rosenblatt to ask the question about the importance of ratings.

Before I returned to the issue of ratings, I asked:

> Q: Ms. Zigman, the gentlemen who just made an objection and came up here is your lawyer, Mr. Rosenthal?
> A: Yes sir.
> Q: And every time you've had a statement taken in this case and every time I've taken your deposition or tried to take your deposition, your lawyer has been present protecting your interests, correct?
> A: Yes sir.

Witnesses have to listen to questions very, very carefully because the significance of words is usually not lost on jurors. If Leisa had been listening carefully she would have said that she doesn't have any "interests" in this case and certainly not any interests that need protecting. But she really didn't hear the way I phrased that question. Her interest was in looking good both professionally and personally. She and her employer would look very bad if the jury did not believe her story about the disappearance of the tapes or if they felt that she had exploited Peter so that she could continue with her scoop.

I asked her the question about Al Rosenthal because I thought the jury would resent this very well-dressed and immaculately neat Miami lawyer interfering on trivial points when my client's life was at stake. My cross examination continued:

Q: Ms. Zigman, you know for a fact that if a television station is number one in a given market it can charge advertisers more than a television station that is, let's say, number four in the same market. Don't you know that?

A: Yes sir.

Q: And you knew and everyone at Channel 20 knew that this was dynamite television.

MR. RUSSELL: Object to the form of the question as to what other people at Channel 20 knew.

THE COURT: Rephrase it. (*I love rephrasing questions because it provides me with the opportunity to repeat and emphasize a given point.*)

Q: All your superiors knew, because anyone with an IQ of 100 who has been in the television business for one hour would know that a beautiful woman, age forty-three, dying of cancer, allowing her head to be shaved, and being given chemotherapy treatments, is terrific dynamite television in terms of ratings, isn't that so?

MR. RUSSELL: Same objection and editorializing.

THE COURT: I sustain the objection to the form of the question. (*The jury had heard the question and I could continue my pursuit.*)

Q: You knew it was dynamite television. Forget about everyone else?

A: I knew it was a dynamite story, yes sir.

Q: And, Ms. Zigman, you knew it wouldn't hurt your career, could only do you good, right? Do you have a problem with that?

A: No sir. (*She gave that answer in spite of her look of injured innocence.*)

Q: Obviously a dynamite story, terrific television, quality television. If it's your story, you're the reporter, you're the editor, it's going to help your career, isn't it?

A: Couldn't hurt.

Q: Couldn't hurt. Now you're the 11:00 P.M. news anchor. Back then you were a medical reporter before you ever met Mrs. Rosier, so it helped?

A: I would hesitate to say that story put me in the anchor spot, sir.

Q: Is it not true, Ms. Zigman, that in the history of local television in Fort Myers no man or woman suffering from cancer ever allowed their heads to be shaved on camera?

A: In the four years that I've been there, no sir, I have no recollection of that.

Q: Geraldo Rivera would love that kind of film and so would Oprah Winfrey. You're smiling because you know I'm 100 percent right. That's dynamite television, isn't it?

A: In the television industry it's important to have pictures that you're talking about. If I'm talking about Pat Rosier shaving her head, sure, it's great to have the pictures of it.

Q: Ms. Zigman, don't you know that if the business end of a newscast can go out to advertisers and say we're number one in the market, they can charge more money to advertise if they are the number one station, isn't that correct?

MR. ROSENTHAL: Objection, Your Honor. We have to approach the bench. (*I mumbled to Susan making sure that Rosenthal could overhear me: "I didn't realize that D'Alessandro had hired another assistant."*)

　　Basically the same objection as before, but now we're getting into the sales policies of WBBH. She doesn't work in the sales department. If Mr. Rosenblatt's style is such that he believes that he can shout at the witness as he's been doing, and intimidate her with these questions to benefit his client, that's up to him, but there's a privilege here.

MRS. ROSENBLATT: These questions are certainly relevant as to her motivation, as to her credibility. And obviously there is motivation to put this on to increase ratings, to get more advertisers, and that's the whole idea of why she was chasing after the Rosier children, and trying to get Peter to say things.

She says, well I went back for fairness (*to do the second interview*).

MR. ROSENBLATT: She got promoted on Dr. Rosier's back. This was very important to her career. We don't have to put our heads in the sand in terms of realism.

MRS. ROSENBLATT: And this man did not go on television to plug his book, he went on television because he was talked into it by this witness. We have a right to present that and present the fact that this was a very big deal to her.

The judge ended up giving me appropriate latitude in the direction of ratings and television profits. Judges are human and many times they make these highly subjective rulings on the admissibility of evidence based on their concept of fairness in a given situation. I knew that Judge Thompson did not like Dr. Rosier, but I felt he had his own suspicions as to the disappearance of the tapes. I next attempted to demonstrate that Channel 20 was not the least bit interested in being fair to Dr. Rosier. Instead, they were interested in getting an exclusive dynamite television story if they could do so without jeopardizing their own position. I asked Ms. Zigman about the release and any instructions she received from the former news director, David Cromwell, whom the State never called as a witness.

Q: Didn't Mr. Cromwell tell you that it looked as though Dr. Rosier didn't know what he was saying, or that he was overly emotional?

A: Mr. Cromwell questioned whether Dr. Rosier knew what he was saying, yes sir. (*Well that's pretty damn basic and certainly lent credence to Peter's account that both he and Leisa were crying during the interview.*)

Q: The release didn't protect Dr. Rosier. The release only protected Channel 20, right?

A: I really can't answer that, sir.

Q: Well, look at the release.

A: Okay.

Q: You know very well that the release only protects Channel 20, right?

A: No sir, I don't know that.

Q: What did you think the purpose of the release was?

A: Well, my news director instructed me to have it signed. I was interested in the story. I really don't know.

Q: Well, think about it now. You've read the release, you've got

common sense, don't you? You understand that the purpose
of the release was to protect Channel 20?

A: Sir, I haven't read the release in two years.

I loved these answers because the release was a very simple, straightforward document, and it would be obvious to every member of the jury
in twenty seconds that the entire purpose of it was to protect Channel
20. It was an intelligent thing for Channel 20 to do. It was a serious error
for Zigman not to admit the obvious. By failing to do so she impaired
her credibility. She still could have maintained that Dr. Rosier knew exactly
what he was doing and understood his criminal liability, but nonetheless
agreed to grant the interview as a means of advancing his ideas on euthanasia.

Leisa Zigman and WBBH TV Channel 20, Waterman Broadcasting,
obtained a general release from Dr. Peter Rosier on October 31, 1986
(exactly two years to the day before the commencement of his trial)! It
released "Waterman Broadcasting Corporation d/b/a WBBH TV–20, Leisa
Zigman, and all of its reporters, editors, and employees individually," of
all actions, claims, and anything and everything from "the beginning of
the world to the day of these presents,"

> including but not limited to any criminal or civil charges or claims which
> may result from any interviews I have given to WBBH TV–20, Waterman
> Broadcasting or any of its reporters in connection with the death of
> Patricia Rosier.

Leisa was similarly evasive when I asked her about the missing portions
of the interviews:

Q: The portion of Dr. Rosier's interview that was shown on
Channel 20 to the public was approximately how long?

A: About two or two and a half minutes.

Q: How long was the interview altogether?

A: About ten minutes.

Q: In television lingo, what do you call the two or two and a
half minutes that the public sees? Does that have a special
name?

A: They are called sound bites.

Q: And what do you call the seven and a half minutes that the
public never got to see?

A: It's called raw tape. (*Peter would testify that the unaired portion
of the interview was much longer.*)

Q: The raw tape of the interview with Dr. Rosier that was never shown to the public, what happened to it?

A: The raw tape was given to my news director.

Q: And what did Mr. Cromwell do with it?

A: I don't know, sir.

Q: Obviously since Mr. D'Alessandro went on television the day after the interview appeared and announced that he was going to conduct an investigation, am I safe in assuming that you made inquiry to find out whether that raw tape exists?

A: Yes sir.

Q: Does it exist?

A: I don't know. I haven't seen it in two years.

Q: If it does not exist, who destroyed it?

I used the word "destroyed" intentionally since I wanted to plant that seed in the jury's mind.

A: Well, I have third-hand information I'd be willing to tell you about.

Q: Sure, tell us.

A: My news administrator told me he talked to the news director and the news director told him that he left the tapes behind when he left WBBH TV.

Q: You mean he left them sitting on a desk?

A: Sitting in his office, yes sir.

Q: Are they still there, do you think? (*By this time my voice and manner were dripping with sarcasm.*)

A: Well, we moved buildings, we switched from an old newsroom to a much bigger one.

Q: Think maybe they got lost in the moving? (*I would periodically look over at the jury and roll my eyes.*)

A: I think it's a possibility.

Q: That's as good as you can do for us?

A: I haven't seen them in two years, sir.

Q: You think they exist or you think they were destroyed? What do you think?

A: I don't know.

She was tired and very disgusted with my questioning, otherwise she would have denied the possibility that they could have been destroyed on purpose.

Q: Are you telling us, Ms. Zigman, that a prominent television station, which is an affiliate of the National Broadcasting Company, has tapes within its possession in the nature of a murder confession, the state attorney goes on television the following day, the only evidence being that television interview, and no one at Channel 20 can tell us what happened to the raw tape that the public never got to see?

A: Perhaps Mr. Cromwell could.

Q: And you've asked around Channel 20 and apparently nobody has any more specific information concerning the existence of the raw tapes than you do, correct?

A: Yes sir.

Q: Let's go back to the interview you did a week before when there was no release. How long was that interview?

A: About ten minutes too. (*Again, Peter would testify that it was substantially longer.*)

Q: And no part of that ten minutes was ever shown to the public, correct?

A: Yes sir.

Q: Where are those ten minutes?

A: I believe they have been recycled and put back into normal use, which is standard.

Q: (*I asked in utter astonishment.*) Which is standard?

A: Yes sir.

Q: Sure, if it's run-of-the-mill tape. But it certainly is not standard for any television station anywhere in America, when a doctor describes the circumstances of his wife's death, which may constitute a crime—are you telling us it is standard television practice to recycle, destroy those raw tapes?

There was an objection by Mr. Russell which was sustained, so I asked this question:

Q: When you say that you believe the ten-minute raw tape of the earlier interview has been recycled, in practical terms that means it's been destroyed? (*Again my choice of the word "destroyed" was not accidental.*)

A: Right. Now, I said I believe that. Those tapes could have been part of the ones I gave to Mr. Cromwell. I just don't remember.

Q: Who is your news director now?

A: Chere Avery.

Q: Chere Avery and Mr. Russell were husband and wife back in January of 1986, weren't they? Mr. Russell (*pointing*), this Mr. Russell, the Assistant State Attorney and your present news director, Chere Avery, were husband and wife back then, weren't they?

A: Yes sir.

Russell managed to maintain his poker face as my thumb was extended in his direction but he was seething with anger. If this was one of my cheap shots, at least no one could go to the electric chair because of it. Leisa kept insisting that the second interview was done in the name of fairness since Peter had been "upset, very emotional" during the first interview. And she agreed with her news director when he "questioned Rosier's state of mind during that interview, whether he was on the verge of a breakdown."

I returned to the release because it demonstrated that the reason for the second interview had absolutely nothing to do with fairness.

Q: Read it over, Ms. Zigman, and then answer my question which is—the purpose of that piece of paper is to protect Channel 20 and make sure that Dr. Rosier does not sue them for airing the interview.

A: (*Witness reading, and after some hesitation*) Yes sir.

Q: With respect to wanting to be fair to Dr. Rosier, did you or Mr. Cromwell ever say to him anything along this line? Hey, this is heavy stuff. I think you ought to talk to a lawyer before you give this interview. You didn't do that, did you?

A: My job is a reporter. I'm supposed to gather the news. To offer legal advice on any subject, it's not my job to do that.

Q: You would agree, would you not that both you and Mr. Cromwell were well aware of the significant legal consequences to Peter as a result of airing this interview, correct?

A: I would say yes, that is a correct statement.

Channel 20 had lawyers who could read the criminal statutes and they knew of the Roswell Gilbert precedent; that's why although this was powerful television, Channel 20 was very worried. They created and had exclusive possession of critical evidence in a first degree murder trial.

Q: I would like for you to explain to the jury as best you can how you, as a knowledgeable television person, and how Channel 20, as an NBC affiliate, could allow tapes of a confession to possibly murder be destroyed or erased over. How does that happen?

If I was doing my job properly, the jury would be very interested in the answer to this question. The answer they heard had to be very unsatisfactory.

A: I don't think anything was allowed, sir. I don't know. I can't answer that question.
Q: Well, let me ask it another way. In view of the fact that Dr. Rosier's interviews were incredibly sensitive and incredibly unique, how is it that someone didn't put them in a safe place, to make sure that the station would not be involved in the possibility of destroying evidence in a criminal case?
MR. ROSENTHAL: Your Honor, I object. May I approach the bench?
THE COURT: Yes.

Zigman's lawyer was way back in the bleachers and he had to make the long trek over to the judge. When this occurred I would usually glance over at the jury with a look of total disgust. It was not a look I had to fake. I would deliberately stand at our table and watch Rosenthal walk to the front of the courtroom; I had more freedom when his back was in front of me. Volz, Russell, Susan, and I followed for the whispered discussion.

This kind of objection and the timing of it actually underscored the importance of the point I was making. It's a big deal in the jury's mind when five lawyers and the court reporter snuggle up to the bench to discuss an objection. Many lawyers have tunnel vision and Rosenthal wanted to somehow vindicate the law of evidence and show his clients that he was scoring points on the legal privileges of reporters. From the standpoint of trial technique, when a jury is very anxious to have a question answered they can resent the lawyer who tries to prevent them from hearing the answer. Cases are not won or lost based on which side gets more objections sustained or overruled.

MR. ROSENTHAL: I am a little bit annoyed at the accusation of criminal conduct, and I'm tired of Mr. Rosenblatt accusing

my client of committing a crime. I am tired of it, I don't
have to stand for it.

I whispered to Susan: "Our client could spend the rest of his life
in prison but Zigman's lawyer is terribly offended. The poor thing!" He
argued it was "ludicrous and insulting" for me to even imply that Channel
20 and/or Zigman deliberately lost the tapes. How dare I do such a thing?

At one level we were simply outraged that Judge Thompson permitted
a private lawyer to have this much standing to sidetrack me. At a much
more important and positive level we felt that Rosenthal, by the manner
and timing of his objections, hurt very substantially the credibility of Channel
20 and its anchor person. Anyone would look askance at the fact that
these critically important tapes were missing and we had a right to expect
a reasonable explanation. This was not some seminar about freedom of
the press or arcane constitutional privileges. I was trying to save Peter
Rosier's life and the future of his children.

Rosenthal had wanted to stand by the witness as I was questioning
her, but I protested vigorously, complaining that I did not want to be
looking directly at him as I was interrogating the witness. I would have
gone berserk had that been permitted. Judge Thompson made him sit
behind us, nearly into the audience so that when he made an objection
he had to march to the bench, thereby making his conduct all the more
noticeable.

MRS. ROSENBLATT: It was certainly incumbent upon the station
and its reporters to make sure that evidence would not be
destroyed, evidence we believe very strongly would have been
favorable to us in its entirety, and I think Stanley asked a
very appropriate question. For these tapes to be destroyed
or erased or misplaced when there was an ongoing criminal
investigation is absolutely inappropriate, and actually in violation of the statute. There is a Florida statute on point that
talks about destruction of evidence, and here it's pretty clear.
Certainly it is highly suspect as to what else was on the missing
interviews, and perhaps what is lost would have hurt the station,
would have made them look very bad based on their coercion
in getting this defendant to go along with the interview.

Judge Thompson overruled the objection and allowed me to pursue
this line of questioning.

Q: Do you know why neither you nor Mr. Cromwell nor anyone else at Channel 20 saved the raw tapes?

A: Well sir, I handed them to my news director because we were going to save them. (*Of course they were to be saved; exactly my point.*)

Q: So somehow Mr. Cromwell screwed up? Is that your testimony? You gave them to Cromwell and he lost them?

A: I don't know, sir.

Q: After D'Alessandro announces to the world he's conducting an investigation, and this is way before Cromwell leaves WBBH, you never asked: What happened to the tapes I gave you, boss?

A: I haven't seen those tapes in two years, sir.

Q: That's not my question. My question is did you ever ask Mr. Cromwell: Where are those raw tapes of my interview with this criminal?

I would point to Peter or walk over to him when asking such a question. Sitting there teary eyed and meek, he looked like anything but a dangerous criminal.

A: No sir, I never asked that question.

Leisa Zigman testified that she never had any contact with David Cromwell after the grand jury returned its indictment in September 1987. It was incredible to me that neither she nor anyone else at the station ever made it their business to pin him down as to what he knew about the location of the missing tapes. I hoped it would seem incredible to the jury as well. Our strategy was to divert the jury's attention away from Peter's confessions and the clear language of the Florida statutes.

I had located Cromwell who was working at another television station in another state. Since I had been able to locate him easily, there was no doubt but that Fitzpatrick, with all his knowledge and resources, would have found him as well. The State obviously didn't plan to call him because he was unwilling to confirm Zigman's version. Cromwell was an ace in the hole for us since he would shoot down or at least contradict much of the testimony that had been given about him and the lost tapes. I returned again to the bottom-line question and I was not the least bit worried about being accused of being repetitious.

Q: Does anyone at Channel 20 know where the missing tapes are?

A: I don't know, sir.

Right! A prominent doctor confesses to murder in an exclusive interview with your television station and the station does not preserve every word. To us, that was simply unbelievable and particularly so in view of the first degree murder conviction of Roswell Gilbert. Local affiliates love it when one of their pieces is aired nationally on the network; for that reason alone the unedited tapes would be preserved.

Channel 20 was a modern, well-equipped, financially successful television station covering a five-county area in southwest Florida and yet, according to it, most of the tapes were discarded or lost as though they were so many old candy wrappers. As a trial progresses it is my custom to write myself reminders in a special notebook called "Ideas for Final Argument." I would have much to say about the mysterious and unexplained disappearance of the tapes, and I would not be diplomatic in my comments.

I asked Zigman for the name of the cameraman who accompanied her to either of Peter's interviews in October. She couldn't recall the identity of either one but was pretty sure there was a different cameraman for each interview. I kept stressing the fact that these were not run-of-the-mill interviews where a reporter would forget details. Leisa agreed this "was a great story." A doctor confessing to murder would be a great story in television terms under any circumstances, yet it becomes far more compelling when the confession relates to a hotly debated national subject such as euthanasia, regarding which there had recently been a highly publicized first degree murder conviction in Florida.

Leisa Zigman admitted that at various times she took notes while talking with Peter and Patricia. Of course, her notes were lost as well. The tapes were nowhere to be found, her notes were gone, no cameraman was corroborating Zigman's account of the interviews, David Cromwell would not be corroborating her account, and the release was supposedly signed because the station wanted to be fair to Peter. I was writing all this down in my final argument notebook, since part of our strategy was to put both Channel 20 and the Delmans on trial. Anyone but Peter!

Through Leisa Zigman the State corroborated the television confession since she independently stated that Dr. Rosier told her he had helped end his wife's life. The State also introduced into evidence, through Leisa, portions of the manuscript of "The Lady" that Peter had provided to her at the first interview following Patricia's death. While she lost all other evidence of the interviews, Zigman held on to Peter's manuscript. One of the most dramatic portions of the trial was the reading of chapter 34: the jurors read along with their own personal copies of the entire chapter.

The court had overruled our strenuous objections to the admissibility of this chapter. We couldn't argue that this was some kind of coerced confession; Peter had after all written the manuscript voluntarily and had done everything within his power to get it published. Whether the rest of "The Lady" would be admitted in evidence remained an open question.

I at least wanted to make sure that chapter 34 was read with the correct emphasis and nuances. After much discussion it was decided by Judge Thompson that Deputy Clerk Ann Davis would read chapter 34 to the jury. Ann Davis was part of the Fort Myers courthouse staff that accompanied Judge Thompson to St. Petersburg.

Much to my surprise, the deputy clerk read the twelve pages beautifully and with appropriate inflections. Court clerks as a group tend to be very low key and officious and I was afraid that the reading of this chapter would be done in a boring monotone that would emphasize all the wrong things. My fears were unwarranted and we got a very fair reading. What follows is some of what the clerk read to the jury from "The Lady" after Zigman had completed her testimony.

> I followed Pat into the bedroom. She took off her bathrobe and changed her nightgown. She put on another simple, plain white nightgown. It had no frills and was quite severe. She got into bed and sat with her head propped up against the pillow. I went into the bathroom and counted out twenty 100 mg Seconal capsules and placed them in a small dish. I brought the dish in and a glass of water to Pat. We were holding hands now and I was crying. We kissed goodbye gently and she turned and without hesitation swallowed the twenty Seconal capsules and water.
>
> Her brothers, Farrell and Russell, came into the room now. After a while Pat said, I'm getting a little sleepy now. Russell was whispering what he thought were magical things, such as, "let go, you're going to a wonderful place, just follow the light. Go to the light. It's wonderful. Just let go." He said these things in sort of a hypnotic and urging whisper; and every now and then Farrell would whisper, "yes, yes, it's wonderful." Pat was relaxed and smiling and unafraid. She did not cry. Russell kept his incantations going and Farrell kept interjecting with his, but Pat paid them no attention. She held my hand tightly. Then she said, "I'm a little scared," to which I replied, "Don't be scared,

my love. All of those who have lived before us have done it. It's no big deal." She had opened her eyes when she spoke and now she closed them once again, and I said "bon voyage, my love, my love, bon voyage, my love."

At the point when the judge interrupted the reading by the clerk, Peter was sobbing so heavily that he simply had to leave the courtroom. As the defendant, Peter had an absolute right to be present at every stage of the proceedings. His waiver of that right had to be done in a fairly formal manner, and that's what the judge was worried about. "That camera is driving him crazy," said the judge.

THE COURT: Just a moment. Approach the bench. I'm willing
    to accept the waiver of Dr. Rosier's presence.
MR. ROSENBLATT: He can't handle it. He's going to be crying.

At this point as during most stages of the trial, the huge courtroom was filled with television equipment, reporters, and still photographers. One photographer in particular who had very large and intrusive equipment was just clicking away constantly at the deputy clerk as she was reading, at the judge, at the jurors, at the State's table, at the defense table, and in particular Dr. Rosier. At times some of these photographers acted as though they wanted to take pictures of Peter's tonsils.

At the outset of the trial the St. Petersburg court administrator and Judge Thompson cautioned the media that they were not to interfere with or interrupt the judicial proceedings. Private media that had planned to televise the entire trial proceedings on cable TV were banished from the courtroom, over much protest by their counsel.

If ever there was a media circus this was it; there were wires and cables all over the floor of the courtroom, and a separate room had been set up to connect the television camera in the courtroom to feed into all the other television equipment positioned outside the courthouse so the latter could feed off the original film and satellite it to stations all over the country and the world. An English friend was kept fully informed by the BBC. Ironically, the television camera in the courtroom was from none other than Channel 20—the home team advantage no doubt. During my final argument I would stick my finger right into the lens of the camera and scream, "Channel 20, you should be ashamed of yourself."

MR. RUSSELL: Record should reflect [that] the defendant has
    voluntarily absented himself from the courtroom.

MR. ROSENBLATT: Correct.

THE COURT: The record will.

MR. ROSENBLATT: (*The photographers were still clicking away at the bench conference.*) This is crazy. How many pictures can they take?

MR. VOLZ: It's loud, such a loud click. (*Volz and I finally agreed on something.*)

MR. ROSENBLATT: It's obtrusive. Either get him out of here or just tell him to do it a lot less frequently.

THE COURT: (*The judicial system in general is very wary about doing anything that could be perceived as an infringement upon freedom of the press.*) I'm inclined that he do it less frequently. We may have to move him back.

MRS. ROSENBLATT: (*Susan had followed Peter into the corridor.*) He's going to come back. He just said that he was crying and he had to get tissues and so forth. But he said he was going to be here while the chapter is being read.

THE COURT: He wants to be here?

MRS. ROSENBLATT: Yes, so he'll be back in thirty seconds or so. There. He's back.

Knowing Peter as well as I did, I laughed to myself. Peter had to be part of the action; he was chomping at the bit to testify. He had attended every deposition that was taken and several of them lasted more than ten hours each. They would have been a lot shorter but for Peter's endless stream of suggested questions. I asked many of them simply as a means of maintaining his equilibrium.

Peter was back in his seat to my left as we faced the jury; Susan, as always, was to my right. Some measure of decorum had returned to the courtroom in terms of the positioning of the various photographers. The deputy clerk continued with her reading from Peter's manuscript.

I was holding her hand in my two hands once again and kneeling at her bedside. She had once again opened her eyes and she had spoken to me, but now with me at her side she closed them gently. Her face was peaceful and relaxed and she had a happy smile upon her lips. She was resting easily and slipping into death's slow slumber, but yet she spoke to me and said, "I love you." Several minutes later, she said, "I love you," and several minutes later, "I love you Peter," and she was gone. She was not dead, but she was in a sleep from which she could and would never return.

I found myself in my car with an unopened can of cold beer. I was hurtling down Summerlin Road, and soon I was at the home of Michael and Cindy Carlino. I sat in the Carlino's living room upon the couch and told them of this night. I was drinking the beer I had brought with me. Soon I finished it and began another and another. Time was distorted and reality was distorted, but soon it was 5:30 A.M. I called my home and Farrell [Delman] answered the telephone. I asked him if Pat were dead. He said no. Her respirations were irregular, infrequent and shallow, but this lasted for only a short time and soon her respirations became regular and deep once again.

Thirty minutes later I called back and Pat's condition was unchanged, and thirty minutes later I called again and her condition was unchanged. I now realized that the dose of Seconal might perhaps be lethal but it might not. At worst, she could awaken in many hours; but, equally bad, she could linger unconscious with permanent brain damage until her cancer killed her. Some time after arriving home, I telephoned Michael Carlino and asked him to read to me from the *Physician's Desk Reference,* the toxic dose and effects of Seconal. He read to me that which he found. It stated that two to ten grams of Seconal was lethal. Pat had taken two grams.

Why had Patricia taken only twenty Seconal? They had many more capsules available to them, so why take the risk of not taking enough? This miscalculation caused Peter to involve two additional doctors in an attempt to get morphine and to finish what the Seconal had only begun. In one of the trial's most heated exchanges, during my cross examination of Farrell Delman, he would state with great confidence Peter's true motives in not ending Patricia's life in an effective way. Peter continued in "The Lady":

Several minutes later, Michael Carlino raced into my driveway. Michael went into the bedroom and looked at her and came out and told me that she was stable. There was no sign of impending death. He soon left to go to work, and I called one of Pat's doctors. I said Pat had taken an overdose of Seconal but she will not die. This doctor said, "I did not hear that. I did not hear that. You say she is in a lot of pain, is that what you said? I'll be right over."

Peter was making the point that doctors in these circumstances often pretend to give medication for pain when they know they are actually medicating to cause or at least hasten an inevitable death. As reflected in subsequent trial testimony, Peter was referring to Dr. Daniel Dosoretz, whom he did not name in the manuscript. Dr. Dosoretz had provided the radiotherapy treatment for Patricia's brain tumors.

> He [Dosoretz] had promised Pat two days before her death that if she had an intra-abdominal catastrophy, he would come to our home and give her 100 mgs of morphine to help her on her way. (*This hardly endeared Peter to Dr. Dosoretz.*) When [Dosoretz] arrived he went into the bedroom and he looked at her and came out and said to me, "She's going to die. I don't know when, but she's going to die." I said, "I know she's going to die but please help me—please, please, please." I was crying now and begging this man to help me help my love to make her last voyage. I said, "Please give me some medicine to help her on her way. She kissed her children goodbye last night and they will awaken soon."
>
> He looked at me and said, "I have feelings too, you know. I'll give you something. You say she is in pain." He had not brought any medicine with him. He had brought merely a prescription pad. I was shocked, for he had told me on the telephone that he would help me. He now wrote me a prescription for six milligrams of morphine. I looked at the prescription in disbelief and said to him, "Six miligrams? This is not enough to do anything. Please, please give me more."

Peter returned with eight milligrams of morphine because the Lee Memorial Hospital pharmacy was unable to give him the drug in the precise dosage that had been prescribed. The additional two milligrams were meaningless.

> She was breathing heavily now. I apologized to her as I cleaned her arm with alcohol and gave her the two injections amounting to eight milligrams of morphine. In moments I was once again out of the room, for I could not bear to look at my love as she slipped from me forever. But I knew the dose of morphine was not enough. Her Seconal would soon wear off and she would arise from the deep coma to a lighter coma.
>
> I called another doctor and paged him in the hospital. He

promptly answered his page and I once again began my plea. I said, "Pat took an overdose of Seconal last night, but she won't die. I need some help. Please help me, please." He answered, "I didn't hear that. You say she is in pain?" (*The same fiction was being repeated.*)

He asked me if I wished to transfer Pat to the hospital. She could be placed on a morphine drip. The implication was clear. The nurses could increase the drip of morphine and let her slip away. But why was it all right for nurses to increase a morphine drip within a hospital and it was not all right for me to help my love upon her way in her own bed, in her own home, with her loved ones all around her? But I did not argue. I begged and begged, and finally the doctor agreed to write a prescription for ten 20 mg suppositories of morphine.

Again, Peter did not provide the name of the physician; pretrial discovery and subsequent testimony revealed it was Dr. William Harwin, who had carried out the protocol of chemotherapy that was established by another physician from Sloan Kettering in New York City. Of course, most of Peter's friends and the whole of the local medical establishment could figure out that Peter was talking about Dosoretz and Harwin even though he was not providing their names.

I called an old employee [Peter's secretary, Mary Linden] and asked her to pick up the prescription from his [Harwin's] office, to go to the pharmacy specified, and to purchase the morphine suppositories. Five minutes later I called another employee and asked him to bring me sterile gloves. In a few minutes the morphine was delivered.

This was so very typical of Peter involving two additional individuals in the very sensitive and illegal events which were occurring.

I fully understood the implications of what I was doing. I understood the legalities, but I did not care. I unwrapped the suppositories and I inserted four 20 mg morphine suppositories into the rectum of my love. I kissed her buttocks, and I cried, and I once again apologized to her as I did this. She was breathing with a groaning sound and I thought that I would go mad. I inserted the suppositories and rushed from the room. I did not care if the world knew what I did. She was about to die a catastrophic death, and I merely helped her on her way, and I did not do so because I wished to do so. I had no choice.

As Pat lay dying but not dying, and I did not know what to do, there were discussions amongst her brothers and father. At one point her father said, "If someone would put his hands over her mouth, she'd die quickly, or maybe a pillow. We could put a pillow over her face." I could not bear it. I could not bear the thought of suffocating the love of my life. I thought I would go mad.

I called a local undertaker and told him that my wife was dying and she was to be cremated. I asked for the simplest coffin, a simple pine box. Of course, he responded that they were special, they cost more and he did not have one but could obtain one. I did not care about the price. I wanted a simple pine box for my love. He offered me a rental coffin, for I could rent one if she was to be cremated. I declined. I then called the florist and ordered a blanket of white roses to cover the coffin, and then I sat and sat and waited.

I was now outside my bedroom door and Farrell emerged. I found myself in his arms and sobbing. When he had approached me, I had hated him and did not wish to touch him; but I was now in his arms and sobbing and looking up and begging Pat for forgiveness. A moment later Russell emerged from the bedroom and told me that Pat was dead.

The jury had seen the videotape of Dr. Rosier's confession that aired on Channel 20; it had listened to Leisa Zigman's testimony about Dr. Rosier's confessions on two separate occasions; and the jury had read along with the deputy clerk as Dr. Rosier spoke of how he helped Patricia end her life. Damning testimony—but somehow I had a good feeling.

There were few dry eyes in the courtroom; even reporters reached for their handkerchiefs. Say what they would about Peter Rosier, there had to be some grudging respect for someone who spit at the law and poured his heart out in chapter 34. I felt we were on a roll if we could only discredit the Delmans.

4

In-Laws and Out-Laws:
The Delmans Try to Get Even—
Russell Delman

Dr. Rosier's confessions were legally insufficient under Florida law to support a conviction; in fact, he could not have even been charged with a crime absent independent testimony, since Patricia was cremated. Thus, Peter's in-laws were clearly the State's star witnesses. The Delmans hated Peter and wanted to bury him. My cross examination of the retired Brooklyn dentist, and his sons—a tobacco lobbyist and a body awareness teacher— would need to be very nasty.

Peter involved the Delmans in nearly every aspect of Patricia's suicide/ murder and documented their role in his manuscript. After Mr. D'Alessandro announced he was launching an investigation, Peter's former criminal counsel advised him to tell the Delmans to retain attorneys.

True to form, Peter delegated this job to his secretary, Mary Rose Linden, who called Vincent, Farrell, and Russell out of the blue and told each of them about his potential criminal liability and that Dr. Rosier, on the advice of his attorney, felt they should retain independent counsel. Peter apparently did not think he owed the Delmans any personal explanation as to his reason for appearing on television; nor did he feel that it was necessary to apologize for endangering his father-in-law or his brothers-in-law. Had Peter handled the matter better, he could easily have avoided all the legal consequences flowing from his television confession. The Delmans simply would have refused to testify for the State.

Instead of reassuring his in-laws that he never said a word on television

73

about their involvement in Patricia's death and that they had no vulnerability, Peter, through his secretary, instilled tremendous fear in them, which resulted in their hiring John Patrick Deveney, a criminal law attorney from New York City.

Peter's relationship with his in-laws had been strained over the years, and the secretary's unexpected call infuriated the Delmans. The Delmans had been almost totally out of touch with the Rosiers for many years before Peter invited them to Patricia's surprise fortieth birthday party. The party occurred three years before she contracted cancer. Their involvement with Patricia and Peter became more intense after the cancer was diagnosed in April of 1985. Every time Peter asked them to come to Fort Myers they complied.

When Peter asked Russell to get a prescription filled for Seconal in October 1985 Russell did so. When the Delmans learned in January 1986 that Patricia was terminal they came to Fort Myers and remained through the funeral and beyond. Russell stayed in the bedroom with his sister almost continuously from the time she took the Seconal until her last breath. When Peter needed help with the morphine injections and suppositories, Russell and Farrell did what was requested of them without complaining or second guessing.

The Delmans loved Patricia and they wanted to comply with her wishes. They went through a very tough experience during those January days. The last thing on their minds was murder. They were there to help. They had long since returned to the normal cadence of their lives when Peter's secretary called so unexpectedly. Following the call from Mary Rose, all the old suspicions about Peter rose to the surface; were they in some way being set up to take the fall for him?

When Patricia refused to die some twelve hours after ingesting the Seconal and the morphine (injections as well as suppositories) did not cause her death, Vincent Delman decided he'd had enough. In a strange quirk of fate, Patricia's father, rather than Peter, was with her when she died. We learned during the discovery stage of the proceeding that Vincent had become very impatient and angry at Peter for undermedicating Patricia, and decided to take matters into his own hands. Vincent gently placed two of his fingers over Patricia's mouth and nose to stop her last few faint breaths. In a purely technical and legal sense, we would argue, Vincent, not Peter, had ended Patricia's life; for that reason, Peter was also charged with conspiracy to commit first degree murder. I would repeatedly refer to Vincent's final act as a "smothering" or a "suffocation." A defense was born!

My cross examination of the Delmans had to be very tough. Since it was the State's strategy to have the jury hate Peter, it had to be part of my strategy to have them hate the Delmans even more. I was not comfortable with my role. I knew I would have to be very mean with the Delmans, depicting Vincent as the "killer." To my mind, the Delmans were basically victims rather than villains. But Peter was a victim as well, and his life was at stake.

All the Delmans had been granted total immunity from prosecution. The State had agreed not to prosecute them for anything they did in connection with Patricia's death. The circumstances under which the State attorney granted this immunity would provide the basis for fireworks during my questioning of Farrell Delman, as well as James Fitzpatrick, the lead investigator for the prosecution. Fitzpatrick had been present at the New York City office of the Delmans' lawyer, and it was Fitzpatrick who finalized the immunity deal, a deal that I would characterize throughout the trial as rotten to the core, a deal in which the State of Florida had been defrauded.

Farrell was the natural leader of the Delmans, and those of us at the defense table were amazed by the amount of trust Vincent and Russell placed in him on the very critical and sensitive issue of immunity. They left it entirely up to Farrell to hire their joint lawyer, Mr. Deveney. I asked Russell Delman at trial:

Q: When you met with Mr. Deveney before you ever met with Mr. Fitzpatrick in New York on the issue of immunity, did you tell Deveney of your role and your father's role and Farrell's role in Patty's death?

A: No.

Q: Why not?

A: Well, I had never met with Mr. Deveney. My brother had made the connection to Mr. Deveney; and when I arrived, I never like went into his office and he never asked me what went on or anything.

Q: Are you saying that you never had a private conversation with Deveney before you met with Fitzpatrick to give your statement?

A: That's correct.

Q: Surely you must have had an understanding as to whether Farrell told Deveney about the smothering, or whether the agreement between the three Delmans was to keep that secret from Deveney?

A: I don't know. I don't know to this day what my brother told Deveney; and when I asked him several months ago, after your deposition with me, his comment was, "Let me not tell you until this whole thing is over." And we left it at that.

Fitzpatrick would go to great pains to explain that it was totally irrelevant whether the State had prior knowledge about the smothering before granting blanket immunity to the Delmans. According to him the State had no choice. Since Patricia had been cremated, the State could not prosecute Peter without the corroborating testimony of the Delmans. Peter's confession standing alone would have been insufficient. We didn't think it was quite that simple, and the thrust of my cross examination of Fitzpatrick was that D'Alessandro had been duped.

The State of Florida had been suckered into granting immunity to the Delmans. Fitzpatrick had no idea that one of them had been instrumental in ending Patricia's life. On the stand Fitzpatrick admitted that he almost fell out of his chair at learning of the "final act" during the statements he took from Farrell and Russell. In negotiating the immunity deal with attorney Deveney, Fitzpatrick had been given a general proffer that excluded any mention of Vincent's involvement, referred to at trial as the "final act." In legal terms, a "proffer" tells the other side what your clients will testify to on key issues.

Once he recognized that Vincent Delman's involvement was far more than he had anticipated, Fitzpatrick called D'Alessandro in Florida and, after consultation, deferred taking any statement from Vincent. No official statement was taken until many months later. The state attorney's office recognized that without the Delmans there could be no prosecution. The State of Florida preferred to be tricked by the Delmans and their New York attorney rather than forego prosecuting Peter Rosier.

Under protest from the State, Judge Thompson granted my motion to interrogate Deveney regarding any conversations and meetings he had with the Delmans about the proffer and the granting of immunity. I spoke to Deveney by telephone on two occasions and he said he wouldn't talk to me without a court order. Even with the Florida court order he claimed immunity under New York statutes governing attorney-client privilege. Farrell Delman testified at trial that Deveney did not want to learn the extent of the Delmans' involvement; their discussions were always couched in hypothetical "What if" questions—a cat and mouse game.

I felt the State of Florida and the Delmans were in a no-win situation since, irrespective of what Deveney knew or didn't know, everyone looked bad. The State looked even worse when it was learned during my cross examination of the Delmans that each of them was under the mistaken impression that if they lied under oath, after being granted immunity, they could be prosecuted for murder. In fact, under Florida law the only crime with which they could be charged was perjury. Fitzpatrick admitted that he knew of the Delmans' mistaken belief, but took advantage of their confusion since he thought it would help insure truthful testimony. I hoped the jury was thinking "A plague on both your houses!"

Russell Delman was the first of the Delmans to testify. Russell had many characteristics of a "love child" of the sixties and was basically very engaging and likeable. He had a mellow, laid back, earnest manner which would make his testimony difficult to impeach. He had a very straightforward delivery and could potentially be very damaging to the defense.

Russell Delman's address fit his demeanor: He lived on Lilac Avenue in a small California town, had majored in psychology in college, had attended the Humanistic Psychology Institute in San Francisco for a couple of years, and studied at the Gestalt Institute of Canada. He had taught yoga in San Francisco and had traveled all over the world.

It was very hard for Russell to explain what he did for a living without it sounding flaky and weird to the St. Petersburg jury. He had been a Feldenkrais practitioner for some thirteen years: "I teach a kind of body movement and body awareness work."

Russell Delman had no medical training whatsoever and did not view himself as a therapist. He did not possess any kind of official diploma or certificate saying that he was authorized to teach various Feldenkrais courses. He said that he and his wife started a project to work with Mother Teresa on brain-injured children in Calcutta, India, and they taught the sisters how to work with these kids.

Q: And . . . you teach alternatives, whether to a musician, a lawyer, or a doctor. Your "student" may be sitting in a certain way in a chair, and he may get backaches and you tell him there are alternative ways of sitting?

A: That's correct.

Q: And alternative ways of moving?
A: Right. (*That may sound perfectly fine in the San Francisco area but we didn't think it would go over on the west coast of Florida.*)

Russell, who constantly talked to Patricia during the many hours of her unconsciousness, would say things like: "go toward the light" over and over again. I asked him what this was based upon, and he started talking about Eastern religions in general and about a particular book titled *The Tibetan Book of the Dead*. I invited him to tell us about the book because, again, I didn't think our jury could relate to his explanation.

The idea is that your dying it's not just the end, but as consciousness leaves the body there are potentially wonderful experiences, potentially dreadful experiences. But that there is a light which is very attractive. And the idea is to go toward the light. What can make a death spiritually difficult or painful is fighting the light and trying to stay here.

Russell testified that he and Patricia had discussed how he could help her after she swallowed the Seconal. They both felt that something did live on after death; and as she lay unconscious he would talk to her, reminding her to let go of this world and gently move on toward the light. For the Jewish son of a Brooklyn dentist Russell was hardly mainstream material.

During his direct examination of Russell, Edward Volz established several basic points that were reemphasized through the subsequent testimony of Farrell and Vincent.

(1) Everything the Delmans did in connection with Patricia's death was done at the behest of Peter. Peter was the conductor, the impresario, and the director of all the events leading to Patricia's death. Russell and his wife, Linda, filled a prescription for forty-eight Seconal, 100 mgs each, written by Peter, in October 1985, after the discovery of the brain tumors. All the breathing status reports during Patricia's unconsciousness were given to Peter so that he could assess them professionally.

(2) The intent and purpose of the Seconal and the morphine were not to reduce pain but to terminate Patricia's life. Whatever Peter did, whatever the Delmans did after Patricia ingested the Seconal, was aimed at achieving the common goal of causing Patricia's death. (This common goal was central to the charge of conspiracy to commit murder in the first degree.)

(3) Peter led Patricia to believe that if she did not commit suicide, she would die a horrible and gruesome death. Patricia was very neat and fastidious and feared such an end greatly. Peter caused her to believe that she would "vomit up all her blood." Russell spent the most time talking to Patricia in the days immediately before her death and he testified that her impression was that her tumors would burst and she would choke on her own blood. (Medically speaking, it was highly unlikely that Patricia would suffer such a gruesome death.) Russell testified that Patricia was a very elegant woman who even cared greatly about her appearance in death.

(4) According to the State, Peter further misled Patricia causing her to believe that she could die any day when, in reality, her life expectancy was probably a few months. Russell testified that even after the discovery of the adrenal tumors on January 10, 1986, Patricia would put on makeup and fashionable clothes and interact with guests. Much was made of how good Patricia looked during her television interview of January 14 with Channel 20. Patricia and Russell Delman would take frequent walks around the neighborhood; even on the very night she swallowed the Seconal Patricia was capable of partaking of a lavish, catered lobster dinner.

(5) Peter purposefully and deceitfully led the Delmans to believe that the Seconal and morphine in combination would not kill her. Peter convinced the Delmans that Patricia would awaken in a brain-damaged state, that "she would be a vegetable." This misconception caused Vincent Delman to take the action that he did.

(6) Russell made it very clear that by the time his father acted, Patricia was essentially a corpse, although every minute and a half or so, she would approximate a barely perceptible breath, which he described as "this teeny sound," and Vincent described as something in the nature of a slight hiccup. Patricia had not resisted the morphine injections or suppositories, or Vincent's fingers.

Edward Volz examined Russell:

Q: Describe your sister's movements for this five- or six-hour period before her death.
A: She was stock still. Except for the movement associated with breathing there was no other movement.
Q: There was no movement? She didn't move her hands in any fashion to clutch any part of her body or anything?
A: No. There was zero other movement that could be detected.
Q: She just laid there?
A: Correct.

The State sought to convey the image that what Vincent did with his fingers was the equivalent of gently blowing a feather off the edge of a desk. My purpose was to have it perceived as an aggressive act of smothering that directly caused death. Volz asked:

Q: Were these suppositories put in for any medical purpose to control pain?
A: No, not at all. No. You have to picture my sister: she was like a mannequin at that point. To turn her over was totally like dead weight.
Q: No crying out or anything?
A: Nothing, right.
Q: And the only time her body moved from the time she fell asleep with the pills was when you moved it?
A: That's correct. Except for the breathing.
Q: And as time went on the breathing got softer?
A: Yes.
Q: And the intervals between the breathing stretched out?
A: Correct.
Q: And it's your testimony that these breaths were a minute and a half to two minutes apart?
A: That's correct.

It would be critical for the defense to show that the Delmans smothered Patricia without Peter's knowledge or participation. One of my main themes would be that the Delmans killed Patricia and they were totally free and living the good life, whereas Peter failed in killing his beloved wife and he was on trial for first degree murder. Although legally irrelevant, I needed to persuade the jury that the immunity achieved by the Delmans was absolutely unfair. I needed to convince them that they should refuse to become a part of the State's scenario irrespective of what the letter of the law said. The State's position was that Patricia was just a breath or two away from death anyway and the smothering was accomplished with Peter's knowledge and agreement.

Edward Volz very skillfully laid out the sequence of events leading up to the three Delmans entering the bedroom for the final time. Although these events occurred in a few short minutes, hours upon hours would be spent dissecting them as well as any statements that were made during this time frame.

Q: When you came out of the bedroom, and went to that table on the patio, was there anyone at the table?

[RUSSELL DELMAN]: When I got to the table my brother-in-law, Peter, was there; my father was there; and I believe my brother was getting there. (*If Peter was at the same table with Vincent, then he could hear everything that was said.*)

Q: When you came out of the bedroom did you give a breathing report?

A: Yes. I just said she is breathing at longer intervals, that I thought it was over. I can't believe that it can go on so long, and so long in between breaths.

Q: When you got to the table what did you say?

A: I described the breathing. I thought that any breath now could be it, she would die. They were very long intervals between breaths. I was pretty exhausted, exasperated. I sat down. I remembered smoking a cigarette, feeling kind of dejected, upset, drained. I can remember sitting there and saying, "If I had the guts I'd put a pillow over her face." I can remember thinking that that would be a very humane act to do . . . but I just didn't do it.

Q: Was your father sitting at the table at that time?

A: Yes.

Q: Was the Defendant sitting at the table at that time?

A: Yes. (*So when Vincent arose and headed for the bedroom Peter had to be aware of his purpose.*)

Q: Do you know whether anyone heard your comment?

A: I know that there were two comments that were made. I heard what I thought was my father, [though] now I believe [it was] my brother, saying—I'm not sure who said this—"I was thinking the same thing." And then I can recall my father standing up—because I can remember his hands—coming to the table and saying, "enough is enough." And he left the table.

Q: Your father got up from the table?

A: Correct.

Q: Do you know where he went?

A: He went into the bedroom where my sister was.

Q: What did you do?

A: Well, I continued to sit there. After about twenty seconds or thirty seconds I remember a flash, a light going on in my mind. Oh, is that what he's doing, thinking that he was putting a pillow over my sister's head. And then I had the thought "Well no, maybe he's just checking on her." I wasn't sure that

that was what he was doing. And so I went into the bedroom and my brother came in shortly after me.

Q: Please tell this court what occurred at that time in the bedroom.

A: I saw what my father was doing. I felt startled and supportive.

Q: Was your sister still breathing?

A: There was still movement there. It's hard to call them breaths even. Maybe every two minutes. So there was the slightest bit of movement. My father is on this side of the bed. I go over, put my hands on his back. I could feel him sweating through his shirt. My brother and I both had our hands supporting my dad, and I went on the other side of the bed to continue talking to Patty. . . . My father was positioning his fingers so that the finger of one hand was under the nostrils of my sister and the finger of the other hand was on the mouth. And I remember seeing tears in his eyes. It was a real act of love. (*The jury was obviously fascinated but what the hell were they thinking?*)

Q: Who was the first one to leave the room?

A: My dad.

Q: Did your brother also leave the room?

A: Yes.

Q: Did you stay in the room?

A: I stayed in the room. Again, I didn't feel like my job was over yet. I needed to stay there, keeping a peaceful state of mind and encouraging Pat to move on.

Q: When your brother left the room did you hear anything?

A: Yeah. I could hear my brother and Peter outside kind of in the hall or right near the bedroom door. I remember the door was open, and I could hear kind of a hug, sobbing, and I heard Peter say, "I don't want to hear about the end, don't tell me about the end."

This solidified the State's theory that Peter knew exactly what was going on inside the bedroom; that's why he waited outside the bedroom door, and why he had no need to hear the specifics.

Q: After hearing that did you have occasion to see the defendant?

A: Yes. He, shortly thereafter, walked in the bedroom and again took a pulse and looked at Patty's eyes and said something like, "Well, that's it. She's gone. She's dead." And I think he kissed her and left again.

Under Florida law it was meaningless whether Peter knew the precise means utilized to end Patricia's life; the legal point was that he and the Delmans had precisely the same purpose—to terminate her life. Russell Delman had given the State of Florida two detailed statements regarding all the circumstances of Patricia's death. I had taken his deposition for many hours. Farrell and Vincent gave lengthy depositions as well, plus private statements to the prosecution team. On cross examination, my job was to establish as many areas of conflict as possible between the three Delmans. I also sought to create contradictions between what any one of them said on their statements, or depositions, in contrast to what they were testifying to at trial. The more conflicts the better, since that would undermine their credibility, and I hoped, cause reasonable doubt to flourish in the minds of the jurors. I needed to demonstrate that Peter had absolutely nothing to do with the decision to smother Patricia, or the actual performance of that deed.

[MR. ROSENBLATT]: With respect to what happened in the bedroom when your father smothered Patty, Peter was never in the bedroom at any time during that sequence of events, correct?

A: That's true. (*I was very pleased that Russell was accepting my definition that a "smothering" had in fact occurred.*)

Q: The entire period of time when your father had his hands or fingers over Patty's mouth and nose, Peter was never in the room, correct?

A: That's true.

Q: And during that time frame when you, Farrell, and your father were in the bedroom, Peter never knocked on the door and said, "What's going on? What's taking so long?" Nothing like that happened?

A: That's true.

Q: And as a matter of fact you really have no way of knowing where Peter was or what Peter was doing when you were in the bedroom with your father and brother, correct? You may have made certain assumptions, but you didn't know?

A: That's true.

Q: Not only did Peter not say a single solitary word in response to your comment—"If I had the guts, I'd put a pillow over her face"—but isn't it true Peter didn't say a single solitary word in response to the comment, "Enough is enough," or "I was thinking the same thing"?

A: That's true.

Q: Didn't say a word?
A: I don't recall a word from him during that whole sequence.

I wanted the jury to think, how can someone be a member of a conspiracy when they are not even talking to their supposed coconspirators? I knew that, legally, words need not be exchanged in the forming of a conspiracy, but the jury didn't.

Q: The pact of secrecy that was entered into between the three Delmans in the bedroom was: we will never tell anybody outside this bedroom about what happened. Correct?
A: That's right.
Q: And then on the walk later on in the early afternoon, after Patty's dead and after Vincent had returned from the airport, that agreement between the three Delmans was reaffirmed. Correct?
A: That's right.
Q: Peter was not part of the agreement either in the bedroom or on the walk later, correct?
A: That's correct.

As I glanced over at the jury my expression said: it's really a hell of a conspiracy when my guy isn't even in the bedroom and is not part of the secrecy agreement. The statutes on conspiracy are so broad and confusing that an overly zealous prosecutor could come up with a conspiracy charge against two total strangers at the Rose Bowl game, even though one was sitting on the ten-yard line and the other at mid-field. But in commonsense, practical terms, most people think they know what a conspiracy is. It's when two or more people secretly plot and plan a course of action.

Q: As you sit here today, in all honesty, you have no way of knowing whether Peter Rosier knew what the three of you were up to in that bedroom? You may make certain assumptions, but you have no way of knowing. Correct?
A: There is no way of being certain.
Q: As a matter of fact, when you got up and followed your own father into the bedroom, you weren't positive what he was going to do?
A: I wasn't positive.
Q: You can't even be positive that Peter heard your remark?

A: Again, I can't be positive. He was in the range for the remark,
but I don't know. He didn't respond to it. I have no way
of knowing for sure.

Q: No gestures were made between any of the three Delmans
and Peter?

A: That's right, no gestures.

Q: No gestures and no words?

A: Right.

Spending all those hours with Russell taking his deposition in California
was very valuable. It gave me the opportunity to size him up as to what
he was all about as a human being. Although he was intensely loyal to
his brother and father, I felt that he was fundamentally fair-minded.

Russell was ambivalent in his attitude toward Peter, whereas Vincent
and Farrell were almost totally negative against him. I thought Russell
had mixed emotions about what the verdict should be, whereas I felt that
Vincent and Farrell wanted Peter to be convicted; not for what he did
to Patricia, but for what he put them through. Although Russell also
hated Peter for his ordeal, there was more balance to him. He could
remember the good times from his childhood and youth with Peter and
Patricia, and he would more readily concede that there were virtues in
Peter's character.

The Delmans had every right to be enraged at Peter. Until the immunity
deal was sealed they were on the hook for possible murder charges. Even
after immunity had been granted they were in the humiliating position
of having to explain their actions not only to their families but to the
world. They were part of a "murder," and the victim was their daughter
and sister. The fact that the Delmans had to hire a lawyer to defend
them was both expensive and time-consuming.

I would argue in summation that if Russell, Vincent's own flesh and
blood, was not positive what his father was going to do in the bedroom,
then how could it be assumed that Peter knew? Especially since I would
be able to prove through Vincent that he and Peter were never on the
same wavelength, and never interacted in any meaningful way. From the
time Peter was a teenager courting Patricia, he and Vincent had not liked
each other.

Q: What did you do after your father got up?

A: I continued to sit there; and after another maybe twenty
seconds, I had a flash—where a light bulb went on—where
I said to myself, oh he's going to do it, and I realized I got

to get in there; and then I had the thought—well maybe he's going to check on her, but either way I wanted to get in there and find out what was going on.

Q: Okay Russell, there were essentially two possibilities: number one, he was going to evaluate the situation; number two he was going to end her life. Those were the two possibilities?

A: Yes. I thought of both those possibilities.

Russell and Farrell had been active participants with Peter all night long; Vincent had gone to sleep in the den. He seemed the most unlikely person to take decisive action. Why did he? I had a suggested answer, which I thought would not endear Dr. Vincent Delman to the members of the jury.

Q: When your father realized that Patty was dead, he left the bedroom and he went to the airport to pick up his wife?

A: Yes.

Q: You would certainly admit that it is at least possible that your father, knowing he had to pick up his wife at the airport, that fact might have played a role in his decision to act at that particular time?

A: Possible, yes.

Q: Why were you in a hurry? Why was your father in a hurry to end it? What difference would it have made to anyone if Pat, instead of dying at noon, would have died at, let's say, 1:30 P.M., so what? Who cared?

MR. VOLZ: Objection Your Honor, one question at a time.

THE COURT: I'll allow that question.

[RUSSELL DELMAN]: I'm not sure of my father's thinking about that. I was not in a particular rush.

I was suggesting that Vincent's sudden decision to take charge was dictated by the fact that his wife would be waiting at the airport and that she was not the type of woman who would be mellow about hanging around. The third Mrs. Delman was a New York real estate lady devoted to her poodle, who appreciated efficiency and promptness.

Q: While watching your father end your sister's life, did you ever say to yourself or think to yourself, who the hell gave him permission to do that?

A: Never thought that.

Q: Because Patty never brought your father into the suicide

decision. So from her standpoint, laying there in bed, where did her stepfather, who she had not seen for some twelve years before her fortieth birthday—where did he get the right to do that?

A: Never had that thought.

I wanted the jury to think that the final act of the Delmans encompassed much arrogance. They were all so very positive they had done the right thing. They did not hesitate to describe it as "noble" and "very heroic." Peter had botched the job, but they had performed magnificently. I did not think that cocksure attitude would sit well with the jury.

I also wanted the jury to understand that the Delmans were not objective witnesses simply doing their best to recall facts and testify about them. Rather, they were part of the State's team and wanted the State to be happy with their performances. The State had handed them the greatest gift imaginable, total blanket immunity from being prosecuted for murder or any lesser crime in connection with Patricia's death.

It was similarly important to have the jury understand that the Delmans had spent a lot of time discussing their testimony with Edward Volz, Stephen Russell, and James Fitzpatrick. I firmly believe that witnesses can be "overrehearsed" and that is precisely what I felt occurred here. After the many hours of discussions, and notwithstanding the Delmans' desire to be as consistent as possible, they started contradicting each other, as well as their earlier testimony and witness statements.

Since it was my objective to attack their credibility, I sought to magnify contradictions between Russell's various statements concerning his father's and Farrell's responses to Russell's comment: "If I had the guts, I'd put a pillow over her face." At trial Russell testified that Vincent stated in response, "Enough is enough!" and Farrell responded, "I was thinking the same thing."

Q: When you came out to the patio and said, "If I had the guts, I would use a pillow," what did your father say?

A: He said—I know for sure he said—"Enough is enough." Someone said—either my father or my brother—"I was thinking the same thing."

Q: Now, Russell, isn't it true that when I took your deposition and questioned you on this subject matter, you had no recollection of Farrell responding to your pillow comment?

A: Let me think for a moment. That's true.

Q: It was your recollection then that the only person who might have made a comment in response to your pillow comment, was your father?

A: That's right. And I had thought that he said, "I was thinking the same thing." I hadn't remembered "Enough is enough."

"Enough is enough" was the critical response to Russell's pillow comment because it directly led to the final decisive action. By Russell not recalling this during his eleven-hour deposition, I hoped that would raise some suspicions in the jury's collective mind as to the trustworthiness of his whole account. In the first private statement that Russell Delman gave to the prosecutors, his best recollection was that his father had responded with the words "I was thinking the same thing." I tested Russell's recollection of what occurred after Patricia had died.

Q: After your father and brother left the bedroom and you remained inside, were you able to hear them speaking with Peter, telling Peter that Patty was dead?

A: Yes. I heard a hug and sobs, and I didn't hear a conversation, but I heard Peter say that he didn't want to know about the end.

Q: And it seemed to you that the three of them were together, the hugging, the sobbing?

A: Yeah. I had thought that the three of them were together.

Vincent and Farrell's testimony conflicted with that of Russell. I knew Vincent had testified on deposition that he left the bedroom first and it was he who told Peter that Patricia was dead. According to Vincent, Peter did not respond at all, and he left directly for the airport. Farrell was not with Vincent at this time; yet Russell made it appear as though Vincent and Farrell had left the bedroom together. Vincent would testify that he never heard Peter say that he didn't want to know about the end.

When I later hammered away at Vincent and Farrell on the same subject matter, additional disagreements and contradictions were exposed between the three Delmans. I was as relentless as the judge allowed me to be in pushing the Delmans to explain and attempt to justify the inconsistencies between their statements in depositions, sworn statements, and their trial testimony. Russell came up with an explanation of things happening that would "jog his memory." There were certain things he was 100 percent positive about at trial that he had been uncertain about almost two years earlier. For example, at trial Russell was positive his father said "Enough is enough!"

> Q: Would you agree, Russell, that yesterday in this courtroom was the first time you ever told either the State or myself that it was Farrell who said "I was thinking the same thing?"
> A: No. When we met last month.

He was referring to a meeting that all three Delmans had with the prosecution team in Fort Myers less than a month before the trial began.

> Q: Because something jogged your memory?
> A: That's right.

I tried to be relentless in forcing the Delmans to explain the specific "something" that jogged their memories in each instance, but frequently they could not. Mention of the recent meeting in Fort Myers enabled me to get into an area where I could ridicule the vast amounts of time that the State spent with the Delmans in what I would characterize as rehearsals for getting their collective stories to remain consistent with each other. Referring to that meeting with Volz, Russell, and Fitzpatrick, I asked:

> Q: What was there to talk about last month? You gave two lengthy statements. You gave a 300-page deposition. You met with them for eight hours before your deposition. The time frame we are talking about in this case is from the time Patty takes the Seconal until she dies. What was there to talk about? It was in the nature of a rehearsal, wasn't it?
> A: Yeah . . . something about a pretrial meeting. . . . This was the first time we had all been in a room together talking about this stuff, and maybe to jog our memories with each other.
> Q: Maybe to get more consistent with each other?
> A: One thing I can honestly say sir, for the State has all along really said we only want you to remember what you remember. Tell the truth. They consistently said that.

Nobody needs days and days of preparation if all they are going to do is tell the simple truth. Lawyers always instruct clients and witnesses that if they are asked what was discussed during a pretrial meeting, they should say the lawyer merely told them to tell the truth. Of course, it is never that simple. Lawyers do not have to spell out what each witness is expected to say; when witnesses are together they learn very quickly what the lawyers consider to be favorable testimony for their side. Problems are identified and solutions proposed; witnesses are told what the strategy of the opposition is and they learn very quickly what the party line is. No one is told directly to lie or to change his story simply to be compatible with the story the lawyers want. It is not necessary to do that. When an experienced lawyer such as Edward Volz or Stephen Russell lays out the opposing positions the witness knows where to get on board. Memories get jogged in the right direction.

This scenario refers to ethical lawyers; the unethical ones don't engage in such niceties. They simply tell the witnesses what they must say if they want to help. For example, let's say Farrell says at a pretrial meeting that he doesn't remember his father saying "Enough is enough" and he has no recollection of himself saying anything. If the prosecutor says "Well, your brother and father clearly remember it such and such a way and they are positive," what usually happens is that the prompted witness adopts the memory of others as his own.

All the Delmans clearly understood that it was crucial to the State to convey the message that Peter heard all the comments, saw the Delmans go into the bedroom, and knew what their purpose was. All the so-called memory jogs were designed to strengthen Peter's knowledge of the final act. If there is a line that the witness refuses to cross, the lawyer has to adjust accordingly. Pretrial conferences tell the experienced lawyer how suggestible and pliable a witness may be. Such conferences are perfectly legal, yet juries become suspicious when, in their view, too much time is spent together.

Q: You knew that from the State's standpoint it would be terrific for them if Peter knew that the three of you went into the bedroom to smother Pat. That makes their case stronger if he knew that. Right? You knew that?

A: That's correct. (*This answer is yet another example illustrating that Russell Delman had a basic concept of fairness and honesty.*)

Q: And that's why it's very important that Peter be positioned to hear the comments "If I had the guts, I would use a pillow"; "Enough is enough"; and "I was thinking the same thing." Correct?

A: That's right.

Russell's deposition was the first of the three Delmans. When his deposition was completed he dictated a cassette, which he sent to his father and brother. He wanted them to be prepared for me both in terms of substance and technique. Since they all had blanket immunity, what was there to be prepared for if all they were going to do was tell the truth and if they were neutral on the issue as to whether or not Peter got convicted?

By dictating the cassette, Russell created evidence for the trial. Farrell similarly created evidence smack in the middle of his testimony, which would have a far more dramatic impact on the trial. Farrell's evidence was worthy of a thesis for a doctorate in abnormal psychology (either his or Peter's, perhaps both), and provided him with both a national and an international stage for the trashing of his brother-in-law.

When I learned of the existence of Russell's cassette during Vincent's deposition, I asked Volz for a copy of it. We thought Volz was obliged to provide a copy in accordance with the Florida Rules of Criminal Procedure and the general case law in criminal cases, which tries to avoid unexpected surprises by either side, or what lawyers commonly refer to as "trial by ambush." Volz refused to hand it over voluntarily, which led us to believe that there was at least something on it that would be helpful to us. Susan filed a formal legal motion asking for the cassette and Judge Thompson ruled in our favor.

Russell's cassette led to some fireworks during my cross examination of Farrell. Farrell was forced to admit in the presence of the jury that he had lied about the location of the cassette when I had taken his deposition in New York. All the Delmans admitted at trial they would have also lied under oath about their role in Patricia's death had it not been for the State's grant of immunity. That was a double-edged sword, because the State's position was that with immunity they now had no reason whatsoever to lie. Another great motivation for truthfulness was that lying was the only way their immunity could be affected. If they lied, they could be prosecuted for perjury, but still not for murder. Even so, a juror might believe instead that lying simply becomes a way of life for some people. We hoped the jury would feel that way about the Delmans and would discredit their testimony.

I questioned Russell about his purpose and motive in dictating the cassette. One of the subjects he discussed on the cassette was the excellent preparation for his deposition that he had received from the prosecution team. He referred to Volz and Fitzpatrick by their first names.

Q: By the time I took your deposition, you had spent so much time with Mr. Volz and Mr. Fitzpatrick that you felt comfortable calling them Ed and Jim, right?

A: Right.

Q: (*I quoted Russell's language from our transcript of the cassette.*)

You say it's critical to the State's case, it's probably the most
important feature to them—*did Peter know?*
A: Right.
Q: Did Peter know that the reason the three Delmans went into
the bedroom was to smother Patty? That's what you're saying
is critical, right?
A: What I am saying is that from the point of view of the State,
what's most critical is did Peter know or not, right.

No wonder Volz didn't want to give us the cassette. Russell Delman
had talked on the cassette about the possibility of Peter getting the electric
chair. And of course that was contained in one of my questions, to which
both Volz and Russell objected strenuously.

MR. VOLZ: What we have now, Your Honor, is counsel reading
from a document expressing the fact that the electric chair
is a possible penalty in this case when it is not. It's a total
misrepresentation as to what the conditions of this case are.
MRS. ROSENBLATT: I think we should simply tell the jury the
truth. At the outset of the trial the State announced they were
not seeking the death penalty. At the time this was dictated
the death penalty remained more than a possibility.

I assume the State calculated that going for the death penalty would
seem like overreaching to normal jurors. But they let Peter sweat out this
point until the inception of the trial, which was more than a year after
the grand jury had returned its indictment. Now they were merely seeking
life imprisonment with no possibility of parole for twenty-five years. The
jury was advised that the State was no longer seeking the death penalty.

In a technical, purely legal sense fairness had nothing to do with this
trial. After all, the law is the law, and if it's not fair, we can try and
get it changed. To us the concept of fairness was basic, and I knew that
Russell Delman, as a true liberal, was very much into fairness. I asked
him if he thought it was fair that Peter could spend the rest of his life
in jail while the Delmans returned to New York and California. (Any
other Fort Myers judge would have jumped all over me for asking this
question.)

Q: Is it fair for the three Delmans to walk, considering the fact
that the three of you were in the bedroom ending your sister's
life and for the husband of twenty-two years to be on trial

for first degree murder? You think that's fair? (*Even if Russell were evasive the question in and of itself had a value.*)

A: I don't think it's fair for anybody to be on trial for this case. (*Derek Humphry almost applauded.*)

Q: But better him than you, right? If it has to be someone?

A: If you're giving me a choice of me being in that chair or him being in that chair, I would agree with you.

No matter how the prosecutors would justify the necessity for immunity, the overall situation was simply unfair. Although Fitzpatrick sat at the prosecution table throughout the trial, he also became a major witness for the State and one of his functions was to explain why they had no choice but to grant the immunity sought by the Delmans. His extensive police background in the Washington, D.C., area made him a formidable opponent. Again, on the law, we were dead. Even if the jury totally agreed with me that the relative positions of the Delmans and Peter were terribly unfair, they would be instructed in very clear terms that that was irrelevant and should not be considered by them in arriving at their verdict. The only thing they were being called upon to decide was the guilt or innocence of Peter Rosier, not whether the Delmans got a terrific deal or were very clever and tricky in their negotiations with the State of Florida.

I felt the testimony of Russell Delman, as a whole, raised some doubt in the jurors' minds. Was the wrong man being tried? Did Peter know Vincent entered his daughter's bedroom to end her life? Had the State of Florida proved the essential elements of the crimes charged? I thought we had scored major points with Russell.

Farrell, the tobacco lobbyist, was the next Delman to testify; he would be followed by his father. I was going to cross examine them for as long as the judge would allow. The jury would get to know all about the Delmans. They would not wear well.

5

Farrell Delman: The Ringleader

When Farrell Howard Delman took the witness stand on Thursday, November 10, 1988, he was thirty-eight years of age and resided in Princeton, New Jersey. He also maintained an apartment at 25 Central Park West in New York City. He was president of a trade association called The Tobacco Merchant's Association of the United States.

Like Peter, he was a graduate of Dartmouth College, having obtained a Bachelor of Arts degree with a major in philosophy. Peter had written a letter of recommendation for him and made a modest contribution to the Alumni Fund. Farrell attended the University of Helsinki in Finland, where he received a degree in both philosophy and economics. He had taught tennis for three years in Finland. His first wife, from whom he was divorced, was Finnish; his present wife, the mother of his three children, was French. She worked as a representative for several European textile design firms. We never met the spouses of any of the Delmans. As far as we knew none of them ever came to St. Petersburg during the trial, although the Delman men were there for some two weeks.

When Farrell was born his parents lived on Ocean Avenue in Brooklyn, but before the arrival of Russell less than two years later, the family moved to Woodmere, Long Island. When his parents divorced, Farrell was sent away to a prep school called Worcester Academy in Massachusetts, which he attended from the tenth through the twelfth grades. During his growing up years Farrell was very close to Patricia who was nine years older. He loved her dearly. When Patricia was dating Peter for several years as a teenager, Farrell regarded him as an adored older brother.

Farrell was articulate and very self-assured. He enjoyed the spotlight

95

and was very sensitive to the impression he was creating for the jury. He was a born salesman and would have made a convincing actor. Farrell had a certain presence about him and was the type of person who made an impact; somehow his statements and opinions seemed authoritative. He was a dangerous adversary. One of the first subjects I questioned him about was the manner in which immunity had been obtained for all the Delmans.

Susan and I felt that Farrell's maneuvering in connection with the immunity emphasized his shrewdness. We naturally wanted the jury to view him with suspicion. What set everything in motion in terms of Farrell contacting a lawyer was the telephone call from Peter's secretary to the effect that Peter had been interviewed on television about the circumstances of Patricia's death, and that Peter's lawyer at the time suggested he call the Delmans to let them know they needed a lawyer. At that time, Peter's Fort Myers lawyer, Alan Parvey, fully expected Peter to make that very sensitive phone call himself. Instead, Peter delegated the task, giving vague instructions.

I told Peter that these phone calls to the Delmans may have constituted one of the most ill-advised strategy moves of which I had ever heard. The perfectly well-intentioned secretary was unable to answer the many obvious questions the Delmans had concerning the background and meaning of her call. Her phone call was the final frosting on the cake of distrust and animosity that the Delmans already felt toward Peter, predating Patricia's illness, and as a result of several incidents immediately following her death.

Farrell contacted a lawyer, a close friend named Paul Boylan, who in turn recommended an attorney in Manhattan, one John Patrick Deveney. Vincent and Russell gave Farrell carte blanche to employ Deveney and to tell him or not tell him about the events leading to Pat's death. Farrell made it clear to Deveney that his sole purpose was to obtain total and all-encompassing immunity for all three Delmans so that they could never be prosecuted.

Part of the defense strategy was to show that the State of Florida had been defrauded into granting total immunity without ever knowing about the smothering. Since the prosecution always took the position that they were not tricked and that in spite of Vincent's act they had no choice but to grant the Delmans immunity, Farrell could have simply said he told Deveney the truth about everything and left it entirely up to Deveney to decide what to tell the State in his "proffer."

But nothing was simple with Farrell. There were always detours and subtle nuances. He always thought about contingencies, unlike Russell and

Vincent who were far more direct. In a proffer the criminal defense attorney tells the State's representatives the substance of what his clients will say when their formal statements are taken. Based on the information contained in the proffer, the State can make an informed judgment as to whether it will grant immunity.

Deveney told Fitzpatrick that he knew nothing about the Delmans' role other than they assisted Peter in obtaining drugs and witnessed Peter administering those drugs to his wife. Had Farrell been straight with Deveney? Had Deveney been straight with the State of Florida? Would the attorney-client privilege be waived, and would I be allowed to ask probing questions to Farrell and Deveney?

It made sense to Susan and me that Farrell would figure that if the State knew of the Delmans' more direct role in ending Patricia's life, the prosecution would be less likely to grant blanket immunity. Both Farrell and the State said I was not entitled to cross examine Farrell about conversations he had with Deveney since those talks were privileged communications. In one of the relatively few purely legal battles we won, the court ruled that the attorney-client privilege could not be invoked under these circumstances where fraud was asserted: Farrell would have to answer my questions. Farrell had refused to answer any questions on this subject throughout his lengthy deposition, so I would be pretty much shooting in the dark.

I desperately wanted to question Deveney as well since I was certain there would be conflicts between his testimony and that of Farrell about what was discussed. Since the believability of the Delmans was the absolute centerpiece of the State's case, and since the granting of immunity to "guilty" individuals usually rubs jurors the wrong way, cross examination in this area was critical.

I wanted to know exactly what Farrell had told Deveney about what went on in the bedroom. What the jury heard was a classic cat-and-mouse "what if," hypothetical game played between a very savvy client and his lawyer. Farrell said he never came right out and told Deveney about the "final act" of suffocation, and most amazingly he said Deveney didn't really want to know.

Q: And you said to Deveney, "*What if* the three of us suffocated her?"
A: That's true.
Q: And Deveney never said to you, "Farrell, did that happen?" He didn't want to know. That's what you're telling us?
A: He didn't want to know.

Q: He liked the game; he wanted it on a hypothetical basis.

A: That's correct. I did present information to Mr. Deveney in a *what-if* kind of way. *What if* the three of us suffocated her? . . . Deveney's perspective—this sort of surprised me at the time—was he didn't mind that at all. In fact, he didn't want me to tell a lot that went on and I was surprised about that.

Q: If there was some way to force you to testify without immunity, would you have lied as to the precise manner of your sister's death?

A: If I wasn't given transactional immunity I would have lied, absolutely. There was no way I was going to put my father in jail.

Farrell was being very honest and straightforward about the fact that he would lie rather than endanger his father. Most witnesses would be evasive when confronted with such a direct question. Yet when the key witness against your client admits that he would lie to protect a loved one, that becomes a significant plus for the defense.

There was another actual lie Farrell admitted to, having to do with the location of the cassette Russell sent him.

Q: Now you just used a phrase which you used many times on direct examination, when you said *the nature of the game* was such and such. Isn't the simple truth of the matter that you as a sophisticated New York businessman understood that in a certain respect your negotiation with the State was a game?

A: Yes, but . . .

Q: Hear me out . . . a game in this sense. You wanted to get total immunity for yourself, your brother, and your father without spilling the beans about the smothering; and once you had the immunity, then you'd be happy to spill the beans. So in that sense it was a game? (*"Spilling the beans" was a phrase of Farrell's that I picked up on.*)

A: In that sense it was a game, you know. Yet the word game can get kicked around to mean something not serious. But from the point of view of keeping my cards close to my vest, that's absolutely true.

Q: And it's obvious, Farrell, that you won the game. If there was a gold medal for a con job, you'd have it up on your wall. You got total immunity for all three Delmans without the State knowing that your father smothered your sister. You won the game; don't be modest.

Those were the kinds of statements/questions that drove prosecutors Volz and Russell up the wall. They constantly accused me of asking multiple questions, which could not be answered in an orderly way. They also accused me of phrasing my questions in such a way so that, coupled with my tone of voice, actually became a mini final argument. I suppose I would have to plead guilty to those charges. I would assert, however, that that is simply the way I talk even in nonadversarial circumstances. I either create or get caught up in the emotions of the moment and find it difficult to stop myself. Farrell Delman responded:

A: Gee, I don't think you're right on this con job. I really don't think it was a con job. I wasn't even negotiating with the State. But in terms of it being tricky, yeah it was definitely tricky. Did I defraud the State? I don't believe I did. Deveney did not want to be debriefed, which I had found surprising. What I would have expected is for my lawyer to say to me, "Tell me this and tell me that so that I can know how to defend you." But that wasn't *the game plan* and I was surprised. (*The jury was becoming very sophisticated regarding games played in the legal arena.*)

Judge Thompson had signed an order requiring Deveney to testify. I was very excited because I could not imagine that Deveney would totally support Farrell's version of their interaction. Unfortunately, Judge Thompson's order turned out to be a meaningless piece of paper.

I spoke to Deveney by telephone several times (we never met) and his position was clear: he would not submit to Florida jurisdiction absent a New York court order requiring him to do so. I tried to persuade him by pointing out that he had done such a marvelous job in obtaining immunity for his clients that they had no vulnerability whatsoever, so why should he care? He was rigid and we were not about to get sidetracked by tangling with the convoluted New York court bureaucracy on Deveney's turf. We knew we would lose that battle.

Q: Would you authorize Mr. Deveney to come to Florida and testify about his conversations with you? (*Uncharacteristically, Farrell started to hedge. I persisted.*) My question to you is will you now authorize Mr. Deveney to testify in this courtroom about any and all discussions held with you, your brother, and your father, or will you not authorize that?
A: Why should I do that? Why should I authorize Deveney to

come here out of my own free will? Why should I pay him at all?

Q: It's not going to cost you a penny. I'll pay for first class accommodations for Mr. Deveney to come down. I want to know if I can call Deveney tonight and say Farrell Delman has authorized you to come to Florida to testify. Do I have your permission to tell Mr. Deveney that?

A: I just don't see where that's in my interest at all.

Q: Listen, you're leaving on an airplane when you leave this courtroom. I am asking you, do I have your permission to call Deveney tonight and say that you say it's okay for him to come to St. Petersburg to testify, or do I not have your permission?

A: I'll speak to Deveney about that and ask him what he thinks.

Q: When you say you thought you could blow your immunity you understood it to mean you could lose your immunity and be charged with the murder of your sister, as opposed to only being charged with the crime of perjury, which obviously is far less serious?

A: That's correct.

Q: Where did you get that belief from? Who told you that?

A: I don't know. (*This was a completely erroneous premise the State allowed him to believe because it enhanced its control over the Delmans.*)

Q: It wasn't Mr. Volz?

A: I don't know. I am trying to remember. (*He never did remember.*)

Q: You didn't go to the library and do research on your own?

A: No.

MR. RUSSELL: (*On redirect*) Did I ever tell you to tell the truth, to make sure that's the thing to do? (*Lawyers are very thin-skinned when they feel their integrity is being attacked.*)

MR. ROSENBLATT: Self-serving and leading judge. Aren't I a great guy? Isn't the State terrific? These are not proper questions to ask of this witness, who they gave immunity to.

THE COURT: Allow the question.

MR. RUSSELL: What one single thing have I repeated to you as far as being a witness?

A: Tell the truth, tell the truth just as you see it. (*It is never that simple; lawyers don't need hour upon hour of preparation time if that's all they want their witnesses to do.*)

Why were the Delmans willing to besmirch themselves by confessing? Especially since Farrell admitted to political ambitions, sometimes fantasizing about running for the United States Senate. Farrell was very worldly and in his position as president of The Tobacco Merchant's Association of the United States he had dealt with law firms that had several hundred lawyers on board. He knew he could trust his father and brother. The answer lay in their very deep distrust of Peter, which was certainly reinforced by his television confession and the manuscript. I was pointing out to Farrell how self-destructive it was for Peter to go on television and to write a book. I was stressing how careless he had been and how clever the Delmans had been. I was happy to let the Delmans win the IQ contest since our focus was on an acquittal.

Q: You would agree he's been very stupid throughout this in terms of not looking out for number one, as opposed to the Delmans who have been superbly clever in looking out for yourselves. Because by virtue of what he did he is in that chair on trial, and by virtue of what the three Delmans did, you're all in the clear.

A: I would agree essentially with what you're saying. Except to this day I still don't know why he went on television. I'm still trying to understand the motive there because it was at the very least a very stupid act. (*By that weekend, in the quiet of his hotel room, Farrell would finally figure it all out— at least to his satisfaction. He would give birth to a bombshell!*)

Q: Incredibly stupid, right?

A: Oh, incredibly stupid. Unless there was a video tape of the Delmans and he wanted to get back at us. That's the only way I could possibly understand it.

Q: What are you saying, that you think Peter filmed the smothering?

A: I honestly believe that there could have been a videotape of the final few minutes of Pat's life.

Q: Why do you believe that? (*A dumb question, but I was curious.*)

A: Well, I knew Peter was into photography. There were explicit photos of Pat in the house in full view. To capture their love making and to have Pat live on for him is not something that would have been beyond what I think Peter could have done in that situation.

Every time we attempted to make the State or the Delmans look bad the State would up the ante by trying to make Peter look worse.

Oftentimes the focus of the trial became the nonissues of character and likeability rather than the factual elements of the crimes with which Peter was charged. We didn't kid ourselves for a minute; juries often convict people they hate for irrelevant reasons and just as often acquit guilty defendants for whom they have compassion and affection. Judge Thompson was continuing to allow all kinds of testimony that made Peter look very bad.

There was a fundamental difference in approach between the State and the defense. To the State this was a first degree murder trial where the defendant deliberately ended the life of another person. To us this was a euthanasia case, a mercy-killing case, a private family tragedy. Over and over again throughout the course of the trial and during bench conferences outside the presence of the jury, we would be saying to each other: "What does this evidence have to do with euthanasia? Even from the prosecution's standpoint, what does it have to do with murder?"

Once trials begin they frequently take on a life of their own and can bear small resemblance to the formal charges or the original plans of the opposing lawyers. Edward Volz, Stephen Russell, and James Fitzpatrick were playing hardball and they were good at it. They honestly believed that the relationship of Peter and Patricia had not been anything special. After all, they had read "The Lady," where Peter talked about a lengthy affair and a separation from Patricia when he was leading the life of a carefree, rich, swinging bachelor. They were convinced (Susan and I were as well) that if the jury was allowed to read the entire manuscript, Peter would be convicted; that's why they repeatedly tried to persuade Judge Thompson to admit it in evidence.

MR. RUSSELL: I think the door has been opened up by Mr. Rosenblatt's extensive cross examination—by portraying this defendant and his wife as having this long, loving relationship . . . there was a period of time when they separated and there was an affair. . . .

MRS. ROSENBLATT: Your Honor, this is really outrageous . . . this separation ended several years before Pat contracted the cancer. It has no relevance to this case. My husband said on numerous occasions this family had its problems. It wasn't a perfect marriage but basically they loved each other. To bring in something obviously prejudicial and bringing it up in front of the press, it's really outrageous.

THE COURT: I'm not so sure that's not a proper subject matter of inquiry.

MR. ROSENBLATT: This is the cheapest shot imaginable. The State
has been looking for some angle to get the affair in evidence.

MR. RUSSELL: *What's good for the goose is good for the gander.*
I think we've got every right to put it in perspective. (*The
"what's good for the goose is good for the gander" cliché was
one of Russell's favorites; I felt like strangling him every time
he uttered it.*)

THE COURT: If it's relevant that he's a loving husband, it's relevant
that he's not. I agree it's remote.

After protracted wrangling and a lot of general reciprocal nastiness,
the judge decided that he would allow the jury to learn of the separation
but not specifically the affair. The State was confident the jury would
infer from the period of separation that Peter had affairs.

Farrell Delman was very proud of the role he, his father, and brother
played in Patricia's death. Farrell's basic attitude was that Peter had screwed
it up miserably, making it impossible for Patricia to achieve the dignified
death she wanted. The smothering occurred because the Delmans had to
repair the damage caused by Peter's inability to induce death. Not only
did Farrell feel no guilt about what they had done, he believed his father's
final act was heroic.

[MR. ROSENBLATT]: He screwed up? He bungled it?

A: Yes. He said it dozens of times that night.

Q: Peter and the children should have thanked the Delmans.

A: Oh, absolutely, no question about it.

Q: In all the time that has elapsed since January 15, 1986, right
up until today, you have never felt one shred of guilt for anything
that you did in connection with your sister's death. As far
as you were concerned what you did was moral, proper, and
ethical?

A: Absolutely.

Q: You think maybe that's a little arrogant, to be that sure?

A: No, I don't think that's arrogance at all, I really don't.

State's Attorney Stephen Russell took Farrell through the events that
directly led to Patricia's demise.

Q: Would you describe what happened at that point? (*The critical point when Russell Delman left the bedroom and joined his father, Farrell, and Peter on the screened-in outdoor pool patio.*)

A: Russell gave the breathing report and said, "Her breaths are little quivers, she is breathing little bits of air, just hanging in there. She is just barely holding onto life." And he said, *"If I had the guts I'd put a pillow over her face."*

Q: Do you recall whether anything else was said by anyone or done by anyone at that time?

A: I recall a statement and this is not 100 percent certainty, and I kept thinking that maybe it was my father. But I'm thinking now more clearly that maybe I said it: *"I was thinking the same thing."* I feel very strongly that was said. And then shortly after that my father said, *"Enough is enough,"* or he uttered a sigh that certainly expressed to me *enough is enough.* I'm not absolutely sure he said, "Enough is enough." (*The ever-resourceful Farrell was covering his bases because he knew that I would zero in on his prior inconsistencies during my cross examination.*)

Q: During the process of being interviewed by the State and going through a deposition with Mr. Rosenblatt, has your memory been jogged on some things? (*Aha, the old memory-jogging question to a witness who has lost his way.*)

A: Sure.

Q: When you got up from your chair at the patio table did you see Peter?

A: Yes I did.

Q: Where was he?

A: Peter was heading toward the kitchen area, and I remember this clearly. He had his back toward me and he was heading toward the kitchen area.

Q: From what direction?

A: From the table. (*Under the State's first degree murder conspiracy count it was critical that Peter heard all the pertinent remarks that led to Vincent's definitive action.*)

Q: What did you think was going to go on in the bedroom at that time?

A: We were going to put Pat out of her misery.

Q: What were the intervals between the breaths?

A: Oh, long. Long. It was amazing. Every time we would hear a quiver we were amazed that she was still breathing, that there was still a breath. We figured this had to be it because we'd wait and wait but then we'd hear another one. (*By emphasizing the obvious fact that Pat was so very close to death, the State sought to minimize the impact of the smothering.*)

Q: And what occurred after that?

A: Well, my father had got into one position and felt somewhat uncomfortable, so he moved into another position where he put his right knee on the bed and was holding Pat with one finger under her nose and the other finger on her mouth. His back was stretched over this way so his back was hurting. . . . I was holding my father at the waist to support him so he wouldn't feel like he was alone.

Russell Delman had testified that he wasn't sure what his father was going to do as they all marched to the bedroom. Vincent himself would testify that he wasn't sure what if any action he would take. Yet Farrell knew. I asked,

Q: So it was 100 percent clear to you?

A: For me it was thoroughly clear what we were going to do. We were going to go in there and with the little quiver of breath she had, we were going to shut it off and her lingering would be over.

Q: How come it wasn't 100 percent clear to your brother or your father?

MR. RUSSELL: Your Honor, I object.

THE COURT: Sustain the objection.

Q: You certainly have no recollection of Peter saying anything in response to Russell's pillow remark, correct?

A: I am absolutely certain he said nothing.

Q: And if you said anything or if your father said anything, Peter said nothing in response to any of your comments, correct?

A: Correct.

Q: When your father got up, when you got up, when Russell got up, Peter said nothing—correct?

A: Correct. (*"One hell of a conspiracy," I muttered to Susan.*)

Q: When the three of you went into the bedroom Peter did not follow you into the bedroom, correct?

A: Correct.

Q: What jogged this sudden burst of memory that now you think the likelihood is that after Russell made his pillow comment, you said, *"I was thinking the same thing"?* What triggered that?

A: I don't know. But what I am telling you now is that I feel like I said it. (*In his statement Farrell had said he thought his father said that.*)

Q: Your best recollection today is that you said, *"I was thinking the same thing."* My question is why was that not your best recollection when you gave your statement to the State in December of 1986, or when you gave your second statement in March of 1987, or when I took your deposition in December of 1987? Why did it take until late 1988 for that to become your best recollection?

A: I don't know. I can't answer that. I really can't answer that.

We were ecstatic with this answer yet surprised that Farrell Delman offered such a feeble explanation. I made it clear that Russell Delman had a sudden memory jog on this point as well. Farrell said he remembered it first at the meeting in the state attorney's office in Fort Myers about three or four weeks before the beginning of the trial. After hearing Farrell's memory burst, Russell then said that he remembered it that way as well. What a lovely coincidence!

I was feverishly noting every inconsistency and contradiction in my final argument notebook; while some of these inconsistencies may have been trivial in and of themselves, I felt their collective impact had the potential to be impressive. These kinds of answers also dovetailed very neatly with our cynicism about the true purpose behind the lengthy and repeated meetings with the State's representatives. I reminded Farrell that he brainstormed with the State for eight hours in preparation for his deposition.

There was also a conflict between the Delmans as to what occurred after Patricia died. They all agreed that Vincent left the bedroom first and that his destination was the airport, where he was picking up his wife. All agreed that Farrell was the next to leave and that Russell remained behind.

It was very important to the State to have Peter positioned right outside the bedroom door as Vincent and Farrell left, to add weight to their theory that Peter knew exactly what was going on but had manipulated the Delmans so that he could avoid any direct participation. The Delmans were unified in their testimony regarding Peter's location.

[MR. RUSSELL]: What happened when you left the bedroom?

A: I took one step out of the room and boom, ran into Peter.

And he said to me, *"Whatever happened in there, don't tell
me about it."* I will never forget that for as long as I live.
He looked me straight in the eye and said, "Whatever happened in there, don't tell me about it."

Q: And did that surprise you?

A: Blew my mind, thoroughly blew my mind.

Q: Why?

A: Because I was expecting a hug.

Yet, I was able to develop conflicts on cross examination in this area:

[MR. ROSENBLATT]: By the time you left the bedroom, your
father was nowhere to be seen. He had gone already?

A: That's correct. (*This answer conflicted with his brother who
had testified that he thought Farrell, Vincent, and Peter were
all together.*)

Q: It was your understanding then, and it's your understanding
now, that as soon as Patricia was dead, your father got into
Peter's car so he could go to the airport and pick up Joan?

A: I certainly know that now, yes.

Q: You learned later that when Joan and Vincent returned to
the home from the airport, that Joan had been kept waiting
about a half hour?

A: Right. (*This testimony made Vincent look bad and we wanted
the jury to believe that his fear of being late to the airport
was the motivation for him becoming suddenly decisive. After
all, until the smothering he had been a very passive observer.*)

Q: You don't like Joan very much do you?

A: I tolerate her. I'm not crazy about her personality.

Q: She's bossy, the bossy New York real estate lady, right?

A: Right. She can be bossy.

Q: She's tough. Isn't she tough?

A: Yes, I would say she's pretty tough.

Q: Nicer to her poodle than she is to your father, right?

A: I wouldn't go that far either.

Q: About a tie?

A: No, she's nice to him. I mean you're describing a personality.
She is a tough lady, New York-type person.

Q: Kind of woman that if your father was late to the airport
might yell at him?

A: That's certainly possible.

The State believed that Peter had cleverly manipulated the Delmans by stressing the idea that unless something was done, Patricia would awaken and then remain in a pathetic vegetative state. Of course, had Peter been correct about her life expectancy, she could not have remained that way very long. Peter manipulated Patricia just as adroitly by his repeated assertions that she would suffer a gruesome death by vomiting up all her blood and choking on it.

Patricia had well-documented terminal cancer, which had spread from her lung to her brain to her adrenal glands. She was certainly going to die soon. What was Peter's incentive to have her commit suicide a few days or weeks early? According to the State, a botched suicide followed by a mercy killing added tremendous pizzazz to the overall scenario and would greatly heighten the media's interest in the manuscript and in their love story. According to the State, Peter needed an angle to interest a publisher in his manuscript and to make any book that would be published a best seller, which would then be made into a blockbusting movie.

Farrell had heard that "The Lady" trashed the Delmans (it did); he wanted desperately to read the manuscript but the State refused to make it available. Farrell figured Peter wrote about his father suffocating Patricia, and this was another motivating factor causing Farrell to turn state's evidence. "The Lady" was some 641 pages, yet not once did Peter specifically accuse Vincent of smothering his daughter. There was included a general discussion (contained in chapter 34, which was in evidence) between the Delmans about smothering Patricia, shortly before she died, but in writing his manuscript, Peter did not go the extra step and directly link a smothering to Patricia's death. Had he known, I don't believe he would have been capable of sufficient self-control to exclude it. Everything else was in the book, much of which made him and his family look terrible. So why in the world leave out the specifics of the suffocation if Peter knew definitely that Vincent caused Patricia's death?

My position was that the State wanted Farrell to believe that lie so he would be even more strongly motivated to bury Peter. It was impossible to predict where my cross examination of Farrel Delman would ultimately lead.

Q: Don't you now understand that the reason the State did not allow you to read the book was because they wanted you to believe that Peter knew about the suffocation, and wrote about the suffocation, when in reality he did not?

A: I really don't know what is in the book. Maybe the suffocation is in it.

Q: It's not in the book. (*Technically, I was correct but there was a strong suggestion of a smothering in the manuscript.*)

A: I don't know. I really don't know.

Q: But you'd like to know; that's why you asked to read it.

A: Well sure, I would love to see the other things he said about the Delman family.

Q: You had heard from the State and from other sources that Peter said bad things about the Delmans, correct?

A: I don't know whether I heard it from the State per se. But I certainly did hear it from Mitchell Parnes (*Patricia's cousin*). He did tell me that the book trashes the Delmans.

Q: And is it conceivable to you that in a book where he is trashing the Delmans and he knows that the three of you suffocated his wife, is it conceivable that he will protect you and not mention that?

A: No. In that situation I assumed the worst. I assumed that he put that in the book, okay. And that's what I had to protect myself against.

Q: Exactly, Farrell. Why didn't you just flat out ask Mr. Russell, Mr. Volz, or Mr. Fitzpatrick, "Does Peter in the book talk about the smothering?"

A: I did ask them.

Q: What did they say?

A: They wouldn't tell me. (*This refusal led to the most unexpected twist of a very winding trial.*)

Q: And obviously, they didn't tell you because they wanted you to continue to hate Peter and be worried that he had mentioned the smothering in the book. What other reason . . .

MR. RUSSELL: I object to the question.

THE COURT: Sustained.

Q: I'd love to tell you what's in the book but they object when I do that. (*This wise-guy comment was shoved down my throat.*)

MR. RUSSELL: Your Honor, we have no objection to the book going into evidence right now. (*Although the State had asked many times that the book be admitted, this was the first time that the request was made in the presence of the jury.*)

MR. ROSENBLATT: Chapter 34 is in evidence; let's give it to him to read.

MR. RUSSELL: The whole book, let's put it in evidence. (*Russell never gave up. Susan and I were convinced that if the judge weakened and allowed the entire book to be read by the jury, that would constitute reversible error. It would also add weeks to the trial.*)

Judge Thompson sustained my objection to the entire book but permitted Farrell to read chapter 34, which was in evidence.

[MR. RUSSELL]: (*On redirect*) Based on what you know of the defendant, how would you describe him in terms of ego?

A: Oh, tremendously egocentric, very strong ego. But a lot of that was a facade. To a great extent he was a little boy inside.

MR. ROSENBLATT: Your Honor, unless counsel is going to qualify Mr. Delman as an expert in psychiatry, I object to this line of questioning. Pop psychology we don't need.

MR. RUSSELL: Judge, I am asking him for his perceptions and his understandings. I don't see why I can't do it.

THE COURT: Objection overruled.

For some inexplicable reason the State became obsessed with establishing that their motives were pure in denying Farrell access to Peter's manuscript. Who really cared? Talk about side issues! The State's focus on this subject led to the most dramatic and bizarre testimony that I have ever witnessed in a courtroom, testimony that was unique in the history of criminal law. It led directly to Farrell Delman having the golden opportunity to psychoanalyze and trash Peter Rosier before a worldwide audience.

In arriving at that point Farrell inadvertently revealed much of his own psyche. The State, not I, invited Farrell to speculate about Peter's motives in including or excluding certain events from chapter 34. In a very adolescent-type way, yet in a way typical of so many family disputes, Farrell began to get very angry at Peter (as he read chapter 34), underplaying the role of the Delmans in causing Patricia's death. Farrell was incensed that Peter (the wimp, the coward) portrayed himself as the hero and the Delmans as minor supporting characters.

Farrell did not complete his testimony on Friday afternoon so he remained at the Hilton Hotel in St. Petersburg over that weekend. Reading and rereading chapter 34, he had a revelation that he described as a profound religious experience. He said on the following Monday morning during the State's redirect examination:

[MR. DELMAN]: I've been trying to figure these things out the last two and a half years really. But reading this stuff really triggered a true understanding of exactly what took place January 15, 1986. Over the weekend I think I really understand it now, the whole truth of what happened.

[MR. RUSSELL]: And what would be your understanding of that now?

A: Over the weekend I wrote up the precise answer to that question.

Q: What is the essence of it?

A: The essence of it is this: That Peter needed, it's very compli-cated. The events had to be bungled. He could not stand her dead, he could not stand her dying and suffering, okay. The only middle ground left is a world of lingering between life and death, and he let her linger because he didn't have the guts to do it.

I followed up on recross examination:

[MR. ROSENBLATT]: When did you write the analysis that you've told us about for the very first time today?

A: I wrote it starting Saturday afternoon and part of Sunday morning.

Q: Why did you do that?

A: Because I've been trying to figure this whole thing out myself. The death was such a bungled event, it couldn't have been an accident.

Q: Where is what you wrote? (*Stephen Russell never asked him for it or offered it in evidence.*)

A: In my little portable computer in the witness room, you know, where I wait before I come in here.

Q: You're sure it's not at the hotel?

A: No, no, its right here.

Q: You're sure it's not in the car? (*My sarcasm related to the lie that Farrell had told about Russell's cassette.*)

A: No, I have all the other bags in the car.

Q: (*Pointing to Volz, Russell, and Fitzpatrick, I asked*) When did these gentlemen first learn that you had written this analysis?

A: They just learned it right now. They didn't know I did that.

Q: They learned about it happenstance in the courtroom today? You never told them about that before?

A: Absolutely, because I only did it over the weekend. We haven't talked. (*This explanation stretched credulity; they were all at the same hotel.*)

Q: How did you get to the courthouse this morning?

A: Steve Sorenson who works for the State, he's got a truck, and I threw all my bags in the truck because I'm planning on getting home this afternoon if I can. I didn't want to leave this $8,000 computer in the truck.

Q: What I'm going to do—and its time for a break now or shortly— what I want to do is have you bring in your computer because I want to read what you wrote. Any problem with that, Farrell?

A: No. I don't have any problem with that.

Q: You can get it up on the screen so that all of us can read it, correct?

A: Yes.

Q: Are you planning on writing a book after this trial?

A: Thinking about it, yeah. (*We got to know many of the reporters and television people covering the trial, and it seemed like half of them were planning books as well.*)

MR. ROSENBLATT: Would this be a good time to break, Judge?

THE COURT: Close enough. Take about ten minutes, ladies and gentlemen. (*Addressing the lawyers*) How do you want to handle this thing? Y'all want to look over his shoulder and have him read the thing or . . .

MRS. ROSENBLATT: No. What we want to do is see what it says, obviously, before we cross examine him on it. We want to determine whether or not we want to use it. If it's something that he prepared, we have a right to look at it. We don't want to publish it necessarily.

THE COURT: You don't want to take it cold?

MR. VOLZ: We don't know. We have never seen it.

THE COURT: Everybody want to look at it?

MRS. ROSENBLATT: Yes.

Lawyers, judges, and law professors preach ad nauseum that there is no substitute for diligent preparation. Who would want to argue with that premise? The consensus is that thorough preparation is far more important than occasional flashes of brilliance.

This unique evidence did not exist before the trial, nor did it even exist when Farrell began testifying on the previous Thursday. Susan and I had to make an almost instantaneous decision as to whether we would allow the jury to read along with Farrell. The decision was entirely ours;

the State had not offered it and even if they had I am confident the judge would not have admitted it over our objection. Susan and I were fully aware that if we guessed wrong and Peter got convicted, we would be severely criticized by our fellow lawyers, who are among the greatest second-guessers the world has ever known.

One of the dumbest clichés expounded repeatedly by lawyers (most of whom have never seen the inside of a courtroom) is to never ask a question to which you don't know the answer. I can only assume this advice comes from lawyers who work for five-hundred-member firms with armies of investigators and unlimited funds. The rule cannot be followed in the real world, because trials take on a life of their own and are unpredictable.

After reading Farrell's opus, I said to Susan: "Farrell paints Peter as a hideous human being with almost no redeeming qualities. Yet his bottom line is that Peter never intended to kill Pat, and therefore committed no crime."

"Neither law school nor handling hundreds of appeals ever prepared me for this," Susan gasped. "This is just a shocker, and I don't know whether to laugh or cry. By allowing this in we are giving Farrell a soap box to offer expert opinions in the field of abnormal psychology. It's just unheard of for a layman to do that. And then when he starts distinguishing between morality and legality, he becomes an expert both on the law and situational ethics. And if the jury believes Farrell on the conspiracy, Peter is dead."

"I know the judge will instruct the jury that Farrell's legal opinions are worthless," I said, "but I love them and think the jury will be influenced by them."

Susan looked at me: "I think it's a mistake to let this in evidence; the jury could really grow to despise Peter."

While the jury was in recess Peter had read along with us, the judge, Volz, Russell, Fitzpatrick, the bailiff, the court reporter, and every member of the media who could squeeze in for a view of the computer screen. Peter winced at every insult, he recoiled at Farrell's conclusions, and he hated the fact that Farrell was basking in the spotlight.

After the first page or so Peter became totally disheartened. As Farrell remained the center of frenzied attention Peter slowly retreated to his seat. He slumped downward almost disappearing under the table; perspiration had soaked through his lightly colored suit jacket. When I asked Peter what he thought we should do, he flung his arm in utter disgust and said he didn't give a shit.

I said to Susan, "Input from Peter we can forget about. Look . . . we have discussed this time and again. I will concede to the jury all of Peter's faults. He's not being charged with being an arrogant asshole. I may tell the jury that as long as they find him not guilty they can consider him a selfish putz if they want to. I say let it all hang out. What say you, coach?"

"What the hell, go with your gut."

"As you well know, my gut has gotten us into a lot of trouble."

"You and I get heavy about the trivial decisions, but on the biggies we decide fast."

"Like having six children within seven years."

"The judge probably thinks we're having some intellectual, law review-type discussion here."

MR. ROSENBLATT: Judge we want this to come into evidence, to be read to the jury. (*The State did not object.*)

THE COURT: Okay. I approve. Farrell is going to read what he has written, after which he may be questioned on it.

Farrell Delman began reading: "Facts Explained by Peter's Gutlessness."

Since January 15, 1986, I like many of you, have been trying to pull all these facts together into a coherent whole. It was only with my reading from Peter's book and the recognition that he has tried to make himself a hero that I found the final pieces of the puzzle. Patty's death was a gruesome ordeal. In fact, it was so badly bungled that one has to wonder whether such a bungling could possibly be accidental. Of all currently living people, I would guess that I know Peter the best. For many years I was the only family member who maintained a relationship with the defendant. Let's review some facts about who the defendant is and how he acted in the events surrounding the death of his wife, my sister.

First, Peter's personality. . . . For most of his life he was a hypochondriac that forced attention on himself. . . . His fear of death drove him into medicine. . . . Did his fear of death make him unable to kill Pat?

Second, Peter, the malignant narcissist, is self-centered, has a self-image of perfection, scapegoating, badmouthing, [and] unceasingly engages in an effort to maintain the appearance of moral purity. Peter was never wrong. Think of his book and the hero that he makes himself into. He imposes his will upon others by covert coercion. . . . I don't think he ever had a friend for more than a year or two. . . .

Third, Peter the wimp. Think of Peter as the guy who is whimpering and sobbing around the home, who even in Pat's death had to be the center of attention. How are we to understand this self-centered narcissistic, strong-willed, scapegoating personality? What sort of person needs to have such a tough exterior personality? Answer—A weak, unformed personality. This exterior was little more than a facade, a house of cards that concealed the weak little boy of eight. Inside, the weak little boy was emotionally frozen. . . . Sometimes the little boy would invite me in. Sometimes the Mount Everest hard exterior would keep me out. For this reason I would have a love-hate, hot-cold relationship with Peter over the years. . . . Peter could never commit suicide, because he lacks courage. He's incapable of it and Patty knew this. . . .

Peter could not tolerate the process of Pat dying and he could not tolerate her death. . . . Since she was his life, her death was tantamount to his dying. . . . If Peter really wanted to kill Patty, then why all the bungling and why all the involvement of so many other people? For the resolution of his fatal flaw—his lack of courage, his basic cowardice. . . .

How is it, then, that an expert on death is unable to kill? Why involve other doctors? Why didn't this expert on death know that twenty Seconal would not do it? Why didn't this doctor have other drugs available to him? . . . He needed to involve other people to provide the courage that he lacked. . . .

Why didn't he take his own breathing reports? . . . He clearly heard Russell say, "If I had the guts I'd put a pillow over her face." . . He knew where we were going and what we were going to do. . . . He could not bear having her die whether by her suicide, by his act, or by the act of others. Peter the wimp won out. . . .

Because of Peter's lack of courage and [his] gutlessness, he performed immorally. If his book describes him as a hero, this is also a coverup for his guilt, the guilt that he left his wife hanging, unable to put her out of her misery.

And this very same guilt forced him to appear on television. While it was a stupid act, it was a necessary one. But because he performed immorally, he may well have performed legally, to the extent that Peter never intended to kill Pat but led me, my brother, my father, Mary Linden, all the doctors involved on a not-so-merry chase. . . . With Peter energizing

us with talk about becoming a vegetable and the phrase "death
rattle" used to imply [that] the event could go on endlessly.
We wanted Pat to die and we did suffocate her, to take her
out of her misery. We acted morally. We also acted illegally.
. . . In her death as well as in her life Peter's wishes came
first. . . . Sitting before you is a despicable, immoral human
being. . . . What I have just read is one man's opinion only;
it is nevertheless the truth and the whole truth of what took
place on January 15, 1986, a day I will never forget.

The jury appeared to be transfixed. One could be the most experienced lawyer in America and it would still be next to impossible to assess
the impact this would have on the jurors. We were truly in unchartered
waters. In some ways Farrell's analysis was brilliant.

Did the jury like Farrell? Did they believe him? Had we made a huge
mistake? Had Farrell succeeded in painting Peter's portrait more miserably
than the State could have ever hoped for? Was this part of the State's
plan? We had taken our gamble and would have to live with it. Susan
and I hoped that Peter would not have to rot in prison because of our
miscalculation.

I wanted the jury clearly to understand that, at least from Farrell's
standpoint, Peter had committed no crime.

Q: What you have figured out, what the bottom line to you is
that Peter Rosier did not want his wife to die. He did not
have the guts to do it himself, so you think that you and
your brother and your father were somehow manipulated,
correct?

A: That's absolutely correct. (*I figured, psychologically, that if
my questions included insulting Peter, it would make it much
easier for Farrell to agree with me.*)

Q: Now you realize, after having figured all this out, that Peter
did not have the requisite intent to kill Pat, because he didn't
have the guts.

A: I think that's strangely true.

State's Attorney Russell was put in the very weird position of coming
close to impeaching his own witness; he needed to demonstrate that when
it came to the law, Farrell didn't know what he was talking about.

[MR. RUSSELL]: Do you know what the law is in the State of
  Florida on proof of motive in a criminal case?
A: Absolutely not.
Q: Do you know what the law of the State of Florida is in aiding
  and abetting another individual to commit a crime?
A: No.

When Farrell had concluded testifying, the State requested that Judge
Thompson again instruct the jury to the effect that Farrell's legal opinions
were meaningless. Typical of lawyers, the State wanted to have its cake
and eat it, too. They wanted the jury to believe Farrell's character analysis
of Peter but they wanted them to throw his legal conclusions into the
garbage can. Judge Thompson complied with the State's request and the
jury was instructed as follows:

THE COURT: The decision as to whether a particular act was
  a violation of the law is for the jury to make based on the
  evidence, and the court's instructions on the law at the close
  of the case. You have heard testimony from certain witnesses
  as to their opinions on these matters. Witnesses' testimony
  that a particular act is moral or immoral, or legal or illegal,
  is not to be considered by you in determining whether an
  act is in fact an illegal or legal act.

Judge Thompson was always kind enough to recess early on Fridays
(we would go from 8:00 A.M. to about 1:00 P.M. with one or two short
breaks) so that Susan and I could fly home and spend the weekend with
our children and not violate the Sabbath by traveling. Knowing this the
State pushed me very hard to rush through my cross examination the
Friday before so that Farrell could finish his testimony and not have to
return to the courtroom on Monday morning. Farrell had been on the
stand all day Thursday as well.

The judge engaged in some psychological warfare, saying if we had
to work late this Friday, so be it. He definitely wanted to be finished
with Farrell Delman. We refused to be intimidated even if it meant having
to spend the weekend in St. Petersburg. Susan and I knew we would
be walking out of the courtroom before sundown come hell or high water.

In one of the supreme ironies of the trial State's Attorney Russell
did a total about face and said he agreed that we could quit at the usual
time that Friday even though this guaranteed Farrell's reappearance on
Monday. If Farrell had finished on Friday, he never would have written

his analysis of Peter. The background of this reversal involved the State's fervent desire to get Peter's entire manuscript entered into evidence.

> MR. RUSSELL: Your Honor, at this time the State would move to admit into evidence the entire book, State's Exhibit 4.
> MR. ROSENBLATT: This is a ploy for the press, Judge. Your Honor has ruled on that already.
> THE COURT: Approach the bench gentlemen.
> MR. RUSSELL: Judge this will require very extensive argument, perhaps if the Jury was taken out.
> MRS. ROSENBLATT: How can he ask to have the book introduced through this witness, who never read it?
> MR. VOLZ: We don't need a witness to introduce the book. We may be asking this witness to read portions of the book Your Honor. (*Was this part of a strategy to enable Farrell to write his piece trashing Peter? We would never know for sure.*)
> MRS. ROSENBLATT: If you want him to read the book, why can't we break at 1:00 P.M.?
> MR. RUSSELL: I have no problem breaking at 1:00 P.M. (*They could have knocked us over with a feather.*)

A local lawyer has a significant advantage over an outsider. After trying many cases in front of a particular judge, a lawyer becomes expert at predicting the judge's rulings on objections and the admissibility of evidence. This was particularly so here because Volz and Russell were intimately familiar with Judge James Thompson's track record when he worked for their boss, State Attorney Joseph D'Alessandro. Judge Thompson had a kitchen-sink philosophy on the admissibility of evidence. When in doubt he would allow the evidence to be heard by the jury; he let everything in including the kitchen sink. Surprisingly, Judge Thompson agreed with the defense that the whole of "The Lady" should not be admitted into evidence—only chapters 33 and 34.

The State's case made a high-risk defense strategy just about mandatory. In the "good guy, bad guy" category, I even touched upon a subject that is considered off limits by nearly every trial lawyer—religion. Susan whispered to me, "Fools rush in where angels fear to tread." I continued questioning Farrell Delman:

> Q: Although you studied some Asian religions, do I understand correctly [that] you don't practice any religion?

MR. RUSSELL: Your Honor, I object. Ask to approach the bench. There is an evidentiary rule against going into religion.

MR. ROSENBLATT: I don't intend to dwell on it. I want to establish, as I did with Russell Delman, that he is not a follower of any organized religion. He has no system of religious beliefs which guide his life. Therefore, he would have no dilemma with lying. (*The judge made it obvious he wanted me to stay away from this area and I complied for the most part.*)

Q: Your statements to Pat when she was unconscious were not based on any system of religious beliefs that you adhere to, correct?

A: That's correct.

Q: Were you chanting to your unconscious sister because you thought your words had any practical effect? Did you believe that by saying those words from the *Tibetan Book of the Dead* that you were helping your sister?

A: I believe so and I believe so to this day.

According to Russell and Farrell the *Tibetan Book of the Dead* describes the death process as feeling like the person is flying effortlessly through the air. The Delman brothers were repeatedly chanting things like, "Go for the light, let go." This testimony coming from two Long Island Jews would make them appear very weird or worse, especially to any Jewish juror. I knew we had one Jewish man and one Jewish woman on the twelve-member jury.

I touched upon the controversial topics of religion, drugs, and the Vietnam War during my cross examination, even though I had little idea how this strategy would cut. We sure as hell hoped we had liberals on the jury, although defining liberalism in the context of a euthanasia trial is very tricky. Liberals would have a spirit of kinship with the Delman brothers. Peter was probably to the left of both of them; the favorite presidential candidate of the Rosier family was Jesse Jackson.

Susan and I had told Peter long ago, and he agreed, this was going to be a "pull out all the stops" defense. That strategy became more pronounced after we saw the direction of Judge Thompson's rulings. If I was polite and professional and played the "respect game," Peter would be going from the courthouse to prison. If I was offending certain members of the jury, that was a risk I simply had to take.

I sought to portray Farrell as selfish, as always looking out for himself.

Q: You were looking out for number one, number two, and number three, right?

A: Yes.

Q: And you succeeded royally, correct?

A: We succeeded.

Q: Don't be modest. Not only did you succeed royally in looking out for the Delmans but you managed to put yourself in the absolute catbird seat, because by doing that you were able to hurt that man (*pointing to Peter slouched in his chair*). So you could get at your enemy as well as protect yourself, and that's really the best of both worlds.

I knew there would be an objection to the question (or questions) and I knew the objection would be sustained. Yet from a tactical standpoint, the question itself had a value irrespective of any answer I might get.

Since Farrell was into the *Tibetan Book of the Dead,* and since he had married one woman from Finland and another from France, I wanted to ask him if it wasn't true that, psychologically, he was running away from his heritage. If he could psychoanalyze Peter, why couldn't I do the same with him? Susan thought I was well over the line already, so that was one of many questions I crossed out.

Susan turned to me and said: "Enough already. You're really beginning to repeat yourself. I feel strongly you've scored all the points that you're going to score."

"You're right, but believe it or not I enjoy dueling with this guy. He's intelligent and he's got street smarts, an unusual combination. Okay, I'm going to wind it up by drilling a few clean singles if I can."

Q: In all your discussions with the State Attorney's Office did you ever ask them this question: "With all the murderers and rapists and armed robbers walking the streets, why are you putting so much manpower and money in this case?"

RUSSELL: Your Honor. . . . (*That's all the judge had to hear.*)

THE COURT: Sustain the objection.

Russell asked Judge Thompson to hold me in contempt for asking that "outrageous" question. I felt the question was perfectly valid from a commonsense, taxpayer standpoint. Judge Thompson thought it was a bad question (not lawyerly) but it hardly reached the level of being contemptuous. I was losing track of the number of times that Joseph D'Alessandro's soldiers demanded that I be held in contempt.

I expected Farrell to be honest and direct enough to admit that there were reasons for Patricia to commit suicide, reasons more powerful than her fear of an ugly death. He did not disappoint me.

Q: You testified earlier that Pat did not want to vomit up all her blood on the kitchen floor. Isn't it equally true that Pat's rational decision to end her life took into account the following: that she was in great pain, she did not want to waste away, and she did not want to lose her mental faculties?

A: Absolutely true.

Q: Based on your knowledge of Patty being meticulous, and being very much into esthetics, you would agree that just the mental image of knowing she had all this cancer throughout her body must have been very distasteful to her?

A: Absolutely correct.

Q: Regardless of any talk about a death rattle or Patty becoming a vegetable, the fundamental truth is that the reason you, your brother, and father decided to end Patty's life is, number one, she had terminal cancer; number two, she had made a rational decision to commit suicide; and number three, you all knew that she did not want to get up? (*She didn't want an unsuccessful suicide attempt.*)

A: Absolutely true.

Q: If someone had said: "Well maybe the Seconals are not working. Let them wear off and when Pat wakes up we'll ask her if she wants to take this time thirty Seconal." You would have said that's totally crazy, right?

A: Right.

Q: There was nothing to rediscuss with Patty. She had made her intention one thousand percent clear, she had decided to die and she did not want to get up?

A: That's true.

Farrell loved Patricia as much as he hated Peter. Without equivocation he admitted that the Rosiers had a great relationship. "Pat was always on a pedestal for Peter. . . . She was his life, they were one person to an amazing extent."

From our standpoint that was great testimony, but Farrell went even further: "I don't think anyone in this room has that kind of relationship with their spouse."

Wow, what a way to end up the longest and probably the most

important witness for the State. That comment by Farrell would allow me to argue with much justification: Who other than Peter Rosier had the right to participate in Patricia's exercise of her freedom of choice? How could he or any loving spouse refuse to assist their life partner's last wish? How could the Delmans, who had been estranged from Patricia for years, arrogate unto themselves the right to decide her moment of death?

"Susan, I'm ready to call it a day. Anything else?"

"No. The Delmans really do have some mensch qualities."

"Two Delmans down, one to go."

6

Vincent Delman Takes Matters
into His Own Hands

Dr. Vincent Delman had practiced dentistry in Brooklyn for forty-one years prior to his retirement, which occurred about a year before the trial began. He had married Pat's divorced mother, Lorraine, when Patricia was eight years old and he testified that he adopted Patricia shortly thereafter. Patricia had no contact whatsoever with her natural father, a printer, although he continued to live in the New York area.

Vincent testified that he was very close to Patricia during her growing-up years, loved her as he loved his two sons and described her as "lovely, absolutely adorable, charming." I believed him as I believed Russell and Farrell when they described their feelings about Patricia. That was a major reason why I could take no joy in discrediting the Delmans.

Patricia's mother was incapacitated periodically because of alcohol and drug problems ("uppers and downers") and Patricia was a great help with her much younger brothers. Lorraine was actually institutionalized on occasion—once remaining at Rockland State Hospital for some two months. Patricia worked in Vincent's office and subsequently became a dental hygienist.

Prosecutor Stephen Russell knew I would bring out the fact that there was no contact between father and daughter for some years prior to her fortieth birthday, when Peter threw a surprise party and invited all the Delmans to Fort Myers. Within weeks of that event Jacob celebrated his bar mitzvah and the Delmans attended that as well.

The effect of cross examination can be blunted considerably by bringing out potentially damaging areas in a forthright way on direct exam-

123

ination. Both Russell and Volz displayed much skill in employing this technique.

> [MR. RUSSELL]: Let's say from around 1969 up to 1982, did you have much contact with your daughter and son-in-law?
> A: I didn't have any contact with them.
> Q: Why was that?
> A: Well, number one, Peter and I never got along well. We tolerated each other. And the second thing is I had the impression that there would be very serious problems if she remained in contact with her family. And it would be better off for her if the contact was kept at a very, very long arm's distance. (*This description seemed totally consistent with a character trait of Peter's attested to by his former friends and even some of his current ones; he was extremely possessive and wanted to have Pat exclusively devoted to him.*)
> Q: Now regardless of the infrequent contact you had with Pat during that period of time, did you maintain a love and affection for her?
> A: Absolutely.
> Q: Did you have occasion between April of 1982 (*Patricia's fortieth birthday*) and April of 1985 to see Pat in New York?
> A: Yes. I saw her several times. We had dinner. Russell got married in January of 1984 in Philadelphia and Pat was there with [their daughter] Elizabeth.
> Q: Did you have occasion through 1983–1984 to see the defendant and Pat in Miami?
> A: Yes I did.
> Q: What were those occasions?
> A: Well, several times they had their own airplane or part of an airplane and they would fly into Miami. I would pick them up at the airport. And I think at around that time they were purchasing an automobile or two in Miami. (*This line of questioning was useful to the State in that it demonstrated that the Delmans had become much closer to Pat since her surprise party, and it let the jury know that Peter had accumulated substantial wealth.*)

On December 12, 1986, the three Delmans met with the State's lead investigator, James Fitzpatrick, in their attorney's Manhattan office. Vincent testified that he never at any time had a discussion with John Deveney about the events surrounding Patricia's death or anything else. This was extraordinary since Vincent smothered her, yet it was totally consistent with Farrell saying Deveney didn't want to know the facts. Vincent said he never even had a discussion with Farrell regarding what Farrell would tell Deveney about the final act or the events leading up to it. He and Russell gave Farrell total discretion as to the strategy he would employ with Deveney.

Stephen Russell wanted to make it crystal clear that the Delmans would not have testified absent the grant of total immunity. He reemphasized the state's contention that they had no alternative but to grant immunity; without the testimony of the Delmans, Dr. Peter Rosier would get away with murder.

Vincent went to sleep on the couch in the den about midnight, knowing absolutely nothing about any planned suicide. He testified that he was awakened at twilight by loud voices, he walked toward the kitchen, where he saw Peter arguing with Dr. Daniel Dosoretz. Steve Russell asked:

Q: What did you hear of the conversation?
A: Well in essence, "I need it, it didn't work and it wasn't strong enough," that type of thing. (*It was important for the State to show that Peter was the leader and wanted sufficient drugs to end Pat's life, that that was his intent.*)
Q: And when you went to the kitchen, what happened?
A: Peter told me to get out, so I went back into the den.

I was confident that when Dosoretz testified, I would be able to demonstrate substantial conflicts between his recollections of the events and those of the Delmans.

Hearing part of the loud, nasty argument between the two doctors caused Vincent to realize that something significant was in progress. He searched out Farrell and started asking questions. Farrell filled him in on Patricia's suicide, the breathing reports to Peter, and their great dismay at the fact that she was still alive. From that point on Vincent was kept current on all developments; he agreed totally with the object of ending Patricia's life.

Watching Peter's behavior the morning of January 15, Vincent became disgusted with his son-in-law's incompetence. Peter appeared to be out of control, and his extreme agitation and crying jags were very unsettling. Peter's worst fear was that Patricia would wake up. He kept telling the Delmans, "She could be brain damaged, remain as a vegetable."

The State established through Vincent and his sons that Vincent was energized into action by virtue of Peter stressing the likelihood of a violent death, and by Peter making it appear that Patricia could linger in limbo almost indefinitely.

[MR. RUSSELL]: What did he say?

A: He said that the tumor, the size of a melon, was pressing on a blood vessel, and she could bleed to death, with feces and vomit on the kitchen floor.

I successfully defused that testimony on cross examination:

MR. ROSENBLATT: When you finally heard from Farrell about the suicide, it was clear to you that your daughter had made a rational, definite decision to end her life, correct?

A: That is correct.

Q: And it is precisely those two facts and those two facts alone— she had terminal horrible cancer and she had made a rational decision to end her life—those two facts in and of themselves with nothing else caused you to agree totally with her?

A: Yes.

Q: So all this talk about whether Patty would come back as a vegetable or suffer a violent death, that had nothing to do with your fundamental belief that since she had terminal cancer and wanted to die, you agreed that she should die, correct?

A: Yes. But I would not have participated if I didn't think that she would have come back as a vegetable. I would not have gone into the bedroom to end her life, but I was concerned that she would come back as a vegetable. (*I did not like that answer at all.*)

Q: You were satisfied that she wanted to die?

A: Yes.

Q: If somebody had suggested to you: "Well, let Patty wake up and then we'll discuss whether she wants to try to commit suicide again, only this time with more drugs," you would have said that's absolutely crazy, right?

A: That is correct.

Q: And you agree there was no point in Patty awakening, even if she would have been fine when she got up—that would have been cruel?

A: That's correct. (*I hoped that would shoot down Peter's "vegetable" talk as supplying Vincent's primary motivation.*)

Actually, it was very much in our interest to agree that Peter was behaving in an irrational way so that he would lack the ability to function as the leader of a criminal conspiracy. I asked Vincent:

Q: He was not functioning as a physician; he was functioning pretty much as a lunatic?

A: Yes . . .

Q: Wouldn't you agree that for a physician who wants to end someone's life, that's very simple to accomplish if you have the necessary drugs?

A: I would agree.

Q: And that's one of the things that got you angry. . . . Here's this guy: he's board certified in his specialty, he's a pathologist, his wife decided to commit suicide, why are we hanging around for eleven or twelve hours? End it. He's not ending it, I'll end it. That was essentially the atmosphere?

A: Basically.

Q: Because it was incomprehensible to you that he couldn't end it?

A: I agree.

Stephen Russell laid the ground work for the smothering. It was close to noon on January 15; Russell Delman came on to the patio to give Peter a breathing report; Vincent and Farrell were there, too.

[MR. RUSSELL]: Did Russell say anything else at that point?

A: He said that if he had the guts he would cover her face, or cover her with a pillow. I believe I said—but I'm not sure— "Enough is enough."

Q: Did you think that at that time?

A: I know I thought it. Whether I said it, I'm not sure.

Q: Now as far as those specific statements, have you had trouble as far as your recollection and memory goes on those?

A: Yes. (*Stephen Russell knew I was prepared to zero in on the inconsistencies in Vincent's earlier testimony about what was said on the patio immediately before the final act.*)

Q: And after that discussion, what occurred?

A: I got up. I went into the bedroom.

Q: Were you relying on the defendant as far as his assessment of Pat's condition?

A: Absolutely.

Q: What occurred in the bedroom?

A: First thing I did I took Patty's pulse and I didn't get a pulse. (*This was great testimony for the State since they were contending that for all practical purposes Patty was dead already. Vincent simply blew the feather off the edge of the table.*)

Q: Was there anyone there with you?

A: I was followed into the bedroom by Farrell and Russell.

Q: What occurred after you tried to get a pulse?

A: I put my hand by her nose and mouth.

Q: Did you determine whether or not she was breathing?

A: Well, I heard, it sounded like a very slight hiccup.

Q: Were there any indications of pain at that time?

A: No, there was no movement, not a spec of movement in her body. Not an eyelash, nothing.

Q: What did you do after that?

A: I put my finger over her mouth and over her nose.

Q: Why did you do that?

A: Well, to make sure that she was deceased. I was worried about her coming back and being a vegetable with the pain that she had prior, and the cancer and brain damage and everything else.

Q: Did you determine whether or not you terminated her life?

A: I took the pulse again. I didn't get the pulse any better than I did when I first went in, but I didn't hear any more hiccup.

Q: What did you conclude?

A: I concluded that she was dead.

Q: Dr. Delman, would you have terminated your daughter's life if Peter had said when you got up "Don't smother her. Don't go in there and do anything to her"?

A: I would not have done anything.

Stephen Russell was focusing on the murder conspiracy count and Peter's manipulation of the Delmans so they would act, and he could be passive. I thought Russell became somewhat careless in the use of language when he acknowledged that Vincent "terminated" Patricia's life. During another question, when again he was stressing Peter's orchestration of events, Russell asked, "Would you have gone in and killed your daughter?"

Although legally irrelevant, it was crucial to our defense that the jury understand that the Delmans "killed" Pat and yet they were going to escape punishment completely.

[MR. RUSSELL]: When you made the decision to go into the room, did you rely on what the defendant had been saying about her condition?

A: Yes I did.

Q: Why was it that you decided to go in and *terminate* your daughter's life?

A: At that time I was worried that she would come back as a vegetable . . . because there was zero resistance.

Q: How did you know she was going to come back a vegetable?

A: I didn't know. The thought was placed in my mind when Dr. Rosier had stated that she could come back like that.

Q: Was that the reason you went into the room?

A: Yes it was. (*So, it was all Peter's fault.*)

In my cross examination of Dr. Delman I moved quickly to the pivotal circumstance which led to action to demonstrate that his recollection on crucial matters could not be trusted.

Q: In the statement you gave to the State of Florida in March 1987, way before I took your deposition, you were asked if your son Russell said anything before you went into the bedroom.

A: Yes.

Q: Your answer in March 1987: "I don't remember Russell saying anything"?

A: That is correct.

Q: And you were even told during that statement that your son Russell said "If I had the guts I would use a pillow," but even that failed to refresh your recollection?

A: At that time, correct.

Q: Because even after you were told that by Jim Fitzpatrick, you said "I don't remember," right?

A: That is correct.

Q: You were also asked in March 1987 that, assuming Russell said "If I had the guts I would use a pillow," what did you say in response to that, and your answer was "I didn't say nothing or I don't remember saying anything"?

A: I think that's more accurate.

Q: So fourteen months after the death of your daughter, you had zero recollection of Russell saying "If I had the guts I would use a pillow," and you had no recollection of whether or not you said anything in response to that?

A: That is correct. (*Those three days in Fort Myers being prepped by the State Attorney's Office really worked wonders.*)

It was very important to establish that Vincent made the decision to end Patricia's life in the bedroom rather than on the patio. Peter was never in the bedroom at any time during the final act; all three Delmans acknowledged that. I sought to distance Peter from the so-called conspiracy.

[MR. ROSENBLATT]: You sat down after taking her pulse. You thought about things and then you just decided to do it?

A: That is correct.

Q: Can I assume in all fairness that you made the decision to smother Patty within a second or two before you actually put your hands on her face?

A: Yes. (*Psychologically I thought Vincent would feel that he wouldn't look as bad if his action was closer to a snap judgment rather than being premeditated.*)

Q: The decision was made in the bedroom, not on the patio?

A: That is correct.

Q: When you were walking to the bedroom you weren't even sure what you were going to do, right?

A: I didn't know what I was going to do.

Q: How could anybody else know what you were going to do when you yourself weren't sure? (*Farrell testified he knew.*)

MR. RUSSELL: Your Honor I object. He's being asked to speculate what other people would know without a factual predicate.

THE COURT: Rephrase the question.

Q: Doesn't it make sense that since you did not know for sure what you were going to do, and you had no discussion with your sons, they couldn't know?

A: That is correct. (*So how in the world could Peter know, even assuming he was in a position to hear the various remarks leading up to the trip to the bedroom?*)

Q: The decision you made to put *your hands* on Patty's face, was your decision and your decision alone? (*I talked about hands rather than fingers because I wanted to make the final act as aggressive as possible.*)

A: Yes.

Q: You didn't ask Russell "what do you think of this?" or "Farrell, what do you think of this?" You just did what you would have done if you were 100 percent alone?

A: That is correct. (*I felt that normal nonlawyers could not conceive of a conspiracy when people are not talking to each other; I likewise knew that Vincent was very protective of his sons.*)

Q: When you made *the decision to terminate* your daughter's life, and during the time that you were doing that, did you ever say to yourself "Do I have the right to do this?"

A: No.

Q: You felt you had the right?

A: Yes.

Q: You see no arrogance in that?

A: No.

Vincent had stressed, in answering the State's questions, that had he encountered any resistance whatsoever from his daughter, he never would have smothered her. That again dovetailed perfectly with our point that no decision was made on the patio, no conspiracy was entered into on the patio, not even as between the Delmans, let alone with the defendant.

Q: (*Referring to resistance*) So that was the key. That's why you made your actual decision, not before you got to the bedroom but in the bedroom?

A: That is right.

Q: And what was critical in your decision was that as you looked at her and assessed her situation, you got no resistance whatsoever?

A: That's correct. If there was any resistance I would have chickened out. I wouldn't have had the guts to do it. But there was no movement, nothing at all. (*This answer would make Dr. Dosoretz look foolish when he claimed he gave Patty morphine to keep her comfortable.*)

Q: You figured: "She is very close to the edge. My sons have been through this horrible experience. Rosier is acting like a fool. He can't get the job done, [so] I'm going to end it."

A: That is correct.

Q: And you did end it?

A: Yes I did.

Q: This seemed the humane thing to do?

A: Yes.

Q: What was inhumane was allowing her to linger?

A: That is correct.

Q: Your personal belief at that time, you thought it was morally right or wrong?

A: Morally for me, it was right.
Q: Did you think it was legally right or wrong?
A: I knew it was not right legally. I don't know if I gave that much thought at the moment.

When Vincent left the bedroom he immediately saw Peter, which strengthened the State's contention that Peter knew exactly what was going on. This went along perfectly with Farrell's theory that Peter, "the wimp," did not have the guts to be an active participant.

Vincent told Peter that Patricia was dead and, according to Vincent, Peter said nothing at all in response. Farrell testified that Peter said he didn't want to hear about the end. When Vincent left the house to go the airport to pick up his wife, he said that both Farrell and Russell remained in the bedroom. Russell thought he heard interaction between his father, brother, and Peter just after the final act.

Although Vincent admitted that Peter acted like a big brother to his sons and helped Patricia with her schoolwork during their teenage years, he could never stand Peter. How do you form a conspiracy with a person you detest and with whom you almost never converse? Vincent had a tough childhood, things did not come easily to him, either intellectually or financially. Even his early years as a dentist were a struggle.

Vincent looked upon Peter as a spoiled, rich, know-it-all little punk who basically had everything handed to him on a platter. That's exactly how the State hoped to present Peter to the jury. I didn't think that assessment of Peter was fair because, in reading his manuscript, it was obvious that although he was loaded up with material benefits, his emotional life was utterly devoid of warmth or love. That's why his parents' housekeeper became a surrogate mother.

I questioned Vincent about his nonrelationship with his son-in-law.

Q: You didn't like each other?
A: That is right.
Q: And certainly the one thing that really never occurred was for you and Peter to sit down and have a conversation?
A: Absolutely correct.
Q: You guys didn't discuss football or movies? You basically had nothing to say to each other?
A: That is correct.
Q: And that never changed to this day.
A: That is right.

As in so many long-standing family feuds the original reason for the enmity isn't even recalled specifically, or the incident that caused the breach doesn't seem like a big deal at all to an outsider. In trying to nail down the background of Vincent's hostility, I asked "Did you ever have an actual physical fight with Peter?" "Did he ever curse you?" "Did he ever insult or belittle you publicly?" Vincent's answers were no. So I said, "Tell me the worst incident you can ever recall involving Peter." After searching his memory Vincent said: "I was invited to dinner at Patty's home and Peter and I were sitting down and having dinner. Patty had cooked a meal and he went like this (*snapping fingers*). Patty jumped up from the table to light his cigar."

In Vincent's perception, Patricia was degraded by responding obediently to Peter. Peter told me this amounted to playful bantering between them, which signified nothing; he was certainly in no way trying to demonstrate his dominance. Yet it was but another example of Peter's lack of sensitivity. How did he think a father would react?

The Delmans' distrust of Peter was so manifest they that suspected he could have had a secret camera filming the final act. He didn't, but this suspicion was the fundamental reason the Delmans turned State's evidence against Peter; that coupled with Peter's "advice" to get a criminal lawyer.

Q: Is it not true that the only reason you told the truth about the smothering was because of this fear of the possibility of a camera in the bedroom?

A: That was very instrumental, yes.

Q: If there would have been a way to satisfy you 100 percent that there was in fact no camera in the bedroom, then there really would have been no need to tell the State about your role?

A: That is correct. (*This answer at least implied that Peter did not know what went on in the bedroom.*)

Q: So you never would have told the State the truth?

A: That is correct.

Q: And as a matter of fact, from the time you awoke the morning of January 15, 1986, until the time you left the house to pick up your wife at the airport, you never had a conversation with Peter?

A: That is correct.

Q: From the time Russell came out and during those minutes before you walked into the bedroom, Peter said nothing?

A: While we were sitting at the table, he said nothing. He did not answer anything. (*Hardly the role of a supreme manipulator; my argument would be that Peter was in his own private world, oblivious to everything.*)

Q: When you got up to go into the bedroom, you did not signal Peter in any way?

A: That is correct.

Q: So, could you tell me how two people like that can form a conspiracy, two guys who never talk to each other, who don't like each other? (*I knew Russell would object and he did not disappoint me. He could object till he turned blue; the point was in the question, not the answer.*)

MR. RUSSELL: Object, unless he knows what a conspiracy is in Florida.

THE COURT: Sustain the objection.

Q: Do you know what a conspiracy is?

A: When two people get together and do something, I would think.

What a wonderful definition. It takes legally trained minds to create a fictional definition of conspiracy that is alien to common sense. (I remember in college reading about Clarence Darrow and being very impressed with his defense of labor leaders where the laws of conspiracy were used in draconian fashion to protect industry against its perceived enemies.)

Q: You and Peter didn't get together and do something . . .

MR. RUSSELL: Same objection as to whether he knows what a conspiracy in Florida is. (*There's not one lawyer out of five hundred who knows what it is either.*)

THE COURT: I'll allow that question.

A: No, never got together.

Q: You never in your lives got together to do anything?

A: That is correct.

Peter's father was a respected physician on Long Island, and Vincent described Peter's mother as one of America's most successful interior decorators, a woman who introduced to the world a fashion in decorating known as Country French. I attempted to make Peter's privileged background somewhat of a virtue.

Q: When you said Peter was spoiled, I assume you mean in the sense that, economically, as a kid, he was in much better shape than Patty was?

A: He was in better shape than I was.

Q: Okay. That was not his fault.

A: No.

Q: He was born into that family.

A: Yes.

Q: To his credit, he wasn't looking for some rich girl to marry; he was willing to fall in love and marry a poor girl. That's to his credit, right?

A: Right.

Q: And he may have been spoiled but he went to medical school and he studied hard and he picked pathology and he did autopsies and he became board certified in four subspecialties of pathology, right? (*I neither expected nor needed an answer to this question. Of course, Mr. Russell objected and was sustained. I followed with another question that fell in exactly the same category.*)

Q: And you know that a selfish, spoiled teenager—the last thing in the world that he wants around is his sweetheart's two kid brothers, whose noses have to be wiped—yet Peter took your boys with him and Patty all the time? (*Another objection, same ruling.*)

I liked Vincent. He was truly a guy who had paid his dues. He was not interested in being cute; he was not trying to outsmart me at every turn; he was not calculating every response; and he would give credit to the devil if he felt credit was due. Take the instance of Gertrude Ahlbrecht.

Q: Peter may have some lousy qualities, but he's also got some very good qualities. It was, after all, Peter who reunited the Delmans with Pat by inviting you all to the surprise fortieth birthday party and then [to] Jacob's bar mitzvah?

A: Got some very unusual qualities; done some things above and beyond what a lot of people would do.

Q: His relationship with Gertrude and Fred was much better than most adult children have with their flesh-and-blood parents?

A: That's absolutely true. Gertrude and Fred always lived with them, and after Fred died, Gertrude continued to live with them, which is unusual for a young married couple to have

somebody live with them all the time. And of course, she
wasn't really a mother. It's very rare in this country.

Q: Gertrude and Fred had no children?

A: That is correct. They were basically employed in the house
and Peter became very attached to them, and they became
very attached to him.

Q: And when they got older and sickly, Peter was there for them.

A: That is correct. (*This testimony humanized Peter and we loved it.*)

Q: Although there was no legal obligation?

A: Absolutely not.

Edward Volz, Stephen Russell, and James Fitzpatrick would get livid
when I would introduce this kind of testimony on cross examination. From
their point of view, Peter's bad qualities outweighed his good points at
least 50-to-1.

Gertrude was probably the best thing Peter had going for him. She
was now in her eighties, a lovely, kind woman with an angelic face and
regal bearing (in spite of her walker). I would make sure that she had
a ringside seat during my final argument. Subliminally, Susan and I would
be saying to the jury: "How bad could our client be when this angel loves
him so much?" We would also be saying, perhaps not so subliminally:
"If you convict her employer/'son,' what do you think will become of
Gertrude Ahlbrecht?"

In the Rosier "good-guy" category, it was Peter who got the Delmans
together with Patricia by inviting them to her surprise party and shortly
thereafter to Jacob's bar mitzvah. In the Delman "bad-guy" category was
the fact that Vincent never saw Jacob till Pat's birthday; he provided nothing
to her children in his will. Also, Vincent once gave Patricia $5,000 and
then asked for it back.

Q: At Patricia's birthday party you introduced yourself to Jake?

A: That is correct.

Q: You had never seen him?

A: No, never saw him.

Q: Not even as a baby?

A: Didn't know he was born. I had no contact. They didn't even
let me know when he was born. I didn't know where he was
born.

Q: Would you not agree that it is a little unusual for a father
who is a successful dentist in New York to give his daughter
$5,000, and a few years later want it back?

A: I don't think so.

Q: Why couldn't you just say: "Hey, you need $5,000; here it is—after all you are my daughter"?

A: I needed it at the time when I was short.

Q: You needed the $5,000? Come on.

A: Maybe you have never been short. For me, when I had bills, I was being pressured and I had parents in Miami.

Q: I've been short but I would never go to my daughter and ask for a lousy $5,000 back.

MR. RUSSELL: Object to the comment as to what Mr. Rosenblatt would do.

THE COURT: I'll sustain the objection as to Mr. Rosenblatt.

Q: You kept Patricia's children out of your will, not because Peter had money but because his children are basically strangers to you?

A: That is correct.

Q: And you didn't change your will after attending Pat's party and the bar mitzvah?

A: No.

I wanted the jury to know that Dr. Delman had done more than okay in the practice of dentistry. I did this by establishing that at one time he was one of the larger Medicaid recipients in all of New York State.

Vincent spent more time alone with his sons in St. Petersburg than he had at any time since they were nine years old. With some pathos he said, "I don't think we'll ever do it again."

I was going to say, "Well, you have Peter Rosier to thank for that," but Susan wouldn't let me.

I continued to utilize the technique of allowing the Delmans to elevate Patricia and knock Peter; if I conceded the moral high ground to them, I was much more likely to get helpful answers.

Q: Do you agree that because of the nature of the relationship between Patricia and Peter, because she was much stronger and because Peter was dependent upon her, he really couldn't let go; he really didn't want her to die?

A: I would say that's true.

Q: That's pretty much what Farrell's analysis was yesterday. Would you agree with that?

A: I would.

At the end of Vincent's testimony, Susan turned to me and said: "Two of the Delmans, the State's superstar witnesses, have now testified that Peter didn't want Pat to die. Therefore, Peter lacked criminal intent. This is a terrific place to stop."

"I agree," I said. "I almost hate to see the Delmans go. I like them a hell of a lot better than the coming contingent of medical prima donnas."

7

Dr. Michael Carlino:
Best Friend, Worst Enemy

Michael Carlino had been Peter's best friend in Fort Myers, probably his best friend in the world. After Patricia's death, their relationship had so deteriorated that Dr. Carlino refused to speak with Peter, the Rosier children, or me. Peter had made a media circus of his wife's death, so the son-of-a-bitch should rot in hell—that was Carlino's attitude.

The State intended to show through his testimony: (1) that Peter definitely intended to kill his wife and he sought drugs for that purpose; (2) Peter concocted a fraudulent scheme to cheat the government out of estate taxes; and (3) Peter was very rich.

Although Dr. Carlino and many others knew of the general circumstances surrounding Patricia's death, neither he nor anyone else considered reporting anything to the authorities. Suicide and even euthanasia were perfectly all right so long as they were kept private.

[MR. ROSENBLATT]: Is it fair to say that neither you nor your wife nor your best friends, the McMahons, nor anyone else who had heard about the rumors of Patricia taking her life ever said one single solitary word along the line of, "Hey, let's report this"?

A: No sir. No one said that.

Q: About what time did you get to the Park Meadow Tennis Club on January 14?

A: Probably around 5:00 to 5:30 in the evening. While I was there I began to hear some rumors that this may be Pat's

139

last day. . . . I had also heard rumors that Patricia was making arrangements for food and beverage for the period of mourning following her death. Being a friend of the Rosiers, I wanted to find out what was going on so I went to their home. . . . I could see the whole family at the dining room table. The men were dressed in suits and ties, the women had dresses on, and my impression was that it looked like a last meal together.

Q: Upon leaving the Rosier home what did you do?

A: I went to my home and, as I recall, my wife had also heard some rumors that day. In fact, she received a gift. When she said she would thank Pat tomorrow, she was told that tomorrow may be too late. We called friends of ours, Bob and Landis McMahon, and they had also heard similar rumors, and we went over to the McMahon house that evening.

Q: When you got to the Rosier house and sized up the situation and saw the last supper scenario—by the time you left you said to yourself, the rumors are true?

A: I said to myself, it may very well be true.

Q: Did any of the four of you ever say, "Well, maybe she is committing suicide and maybe we should report this to somebody? Because it's against the law?" Did any of you say that?

A: No sir.

Q: When Pat hugged you as you left her home on January 14, and said, "Take care of my boys," you pretty much concluded that the likelihood was that she would commit suicide, correct?

A: Correct.

Q: Why didn't you ask Peter or Pat about these rumors and say to them, "Is it true that you are going to end your life?"

A: I didn't feel it was my position to question them on that. I felt this was a private decision of theirs.

Q: (*That answer allowed me to make a very important point.*) Certainly not the business of government, correct?

A: I feel that a person who has a terminal illness, who has nothing to look forward to but pain and suffering, and who knows the full facts of their illness and is rational may have the right to make a decision whether to live or die. Now, should they choose to die, I disagree with that. That is my own personal feeling.

This answer was very much a part of the worldwide euthanasia debate and illustrated the medical and legal hypocrisy surrounding the subject.

Carlino knew of the morphine injections and suppositories, yet he never considered reporting anything. Carlino was saying in effect: "Whether I agree or disagree with the decision, it is not really my business, and it is certainly not the business of Joseph D'Alessandro or any other prosecuting attorney."

If our jury had that belief and if they were not cowered by the clarity of the court's instructions, we would be in good shape. Sure, Peter brought it all on himself by going public and that may have made him a Grade A putz, but it certainly didn't make him a killer. It is because Carlino's belief is so widely held by doctors and nurses that assisted suicide or euthanasia in the terminally ill is generally winked at. But if an enemy or someone with a real or imagined grievance against the perpetrator learns of the act and reports it to the legal authorities, the authorities are duty bound to take action. Euthanasia is against the law in every state in America!

Considering the gifts, Patricia saying her last goodbyes, Peter telling guests that Pat would not be around tomorrow, and the last supper, it did not take a genius IQ to figure out what was going on. The Carlinos and the McMahons had a night of gossip and speculation. At 3:30 on the morning of January 15, 1986, Peter knocked on the Carlinos' door and told them that Patricia had taken an overdose. Peter told Dr. Carlino that Russell and Farrell Delman were conducting a bedside vigil, and that he was surprised Patricia was still alive.

> MR. VOLZ: When was the next time you heard from the defendant?
> A: About a half hour after Peter left my home, he called me. He asked if I had a *Goodman and Gilman Pharmacology Textbook.* I told him I did not, but I had a *Physician's Desk Reference.* (*A* Physician's Desk Reference *is a book that nearly every doctor has since it contains the basic information from the manufacturers as to every drug available: what the drug should be used for, dosage, contraindications, etc.*)
> Q: You looked up Seconal?
> A: I looked up Seconal and I started to read the information, and when I got to the part about the lethal dosage being between two and ten grams, Peter's response to me on the phone was "Oh my gosh, Gerson told me that would be enough." He asked if I would stop by the house.

Why would Peter need Carlino to look up the lethal dosage of Seconal? Peter had ready access to the same books and medical libraries. He had been talking about a single or double suicide for months and he was not working, so he had all the time in the world to conduct research. Could I argue reasonably that this lack of research on materials readily available was proof that he lacked criminal intent? Was Farrell Delman to become my free expert witness on the psyche of Peter Rosier?

Michael Carlino, as a dear friend, took off for the Rosier home with the *Physician's Desk Reference* in hand, arriving there at about 7:15 A.M. He went into the bedroom to see Patricia because Peter asked him if he would. As a radiologist Carlino did not deal directly with patients; he interpreted their X-rays and reported his findings to the primary physicians. Carlino looked at the unconscious Patricia as a friend.

MR. VOLZ: Did you examine Patricia Rosier at that time?
A: No, I did not examine her. I just observed her for a period of between thirty seconds and a minute.
Q: Did you touch her at all?
A: No sir. (*Dr. Carlino wanted to get out of that bedroom and out of the house just as quickly as he could. He was scared and felt vulnerable because he fully realized what was going on.*)
Q: What did you do when Peter asked you to look up the lethal dose of morphine in the *PDR*?
A: I told Peter I could not find the dose for morphine. I didn't even look. I only pretended to do so. Pat was no longer in control; Peter was trying to end her life and I considered that to be very dangerous territory and I did not want any part of it.

Dr. Carlino was still at the house when Peter put in a call to Dr. Dosoretz. Carlino made sure he left before Dosoretz arrived.

MR. VOLZ: But could you hear what the defendant was saying on his end of the line?
A: The only thing I can remember with certainty that Peter said to Dr. Dosoretz was that Patricia was in a lot of pain, and would he come over.

I established on my cross examination that Dr. Carlino was confused about who was at the Rosier house that morning.

[MR. ROSENBLATT]: On the morning of January 15, other than
for the very brief time you were in the bedroom, the balance
of the time you were in the den or the television room?

A: That's correct. (*I was setting up conflicts because, if that were
true, how could he not have seen the sleeping Vincent?*)

Q: Generally speaking, the den was the hub of activity within
the house, correct?

A: Correct. When my wife and I would visit Peter and Patricia,
the vast majority of our time was spent in the television room.

Q: You never saw Vincent Delman in that room, did you?

A: I cannot recall with 100 percent certainty who was at the house
other than Peter, Patricia, and Russell. Someone asked me
if I wanted a cup of coffee while I was there, and my best
recollection is that it was Vincent, but I am not totally certain
on that. (*According to Vincent's testimony, he was first
awakened by the argument between Dosoretz and Peter, so
he would necessarily have been asleep when Carlino was at
the home earlier.*)

According to Carlino, Peter told him of his and Pat's plan for a double
suicide. The deal was for Carlino to come to the house and examine the
bodies, and declare that Patricia was dead but that Peter still had a heart
beat. Peter's insurance man, Carl Sousa, would explain to the jury the
significant savings in estate taxes that could be achieved if it was determined
that Patricia predeceased Peter.

MR. VOLZ: What did he tell you about the double suicide?

A: Peter told me that the way their estate was set up, it would
mean money saved to the children if Pat's death preceded
his. Peter told me that his life would be no good without
Patricia and he could not see going on without her. (*The State
contended that Peter never truly meant to take his own life.*)

Q: Were there any figures mentioned in terms of the value of
the estate?

A: I remember a figure. (*Susan objected vehemently and there
was a bench conference. Again she argued that this was another
attempt to inflame the jury about Peter's wealth, but it had
nothing whatsoever to do with the criminal charges against
him. Predictably the judge overruled Susan's objection.*)

Q: In talking about how much money this would mean to the
estate, were there any figures discussed?

A: There was a figure that I recall being between $2 and $3 million, but I do not remember what context that figure was used in.

Q: What was your reaction to this?

A: I was stunned, shocked that I would be asked to take part in this.

Q: Why?

A: It's something that I found shocking: two people wanting to end their lives like that. I can't agree with that. I also, however, wanted to be helpful and supportive, as Peter was a friend and it seemed to me the appropriate thing to do at that time was to lie to him and tell him I would do that, but I never had any intention of actually doing that. (*Carlino knew I would use the word "lie" so he used it first.*)

Q: Did you ever tell that to Peter?

A: Yes. I told him that I had learned to love him like a brother and I was not going to take part in the suicide.

Q: And what did he respond to you?

A: Peter's response was that he understood. He said he had decided not to take his life anyway, because of the children.

Q: This was some time around Christmas or New Year's 1986?

A: Yes sir, around the holiday period.

Carlino's testimony left unanswered questions that I explored on cross examination.

[MR. ROSENBLATT]: Why did you lie to Dr. Rosier when he and Patricia told you about the double suicide? Why weren't you man enough to say to them: "This goes against my grain. Peter you're a good friend, but I think it's wrong and I'm not going to be a part of it." You didn't say that, but that's what you thought. Why?

A: Because I felt at that time Peter was reaching out for help. I thought the best thing to do was to be supportive, and therefore I lied.

Q: And another lie you told was on the day that Pat died and you were in the house looking up morphine in the *Physician's Desk Reference,* and again you didn't say to him: "Hey, this is dangerous territory. I don't want any part of this." You faked that you could not find morphine in the book, correct?

A: I thumbed through the book, pretended to look—told him I could not find it.

Q: Pretended. You could have found it like that (*snapping my fingers*) but you pretended that you couldn't find it?

A: That is correct. (*Carlino had admitted to two lies, his testimony conflicted with the Delmans about the morning of January 15, and he obviously hated Peter and his lawyer. I hoped the jury would not be impressed.*)

Q: You would agree that any doctor who is interested in knowing the amount of a drug it would take to kill someone could find that out in ten minutes in a medical library?

A: Correct.

Q: You don't have to do heavy, deep research to find out the lethal dosage of drugs?

A: No sir, you do not.

Q: And although you told Peter that you could not locate the lethal dose of morphine in the *PDR,* he never took the book and looked for himself.

A: No.

This testimony was very supportive of our theory, echoed by Farrell, that Peter lacked the criminal intent to kill his wife. He possessed far more Seconal and morphine than he actually used. As Farrell pointed out very accurately, Dr. Rosier, as a pathologist, was an expert on death; certainly he would know how to kill someone.

The State's answer would be that Peter consciously manipulated events in order to create the atmosphere for a best-selling book and blockbuster movie so that he could become a national figure on the subject of euthanasia and make a ton of money. Would the jury hate him that much, would they believe he could be that cynical?

Susan and I had been sympathetic to the original predicament of Drs. Carlino and Dosoretz. They both came over to the Rosier home on the morning of January 15, 1986, to help a friend and colleague deeply involved in a very private and sensitive matter. Patricia died and was cremated—it was all over. But it wasn't over, because ten months later Peter appeared on television saying he would challenge Florida's criminal statutes. As a result of the investigation necessarily conducted by the State Attorney's Office, Carlino and Dosoretz were implicated. They had to hire lawyers and give statements. The Rosier case became one of intense media coverage; their photographs appeared in living color on the front page of the Fort Myers *News-Press.*

I did not blame Carlino and Dosoretz for hating Peter; all I asked for was some balance. It was now some two years later; everyone had full immunity; they continued to practice medicine; they were all making big money and living the good life. These doctors had every right to regard Peter as a loud-mouthed, arrogant, grandstanding, publicity-hungry windbag. But, come on; he didn't deserve to die or spend the rest of his life in prison. Elizabeth and Jacob were innocent victims who had already lost their mother; if Peter were convicted, what would become of them?

I wanted Dr. Carlino to at least talk to me. He was a professional, and I respected that; but he had to understand that I was just doing my best to represent a client. Yet Carlino snubbed me. I was incensed, and that attitude came out in my cross examination.

Q: Why are you so angry at Peter?

A: I am not angry at Peter. What angers me is the fact that he went on television.

Q: Don't you think that's a word game? You are angry at Peter period.

A: No sir. . . . What angers me about the fact that he went on television is that he turned this into a three-ringed circus. . . . The other part of it is that by going on television Peter has taken a very private, a very personal and emotion-filled time of my life and has opened it up to public scrutiny.

Q: And I suppose that's the reason when I called you the other night, and tried to speak with you that you told me you would not speak with me, and that you didn't like me, correct?

A: That is correct. And the reason I told you I didn't like you was because you made my wife cry. You upset her, and that in turn upset me. (*How wonderful it was to be back in kindergarten. I would show Carlino that he refused to speak with me before his wife cried during her deposition.*)

Q: Does it not strike you as rather incongruous Dr. Carlino that you were a close personal friend of Dr. Rosier's; you loved him like a brother; you were tennis buddies; you went to his son's bar mitzvah; you invited him to your fortieth birthday party; you spent some New Year's Eves together; you were frequently at the Rosier home during the terrible months of Patricia's illness—

MR. RUSSELL: Objection Your Honor. We are going through a whole list—

MR. ROSENBLATT: Exactly right. I have the right to ask a long question. Not every question has to be short and to your liking.

THE COURT: I will allow the question, but I'm going to reinstruct the jury that they are not to regard what the lawyers say as evidence.

Q: With what I've just enumerated and with your former friend being charged with first degree murder, you will sit down time and again and talk to the people who are prosecuting him but you refuse to speak to the lawyer who represents Dr. Rosier? Is that not incongruous?

A: I have spoken to you, Mr. Rosenblatt. I gave you a deposition several months ago. (*I regarded this as a very silly answer. He was required to give deposition testimony and that was done in the presence of the State and a court reporter. He refused to speak with me privately, although he did that many times with the State.*)

Q: You have refused to ever speak with me privately. Isn't that true?

A: As I understand it, it was my option and I chose not to speak with you.

Q: You are right. I could not force you to speak with me. But my question is: is it not incongruous to you that you are willing to speak privately with the State but you refuse to talk to the attorney who is representing your former friend and colleague?

A: I don't know, Mr. Rosenblatt. A lot has happened in the last two years.

Q: Your kids were friends with Peter's kids, right?

A: Correct.

Q: You saw Peter's kids today in this courtroom, and you wouldn't so much as look at them or even say hello, correct? (*I wanted the jury to fully understand both his coldness and his motivation.*)

A: I believe I did not see with certainty who the individuals were standing in the hallway. It may very well have been Elizabeth and Jacob. (*Please, give us a break!*)

Q: You didn't want to see them?

A: Mr. Rosenblatt, I would be very happy, after this trial is over, to speak with the children. I have always liked Jacob and I would welcome him to my house at any time when this trial is over. (*Oh, I'm sure if Peter were convicted his children would be ecstatic to have brunch at your house.*)

Q: I made your wife cry on her deposition. That's the fundamental reason you refused to talk to me?

A: The reason was because I did not like you. (*Hate at first sight would have been more like it. He would not be the first person to react that way, but I was stupefied by his lack of originality.*)

Q: You and I met at your deposition—at no other time—correct?

A: Correct.

Q: I called you from Peter Rosier's home a long time ago and asked to speak with you about this case before I ever took your deposition or your wife's, and you refused to talk to me. So you couldn't have learned to dislike me yet. Don't you remember that?

A: I remember that, yes.

Q: Didn't you say in this courtroom a few minutes ago that the first time I ever asked to talk to you was a couple of nights ago?

A: I forgot about that incident. As I recall that afternoon, it was the first call I had received from Peter in a long time. I was absolutely shocked that he was calling me. I believe he called back a second time, but by then I had instructed my people at work to screen the calls. Then, when you called, I told you how Peter had turned my life upside down and I did not wish to speak with you.

So now the jury understood that he refused to speak with me because he hated Peter, and it had nothing to do with his wife's deposition or him not liking me. He would have been far more effective for the State had he been willing to speak the simple truth: he is a very private person; the situation with Peter caused him great stress and caused problems in his family relationships; he had voluntarily gone out of his way to assist a friend in need; and from his standpoint Peter had turned on him and now he hated Peter and wouldn't talk to him or his lawyer. But when witnesses spend a lot of time conferring with lawyers, they can lose all their natural anger and spontanaeity.

[MR. ROSENBLATT]: Before I called you two nights ago, my secretary called you and asked if you would be willing to speak with me, correct?

A: Correct.

Q: And your answer to my secretary was that if the State says it is okay, I will?

A: That is what I said, but I later found out I was wrong in saying that. (*This was further evidence of the fact that Carlino*

was under the thumb of the State and would do their bidding.
Of course he had the right to talk to me.)

Q: You attended this kid's bar mitzvah when he was thirteen years old; he calls you in the middle of his father's trial for first degree murder—

MR. VOLZ: Objection.

MR. ROSENBLATT: And you won't even talk to him, correct? You won't give him the time of day or night?

MR. VOLZ: Objection.

THE COURT: Wait a minute.

[MR. ROSENBLATT]: It's a perfectly legitimate question, Judge.

THE COURT: I'll allow the question.

MR. VOLZ: Improper recross. This was not an area that we went into on redirect examination at all. Nothing about any bar mitzvah or anything else like that.

THE COURT: All right, I'll allow the question. I want to end this in a very short period of time, so go ahead.

MR. ROSENBLATT: Judge, your patience always seems to be running out when I'm doing the questioning and getting somewhere.

THE COURT: Ask a question. Time's running.

Q: For maybe the fourth time, why did you refuse to speak to Jacob?

A: I didn't think it was appropriate that I talk to him. Maybe we can get together once this trial is over and talk. It did not seem to me to be appropriate to talk to him the day before I was driving up to St. Petersburg. (*"Appropriate" is one of the legal world's very favorite words.*)

Q: What do you mean by appropriate? He's lost his mother. His father is on trial for first degree murder. You know the boy, he calls you and wants to talk to you, and you don't think it's appropriate?

A: Not at that time, no.

Q: In a legal sense, in an ethical sense, how are you using the word "appropriate"?

A: In my sense.

Q: The bottom line is, you didn't talk to Jacob?

A: That's correct.

Q: But you['ve] got all the time in the world for these guys, right? (*I pointed with my thumb to the three musketeers at the State's table.*)

A: Correct. (*He was weary by this time and didn't mean to give that one-word answer without an explanation.*)

I wanted to make it crystal clear to the jury that in spite of Carlino's handwringing anguish, he never had any real fear of criminal exposure. Once you receive a subpoena from the state attorney to come in and give a statement, that subpoena by itself is your guarantee of total immunity pursuant to Florida law. Naturally, Carlino's attorney arranged for a subpoena. Would I get straight answers on this subject?

Q: Surely Mr. Parvey [Carlino's attorney] explained to you that if you were subpoenaed and gave a statement to the State, you would have immunity for anything you may have done in connection with Mrs. Rosier's death, and you would be totally in the clear?

A: I cannot recall having a conversation with Mr. Parvey with regards to the immunity.

Q: Wasn't that the whole reason that you hired a lawyer, to obtain immunity for you?

A: No sir. . . . I am naive when it comes to the law. Alan Parvey told me to ask for a subpoena. So I asked for a subpoena. The reasons I don't know.

Q: Didn't Mr. Parvey explain to you that the reason he told you to ask for a subpoena was because once you are subpoenaed, under Florida law that guarantees your immunity? Didn't he tell you that?

A: He may have, Mr. Rosenblatt, but I cannot recall the conversation where a discussion of immunity was made between Mr. Parvey and myself.

I could not understand why this intelligent doctor was being so obviously evasive. The jury would not hold it against him that he sought to protect himself. It was perfectly normal behavior. How could he have been prepped on this subject and still have given these absurd answers? The problem with many smart and sophisticated witnesses is that they get caught up in mind games trying to figure out why the lawyer is asking particular questions and where the questions are leading. The much wiser course is to deal with questions in a straightforward way without subjectively reading other things into them. I knew that Peter would fall into the same trap when his turn came to testify. Nearly all doctors do.

Carlino obviously forgot that he already made this concession in earlier sworn deposition testimony when he said, "My attorney told me to get immunity." I reminded Carlino of this testimony from his earlier deposition:

Q: Mr. Parvey told you that before you gave a statement you should get immunity, and you followed that advice?
A: Correct.

I felt strongly that Carlino had unnecessarily damaged his credibility in the meaningless area of immunity. Susan, as always, would hand me the applicable statement or deposition of a witness I was seeking to impeach so that I could immediately zero in on any inconsistency.

The former friend again hurt Peter in describing why their friendship broke up after Patricia's death.

[MR. ROSENBLATT]: Dr. Carlino, do you feel that you broke your promise to Patricia to look after her boys?
A: If circumstances remained as I would have anticipated, then I would not have broken my promise to her. (*This broken promise made his refusal to talk to Jacob even more egregious, but in his own mind Carlino could justify that because Peter had committed the capital crime of going public.*)
Q: When did you stop loving Peter like a brother? (*I never should have asked this question.*)
A: We tried to be friendly with Peter. We invited him over to our home for dinner, and there would be occasions where Peter would call and cancel at the last minute. On one occasion he told us, "I'm sorry I'm late but there was a good-looking girl in the car next to me at the stoplight and I followed her for a while." That upset my wife.

This cheap and very mean shot was consistent with Carlino's friendship with the McMahons, who were so anxious to bring out the alleged fact that, at Mr. McMahon's birthday party a week after Pat's death, Peter allegedly said he was the most eligible bachelor in Fort Myers but couldn't even get laid. Following Carlino's testimony, the judge said something really amazing about this point.

THE COURT: I don't want to suggest anything that might not be a problem, but the State got a minor gift in the thing and I don't know if you are going to try to make more of it or not.

MR. VOLZ: On what, Your Honor?

THE COURT: The testimony about one of the reasons Dr. Carlino was irritated at Rosier. (*By the expression on our faces Judge Thompson realized that neither Volz nor I really understood where he was going.*) I'm talking about the possible womanizing, seeing the girl in the car.

Susan and I were shocked out of our minds. The judge was going out of his way to help the State. Maybe he thought he was still working for the State attorney. There was plenty of testimony that Peter was still very interested in women after his wife's death, and perhaps it was much too soon. Such behavior may very well have deserved condemnation, but it was wrong to prejudice the jury against him on collateral matters relating to his character or lack thereof. To his credit, Volz did not pursue the judge's suggested line of inquiry at that time.

Dr. Carlino turned out to be very helpful on the issue of whether Dr. Rosier knew anything about the final act of suffocation. Carlino admitted that Peter never mentioned it to him.

[MR. ROSENBLATT]: Doesn't it make sense to you, based on your relationship with Peter, that if he knew the Delmans had smothered his wife, he would have told you that?

A: Yes.

Q: So since he didn't tell you that, your assumption is he didn't know?

A: Correct. (*Carlino knew Peter well enough to know he was addicted to talking, and could not have remained silent had he known.*)

Since my methods are often unorthodox the State probably did not figure I would pursue the latter line of questioning with a witness who was programmed to hurt us. I felt there was very little risk involved; if Carlino was going to say Peter knew of the smothering, the State would have covered that with him on direct examination.

The State's next witness would be another visitor to the Rosier home the morning of January 15.

8

Dr. Daniel Dosoretz:
Brother, Could You Spare Some Morphine?

There is controversy about the therapies administered by cancer specialists like Daniel Dosoretz and William Harwin, where many patients, like Patricia, were not benefited by the treatment. They undoubtedly extended lives by a few weeks or months but at what a terrible cost: excruciating pain, nausea, vomiting, hair loss, and the like.

Dr. Dosoretz is a radiation oncologist, a cancer specialist who treats his patients with radiation. Like Dr. Harwin (who administered chemotherapy to Patricia) his medical background was quite impressive. He was born in Buenos Aires, Argentina, and graduated from the Buenos Aires Medical School in 1975. He never practiced medicine in Argentina; rather he became chief resident at Massachusetts General Hospital, the main teaching hospital for the Harvard Medical School. After completing his residency he remained at Massachusetts General two more years as a staff attending physician; he was an assistant professor at the medical school as well.

I felt the State was neurotically compulsive about presenting their evidence in methodical, chronological order. Because of that strategy they would call Dr. Dosoretz to the witness stand twice, several days apart. Edward Volz saved his questions about Dosoretz's visit to the Rosier home on the morning of January 15 until Dosoretz's second appearance.

In his first round of testimony Dosoretz explained the medical aspects of the case to the jury. Dosoretz had taught many medical students; he had developed a caring style for dealing with terminal patients. The jury would be impressed with his expertise and, more importantly, they would probably like him. The State correctly anticipated that he would gain much credibility for his subsequent testimony about January 15, 1986, and it would be difficult for me to attack the witness in his second appearance on the stand.

Dr. Dosoretz's first contact with Patricia was on October 23, 1985, the date a CAT-scan was done in Dr. Donald Gerson's office, at which time four brain tumors were discovered. Dr. Dosoretz gave Mrs. Rosier two radiation treatments that very day. The radiation machinery is complex and expensive; it is designed to hit and kill the nucleus of the cancer cells. Unfortunately, healthy cells are killed as well. According to Dr. Dosoretz, "The trick is to kill more bad cells than good cells." The side effects of radiation can be devastating, the most serious in this case being brain damage.

One of the most important points Volz made through his direct examination of Dr. Dosoretz was that Patricia could have anticipated a peaceful death while on an intravenous morphine drip, and there was no chance at all that she would suffer a gruesome end. There is one universal thing that doctors in America do not do. They don't guarantee results. So I asked on cross examination:

Q: If Mrs. Rosier had said to you: "It's one thing if I die in my sleep, but I sure don't want to die a painful and gruesome death. Danny, I want you to guarantee me that I won't have a painful death," you're not about to guarantee anything of the kind are you?
A: Correct.
Q: You won't do it, right?
A: I don't guarantee anything, no.

Edward Volz made his point again on redirect.

Q: Now in response to Mr. Rosenblatt's persistent questioning, you have said you suppose a horrible death was possible, this gruesome death of vomiting up her blood. Is it possible that it will snow in St. Petersburg?
A: Possible—it's possible it's going to snow I mean. Very unlikely, very inappropriate. . . .

I wanted the jury to recognize that the real killer of Patricia Rosier were cancer cells that had spread uncontrollably. I asked Dosoretz to explain how the cancer had conquered the chemotherapy and spread to the brain.

He said that the vast majority of drugs used in chemotherapy simply do not reach the brain and frequently "the brain acts like a sanctuary site" for the formation of destructive lesions. Lung cancer spreading to the brain is, therefore, a very common phenomenon in spite of chemotherapy.

> [MR. ROSENBLATT]: Obviously, there is no good kind of cancer. But lung cancer is one of the worst in terms of prognosis, correct?
> A: Correct.
> Q: Because it usually metastasizes?

One of Patricia's brain tumors caused Dr. Dosoretz particular concern. The skull is a rigid box and the brain itself is of mushy consistency. If a brain tumor grows, it will compress the brain because it cannot penetrate the skull. One of the tumors was very nearly invading the third ventricle, close to an area that connects the brain to the main spinal fluid. When the brain fluid doesn't circulate, increased intracranial pressure results and if there is a buildup of enough pressure something must give.

Patricia had received two radiation treatments a day from October 23, 1985, through October 29 and then one-a-day treatments from October 30 until November 29. A repeat CAT-scan of the brain was done on November 15 and actually showed a shrinkage of the tumors. A CAT-scan of the abdomen and chest was performed on November 19; it showed no evidence of metastasis, and the Rosiers were actually becoming hopeful once again, although certainly Peter should have known better.

This optimism was short lived, for on January 10, 1986, the final blow struck in the form of another CAT-scan of the abdomen, which demonstrated huge masses on both adrenal glands. Patricia would be dead in five days. It was extraordinary that the CAT-scan of the abdomen of November 19, 1985, was clear, and yet the scan of January 10 showed gigantic tumors. The spread of Patricia's cancer had been explosive, and the chemotherapy and radiation had accomplished nothing.

Dr. Dosoretz testified that the life expectancy of patients with brain metastases was on the average three to four months, with treatment. Once the adrenal tumors were discovered he estimated that Patricia's life expectancy was from seven days to three or four weeks. Responding to my questions, Dr. Dosoretz reduced her life expectancy even more: from five to seven days to three weeks. It was legally irrelevant whether Mrs. Rosier's life expectancy was one hour or one year, yet we strongly felt that the shorter the life expectancy the more sympathetic the jury would be to our position.

Patricia never had much confidence in the chemotherapy or the radiation. She had heard Peter talk about lung cancer over the years and she was a voracious reader on medical subjects. With the discovery of the adrenal cancer, Patricia had had it; she felt liberated in a strange way. She was finally finished with doctors, machinery, and drugs. She no longer needed to pretend that she believed in the possibility of a cure.

Dr. Dosoretz knew her situation was hopeless, yet he recommended steroids and other measures to control pain and ease her vomiting. He wanted to give her medications to replace the hormones normally produced by the adrenal glands. Although he had no faith whatsoever in various experimental regimens that were available, he at least wanted to discuss every possibility with the Rosiers. They were through listening; they knew the fat lady had sung!

Dosoretz conceded that the adrenal tumors were probably only the tip of the iceberg.

> [MR. ROSENBLATT]: The tip of the iceberg is the tumors that you can actually see on the adrenals, but the iceberg itself you figured was all over her body?
> A: Right. I said let's repeat the CAT-scan because she might have new lumps we don't even know about. In fact, I wanted to repeat her brain scan and she wouldn't let me do that.

Through my cross examination we were able to let the jury enter the world of medical reality in terms of dealing with patients who are in pain and who realize they are going to die very soon. Dr. Dosoretz's answers made it clear that American criminal law has been a very ineffective and arbitrary instrument in dealing with euthanasia.

> [MR. ROSENBLATT]: Generally speaking, when cancer patients have a tumor removed and yet they keep getting bad news after that removal, as Patricia Rosier kept getting bad news, it is not unusual in your experience that at some point the patient says, "I've had it, I'm not going to fight any more"?
> A: True.
> Q: The choice is not yours; it's theirs?
> A: Absolutely theirs, yes. (*Certainly in these kinds of conversations the clear implication is that the patient may commit suicide, yet in the real world the doctor does not ask probing questions and certainly does not consider reporting his suspicions to legal authorities.*)

Q: It's not unusual in your practice for you to hear from your patients something to this effect—that life just isn't worth living like this, [they] don't want to go on any more—correct?

A: I hear that statement—"Life is not worth living" or "When is this going to end?"—two or three times a week. (*If one doctor in Fort Myers hears this two or three times a week, it is obvious that terminal patients often hasten their own deaths either alone or with help.*)

Q: Would you agree with me, as a general proposition, that with most cancer patients it is almost easier for them to accept the idea that they are going to die than it is for them to accept the fact that they will be in a lot of pain? They are more worried about the pain than their impending death. Is that a fair statement?

A: Yes. . . . They are destined to die, that's not the problem. . . . They fear being abandoned, they are afraid of pain, they are afraid of suffering. That's the main concern.

We were again getting far away from the statutory elements of first degree murder, and we were neck-deep in sensitive waters where the medical insiders usually have a "Keep Out" sign meant for civilians.

Q: Isn't it true that morphine drips generally serve to speed up a person's death?

A: When I start . . . patient[s] on a morphine drip, I don't want to hasten their death. We try to keep them comfortable. The practical effect may be that they are unconscious and they are breathing a little less. (*Of course, and it follows that their respirations become more and more depressed and they die more quickly.*)

Q: Well, one of the reasons the hospice movement developed was because there's really no point in keeping a terminally ill patient in an expensive hospital in unfamiliar surroundings?

A: Correct.

Q: Such patients laying around in a hospital where they couldn't effectively be treated, they had the feeling of abandonment, correct?

A: Yeah. What happens is doctors and nurses get very frustrated at seeing a human being suffering. There is nothing you can do and emotionally you say, "I'm not going into that room." You try to spend as little time as you can with that patient.

(*Dosoretz seemed to ache as he said this and I felt he was being very honest on this point, and conveying at least a tinge of guilt for this very understandable attitude.*)

Q: "What is the point of being around if I'm not going to have all my mental faculties but will be in a kind of twilight zone, in and out?" Certainly you've had patients say that?

A: This is a cry of desperation I hear at least two or three times a week. "How long is this going to go on?" or "I pray I am taken soon." (*How could anyone doubt that some patients or their families or their doctors intervene?*)

Q: There is only one way that a patient in that circumstance can help himself, and that's to take his or her life, isn't it? If they refuse your offer to keep them comfortable on a morphine drip, their only option is to end it?

A: Perhaps, I just happen not to agree with that, but. . . .

Q: Mrs. Rosier never complained or said, "Why me? Why is this happening? It's so unfair. I have so many things I'd like to do."

A: She was always concerned about me and Dr. Rosier. She was always trying to please me and please everybody else.

Q: You haven't in your career really seen many tumors on both adrenals that have been larger than Mrs. Rosier's. I mean these are among the largest you have ever seen, isn't that true?

A: I told you before I don't keep score on those things, but these were among the largest I've seen.

Dr. Dosoretz's first appearance in court was low key; he was being questioned about scientific matters and philosophical issues related to the broad field of euthanasia. When the State called him back several days later, it was more as a fact witness than an expert. Edward Volz wanted to demonstrate that it was the grand manipulator, Peter Rosier, who desperately wanted to obtain sufficient morphine for the purpose of ending his wife's life. As a practical matter, the prescription Dosoretz wrote for six milligrams of injectable morphine was so trivial it could have had no bearing on whether Patricia awakened or not.

It was further evidence of Peter's irrational behavior that he did not recognize how it was pointless to fill the prescription or his vulnerability in doing so. Peter went to the Lee Memorial Hospital pharmacy, where he was actually given eight milligrams of morphine (a meaningless difference) because the pharmacy did not stock the drug in the precise increments ordered by Dosoretz.

My stategy with most witnesses on cross examination is to get them committed to a position before I start to get tough. Sometimes it's unnecessary to get tough at all. Many lawyers come on very strong for no purpose, simply to show how clever they are or to assert their dominance over the witness. If a witness is agreeing with my primary themes, there is nothing to be gained by this approach. Many lawyers lose sight of their objective and act as though they are conducting some kind of seminar on the art of ruthless cross examination. Psychologically the attorney is feeling the witnesses out, and many times intelligent witnesses will sense that if they concede what they should, the attorney may never seek to embarrass or contradict them. Frequently they are correct.

In terms of Dr. Dosoretz's argument with Peter, I was not trying to get him to agree with the Delmans' account: the more inconsistencies between them the better. If the jury believed Dosoretz over the Delmans, that was fine with me. I knew that when James Fitzpatrick took Dosoretz's statement, Dosoretz originally denied having any argument with Peter. When Fitzpatrick told Dosoretz's lawyer that he could prove Dosoretz participated in the argument, Dosoretz suddenly verified the argument.

I could never fully understand why Dosoretz denied having the argument with Peter, an argument that actually made him look good because he was refusing Peter's request for enough morphine to kill Patricia. The most likely explanation for this is the etiquette and image games doctors play: Dosoretz saw himself as a high-class guy who took pride in speaking quietly and being scientifically objective. I think he thought that it looked bad for two highly qualified specialists to engage in a loud argument where profanity was used.

Dosoretz testified that Peter called him twice the morning of January 15 begging him for medication. The second call was approximately 7:00 A.M., and Dosoretz arrived at the Rosier residence shortly after 8:00 A.M.

MR. VOLZ: What did Dr. Rosier say to you?
A: He said, "My wife's in a coma but she's not dying." I said, "What happened?" He said she took an overdose. I asked him: "She took an overdose of what?" He said she took an overdose of Seconal. . . .
Q: And as a result of that conversation what did you do?
A: I told him I was going to go and examine my patient. I was shown the room and I went in there.

Q: Was there anyone else in the room when you were with Mrs. Rosier?

A: To the best of my knowledge, I was all by myself there. Dr. Rosier didn't come in with me. . . . (*This was but one of many conflicts between Dr. Dosoretz and the Delman version. Both Russell and Farrell Delman testified that Russell was in the bedroom when Dr. Dosoretz entered.*)

Q: What was Mrs. Rosier's condition?

A: I touched her abdomen and she grimaced. (*This was going to be his justification for prescribing morphine. The legal no-no is that you cannot under any circumstances give medication if the object is to hasten death.*) I decided I was going to keep Mrs. Rosier *comfortable*.

Q: What do you mean by keeping someone *comfortable*?

A: I didn't want her to have any suffering or have any pain or anything like that, and I didn't want her to be restless. So I walked out of the room and my decision was to keep her *comfortable*. I said, "I'm going to keep her *comfortable*."

Q: The only sign of pain that you observed was when you poked her abdominal area and saw a grimace?

A: Correct. My definition of comfort is not just pain, Mr. Volz, it's just to keep her so [she is] not restless, so people don't suffer when they die. (*This was a total fiction as far as I was concerned. Patricia Rosier was unconscious and would remain so; she was not in pain and she was not restless.*)

Q: What else was said?

A: He says, "How long is this going to go on?" I said, "I don't know. We're going to keep her *comfortable*." I said, "We're going to give her morphine." (*The prescription was for morphine sulfate, two milligrams in three separate injections.*)

Q: That's done to control pain?

A: To keep the patient *comfortable*, not to be restless, not to be fighting their death; just to be *comfortable*.

I turned to Susan: "If he says comfortable one more time I'm going to puke." I felt we were witnessing a bizarre event psychologically. In order to emphasize that he would have no part of a mercy killing, Dosoretz had to convince himself that he was medicating her to relieve pain.

Q: What was his [Dr. Rosier's] tone of voice at that time?

A: He was starting to scream at me. It was loud, he was emotional.

He said, "You're supposed to be kind—put an end to this misery. How long will this go on?"

Q: And he wanted you to do something?

A: I told him I'm only going to do what my license let's me do.

Q: Was it your interpretation that he wanted you to give him more medicine?

A: In my mind that's what he wanted me to do, yes sir.

Farrell and Vincent Delman clearly said the argument between the two doctors occurred in the kitchen, so I asked

Q: This conversation occurred out by the pool?

A: In that area, yes.

Q: Look, this whole argument—all that occurred around the pool area—isn't that so?

A: Yes. Again, as I said before, I don't remember precisely where. I testified in the deposition and you tried to pinpoint me— where did this happen, where did that happen? I think it happened outside the bedroom toward the pool deck. (*You bet I tried to pinpoint you.*)

Q: I understand you may not be 100 percent certain, but what you said in your deposition and what you are saying today is that your best recollection is that after you left the bedroom, the entire argument was in the area of the pool deck?

A: Correct.

Q: Other than walking through the kitchen on your way to the bedroom and other than walking through the kitchen as you were leaving the house, you spent no time in the kitchen?

A: True. I don't think I washed my hands or had a drink. I just, as I remember, went back and forth.

Who cared precisely where the argument occurred? I did. Wasn't the important thing the substance of the argument rather than the location of it? Yes and no.

Unlike in a civil case where the plaintiff has the burden of proving his or her case by the greater weight of the evidence or by the preponderance of the evidence, in a criminal case the State has the burden of proving guilt beyond and to the exclusion of every reasonable doubt. I was interested in any factual conflict that could create reasonable doubt in the jurors' minds. If a witness is wrong about a relatively trivial subject, the jury may reasonably conclude that the witness is also wrong about a far more critical topic.

Dosoretz testified that while he was at the Rosier home he momentarily saw a young man, in his thirties. Vincent was sixty-six years of age then and had testified that he and Dosoretz saw each other, and that Dosoretz witnessed Peter telling him to leave the kitchen. So naturally, I asked

> Q: You never saw an older man?
> A: I don't remember that. I don't think I saw an older man.
> Q: And the person who Peter motioned away, was that a young man?
> A: Yeah.
> Q: And you certainly never saw anybody that morning sleeping on a couch or lying down in the den area, did you?
> A: I don't remember that.

The jury had to be wondering about both the memory and truthfulness of the Delmans as well as Drs. Carlino and Dosoretz. Dr. Delman testified that he was asleep in the den until he was awakened by the loud argument between Dosoretz and Rosier, yet Dr. Carlino, who was in the den while Vincent would have been asleep, never saw him. Vincent testified that he took a step into the kitchen during the angry confrontation and Peter motioned him away, yet Dosoretz says he never saw Vincent.

Confusion would work to our advantage. For any jurors motivated to help Peter, I wanted to provide them with an abundance of ammunition to argue that the State had not proven its case beyond and to the exclusion of every reasonable doubt. Somebody was screwed up on some basic facts; January 15, 1986, was not just another Wednesday.

The State's next cancer specialist, who I called "the suppository doctor," disliked me even more than Carlino did. But unlike Carlino, William Harwin had never been friendly with the Rosier family. It's actually fun to cross examine a hostile witness.

9

Dr. William Harwin: The Suppository Man

William Neil Harwin, M.D., signed Patricia Rosier's death certificate on January 15, 1986, attesting that the cause of her death was cancer. Since he didn't make house calls, he did not see his patient on January 15; but he did prescribe morphine suppositories by telephone. In terms of the procedures established by the medical examiner of Lee County, this death certificate was a key element in avoiding an autopsy. The state, of course, ascribed sinister motives to Peter for having Patricia cremated without an autopsy.

When Edward Volz would scream in final argument, pointing at Peter, that "He burned the evidence," Peter would sob and heave; his fingernails would literally tear the rugged leather of his courtroom chair—or my arm if I wasn't careful.

Harwin was the oncologist (cancer specialist) who supervised the administration of Patricia's chemotherapy treatments. The chemotherapy accomplished nothing; the lung cancer spread to her brain and then to her adrenal glands.

Harwin, like Doctors Carlino and Dosoretz, felt betrayed by Peter. He had given Peter all the drugs he requested and, most importantly, he signed the death certificate. By observing Dr. Harwin's very cold countenance and his body language on deposition, I was convinced that he despised Peter but, of course, he would never admit to this honest and elemental emotion. Dr. Harwin may have felt vulnerable to professional or even possible criminal problems, but he would never admit to that either. It seemed to me that Harwin went out of his way to hurt Peter.

When an expert expresses an opinion, he can emphasize selected facts.

163

At most, his opinion can be proven to be wrong or perhaps even illogical. Whether Harwin was expressing an opinion about Patricia's life expectancy or the likely manner of her death, he appeared to take pleasure in answers that were harmful to Peter's defense.

Like Dr. Carlino, he refused to ever speak with me privately. He would become outraged when my questions implied that the State owned him and he was at their beck and call. He became even more outraged when I questioned his professional judgment by pointing out the uselessness of the chemotherapy and the fact that Dr. Rosier was way ahead of him in detecting the spread of Patricia's cancer.

Patricia's first visit to Dr. Harwin was May 28, 1985, one month after her lung surgery. His function was to administer a program of chemotherapy that had been established by an oncologist at Memorial Sloan Kettering in New York City. Chemotherapy was intermittently given to Patricia between June 3 and September 2, 1985. As Patricia's primary physician, Harwin continued to see her periodically through early January.

Edward Volz asked Dr. Harwin about Pat's condition the first time he saw her.

> A: Her condition was excellent at that time. The tumor had been removed and there was no known disease present.

How could a medical professional describe her condition as excellent considering the horrible prognosis that lung cancer has? Dr. Harwin himself admitted that 90 percent of patients who contract lung cancer are dead within five years. This was consistent with his damaging opinion on life expectancy and his suggestion that Patricia played vigorous tennis three weeks before her death (implying that she was in terrific shape).

> MR. VOLZ: What was the purpose of her visit on December 26?
> A: At that time she was complaining of low back pain, which had been present for approximately five days, and she gave the history of it starting after playing vigorous tennis, but the pain continued. And I saw her and examined her and we prescribed an anti-inflammatory medication as well as Valium, a muscle-relaxing medication. (*Patricia may have been hitting some tennis balls but there is no way in the world that she was capable of engaging in vigorous tennis.*)
> Q: Could you tell us in your opinion what the life expectancy of Mrs. Rosier would be?

A: At that point I thought the life expectancy was a few weeks to a few months.
Q: How accurate are medical predictions of life expectancy?
A: They are very inaccurate. It's very difficult to predict unless someone is at the very very end.

He agreed that Patricia was terminal when the brain cancer was discovered and that she had less than a one percent chance of survival. He agreed that her tumor was superaggressive. It was unrealistic to suggest that Patricia could have lived for several months.

MR. VOLZ: Have you ever seen that type of death [vomiting up all of her blood and choking on it] from this type of cancer in your practice?
A: No, I have not.
Q: Have you ever received a report of such a death from any other doctor, nurse, or from anyone involved with any hospice program?
A: No, I have not. Such a death is not even a significant possibility. I see cancer patients all the time and they just don't vomit up their blood.

Dr. Harwin backed off a bit on cross examination:

[MR. ROSENBLATT]: If a terminal cancer patient is having intractable vomiting, it's possible that they could then bleed from a tear in the esophagus and hemorrhage?
A: Yes, that's possible. (*Harwin had to admit that his history said Patricia was having a lot of vomiting. Harwin had made the point that death from cancer is a gradual wasting-away, not a sudden event. That was my opening as to why many people believe that suicide is justified.*)
Q: It's a horrible wasting-away in a terminal cancer patient?
A: Yes. Definitely.
Q: And is not that in fact one of the most common reasons that family members frequently ask doctors to do something, because the wait and the lingering and the suffering is so very horrible to watch?
A: Yes. (*From our standpoint this was a great answer and tied in beautifully with Dr. Dosoretz's euthanasia testimony.*)

On redirect, the State opened the door to later testimony on euthanasia:

> [MR. VOLZ]: Have you ever administered or are you aware of any other physician ever administering morphine to a patient to terminate a life?
>
> A: No, I'm not. (*The State as usual chose to indulge in fantasy.*)

This also opened a further line of inquiry for me:

> [MR. ROSENBLATT]: Do you believe for one minute that in the history of medicine in the United States that there has never been a circumstance where a doctor, out of sympathy and out of complying with a patient's wishes and the family's wishes, did in fact increase the morphine drip to cause death? Do you think that's ever happened?
>
> A: Yes.
>
> Q: Of course it's happened. And that is what I was asking you before when I said there are some things doctors will talk about privately that for obvious practical reasons they would not make public, correct?
>
> A: I don't agree with that. . . . I'm sure if and when they do occur that they probably occur with people who are literally within hours or a day or two or three of dying.
>
> Q: Dr. Harwin, no doctor in his right mind would write an article for let's say the *New England Journal of Medicine* saying he did such a thing, because of the possible legal consequences, correct?
>
> A: I would say, yes. (*Amazingly between the end of the trial and my completion of this book a Dr. Timothy Quill of Rochester, New York, wrote precisely such an article.*)

Volz again hammered away:

> [MR. VOLZ]: Dr. Harwin, you have never administered any morphine to any terminal cancer patient with the intent to terminate a life, have you?
>
> A: No, I have not. (*Give that man a box of cigars.*)
>
> Q: Why not?
>
> A: Well, for one thing it's against the law. (*Does that mean if it wasn't against the law he would do it?*)
>
> Q: It's murder, isn't it?
>
> A: Yes.

That type of answer is why I went out of my way to be tough on Harwin. How does he know what murder is in this context? But he seemed anxious to agree with the label if that would hurt Peter. Volz asked this question out of frustration because the State had repeatedly asked the court to instruct the jury that witnesses' opinions about the legality or illegality of certain acts were worthless.

The death certificate that Dr. Harwin signed was great for us. He prescribed much more Seconal and morphine than Peter actually used, which was likewise very helpful on the issue of criminal intent (why didn't Peter use more drugs?). Had he agreed with Dosoretz about life expectancy and recognized at least the possibility of a gruesome death, my cross examination would have consisted of little more than marshmallows.

On January 10 when the huge masses on both adrenal glands were discovered, Dr. Harwin had multiple telephone conversations with Dr. Rosier. On that date he prescribed 50 Seconal, 100 mgs each, plus 50 morphine capsules, 100 mgs each, plus Tylox (a very strong pain killer) and methadon. Harwin did not actually see his patient on January 10.

[MR. ROSENBLATT]: And as far as you know the Seconal she ingested when she tried to commit suicide, these were Seconal from January 10, correct?

A: I suspect it was.

Q: But of course you had no idea or suspicion that your Seconal were going to be used for that purpose?

A: That's correct.

Q: And you had no idea or suspicion that the morphine suppositories that you prescribed on January 15 were going to be used for the purpose of terminating her life, correct?

A: That's correct.

Q: Do you consider yourself to be a naive person doctor?

A: No.

Why ingest only twenty Seconal when there were at least fifty available? Why not ingest the morphine capsules as well? Likewise, on January 15 Dr. Harwin prescribed ten doses of rectal morphine sulfate, 20 mgs each; why did Peter insert only four of them? This tied in beautifully with Farrell Delman's theory and the defense thesis that Peter did not possess criminal intent. If you truly wish to kill someone, more is obviously better.

For some strange psychological reason many doctors get very competitive when being questioned by opposing counsel. I am convinced that in large part this is due to the deference with which they are generally treated by patients and lesser medical personnel. No one asks them to explain their decisions or their recommended course of treatment. They resent very much having to give reasons. This attitude is especially pronounced among board-certified specialists, and Dr. Harwin was board certified in internal medicine, hematology, and medical oncology.

He would fight me when there was no reason to fight. I was preliminarily and innocently establishing the obvious point that Dr. Harwin was a young man who had been in practice a short time. I was not foolish enough to attack his training or credentials since they were impressive.

> Q: When Mrs. Rosier came under your care, how long had you been in private practice?
> A: Approximately a year and a third.
> Q: So you were a very new doctor in terms of being out on your own, correct?
> A: I wouldn't consider that a very new doctor at that point.
> Q: You were in private practice one year and three months. Didn't that make you a pretty new doctor?
> A: I think that's open to interpretation, how you consider a new doctor.

I did not regard that as a normal answer or part of a normal conversation. That is what frequently happens to intelligent witnesses who spend a great deal of time being prepped by lawyers; they lose the ability to respond in a natural manner and they become very defensive and picky. I wanted the jury to understand that Dr. Harwin had an ax to grind, that he was not expressing scientific opinions with dispassionate objectivity.

> [MR. ROSENBLATT]: Dr. Harwin, before yesterday you and I met one time when I took your deposition in April of 1988. Is that correct?
> A: Yes.
> Q: You were in this courtroom yesterday and I believe that was the second time that you and I ever saw each other, correct?
> A: Correct. (*He was in St. Petersburg, but he didn't get to testify.*)
> Q: I asked you in the presence of Mr. Volz yesterday—would you be willing to speak to me privately, and you told me no. Is that correct?
> A: That's correct.
> Q: Why? Why would you be willing to speak privately with the State? . . .

MR. VOLZ: Objection.

THE COURT: I'll allow the question.

Q: Why would you be willing to speak privately repeatedly with representatives from the State Attorney's Office who are trying to convict your colleague of first degree murder?

A: Well, first of all, at the time you approached me I was rushing to catch a plane to get back in town, so I had no time to talk with you. Second of all, you have had a chance to depose me, you've had a chance to contact my attorney, you could have approached me numerous times if you had wanted to talk to me, which you never did. And I felt it was somewhat suspicious why you would approach me during the actual trial.

Q: You thought it was suspicious that I would come over to you in front of Mr. Volz, and ask if I could have five minutes of your time, if you would step outside the door and talk to me—you thought that was suspicious?

MR. VOLZ: Objection Your Honor. We're having a repeat of the answer now.

THE COURT: I'll allow the question. (*I felt that Judge Thompson's basic sense of fairness made him curious as to how Dr. Harwin would respond.*)

Q: Why did you think that was suspicious? I was being totally up front with you. Why did you say no to me?

A: For the reasons that I just answered. (*This was a lousy answer for someone as bright as Dr. Harwin; he simply was incapable of saying, "I hate your guts and your client and I hope he gets convicted and I didn't talk to you because I don't have anything to say to you.*")

Q: What was suspicious? What was I going to do outside?

A: I have no idea.

Q: Dr. Harwin, why do you have one rule for the State and another rule for me?

MR. VOLZ: Objection. (*Volz's objections were tactical because Harwin was not handling these questions well.*)

THE COURT: I'll allow that question. (*There was another muddled answer along the same line.*)

Q: What time did you get to the courthouse yesterday?

A: At 9:00 in the morning.

Q: Nine in the morning—yet you didn't show your face in this courtroom until 5:00 P.M. when I requested to speak with you, isn't that correct sir?

MR. VOLZ: Objection, Your Honor.

THE COURT: Sustain the objection as to form. (*I never really understand what such a ruling means and, therefore, I seldom know or care about making my question less technically objectionable. As far as I was concerned, my question was perfectly fine both as to form and substance. Stephen Russell as usual was becoming very frustrated by my questions and I heard a loud stage whisper where he said "Jesus" in utter disgust. That was not like him. I loved it when they lost their cool.*)

MR. ROSENBLATT: Now I object. I just heard Mr. Russell say "Jesus," and I don't think that's professional or appropriate. (*What's good for the goose is good for the gander I thought.*)

THE COURT: Ask the next question. (*This judge was always very uncomfortable in free-form situations where the objections were not on traditional grounds, such as hearsay.*)

Q: Where were you between 9:00 A.M. and 5:00 P.M. yesterday?

A: I was down in one of the witness rooms.

Q: All day? (*I knew how furious Harwin had to be, sitting around all day yesterday without ever being called to the witness stand. Patients wait for him all day, never the other way around.*)

A: Well, I went out for lunch.

Q: Obviously you didn't feel it was incumbent on you or appropriate for you to let Dr. Rosier or his children or me know that you were here the entire day so that I could have the opportunity to perhaps speak with you for ten minutes during the lunch recess? (*As far as I was concerned this sequence told the jury everything about where Dr. Harwin was coming from; it would enable me to make the point that the State owned him.*)

Q: Isn't that correct, Dr. Harwin?

A: Would you restate the question? (*This very smart doctor had not forgotten my question; he was now assisting Volz with throwing me off track and it was working. When I restated the question Volz objected again. I was getting furious since Volz was giving the witness time to think.*)

MR. ROSENBLATT: This is outrageous, these constant speaking objections. I didn't object once when Mr. Volz was questioning Dr. Harwin.

THE COURT: I'll allow the question.

Q: Do you remember the question, doctor?

A: For what reason should I feel that it is incumbent upon me to let you know I was here or Dr. Rosier or his children? (*I loved the opportunity to answer that.*)

Q: Fairness, Dr. Harwin, fairness.

A: If Dr. Rosier or his children wanted to talk to me they could have called me. (*Just how cold can someone be? Maybe like Carlino he'll invite them over for dinner after the trial is over.*)

Q: The reason you went out and hired an attorney is because you felt that you had criminal vulnerability in connection with Mrs. Rosier's death. Isn't that true sir?

A: That's absolutely incorrect.

Q: You were not the least bit concerned about your having given Dr. Rosier suppositories and having prescribed Seconal and morphine for Mrs. Rosier?

A: Not at all.

Q: Well you got a subpoena when you went to the State Attorney's Office to give your statement. You didn't go voluntarily. You got a subpoena?

A: I honestly don't recall.

Q: Didn't your attorney tell you that a subpoena from the State is equivalent to a grant of immunity? Once they subpoenaed you, you got immunity.

A: I did not seek immunity. I did not at any time say I won't talk unless I am given immunity.

That's the same way Michael Carlino handled the issue of immunity, as though it was a matter of personal indifference. The first question a normal person would ask a lawyer under these circumstances is "Do I have any exposure?" And the advice is so very simple in Florida: don't voluntarily give the State a statement unless you get a subpoena, because once you get the subpoena you cannot be prosecuted.

Harwin returned to Fort Myers and had to come back to St. Petersburg the following day. Edward Volz had not asked Harwin any questions about the events of January 15, so we did not need to be prescient to figure out that Harwin would return yet again when his testimony would fit more neatly into the State's chronological niche. We knew that all busy doctors hate to reschedule many patients and to have their routines disrupted.

So I thought I would needle the chemotherapy man. What the hell? If you're going to hate me for no reason, I'll accommodate you by giving you some reasons.

Q: Before you testify the second time, Dr. Harwin, I'm going
   to want to speak with you privately. Will you show me the
   courtesy of talking to me or is that a privilege only the State
   enjoys in this case? (*There was fire in his eyes but he said
   nothing.*)
THE COURT: I'll sustain the objection. Disregard the question.

Damnit, there had been no objection. This happened to Thompson
every now and then where he became irascible and thoroughly disgusted
with a given topic. He figured I had made that point already and was
now looking to grind the witness's nose in the dust. He was probably right.

But my needling continued when Harwin returned to the witness stand
a few days later, particularly in view of the fact that the State only asked
him a few questions about January 15. Volz was mainly concerned with
establishing that Peter called Harwin on January 15 searching for more
morphine, since Dosoretz's prescription had accomplished nothing. Harwin looked foolish prescribing suppositories, for when I asked Dr. Dosoretz
about this route of administration he testified that he never in his life
prescribed suppositories and had no idea they were even available in this
form.

Steven Kelsey, the pharmacist at Lee Memorial Hospital for over eleven
years and who had filled Dr. Dosoretz's prescription for Peter on January
15, testified that he had never filled a prescription for morphine suppositories. The State brought in the owner of the pharmacy, who had filled
Dr. Harwin's several prescriptions on January 10. In response to my
questions, this pharmacist stated that his drugstore did not carry morphine
suppositories since there was no demand for them. I asked Dr. Harwin:

[MR. ROSENBLATT]: Does it not strike you as rather incongruous
    that since you were here testifying for the State several days
    ago that they would bring you back for four minutes of
    testimony?
A: Having never been in a situation like this before, I really have
    no comment.
Q: And it didn't occur to you a few days ago to ask the State
    "Why do you need me back on a separate trip to answer
    a few more questions? I'm here now, I have a busy practice,
    I'll answer all your questions now." That never occurred to
    you, right?
A: Would you repeat the question? (*I just glared at him and
    looked over at the jury with total disgust etched on my face.*)

... I basically just follow the instructions. (*Right, the State says jump and you say, "how high?"*)

MR. VOLZ: I object to this subject matter. Can we approach the bench? (*We do.*) We went into that in great detail the last time this witness was here.

MR. ROSENBLATT: This is a busy doctor who comes back willingly and never even raises the issue with the State or shows any degree of normal annoyance that he's being called back to travel over 200 miles round trip to answer less than ten questions. The jury has the right to infer that in practical terms the State owns these people.

THE COURT: I'm going to allow the question, but I don't want to spend but just a very few questions on the subject.

A: I think you've had ample time to ask me questions. You took my deposition for two and a half hours, you had me on the stand for several hours the other day, I'm here to answer any questions. I don't see any reason why I need to meet with you in addition to that.

Q: Why the different treatment between me and the State? Is it because you dislike Dr. Rosier so much, or is it because you dislike me so much?

A: Has nothing to do with Dr. Rosier, I think it has to do with your personality. (*I was just flabbergasted; two grown people, two doctors who would not talk to a lawyer in a first degree murder case because they didn't like him.*)

I said to Susan: "I guess he and Carlino were prepped at the same time. Can you believe it, they won't meet with me because I'm so obnoxious. You deserve a medal for sticking with such a terrible person."

I rubbed in the points that Peter had been a far better diagnostician than he and that Harwin's treatment had proved worthless. I established that he signed the death certificate without ever examining the body and I reiterated the fact that he prescribed large amounts of drugs both on January 10 and January 15 without ever seeing or examining his patient.

Q: The doctor who was suspicious that the cancer had metastasized to the brain was Dr. Peter Rosier, isn't that correct?

A: Correct.

Q: It was he not you who ordered the CAT-scan in late October, which showed the brain tumors, correct?

A: Correct.

Q: You didn't go over to the house to check your patient on January 15?

A: I generally don't make house calls. (*What an incredibly careless answer. The refusal of doctors to make house calls is grist for every stand-up comedian in America.*)

Q: Mrs. Rosier had a very unusual kind of lung cancer, didn't she?

A: I don't think we've ever absolutely established what kind of lung cancer she had. I think probably she had some kind of atypical carcinoid which would be an uncommon type.

Q: You are aware that Dr. Rosier took slides to some of the best pathologists in the country and there was disagreement among them as to exactly the type of tumor which was involved?

A: Yes.

Q: I take it that it's your belief that although the November 19 CAT-scan of the abdomen was read as negative, probably there was cancer in the abdomen then but not in a form that was yet able to be picked up, correct?

A: I would say definitely, not probably.

Q: With the benefit of hindsight you would agree that the back pain that Mrs. Rosier was complaining of was related to the abdominal tumors, which showed up later?

A: Yes. (*Not due to any vigorous tennis.*)

Q: You say in your records regarding Mrs. Rosier's back pain that you have felt all along it is not related to metastatic disease since it followed heavy activity, etc. But with the benefit of hindsight it's obvious to you that her back problems were related to the spread of the cancer?

A: Yes. For the fifth time.

Yes, the doctor was becoming testy every time I pointed out that he missed the obvious. How could he think the back pain was unrelated to the spread of cancer? How could he have thought that in January Patricia was engaging in heavy, vigorous activity?

Finally Dr. Harwin was finished.

MR. VOLZ: Your Honor, may this witness be excused from all the subpoenas?

MR. ROSENBLATT: No, I may want him for my case.

MR. VOLZ: A third time, Your Honor?

MR. ROSENBLATT: Yes, sure. You got it.

I had no intention of calling Harwin in my case, but since he went out of his way to hurt us, I was not about to provide him with any peace of mind.

"Harwin and Carlino have destroyed the myth that doctors always stick together. Susan, can you believe it? I actually like the State's next medical witness and, hold onto your hat, he thinks my personality is outstanding."

"It figures, all his 'patients' have no personality whatsoever."

10

Dr. Wallace Graves, Jr.:
The Medical Examiner, Who Else?

The State sought to make Peter look very devious in the manner in which he avoided an autopsy and had Patricia cremated. The prosecution called to the witness stand the medical examiner of Lee County, Wallace Graves, Jr., a not inappropriate name for his line of work.

I liked and respected Dr. Graves. He had no hangups about lawyers, and he was a professional who was intimately familiar with the legal system. By necessity a medical examiner works very closely with the State Attorney's Office and other law enforcement agencies. In addition Dr. Graves was a forensic pathologist: he worked daily with the legal as well as the medical aspects of pathology and was schooled in being an effective and understandable witness.

In one of many ironic twists involving witness relationships, Dr. Rosier had worked for Dr. Graves for some three years during the 1970s. It was Dr. Graves who recommended to the State a forensic toxicologist named Robert Forney who became the State's chief expert witness against Peter. Graves's current executive secretary had been employed in Dr. Forney's department at the Medical School of Toledo (Ohio).

Dr. Graves agreed with my characterization of Peter as a highly skilled pathologist who was conscientious in his work. Likewise, he expressed a high opinion of Patricia as a bright, energetic woman who cared about the less fortunate and was involved in many community activities.

Dr. Graves was board certified in anatomic pathology. He obtained his medical degree from the University of Chicago and did his pathology training at Jackson Memorial Hospital in Miami. He was the president-elect of the Florida Society of Pathologists and a member of the board of directors of the National Association of Medical Examiners. His jurisdiction extended over two other Florida counties in addition to Lee County, a post he had held since 1973. His office was constantly in the newspapers and he was a well-known and well-respected figure in southwest Florida. Unlike the situation in more populous areas, Dr. Graves was permitted to have a private practice in addition to his public duties.

A medical examiner, like a state or district attorney, is vested with enormous discretion: deciding when and what to investigate, whether or not to perform an autopsy, and so on. In certain categories of deaths an autopsy is mandated under Florida law; these include all gunshots and all possible suicides. Dr. Graves said: "If I had information that someone had committed suicide, whether they were about to die the next day or not, statutorily I am obliged to investigate that death. I have no option."

It was Dr. Graves who established a procedure called the "expected death list," the purpose of which was very pragmatic and provided a means of avoiding navigating through a bureaucracy; it spared grieving family members much anguish. Through this "list" the medical examiner's office was notified of all home deaths. In a case of a natural death confirmed by the attending physician, without any evidence of foul play, the medical examiner had no jurisdiction to perform an autopsy. The expected death list procedure allowed the body to be removed from the home by the funeral parlor, thus avoiding any contact at all with the medical examiner's office.

Peter complied with Dr. Graves's procedure in a straightforward way. When Peter called Dr. Graves on January 14, 1986, at 11:25 A.M., Dr. Graves happened to be out of town. Peter spoke with an associate medical examiner and explained that his wife was terminal and could die at any time. Patricia's steady downhill course was well known throughout the medical community of Fort Myers. This physician spoke with Dr. Harwin who said he would sign the death certificate giving cancer as the cause of death. With that assurance from the primary physician, Patricia was placed on the expected death list. This same pathologist granted authorization to the funeral home to cremate Patricia.

When I took Dr. Graves's pretrial deposition testimony I was very careful to limit him to factual matters; he agreed with my characterization of his role in the case to the effect that he would not be expressing expert opinions. We knew that his opinions would probably hold greater weight with the jury than the same opinions expressed by a less well known doctor. But the State took their best shot at getting favorable opinion testimony about the unlikelihood of a gruesome death.

MR. RUSSELL: How likely is it that a large, rapidly growing cancerous tumor on the adrenal glands would erode through the stomach so as to cause a person to vomit up all their blood?

MR. ROSENBLATT: Objection. When I took Dr. Graves's deposition I asked him very specifically whether he had then or intended in the future to express any expert opinions and his answer was clearly no. . . . He saw himself strictly as a factual witness, and this comes as a total surprise.

MR. RUSSELL: I am not intending to ask anything more than this one area. . . . If he's qualified to give that limited opinion, I would not ask any more direct questions than I just asked. (*The judge overruled my objection.*)

A: I have never personally seen such a case and I am not familiar with that particular scenario happening . . . that's not to say that it couldn't happen. But I'm not familiar with such a case.

I revisited that area on cross examination.

MR. ROSENBLATT: Would you agree that rapidly growing tumors that become huge and cystic and necrotic can hemorrhage into themselves and perhaps erode blood vessels?

A: They can.

Q: Taking into consideration that Mrs. Rosier died on January 15, there is no way to know whether if nature had been allowed to take its course, what the size of the adrenal tumors would have been—let's say on January 25?

A: There is no way of knowing.

Q: You would agree that before injectable morphine was around, most cancer patients died horrible, agonizing, and gruesome deaths?

A: Many did. (*I very much appreciated Graves's honesty and no-nonsense approach in dealing with my questions; he was not trying to duel with me over every nuance.*)

Q: When speaking about an individual specific case, no one can be 100 percent certain as to precisely how someone is going to die from a terminal disease, correct?

A: True.

Q: You said when you were asked by Mr. Russell about this horrible death—the vomiting up of the blood—you said that such a death, in your experience, would be uncommon or rare, but certainly it's possible?

A: It's possible.

These opinions opened the door to my directly questioning Dr. Graves about general euthanasia issues. So it turned out to be a huge plus that the judge had overruled my objection.

Q: In your work, Dr. Graves, you have seen hundreds of suicides. Isn't that correct?

A: Yes, sir.

Q: Yet you have never had occasion to investigate a charge brought by a prosecutor against a person for assisting a suicide. Isn't that correct?

A: That is correct. (*This answer lent great weight to my argument that the State was out to get Peter.*)

Q: In your work as a medical examiner you have learned that there are a lot of suicides among the terminally ill. Isn't that correct?

A: There appear to be increasing numbers as our aging population increases and more people develop terminal diseases. And I think this is a nationwide if not universal phenomena—we see more and more suicides among the elderly and particularly with those who have terminal disease. (*Derek Humphry and many members of the audience were nodding in agreement.*)

Q: You must be aware of situations where a terminally ill patient told a treating physician that they were going to go home and commit suicide—you never heard of any physician reporting such a conversation to the authorities—isn't that correct?

A: That's correct. I'm not personally aware of that ever happening.

Q: You have a general awareness that doctors treating terminally ill cancer patients who are in great pain with no chance of recovery occasionally increase the morphine drip to the point where they end that person's life?

MR. RUSSELL: Your Honor, I have an objection.

THE COURT: Sustain the objection. (*It was unusual for Judge Thompson to sustain an objection without at least hearing argument from us, but he had expressed his attitude on many occasions about not allowing me to go too far into broader euthanasia issues. The State wanted to equate Peter with a robber who killed a store employee during a holdup. The criminal law did not distinguish between them.*)

Q: There is no doubt in your mind, is there, that occasionally physicians who are treating a terminally ill cancer patient in great pain will deliberately increase the morphine drip to hasten their death.

MR. RUSSELL: Your Honor, I object, unless it's established that Dr. Graves has personal knowledge of the facts first.

THE COURT: Sustain the objection.

Q: Is it not true whether it was at a medical meeting or a cocktail party with only doctors present where you have heard some doctor—don't worry I'm not going to ask you for the name of the doctor or the patient—admit that he had increased the morphine drip for that purpose?

MR. RUSSELL: Your Honor, same objection.

THE COURT: Sustain the objection.

I was appealing to the jury's sense of fairness. Although two wrongs don't make a right and the fact that everybody may do it is no defense, the fact that there is very selective and random enforcement should be a turn-off to a decent jury.

This was terribly frustrating to us because Dr. Graves had already said some very heavy things of which the national and international media in the courtroom had to be acutely aware. We yearned for the opportunity to open wide the curtain of secrecy and hypocrisy that envelops the subject of so-called mercy killing. Very uncharacteristically, Susan simply walked up to the judge's bench and started whispering.

MRS. ROSENBLATT: The relevancy is that doctors put people on morphine drips to avoid a violent death. That's the answer to the issue they are creating, so its very relevant. Dr. Graves rendered an opinion as to the nature of the death that would have occurred. I believe he can be cross examined on the entire issue of—would that death be avoided if you put someone on a morphine drip.

THE COURT: Ask the question. (*This was a beautiful thing about the character of Judge Thompson; he was not embarrassed to change his mind and he was open to persuasion. Most judges become stubborn in similar situations.*)

[MR. ROSENBLATT]: Isn't it true, Dr. Graves, that doctors who are treating terminally ill cancer patients, where there is no hope of recovery and where the person is in great pain, occasionally deliberately increase the morphine drip so as to cause death?

A: I have no personal knowledge of that. (*That certainly was not the answer I hoped to get. Everyone gets off the hook by saying they have no personal knowledge. The psychology of the State's repeated objections worked against us.*)

Q: Dr. Graves, obviously a doctor cannot admit that he's increasing the morphine drip to hasten death; so the fiction always is that he is increasing the drip to control pain and to keep the patient comfortable?

MR. RUSSELL: Objection.

THE COURT: Sustained.

Q: Wouldn't you agree that a doctor cannot admit publicly to deliberately increasing the morphine drip to hasten death, that would be a dangerous thing for a doctor to admit?

A: It would be dangerous.

Then I asked Dr. Graves a question about the famous "It's Over Debbie" letter which appeared in the *Journal of the American Medical Association,* wherein an unnamed physician admitted that he deliberately hastened death. My point was that this goes on all the time and the criminal justice system is simply a bad joke in terms of dealing with it. Let's use this case as a constructive public forum to bring euthanasia out of the closet. Let's start dealing with this problem, which can affect anyone, in a realistic way. Surely the first step must be to tell the truth and get an open debate going. But the State wasn't interested. They simply wanted to convict my client.

MR. RUSSELL: Judge, we did a motion in limine (*a formal motion asking the judge to severely restrict certain areas of interrogation*) when the case started. There is no relevance to the fact that even if some people get away with something, therefore the implication that Mr. Rosenblatt wants to get across is that his client should get away with what is clearly an illegal act.

MRS. ROSENBLATT: That is not the reason we are seeking that information. We are making the point that when people go on morphine drips this hastens their death and they do not die a truly natural death. And that is why cancer is becoming a relatively benign experience—that is, the death process—because of these morphine drips. Fifty years ago people were in pain with tumors exploding, vomiting up blood. And that still happens when people refuse medication. And all the doctors

know that morphine drips hasten death, that's almost an un-
avoidable side effect because it severely depresses respiration.

THE COURT: I'm going to sustain the objection to that area.

After the objection was sustained, I turned to my wife and said, "That's
no surprise. We've gone as far as we can go and I don't think we'd get
any great answers anyway."

"You've more than made the point that morphine drips artificially
prettify cancer deaths," Susan said. "I think these exchanges continue to
portray Peter as a victim himself, which is all to the good."

11

Carl Sousa: Have I Got a Deal for You!

Carl Sousa sold life and disability insurance policies to Peter and many other doctors in Fort Myers. He never obtained drugs for Patricia; he wasn't present at the Rosier residence at any time on January 15, 1986; and he had witnessed no significant event related in any way to the murder charges against Dr. Rosier. Yet he was an important witness for the State of Florida. Why?

Through Peter's transactions with Carl Sousa the State sought to demonstrate: (1) that Dr. Rosier was an astute businessman and very wealthy, and that he manipulated insurance policies as skillfully as he had manipulated his wife; (2) that he sought to minimize estate taxes by attempting to shift the ownership of various policies; and (3) that he collected large amounts of money through disability insurance policies, so that his lifestyle would continue uninterrupted even though he gave up the practice of medicine following Patricia's illness and death. None of this was legally relevant because it did not provide any possible motive for committing murder; nevertheless, Judge Thompson admitted this testimony over strenuous objections from the defense.

Sousa and two of Peter's attorneys were added to an ever-growing roster of Fort Myers residents who knew of the Rosier suicide plans, yet took no step to intercede with authorities, either legal or medical. Carl Sousa had been asked to attend a meeting at the offices of Peter's two lawyers; also in attendance were the Rosiers and their children. The meeting was held on November 1, 1985, shortly after the discovery of Patricia's brain tumors. According to Sousa, Peter announced at this meeting that he and Patricia would be committing suicide together and he wanted to

185

know how that should be handled so as to maximize the assets the children would be receiving and to minimize any payment to the government for estate taxes.

When a married couple dies simultaneously, whether in an airplane crash or by suicide, and it cannot be determined who died first, this can substantially increase the amount of estate taxes. When that was explained to Peter, he said he had a solution that would save the estate (actually the children) a fortune. He had made arrangements to have a doctor friend (Dr. Carlino) determine that Patricia died minutes before he did. Since the lawyers knew in advance who was going to die first, they could restructure the various insurance policies (personal, pension trust, and corporate, totalling fifteen separate policies) to minimize tax consequences.

Sousa testified that he pointed out what he thought should be obvious to the lawyers: that it was improper to change and manipulate ownership and beneficiaries on life insurance contracts in contemplation of death. Life insurance contracts are not drawn by fools; there is a standard provision called a three-year contemplation of death clause, which provides that any significant changes made within a period of three years before death occurs (when death is contemplated in that time frame) results in the changes being deemed null and void. The State further developed this evidence through Carl Sousa.

MR. RUSSELL: What did you indicate at the meeting?
A: I told the lawyers that in my opinion these changes wouldn't fly.
Q: What was the lawyer's response?
A: His response was they'll never catch it.
Q: Explain what contemplation of death means from an insurance angle, what the concern was on your part.
A: Well, the three-year contemplation-of-death provision would have negated the planning that was being done. And it was my opinion at that point that because of the statement about a dual suicide . . . I thought it might very well be illegal.
Q: What specifically do you mean by the three-year contemplation of death?
A: Well, any person who knows that he or she is going to die and maneuvers life insurance contracts with that in mind, falls under these provisions. So there's a three-year window period of time during which you can't do that type of thing. Normally what simply happens is it's disallowed and thrown back into the estate. . . . My specific concern was, because of the suicide

plan, that not only would the three-year contemplation of death be a problem, but that transferring policies could be illegal.

I did my best to establish during cross examination that any impropriety was not Peter's responsibility but rather that of his counselors.

> MR. ROSENBLATT: Is it fair to say your overall impression of this meeting was that here are these attorneys discussing something very sensitive and perhaps illegal in a very open way with witnesses present? That surprised you some?
> A: I was astonished, yes.
> Q: The reason you were astonished is because it sounded illegal?
> A: In my opinion, yes.
> Q: And, basically, the lawyers said don't worry, it's okay? (*I wanted to show that the lawyers were every bit as bad as Peter.*)
> A: The direct quote was, "They will never catch it."

The whole subject was so hypocritical. "Estate planning" has become an industry involving huge numbers of high-priced paper shufflers who devise ways and means of saving money on estate taxes. The complexity of the United States tax code invites these shenanigans, and the prizes go to those lawyers who become adept at predicting what the Internal Revenue people will allow or not allow "to fly." The whole purpose of estate planning is to save on taxes—period, end of story! With the exception of the double-suicide plan, Peter was being very mainstream. He simply wanted to lessen the tax liabilities of his children—a perfectly legal goal.

> MR. ROSENBLATT: Isn't it true that the fundamental purpose of an estate planning meeting with lawyers and accountants and insurance people is to see how an individual or family can save taxes?
> A: Minimizing of estate taxes is normally the reason for the meeting and one of the end results, yes. (*How about that?*)
> Q: Sure. Because it's in everybody's interest to make sure that most of the assets are preserved for family members as opposed to being eaten up in estate taxes?
> A: That's certainly true. Yes.

The prosecutors were intimately familiar with human nature and understood there could be tremendous resentment against Peter for collecting large amounts of money under disability policies. Peter was probably making more money without working than any juror's family collectively earned. This resentment does not exist if someone is missing a limb or is in a wheelchair; but Peter appeared perfectly healthy and the State was convinced that it would have a field-day cross examining Peter on his so-called inability to sit at a desk and look through a microscope. They couldn't understand how Peter had pulled this off; Susan and I could have verified the legitimacy of Peter's disability from our close relationship with him. The disability policy was another nonissue that Judge Thompson permitted the prosecution to pursue.

The State wanted the jury to believe that Peter was disgusted with the practice of medicine, that he wanted to become an author and had cleverly schemed so that his disability income would provide a bridge between his medical earnings and his anticipated earnings as a writer. Peter had become so depressed by Pat's illness and by examining the slides of her lung tissue that he maintained he simply could not handle the analysis of other patients' tissue samples. It did not matter that Peter may have been perfectly capable of performing other medical duties; his disability policy with National Life of Vermont paid off and considered him 100 percent disabled if he was unable to perform the material duties of his specialty. This particular type of disability policy is popular among medical specialists and Peter had every right to assert his claim.

Peter had several disability policies going back to the middle 1970s. As his income increased he would purchase additional policies; there was nothing at all unusual about that. In September 1985, Peter applied to increase his disability benefits from $7,800 per month to $15,000 per month.

The State was eager to announce to the jury that Peter had earned approximately $802,000 the year before Patricia contracted cancer; the income basis of prior years becomes germane in a disability company's decision regarding the total amount of benefits it is willing to write. Peter passed his physical and the potential benefits were increased to $15,000 per month. Peter started collecting under the increased policy on January 17, 1986, only two days after Patricia's death, and he was continuing to receive this income during the trial.

Sousa estimated the net asset value of the estate at between $3 and $4 million; in addition to which there was over $2 million worth of life insurance. We felt this testimony was so damaging and we saw so many raised eyebrows on the faces of the jurors that Susan moved for a mistrial. All of our objections had been overruled.

MRS. ROSENBLATT: We would renew our motion for mistrial.
    I think it is clear from the testimony of this witness that the

purpose of placing him on the stand was to get into the financial circumstances, the great wealth of Dr. Rosier, the amount of money he's getting without working. The simple fact is the disability policy was available had Patricia died from natural causes three weeks later. It really has no probative value whatsoever. (*The court again denied our motion for mistrial and likewise denied our motion to strike the testimony of Sousa.*)

Traditional mainstream lawyers, in cross examining a witness such as Carl Sousa, would limit themselves pretty much to the field of his expertise. To me that would have been a no-win situation since I could not alter the facts of Peter's wealth, his huge earnings, or his disability income.

Sousa was a rarity in that he met with me privately in St. Petersburg prior to trial. I was confident that the State would not have prepped him well on other areas I wanted to cover. One of these was the hostility against Peter on the part of the medical community of Fort Myers. Portraying my millionaire client as an underdog was never easy. I followed up on our earlier conversation with my cross examination at trial:

Q: You know a lot of people who are so angry with Peter they don't want to have anything to do with him, right?

A: Yes, I do know many people like that.

Q: You would agree, would you not, that nobody was angry at Peter or Pat for the fact that she committed suicide, correct?

A: That's correct.

Q: What got Fort Myers and all these doctors crazy with anger against Peter was him going on television, isn't that correct?

MR. RUSSELL: Your Honor, objection. Now he's being asked to give an opinion about everybody he doesn't know. And I think it's improper without giving some predicate that he knows all these people.

THE COURT: I'll sustain the objection.

Q: In terms of the insurance policies you sell, the great majority of your clients are professional people?

A: A goodly portion of them are, yes.

Q: And a goodly portion are physicians, correct?

A: Of those, yes a good portion.

Q: I'm not asking you to name any doctor. I'm simply saying that, wouldn't you agree that, based on those contacts the thing that has made them crazy with anger toward Peter Rosier is not the fact of his wife's suicide or any role he may have played in her death, but because he went on television in November of 1986?

A: Of those that expressed anger, that is what they are mad about, yes.

Q: Is it fair to say that after Peter Rosier went on television he became an ostracized figure in the Fort Myers area. A lot of people just cut him off and stopped talking to him?

A: Yes, that's a fair statement.

This testimony allowed us to reinforce the broad, valid point about the attitude of the American medical community toward euthanasia. As long as suicide and assisted suicide for the terminally ill are kept quiet, as long as they are handled discreetly, no one will make waves. Doctors and nurses are not whistleblowers. The key to avoiding prosecution is observing the etiquette of euthanasia, the rules of the game.

When we were overwhelmed by the State's "bad-guy" material against Peter we could always pull out our ace in the hole, "good-guy" testimony via Gertrude. I was able to enter into evidence through Sousa the fact that Peter and Pat had provided a $300,000 trust fund to be used for the benefit of Gertrude, if they were to predecease her. I made the point that when Peter paid for Gertrude's health insurance, it was quality insurance and he paid for it personally, rather than through his practice. Peter purchased excellent insurance policies for all his other employees as well.

I attempted to shoot down the theory that Patricia committed suicide because Peter convinced her she would otherwise suffer a horrible death. The State expected me to deal with this subject only through doctors.

Q: Did Mrs. Rosier make it clear to you that she would choose to take her own life rather than live a life that was not acceptable to her?

A: Yes.

Q: And you understood that to mean a life where she would be in pain and where she would realize her cancer was incurable, is that correct?

A: That's correct.

Q: You regarded Pat as a strong, intelligent woman?

A: Yes I did. (*This answer helped us rebut the State's repeated contention that Peter dominated her.*)

I knew that many doctors in Fort Myers were millionaires, so I tried to put Peter's wealth in perspective. To his credit, Sousa usually gave straight answers. Referring to Peter's annual income of approximately $800,000, I asked,

Q: Obviously that's a lot of money, right?
A: Yes sir.
Q: A lot of doctors in Fort Myers are making big money now and were making big money in 1985, correct?
A: Yes, that's true.
Q: A lot of those doctors are your clients?
A: That's true.

The State conveyed the idea that Peter benefited in some way by Patricia's death on January 15, 1986, as opposed to some other day. This was nonsense and Sousa helped us show why.

Q: Do I understand very fundamentally that whether Patricia died on January 15 or January 20 or February the 10, let's say, Peter Rosier stood to gain nothing more by virtue of her dying on January 15, as opposed to those other dates?
A: That's correct.
Q: So you are not aware of any financial incentive through insurance or anything else, where Mrs. Rosier dying on January 15 was some kind of magical day? And it would not have mattered one penny to him, whether she died a week later or three weeks later?
A: That's correct.

Stephen Russell was very clever in making Carl Sousa his ally and in setting up conflicts regarding the disability policy and the increase in benefits.

Q: If Dr. Rosier had been unable to work in September of 1985 and had been disabled in the sense of being unable to look at slides and evaluate them, you would not have submitted an application to increase his disability benefits, is that correct?
A: That's correct.

An insurance company would not increase disability benefits to an individual who was already disabled. So Sousa could not say Peter was disabled in September 1985 when the policy increased from $7,800 to $15,000 a month. Patricia's lung cancer was diagnosed in April 1985 and Peter's secretary would later testify that Peter was unable to examine tissue slides after April 1985. The State knew this from the secretary's prior statements and set the stage for this conflict on the clearly collateral issue of the increase in benefits of the disability policy.

Peter's disability policy provided that once National Life of Vermont was satisfied that he was disabled a waiver of premium provision went into effect, meaning the insurance company would pay for Peter's insurance premiums. National Life paid all premiums on all life insurance contracts retroactive to January 17, 1986, which on an annual basis comes to approximately $90,000.

The State figured, all the more reason for the jury to convict Peter. I kept imagining the notes they were probably making in their final argument notebook: "The SOB can take Patricia dancing and to the most expensive restaurants in Paris, but he can't sit down and look through a microscope. He could play tennis and write poetry and close business deals and chase after women, but he couldn't look at slides—the poor baby. He could send his manuscript to half the publishers in America, take writing courses at Harvard, and travel and negotiate about a screenplay, but he couldn't look at slides. Bull!

"Ladies and gentlemen of the jury, the $15,000 a month is just another Peter Rosier scam. It is just further evidence of this man's talent for manipulating people and circumstances to satisfy his own selfish needs."

This potential argument scared the hell out of us. Susan and I weren't sure how to deal with it. What is perfectly legal and customary among medical professionals with six-figure incomes could shock and prejudice a St. Petersburg jury.

MR. RUSSELL: I assume as an insurance agent that you get a commission from policies you sell?

A: That's correct.

Q: That's a continuing thing even after the first year, is that right?

A: Yes. That's referred to as renewal commissions.

Q: And this disability policy, as long as he's disabled, it will go on until his death, is that correct?

A: That's correct.

Q: Did there come a time when Dr. Rosier's psychiatrist ruled that he was no longer disabled?

A: Yes. That was about two years after January 17, 1986.

Q: When that happened, what was the defendant's reaction?

A: His reaction was emotional, he was very concerned about the diagnosis being changed.

Q: Did he seek to reinstate the diagnosis of full disability?

A: Yes he did.

I made the point that Peter had the right to contest the company's stopping the disability payments, and the company had the option to have Peter examined by a psychiatrist of its choice. In any event, National Life of Vermont reinstated the disability payments to Peter. The company was obviously impressed with Peter's disability or it wouldn't have made the payments.

Susan and I were frustrated and angry since all this had nothing whatsoever to do with Patricia Rosier's death. These collateral matters had nothing to do with a first degree murder case. I asked Carl Sousa:

Q: In all your meetings with the State, have they ever explained to you the relevance of all these questions on life insurance and disability insurance as they relate to the criminal charges brought against Dr. Rosier?

A: Have they explained them to me? No.

Q: You must be somewhat puzzled. You're being asked all these questions about insurance in a case where the defendant is being charged with murder, correct?

A: Am I puzzled?

Q: Yes, are you puzzled?

A: I've been puzzled for quite a while, yes.

Q: I'm confused too.

MR. RUSSELL: Objection.

THE COURT: Disregard the comment.

Susan and I were satisfied that the jury understood the purpose of Carl Sousa's testimony, which was to make them jealous and suspicious of Peter. We would eventually find out if the State had succeeded.

The State's next witness, Jules Cantor, would demonstrate Peter's poor choice of friends.

12

Jules Cantor: With Friends Like You . . .

Like Carl Sousa, Jules Cantor knew nothing firsthand of the events at
the Rosier home on January 14 and January 15, 1986. Cantor never obtained
medications for Peter and he never saw Peter administer drugs to Patricia.
So why was he sitting in that witness chair? Cantor was there to unload
another dump truck of garbage on the head of our client. The State's
persistence and Judge Thompson's kitchen-sink philosophy on the admissibility of evidence allowed this to occur. Jules Cantor was living proof
of the old adage "With friends like you, who needs enemies?"

Cantor was a member of the Park Meadow Tennis Club; he was
originally from Long Island, New York, and had lived in Fort Myers
about eleven years. He was part owner of a lumber yard. He and Peter
knew each other casually; that changed within a week or so after Patricia's
death when they suddenly became pals. Their common interest, according
to the State, was finding women for Peter.

The State sought to demonstrate through Jules Cantor that Peter Rosier was a shallow, arrogant, selfish, money-hungry, publicity-seeking
womanizer who got over the death of his wife in a flash. In spite of his
incessant sobbing in the courtroom over the loss of his one true love,
Peter Rosier was at bottom a stinking hypocrite. Instead of grieving over
his irreplaceable loss, Peter only wanted to go out and get laid.

MR. RUSSELL: Did there come a time shortly after Mrs. Rosier's
death that you were aware the defendant was dating?
A: Yes.
Q: And was there an occasion where your wife got involved as
far as fixing him up with a nurse?

195

A: Yes. (*Cantor's wife was a nurse anesthetist.*)

Q: What was the discussion at that time?

A: That she was going to arrange the meeting and Dr. Rosier asked her if she could do it that evening, and my wife said she had no way of contacting Linda. And Dr. Rosier asked her to see if she could call the hospital and get her home number, and she did get Linda's home number but she wasn't at home.

Q: Was he insistent?

A: Yes.

MRS. ROSENBLATT: May we approach the bench Your Honor?

MR. RUSSELL: Judge, if we're going to approach the bench and I know what's coming—my purpose is to rebut three weeks of trying to paint him as strictly whining and crying throughout this whole thing. (*Russell deliberately made this remark so that the jury could hear it.*)

MR. ROSENBLATT: (*I stuck my nose in Russell's face and my finger an inch from his chest, all in the presence of the jury.*) Your purpose is to make people dislike Peter, that's what your purpose is.

THE COURT: Gentlemen, gentlemen. (*To the jury*) I say again what the attorneys say is not evidence. Disregard both the attorneys. Go ahead with the testimony. Overrule the objection.

MR. RUSSELL: Thank you, Your Honor. (*That hurt because the judge wouldn't even listen to Susan. He simply was committed to allowing in all this extraneous and repetitious garbage.*)

Q: Did you and your wife have occasion to go to the Bahamas with the defendant and Linda?

A: Yes.

Q: Did you go to the casinos? Did you have a good time?

A: Yes.

Q: Did the defendant tell you that he took Linda to New York and California during that time?

A: Yes.

Q: Were you aware that he was dating other women?

A: Yes.

Q: Approximately how many?

A: My guess would be approximately three or four over an extended period of time.

My cross examination followed:

MR. ROSENBLATT: What did you say, that the introduction to Linda took place two or three weeks after Pat's death?

A: Approximately three or four weeks.

Q: Could it have been as long as two or three months after her death—big difference? (*That's what Cantor had said on his deposition; he obviously shortened the time frame to help the State.*)

A: It could have been. But to the best of my recollection it was approximately a month. (*I let the jury know what Cantor said at his deposition.*)

Q: You knew [that] from the State's standpoint they would have liked to have the dating occur as soon as possible after Mrs. Rosier's death. You understood that if you said Peter went out with Linda, the closer in time that was to the date of Patricia's death, the more the State would like it. You knew where they were coming from, right?

A: (*After a long pause, with his eyes darting around*) I imagined so.

Q: Peter did not know Linda Maxwell or the other women you say he dated, at any time before Patricia's death. Isn't that correct?

A: Correct. (*At least that was to Peter's credit; there was no evidence whatsoever that he had been fooling around during Patricia's illness.*)

Q: After Pat's death you were the one who initiated the friendship. You felt sorry for him, thought he was depressed, realized he had suffered a great loss, so you invited him over to your home. Isn't that correct?

A: Yes. (*Witnesses will usually agree when they are favorably portrayed.*)

Q: And for about a year you and he remained close friends, right?

A: Yes.

Stephen Russell on redirect:

MR. RUSSELL: Now after that TV story aired, did you ever have a discussion with the defendant concerning money to be made from the book or the movie?

MRS. ROSENBLATT: Your Honor, there is an objection. Could we approach the bench?

THE COURT: (*Outside the presence of the jury*) Is this the one about making a billion dollars? (*Judge Thompson had read the newspapers.*)

MR. ROSENBLATT: Russell is going to ask him about shitting on Fort Myers, and it's very inflammatory. I mean talk about prejudice.
MRS. ROSENBLATT: Not only is it incredibly inflammatory, but again it's not probative of anything in the world.
MR. ROSENBLATT: And he took it as a joke.

Although Volz and Russell frequently did it themselves, they would go nuts when Susan and I would argue the same point. They would accuse us of double-teaming them and they would utilize other insipid clichés that lawyers love so much. Since many judges are most influenced by the very last thing they hear, there was a constant competition at these bench conferences to get in the last word.

MR. RUSSELL: They can cross examine him on that, Judge.
THE COURT: Well, I'm willing to let you do it. Overrule the objection.

[MR. RUSSELL]: I'd like you to tell the jury exactly what was said, using his exact words, even though they may not be appropriate otherwise.
A: We were driving in Dr. Rosier's car and I happened to ask him a question as to what he was going to do with all the money he would make from the book and movie. And his answer was that he hoped to make a billion dollars, and he would buy several Rolls Royces and drive around Fort Myers and shit on everybody in town. (*A fantasy that many lawyers have about opponents and judges.*)

Such an arrogant statement (if believed) made by a wealthy physician who is collecting big disability money could, in and of itself, result in conviction, and lawyers who pretend that is not so are simply not being straight. This testimony had the potential to be devastating because it tied in so beautifully with the State's theory that Peter wanted Pat's death to be dramatic so that he could write a best seller about euthanasia, a subject that can touch anyone.

MR. ROSENBLATT: That comment that you say Peter made as you were driving around, that was not a comment made out of the blue. If he made that comment at all it was in answer to a question you asked—What are you going to do with all that money?—correct?

A: Yes.

Q: You guys were just making conversation. Like hey man, what are you going to do with all that money? Like Ralph Kramden and Art Carney kibbitzing, that kind of man-to-man horsing around. Hey, buddy boy, what are you going to do if the book is a best seller? (*Several of the jurors looked like "Honeymooners" fans to me.*)

MR. RUSSELL: Objection. (*Of course.*)

THE COURT: Sustain the objection. (*Of course.*)

Q: Look, the atmosphere during this conversation was that you were both joking around. Isn't that so?

A: Pretty much so, yes.

Q: And, as a matter of fact, it's your opinion that "shitting on Fort Myers" has been blown totally out of proportion because, at the time it was said, it wasn't a big deal. It's been made into a big deal by the State and by the press, but at the time it was said it was just a passing comment. You laughed and you went on to something else, right?

A: That's right.

Q: The State kept pushing you, asking whether Peter ever said anything about having a profit motive. And after you were pushed and pushed again, you finally talked about this joking remark, shitting on Fort Myers and driving around in Rolls Royces, correct?

A: Correct. (*That was a great answer because it made the State look both petty and mean.*)

Stephen Russell on redirect:

MR. RUSSELL: Now, around the time of the television interview, did the defendant ever express to you any social interest in Leisa Zigman?

A: Yes.

Q: Did he indicate any infatuation with her?

A: In a manner, yes.

Q: Did he ever express any desire to have sex with her?

A: In a manner of guy talk, yes.

Q: Did he ever use the word "love" in guy talk, falling in love with her?

A: Yes.

Q: Did he ever say anything about marrying her, in a loose context?

A: In a very loose context, yes. (*I looked over at the jury and gestured with both my palms upward, and my head tilted back. I hoped my expression said, "Give me a break, please!"*)

What drove Peter particularly wild about Cantor's testimony was that no one else had heard his talk about the Rolls Royces or Leisa Zigman. His comments were totally out of context; he and Jules were functioning like two college sophomores on spring break in Fort Lauderdale. Peter let his defenses down with a good friend and he would oftentimes say things just to get a reaction from his buddy.

I then responded:

[MR. ROSENBLATT]: Did you ever hear the expression "With friends like you, who needs enemies"?
A: Yes, I have.
Q: Don't you think that applies to you?
A: No, I don't.

Right! Now I was ready to spring one of my meanest questions of the entire trial; and I did it without guilt. Cantor had gratuitously dumped on Peter and I felt he deserved it.

Q: Although you're a married man, you go out with other women all the time, don't you?

Cantor was visibly stunned by the question. He reacted as though he had been body-slammed by Hulk Hogan. He closed his eyes, scrunched up his face, and looked skyward. He said nothing.

I did nearly all my questioning at a podium positioned very close to the jury; the courtroom was so huge I was quite a distance from the witness, although I always had the option to move away from the podium and get closer. I decided to hold my ground. You could hear the proverbial pin drop. What was this guy going to say?

I looked over to Susan and Peter who were seated at our table facing the jury. They were to my left, the jury was to my right; the State's table was likewise to my left as I stood at the podium, but closer to me with the prosecutors directly facing the witness, the judge, the court clerk, and the court reporter. I ignored the State's table as I nearly always did since I didn't want to be inhibited by anything they were doing or saying. I folded my arms, looked over at the jury, looked back to the witness, back to the jury, again to the witness. I just kept staring at Cantor with a menacing look which said—"WELL? SILENCE!"

I thought about reasking the question but I didn't. The judge was fidgeting and was visibly embarrassed by this incredibly long pause. I moved in front of the podium, walked several steps toward the witness, and leveled my gaze at him, my arms remaining folded. I did not look toward the jury or our table again. I stood rock still and said nothing.

Cantor's eyes finally opened; his head came down from the ceiling, and he uttered this classic line:

A: "What do you mean, all the time?"
Q: All the time. Not necessarily every day, but frequently?
THE COURT: You want to approach the bench, please.

What the hell was going on? I really had something going with the witness. I hoped his credibility was being flushed down the toilet. There had been no objection. The jurors and spectators were on the edge of their seats, and the judge, by this unwarranted intrusion, was destroying these delicious moments.

THE COURT: I'm inclined not to require him to answer that question.
MR. ROSENBLATT: (*I sputtered in utter astonishment.*) Without any objection from the State?
THE COURT: There is a canon (*of judicial ethics*) that says I'm supposed to exercise some protection of witnesses. I don't think he should be required to answer that question. I'm going to stop it here.

I had difficulty controlling myself. This was insane. My client could spend the rest of his life in prison and the State was allowed to dump all over him every day without restraint. Yet when I asked a tough question to one of the chief manure slingers, the judge was worried about Cantor's sensibilities or perhaps whether his wife would throw him out. I didn't give a damn about that and, amazingly enough, neither did Steve Russell.

Russell was likewise angered by the judge's ruling.

MR. RUSSELL: Stop what? You're going to leave that hanging? We can't go into that? (*He likewise sputtered in utter astonishment.*)

Susan whispered to me: "Calm down, it's not our fight anymore. I was watching the jury as that scene unfolded, you weren't. Russell realizes that that exchange destroyed Cantor. You got the greatest answer in the world when Cantor said, 'What do you mean by all the time?' "

> THE COURT: (*To Russell*) What do you want to go into it for? Well, whether you want to go into it or not, it's not your wants—the witness has some rights.
> MR. RUSSELL: This witness has testified that before his deposition he met Mr. Rosenblatt in the elevator. They went into the bathroom in the courthouse in Fort Myers. That Mr. Rosenblatt indicated to him his concerns about Peter chasing after women. Rosenblatt said, "Listen, you go soft, I'll go soft with you."
> MR. ROSENBLATT: That's vile, Judge.
> MR. RUSSELL: That's vile?
> MR. ROSENBLATT: It's a filthy lie.
> THE COURT: All right.

Again, the State of Florida was going to make Rosenblatt an issue. Susan reminded me that the State wanted to bring out that Peter and Cantor got involved with a number of prostitutes, some of whom the State had listed as potential witnesses. Susan told the judge.

> MRS. ROSENBLATT: We have evidence that the State threatened [Cantor]; they had a decoy that was a prostitute. He picked her up and they said, "We are going to prosecute you on that if you don't help us in this case." This man has admitted this to witnesses.
> THE COURT: I'm not sure exactly what it is Mr. Russell wants to go into.
> MRS. ROSENBLATT: He wants to go into the prostitute thing.

Russell admitted that Susan was correct. His aim was to show that Peter was the instigator in getting the two of them lined up with whores. We were shocked that the State was willing to risk ruining the reputation and marriage of a cooperative witness simply to heap more muck on the defendant. I turned to Russell, in the presence of the judge:

> MR. ROSENBLATT: You're willing to destroy this guy? You are beyond belief.

THE COURT: All right, we can spend a lot of time on this. I don't think the question should have been asked—it was. I'm not going to extend the problem. (*To the jury*) Ladies and gentlemen, I specifically instruct you to disregard the last question asked of this witness and to draw no inference from the question itself.

Yet the judge allowed Russell to inquire into the alleged conversation I had with Cantor in the bathroom immediately prior to his deposition months earlier.

[MR. RUSSELL]: Mr. Cantor, in the bathroom, did you indicate to Mr. Rosenblatt any personal concerns you had about matters that occurred between you and the defendant?
A: Yes.
Q: And they were private matters as far as you were concerned. Is that right?
A: Yes.
Q: And you indicated basically [that] you would prefer that they not come out. Is that right?
A: Yes.
Q: What did he say about the upcoming deposition?
A: Well, he indicated that he would avoid certain topics if I went soft on certain topics.

According to Cantor, the bathroom deal was in effect: "If you don't hurt Peter then I won't ask you embarrassing questions." The State never asked Cantor the first question about this bathroom deal on direct examination; obviously their strategy shifted as a result of my cross examination. Ordinarily, a lawyer is not allowed to bring up on redirect examination a subject that was never covered on either the original direct or the cross examination, but as usual Judge Thompson was as loose as a goose.

The supposed episode in the bathroom, constantly asking the judge to hold me in contempt, repeatedly asserting in front of the jury that my techniques and strategies were improper and unethical were tactics employed by the State to cause the jury to dislike me and be suspicious of me. The message was: "Not only is the defendant a piece of shit, but so is his lawyer. Rosier and Rosenblatt deserve each other." Susan and I did not get intimidated easily.

Q: If I did what you say I did—tried to influence your testimony—
why didn't you report me then to the State or to the bar?

A: I don't know.

Q: You don't know because it didn't happen, that's why. I didn't
need you to go soft. This case has nothing to do with running
around with women. You don't know anything about how
Mrs. Rosier died. Isn't that what this case is all about?

A: Yes.

If this jury didn't recognize that this whole bathroom episode was
total crap, then we were in trouble. I was very confident that during final
argument I could score heavily by pointing out the State's desperation
in focusing on such nonissues. Not only did I want to attack Cantor's
credibility, but I was determined to extract helpful testimony from him.

Q: In all the time that you and Peter were close friends, he never
mentioned anything about Patricia having been smothered to
death by her father. Is that correct?

A: Correct.

It would be hard for the jury to believe that Peter Rosier, this world-
class talker, could have kept the smothering secret from his pal if he had
known about it. Although Cantor was often knocking Peter's behavior,
we were able to turn that around to some extent by getting Cantor to
agree that Peter became a terrible pain because he was obsessed with
Patricia's memory, emotionally overwrought, and would be sobbing all
the time as he recounted things that he and Patricia had done together.
Cantor grudgingly had to admit that he was convinced of Peter's sincerity
regarding how much he missed Patricia.

I was also able to demonstrate, through Cantor, that Peter had motives
other than dollars for confessing on television.

Q: He told you that the reason he went on television was to
further the cause of euthanasia, right?

A: Right.

Q: He didn't say he went on television to make a million dollars
on a book or to make a million dollars on a screenplay, correct?

A: Yes.

Q: And he also told you that he was writing the book to further
the cause of euthanasia?

A: Correct.

Well, Julius Cantor had been just another witness on collateral issues. He had not said a word about Seconal or morphine or suicide or cancer.

The State's next witness, a forensic toxicologist, would address those subjects in exquisite detail.

13

Dr. Robert B. Forney, Jr.:
Have Opinions, Will Travel

When Susan and I traveled to the Medical College of Ohio in Toledo to take the deposition of Robert B. Forney, Jr., he and I disliked one another almost immediately. Like many experts, I saw Forney as a pontificator who was incapable of giving clear, crisp, and forthright answers. I admittedly have a "thing" against experts who voluntarily get involved for either side in civil lawsuits or criminal proceedings. Because lawyers pander to experts and for numerous other reasons, the expert business has become a big-bucks industry. I am convinced that the great majority of expert witnesses are in it strictly for the money and/or the ego gratification of tangling with supposed hotshot lawyers.

The importance of expert witnesses is greatly overrated. I have always believed that juries most often decide cases based on the underlying facts, rather than on the conclusions of experts. Juries nowadays understand that a lawyer can get an expert to say just about anything on any subject if the price is right.

Forney's fees were actually quite reasonable, but many experts charge outrageous sums in excess of $500 per hour, and some even pad their hours on top of that. They travel first class, stay at the best hotels, expect to be paid when they are sleeping out of town, and are accustomed to being treated like royalty both by the law firms who retain them and the presiding judges.

Dr. Forney had a Ph.D. in toxicology from the Indiana University School of Medicine. He was not a medical doctor, but a forensic toxicologist (an expert on drugs), which means he made a conscious decision to become involved in legal disputes, usually of a criminal nature. Dr. Graves, a forensic pathologist, had recommended Dr. Forney to the State.

Forney was frustrated because few of my questions were scientific. He would have loved for me to have been narrow and technical regarding the lethal dosages of various drugs and how and why human beings react differently to various combinations. That way he could have displayed his expertise and created an aura of authority and integrity. But I knew that was his turf and I would not score many points there.

Instead, I asked him many embarrassing questions about how often he testified and on what subjects and how much he got paid; I would get philosophical and ask why he was testifying in this particular case. I basically got him to admit that he was a hired gun who gave opinions (in exchange for money) based on purely hypothetical questions. Most importantly, he admitted that he really had little interest in what the true facts of a given situation were. Perhaps other experts and lawyers could relate to this mind-set, but not normal civilians. I knew that Forney was totally opposed on religious and moral grounds to suicide and he had his own not-so-healthy agenda for becoming involved in the Peter Rosier trial. I had no doubt that Forney wished for Peter's conviction.

Experts love to regale their colleagues with war stories and they love to tell how they outwitted some dumb lawyer, especially when that lawyer enjoys a heavyweight reputation. The Rosier case had incredibly high visibility and would undoubtedly serve as a rainmaker for Dr. Forney (who most likely would be retained in other cases), particularly if Rosier were convicted.

Susan and I tried to convince Judge Thompson to disqualify Dr. Forney as a witness altogether. Susan argued that his specialty was the blood alcohol level in a person's body, and that was the subject he testified about most frequently. His expertise was providing testimony for those accused of drunk driving. It had been a decade since Forney had given testimony regarding either Seconal or morphine. Susan's argument caused Judge Thompson to get off one of the trial's best oneliners.

THE COURT: Okay. I have a very low threshhold. Anybody that knows more than I do is an expert. He knows more than I do. Therefore, I overrule the objection.

Dr. Graves had told James Fitzpatrick to contact Dr. Forney to answer questions Fitzpatrick had about the effect the Seconal and morphine had on Patricia. Forney described toxicology as a medical science having to do with the effects of drugs and chemicals on the body. He explained to the jury in a pretty impressive fashion the properties of Seconal and morphine.

Seconal is the brand name of the drug secobarbital, a barbiturate that is a sedative compound. It is a general central nervous system depressant and it will induce sleep. Morphine is a sedative, a narcotic that comes from the opium poppy; like Seconal it is a central nervous system depressant.

Forney explained to the jury how the rate of absorption of a drug varies significantly based on its route of administration. A drug will impact the body most quickly if it is given intravenously, next if it is given intramuscularly by injection, and lastly if it is swallowed in tablet or pill form.

Many times juries are bamboozled by a string of academic degrees and a plethora of scientific papers the witness has authored. I could take nothing for granted.

The only factual testimony in the case was that Patricia had swallowed twenty Seconal capsules (100 mgs each), received two injections totalling 8 mgs of morphine in her buttocks, and had had four morphine suppositories (20 mgs each) inserted into her rectum. Forney did not believe this combination of drugs would have killed her, and based on my own reading and conferences with our experts I believed he was absolutely correct.

So Edward Volz added Dr. Harwin's drugs to the equation. Just five days before Patricia died, Dr. Harwin's prescriptions for Seconal and morphine had been filled in these amounts: 50 capsules Seconal, 100 mgs each and 50 tablets morphine, 30 mgs each.

By a careful and well thought out series of hypothetical questions, Volz got Forney to assume that Pat had taken substantial amounts of Seconal and morphine during the five days between January 10 and January 15. Assuming that, Dr. Forney could then theorize that the combination of drugs plus the alcohol consumed at the "last supper" could have caused Patricia's death even absent the smothering.

Edward Volz even asked Forney questions about other drugs such as methadone; he was inviting Forney to speculate about the effects of different combinations of drugs, as to whether they could cause death. Experts love these kinds of mind games; case-hardened trial lawyers refer to this process as a form of mental masturbation.

MRS. ROSENBLATT: Your Honor, we object. There is not one shred of evidence saying certain drugs were taken other than the morphine and Seconal. Whether any other drugs were in Mrs. Rosier's system on January 15 is entirely speculative. (*That was absolutely true and most judges would have excluded Forney's "musings."*)

THE COURT: Allow the testimony. You can cover that on cross examination.

Forney was ever so comfortable and secure expounding on dosages of drugs, routes of administration, and the properties of different drugs as well as when they became toxic, when they peaked, and when they became lethal. He became unsettled (as do most experts) when he was challenged and attacked about motivation and technique.

I didn't think our jury could relate to an expert who went out of his way to avoid knowledge of the true facts. Forney didn't even know the cause of death listed on the death certificate.

MR. ROSENBLATT: You weren't even interested in reviewing the medical or hospital records, simply from the standpoint of making yourself more familiar with the background and facts?

A: That's correct.

Q: You knew that medical records and statements of the various treating physicians had been taken but you never asked to review them, correct?

A: That's correct. (*I intended to argue that his philosophy was "Ignorance is bliss; don't contaminate me with the facts."*)

Q: In the course of either Mr. Fitzpatrick or Mr. Volz giving you different hypothetical situations, did you ever say to them —"Hey, what are the true facts, I'd like to know what the actual facts are." Did you ever say that?

A: No, I don't think so.

Q: Because you didn't see that as your role?

A: That's right. . . I have consistently throughout this case refused to render opinions about what are the true facts.

Q: After you read the statements of the three Delmans, you knew that Patricia Rosier had died from being smothered, correct?

A: That's correct. (*To me it was the height of weirdness to read the statements of the Delmans yet not read the statements and depositions of the involved physicians.*)

Q: Did you know the three Delmans were granted total immunity?

MR. VOLZ: Objection again, Your Honor. Where is that relevant to the testimony of this witness?

MR. ROSENBLATT: (*At a bench conference*) Only in the sense that the true facts did not matter to him. I want to establish that this witness is a hired gun. He gets a call from a lawyer and he responds, and whether some habitual drunk driver has been convicted four times before and then kills a golden-haired four-year-old is immaterial to him.

I wanted the jury to appreciate that in spite of knowing about the smothering and the immunity, Dr. Forney was still perfectly comfortable testifying for the State. Let them assess the morality of that. The judge gave me some headway.

Q: Dr. Forney, do you consider yourself a hired gun in the sense that it doesn't really matter which side calls you. (*Usually the effect of calling an expert witness a hired gun is equivalent to an egregious comment about his family tree.*)

A: Yes, I think that's pretty much in line with my view of a moral oath that I would take. I have an expertise which I would like to offer as a service. (*Wonder of all wonders, an expert has admitted in open court that he is a hired gun. Of course, that's precisely what the great majority of lawyers are.*)

Q: The way you operate is that whichever side calls you first and is willing to pay your fee, you will say: "Okay, I'll review the materials. I'll get involved and answer hypothetical questions."

A: I think the Constitution says without regard to age, sex, race, and so forth.

Q: Is it never within your ethical parameters to say that on moral grounds, "I don't like your side of the case" or "I don't like your client or what he or she has done," or "I just don't think it's fair." Or do you put all of those considerations aside?

A: Yes, with the few exceptions I've outlined. Unless there is a conflict of interest or if there is a professionally unethical relationship involved.

Q: If you knew that Vincent Delman, instead of smothering his daughter, shot her in the head, you'd still be testifying. That wouldn't change anything for you?

A: Yes, that's correct. (*I think at this point Dr. Forney lost the jury for the second time; the first time was when he admitted he was a hired gun.*)

Q: Your philosophical position on suicide is that it is never justified under any circumstances, no matter how great the pain?

A: Yes. My personal philosophical position is opposed to suicide.

If we had a juror with this point of view, he or she would be unreachable. People have the same kind of emotional investment regarding suicide and euthanasia as they do about abortion. *If* the jurors had answered my questions honestly, they had open minds on the issue of suicide, depending upon specific circumstances.

I remained unready to broach any scientific inquiry; I wanted this jury to know more about the man beneath the medical jargon.

Q: Dr. Forney, over the years you've testified in hundreds of cases, correct?

A: Yes, I said that. I haven't really kept accurate count. I said dozens, and my guess would be somewhere between one hundred and two hundred cases.

Q: Well, Dr. Forney what you said in your deposition was hundreds. You didn't say dozens. You said that you had testified in hundreds of cases. Both in criminal and civil matters in many states. Did you or did you not say that in your deposition? (*He could see that Susan was ready to hand me the precise page and line of his deposition if he denied it.*)

A: Yes, I did.

Q: Would you agree that in a great majority of cases where you have testified over the years and in many states, your testimony has dealt with the subject of alcohol?

A: I would agree with that. (*I knew there was much prejudice against drunk drivers escaping punishment on technicalities, prejudice which in my view was totally justified.*)

Q: And most of those cases involved drunk-driving allegations?

A: That's correct.

Q: And in the last three or four years you've testified mainly on behalf of attorneys representing the drunk drivers. (*I saw that he was going to correct me with a lecture so I amended the question in midstream.*) . . . the *alleged* drunk drivers. Correct?

A: That's correct.

Q: And, as a matter of fact, when we talked about your testimony as a forensic toxicologist with respect to drugs other than alcohol, your emphasis has been on cocaine and marijuana rather than on drugs such as Seconal and morphine, correct?

A: Yes. I would say that's probably true.

Q: You allow your name to be listed in legal directories letting lawyers know that you are available for consultations and expert testimony? (*Whatever else they may be, frequent testifiers are in business.*)

A: That's correct.

Q: Dr. Forney, you have testified on behalf of criminal defendants charged with some really heinous crimes such as multiple murders and multiple rapes?

MR. VOLZ: Objection, Your Honor. He testified as an expert.

THE COURT: Sustain the objection.

Q: You have testified on behalf of defendants charged with drunk driving who have actually killed people while drunk, haven't you?

MR. VOLZ: Again, Your Honor.

THE COURT: Sustain the objection. (*Susan demanded a bench conference.*)

THE COURT: Certainly a borderline area of inquiry. It's not one in which the result is clear.

MRS. ROSENBLATT: Well, Your Honor, every time it's borderline you seem to rule against us.

THE COURT: I disagree.

MRS. ROSENBLATT: I think we're allowed wide latitude to cross examine. Forney's been doing this hundreds of times and he can certainly handle himself; this is like trying to keep out the truth.

THE COURT: I'm going to sustain the objection. Move on to something else.

Before I moved on to something else, there was another tidbit I wanted the jury to have about Dr. Forney. Animal experimentation has become very controversial, so naturally I brought out that Dr. Forney had been involved in working on various laboratory animals where the animals were eventually put to death. In certain instances their deaths were necessary to validate the experiments. The law of averages made it likely that I had at least one or two animal lovers on the jury. Now I was ready to talk about Seconal and morphine.

Q: For the average person, what would be considered a lethal dose of Seconal?

A: A typical individual would require somewhere between thirty and forty 100 mg capsules to cause death.

Q: If one hundred adults each took twenty Seconal, 100 mgs each, not a single one of them would die from those twenty Seconal. Isn't that right?

A: That's correct. (*Assuming that to be true, that would make Peter Rosier one of the dumbest doctors who ever walked the face of the earth. The only other reasonable explanation would be that Peter at some level did wish to keep Pat in a state of limbo; i.e., he lacked true criminal intent.*)

Q: Would you not agree that [in the case of] a board-certified M.D. pathologist who believed that twenty Seconal would kill an adult, . . . there are only two possibilities: one, he is very stupid and number two, he didn't really want the patient to die?

A: He was mistaken. (*Well, if he was mistaken, he was unbelievably incompetent since even a glance at a superficial source like* The Physician's Desk Reference *makes it obvious that twenty Seconal would not do the job.*)

Q: What is the lethal dosage of morphine by injection? How many milligrams would it take to kill a person?

A: About 100 mgs intravenously, assuming that the patient had not built up a tolerance to the drug. But for a morphine injection given intramuscularly, it would take 500 mgs.

Q: So, obviously, when you are talking about 8 mgs by injection into the buttocks where it would take 500 mgs to be lethal, then 8 mgs is next to nothing?

A: Right.

Q: How much morphine would it take to kill a person if it was administered by way of suppositories?

A: I would say anywhere from 300 to 500 mgs. (*Peter's four suppositories amounted only to 80 mgs and the State's star witness was on record saying that the 80 mgs plus the 8 mgs of injectable morphine plus the twenty Seconal would not have been enough to end Patricia's life.*)

Unwittingly Forney shot down any possibility that there could have been a legitimate need to medicate Patricia after she had swallowed the twenty Seconal. According to Forney, by the morning of January 15, Patricia was totally defenseless; she was in a fairly deep coma and was incapable of experiencing pain. So the State's own expert was in conflict with the testimony of Drs. Dosoretz and Harwin, who said they prescribed morphine on January 15 to make Patricia more comfortable.

Forney thought, absent the smothering, that Patricia would have awakened probably within forty-eight hours, and have been in the same approximate condition she was before taking the Seconal. Susan and I were very happy with this testimony since it underscored our contention that Peter, for all his bumbling, did not intend to end his wife's life.

I asked questions about why one person gets drunk on two drinks and another doesn't on ten. I pointed out the obvious: that there is a tremendous variability between individual responses not only to alcohol but to various drugs. And frequently these different reactions have little to do with building up a tolerance; frequently the true causes are very mysterious. There are simply many things the scientists and technicians do not know.

I wanted to close out my questioning by again emphasizing Dr. Forney's disdain for the underlying facts of the Peter Rosier murder trial.

Q: Since you have not read any of the medical depositions or medical records, the only thing that you can conclude with any degree of real certainty is that up until the time Mrs. Rosier was smothered she was alive. Correct? (*There was a very long pause as though I had asked him to explain Einstein's theory of relativity. Dr. Forney was looking around for help, so I asked.*) Why are you looking at the judge?

A: I have frequently testified that I don't believe that I am an expert with regard to anything other than the effects of drugs. You're asking me a question that is outside of that range. I don't think I'm competent to answer that question.

Q: (*Astonished*) You're telling me you're not competent to say that you know 100 percent that up until the time Mrs. Rosier was smothered by her stepfather, she was alive?

MR. VOLZ: Your Honor, I object. Once again we have testimony drawing conclusions from witnesses and impeding on the function of the jury.

THE COURT: I will sustain the objection to that question.

The judge's ruling was irrelevant. The jury had just been treated to a perfect illustration of what happens when experts get all caught up on leaves and twigs, and no longer see a tree, let alone the forest. I have a six-year-old named David who would understand clearly that Mrs. Rosier was alive until Dr. Delman ended her life. How could Dr. Forney not concede that simple and undeniable fact? I think by this time he was very tired and rattled and certainly had had his full of me.

Great expert witnesses must possess both character and stamina. If they know the facts of the particular case and if they are truly expert in their field, and if they know when and what to concede they can never be shattered on cross examination, no matter how gifted the cross examiner may be. A great expert will convey to the jury brilliance, integrity, and a strong commitment to the justice of the cause on behalf of which he or she is giving testimony. A great expert must be a superb advocate while appearing to be objective.

I have seen a handful of excellent experts in my trial practice; I have yet to see a great one. I have known at least a hundred experts who thought they were great. But I have seen many ordinary, uneducated people come across as great witnesses because they possessed the natural qualities that enabled them to rise to a given occasion—and they weren't charging $400 an hour!

14

James Fitzpatrick: The Cop Who Taught Lawyers How to Testify

James Fitzpatrick, the primary investigator for the State of Florida on the Peter Rosier case, was very good at his job. He was an integral part of the prosecution team and sat at counsel table with Edward Volz and Stephen Russell throughout the trial. In addition, he was an important witness for the State. His overall competence and likability combined with the very professional straight-arrow approach of Volz and Russell made it difficult to attack the motives of the State.

Fitzpatrick had taught courses on courtroom demeanor and knew how to deflect tough questions through long experience, clever evasion, and studied Irish charm. Although only fifty he had served twenty-eight years with the Prince Georges County Police Department in Maryland just outside of Washington, D.C., and had retired as chief of detectives. We were amazed to learn how many retired cops made their way to southwest Florida. Fitzpatrick had a bachelor of science degree in police administration from American University in Washington, D.C., as well as a masters degree in forensic science from George Washington University, also in D.C. He was a graduate of the FBI National Academy in Quantico, Virginia.

As far as Fitzpatrick was concerned, the Peter Rosier case was a black-and-white situation. Patricia Rosier had been murdered and Peter Rosier was the murderer, that was that. Fitzpatrick considered Peter a very bad guy: arrogant, selfish, and manipulative.

According to Fitzpatrick, the granting of immunity is a necessary tool of law enforcement and Joseph D'Alessandro had no choice but to grant all three Delmans immunity. That was the only way in which Patricia

Rosier's killer could be brought to justice. Without the corroboration of the Delmans, Peter's confessions were worthless. Fitzpatrick did not care for the Delmans or what they did, but to achieve his goal (i.e., Rosier's conviction) he had to go through them.

To Fitzpatrick, Peter Rosier was the leader and orchestrator of all the events that caused his wife's death. This hard-nosed investigator was totally convinced that Peter knew of and was responsible for the final act of smothering, but was devious enough to distance himself from it by remaining outside the bedroom. He was just as convinced that Peter had shrewdly manipulated his wife into committing suicide by at first agreeing to a double suicide and then persuading her that she would die a horrible death.

The defense had been shocked to learn that Joseph D'Alessandro had granted all three Delmans total immunity on the telephone, without ever meeting them or their attorney. The proffer that Deveney gave Fitzpatrick in New York the following day was part of a meaningless charade since the Delmans already had their free ride from Fitzpatrick's boss. Deveney had D'Alessandro on tape granting the immunity to his clients.

In his proffer to Fitzpatrick, Deveney said that the Delmans would testify that they saw Peter inject Patricia with morphine and insert morphine suppositories. I had a few questions for Fitzpatrick on this point.

Q: During the taking of the Delmans' statements, when you learned of the suffocation, did you confront Deveney about him never mentioning that?

A: I explained to Mr. Deveney that his client had just exceeded the proffer that he had given to me. Mr. Deveney was shocked. He assured me that he had no knowledge of the suffocation. He indicated that he had never interviewed Russell or Vincent and had only spent a very short period of time with Farrell.

Q: Did you believe Deveney?

A: Absolutely. (*To say otherwise would have tarnished Fitzpatrick's professionalism.*)

Q: So, of what practical consequence was the misleading nature of the proffer?

A: None. The investigation would have ended had we not granted transactional immunity. We had two choices: drop the case or grant immunity. We had no other choice.

If the proffer had been a reasonable fact-finding exercise, Fitzpatrick should have pinned down the amount of time Deveney had spent with the Delmans. I was angry that Fitzpatrick continued to defend Deveney, since it was unthinkable that a lawyer in a first degree murder case gave a proffer to the State after spending "only a very short period of time" with only one of the three critical witnesses.

It was so damn frustrating not to be able to question Deveney, since now I was confident there would be conflicts not only between him and Farrell but between him and Fitzpatrick, too. If Deveney was doing his job, the only thing Deveney had to say to the Delmans was: "Tell me everything you know about the circumstances of Patricia Rosier's death from the time she took the Seconal until she died."

What was D'Alessandro's hurry to grant total immunity to all three Delmans without ever checking out the accuracy of the proffer? Fitzpatrick was so committed to the necessity of granting immunity, he agreed that would have been his recommendation even if the Delmans had used a gun on Pat. I wanted the jury to recognize that D'Alessandro had another choice, one that would have required some political courage.

I asked Fitzpatrick:

Q: . . . Joe D'Alessandro had the option to call a press conference and say to the public: "We got no case! Rosier's confession is not enough and I don't choose to give the Delmans
immunity. The criminal justice system is an imperfect system
and I'm not happy with this result, but that's the way it is.
End of case!"

A: Yes, he could have dropped the whole matter.

I was able to get Fitzpatrick to admit that he was not aware of any other case where the state attorney personally granted immunity. Was there too much pressure from the Fort Myers community? Did D'Alessandro intend to become personally involved in the prosecution of Dr. Rosier? Did he aspire to higher office? Showcase prosecutions can establish state-wide and national reputations. The most common background of United States senators and congressmen is that they were once prosecutors at the local level. Thomas Dewey gained the governorship of New York and twice received the Republican nomination for president as the result of his name recognition from being the chief prosecutor in Manhattan.

It would have been quite normal to explore whether or not the immunity decision was influenced by political ambition. As expected, Judge Thompson had made it clear early on that he would not allow me to delve into this area. I had my suspicions, but this was not the kind of thing that was provable with hard evidence.

I continued:

Q: When you first heard of the smothering, isn't it true that you were angry and thought that perhaps you had been conned by Deveney and/or the Delmans?

A: Oh, I was upset.

Q: That thought entered your mind?

A: Yes, that thought entered my mind.

Q: The granting of immunity can sometimes be a very dirty business, correct?

A: Yes, sir.

Q: But the way you look upon it as a law enforcement professional is that sometimes it's a necessary evil?

A: Yes sir.

Q: And that sometimes it is better to get half a loaf than no loaf?

A: That's correct.

Q: In this case, Rosier is the half a loaf?

A: That's correct.

Q: What percentage of armed robberies and burglaries go unsolved in Lee County?

A: I don't know in Lee County. I have no idea.

MR. RUSSELL: Your Honor, I object to the question. I don't see the relevance of it.

Fitzpatrick's answer surprised me; he certainly should have been ready for that question. He knew exactly where I was headed. Throughout America the majority of such crimes do not result in punishment, and with that pitiful situation staring law enforcement in the face how dare they mount this massive assault on a person who represents no threat to society?

Of course Russell's objection was sustained. Whenever I tried to be creative and attack the criminal justice system or raise the specter of prosecutorial misconduct Judge Thompson would magically become a strict constructionist on admissible evidence. Yet from jury selection onward Susan and I had tried to condition the jurors to glean from even indirect hints the themes we were pursuing. I think the jurors took a certain pride in figuring this out for themselves.

I pursued this line of inquiry:

Q: Do you think Dr. Rosier is a threat to the citizens of Lee County?

A: I think any individual that commits a felony should be held accountable for the act. (*The reality is that relatively few are.*)

Q: That's not what I asked you. That makes about the twentieth time you've ignored my question and answered a question you wished I had asked.

A: Yes. I do think he should be held accountable for his act, yes. (*I whispered to Susan, "I guess the secret of good courtroom demeanor is to be unresponsive while appearing to be responsive."*)

Q: Mr. Fitzpatrick, I asked you whether you felt that Dr. Rosier, who obviously had never committed any crime prior to these charges, whether you honestly believe that if he is acquitted that he would be a threat to the citizens of Lee County or to anybody.

MR. RUSSELL: Objection. (*Actually Fitzpatrick's evasiveness played into our hands because I was able to flesh out the point.*)

THE COURT: Sustain the objection. Disregard the question.

Ah, yes, one of the great myths of the law business: telling the jury, in effect, that they never heard or are not to consider something that they clearly did hear. Days or weeks later, when the jurors are deliberating their verdict, how can they be expected to forget those statements they allegedly didn't hear? Only lawyers and, I suppose, professional expert witnesses believe it's possible to unring a bell.

Most people have the gut feeling that it just isn't right for those who have participated in a crime to go free. There was a situation recently in Miami where a defendant pled guilty to a serious crime and agreed to testify against his codefendants. The plea bargainer received a sentence of only ten years (a light sentence in the context of the crime committed). As it turned out the other culprits went to trial and were acquitted by a jury. The conclusion was that the cooperative guy ends up in prison and the defendants who spit at the State went free. This is but one of many examples of the crap-shoot nature of the American criminal justice system.

The State requested and obtained from Judge Thompson this instruction to the jury:

THE COURT: The general rule of evidence in all criminal cases provides that no confession or admission is sufficient by itself in a criminal case. There must be independent proof of the *corpus delicti* of the crime or the body of the crime. That's a general rule applicable to all criminal cases in the State of Florida.

With this instruction Fitzpatrick, Volz, and Russell could look over at the jury and say in effect: "See, I told you, we simply had no choice." The State was so committed to getting Peter that there was one possibility they never even considered.

Q: Had you known about the smothering, you could have gone to Rosier, granted him immunity, and had him testify against the Delmans. That could have been done?

A: Well, that's an alternative that didn't come up.

Q: But it could have come up?

A: I have maintained from the beginning that I felt that Dr. Rosier was the most culpable individual and that's why I wouldn't grant him immunity.

Q: Well that's not your decision. You are one of what, over one hundred employees in D'Alessandro's office?

A: All immunity comes from the State Attorney.

Q: A policy decision was made at the highest level that this guy (*I walked over to Peter and pointed my index finger at his bowed head.*) embarrassed us by going on television and opening his big mouth, and we're going to get the SOB. Isn't that correct?

MR. RUSSELL: Your Honor, I object to the characterization. That may be Mr. Rosenblatt's opinion.

THE COURT: I'll sustain the objection.

Q: What did the Delmans think would happen to them if they lost their immunity, if they lied?

A: That they would be prosecuted for murder.

Q: You knew that belief was false?

A: Yes, I knew that not to be the case.

Q: What could they have been prosecuted for if they lost their immunity?

A: Perjury.

Q: Did you ever tell them the truth about their mistaken belief?

A: No. It was to my advantage not to. Their attorney evidently told them this. I just didn't argue with it. I said fine, that's exactly the way it is. I agreed with them.

Did this constitute prosecutorial misconduct? Certainly not in a formal sense. Is it okay to lie to witnesses even though your motives may be lofty? Does the end justify the means?

I was doing what I could to smudge the Dick Tracy image of D'Alessandro's warriors. Selective rectitude should be viewed with suspicion. I was also employing this tactic because the State's holier-than-thou approach infuriated me. And I was certainly doing it to get even for the Jules Cantor bathroom incident and five hundred other cheap shots fired in our direction. It also served as a means of diverting attention away from Peter.

Q: And just as you used that tactic with the Delmans, you used a similar tactic with Dr. Dosoretz and his lawyer. After Dr. Dosoretz gave his first statement you went out and told his lawyer that his client committed perjury and you could prove it. Didn't you say that?

A: Yes, sir.

Q: You are well aware that when someone like you, clothed with the authority of the State Attorney's Office, says that to a lawyer in civil practice about a very successful doctor in the community, that would scare any person out of their wits, wouldn't it?

A: I'm sure he was concerned about it when I said it, yes sir.

Q: And just like all the other doctors in this case, you didn't charge him with perjury, correct?

A: That is correct. (*Dosoretz, in his original statement, denied having an argument with Peter on the morning of January 15 about morphine or anything else. After Fitzpatrick threatened him with perjury his memory was restored.*)

Q: That is not an infrequent tactic of the State Attorney's Office of Lee County—threatening someone?

A: Threatening what, in relationship to someone we feel or I know is not telling the truth?

Q: Exactly.

A: Oh, I've done that many times.

Q: Good tactic?

A: Sure.

Q: A good investigator must be somewhat of a con man; you have to gain the confidence and cooperation of a total stranger and you must accomplish this within a brief time frame. You have to do a lot of pretending?

A: I have never conducted an interview in my life where I didn't lead an individual to believe I possess more knowledge than I do.

Fitzpatrick was both charming and disarming. He could talk about lying to a State's witness or scaring the hell out of a prominent doctor and make it all sound totally justified, even civic minded. I would ask him a tough question, he would pause, smile at the jury ever so sweetly, and give me an unresponsive answer. We wanted the jury to understand that Fitzpatrick was a consummate professional, both in terms of preparing the State's witnesses and on how to present himself for maximum believability.

I knew Fitzpatrick had taught a course to police officers and lawyers regarding courtroom demeanor and how to be as believable as possible. After all, he had a masters degree in forensic science, whatever the hell that is supposed to mean. In bantering with me Fitzpatrick said it was the kind of course most lawyers take (he's correct) and he assumed I had taken one. I had not and I said so.

Q: No, I never took one of those courses. I have my own style and I never wanted to become contaminated by even unconsciously imitating someone else. But you've taught those courses?

A: Yes—how to present yourself in Court. . . .

Q: Shoes shined?

A: Absolutely.

Q: Hair combed, tie in place, neat—the whole bit?

A: Absolutely.

Q: Don't look like a slob?

A: That's correct.

Q: Don't use language like slob but use more formal and dignified terms—that's what courtroom demeanor is?

A: Sure. (*I whispered to Susan, "In other words, the art of being a phony."*)

Q: And no matter how tough the defense attorney is, just smile and be cool, as you have been doing all day with me?

A: That's my style counselor, I'm sorry.

Q: That is part of good courtroom demeanor isn't it, because it's disarming?

A: If I am smiling and I do smile, I'm sorry about that if it offends you.

Q: It doesn't offend me at all. It worries me a little bit, because it may be effective. I'm asking you, is it not part of any good course on courtroom demeanor to tell a witness that if you're being attacked on cross, you should be cool and not get excited, correct?

A: Yes, sir.

The Rosiers in their garden after Patricia is diagnosed with lung cancer.

Prior to the murder indictment, Peter Rosier confesses to assisting in his wife's death.

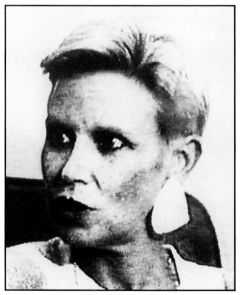

Patricia discussing her struggle with cancer.

Peter's daughter, Elizabeth (left), Gertrude Ahlbrecht (center), and his son, Jacob (right), during the trial.

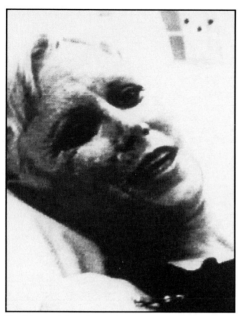

Patricia receiving chemotherapy.

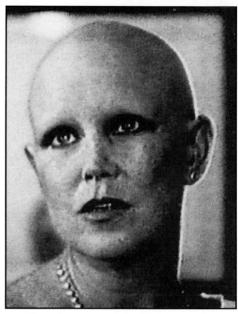

Patricia during her final interview the day before she died.

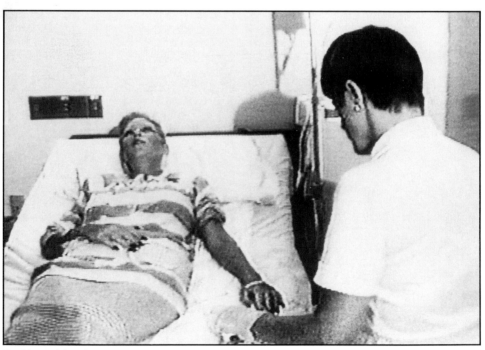

Patricia receiving chemotherapy.

Joseph D'Alessandro, State Attorney

James R. Thompson, the presiding judge

Stanley M. Rosenblatt, Peter Rosier's attorney

Assistant state attorneys Edward Volz (left) and Stephen Russell field questions from the press.

Patricia's father, Vincent Delman

James Fitzpatrick, investigator for the Lee County State Attorney's Office

Patricia's brother Farrell Delman

Mary Rose Linden, Peter Rosier's secretary

Patricia's brother Russell Delman

Jules Cantor, Peter's friend

Dr. Daniel Dosoretz fields questions about the morphine

Television reporter Leisa Zigman

Carl Sousa, the insurance salesman

Dr. Wallace Graves, Jr., the medical examiner

Dr. Robert B. Forney, Jr., the expert witness

1.

2.

1. Stanley M. Rosenblatt examining a witness.

2. State attorneys Volz and Russell at counsel table as the jury hears testimony.

3&4. Stanley M. Rosenblatt delivering his closing argument as the jurors listen intently.

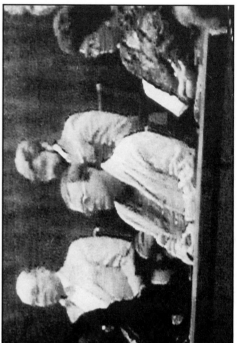

4.

3.

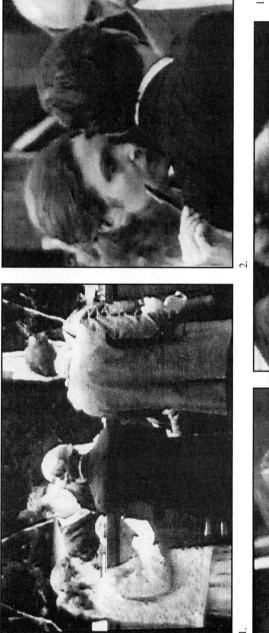

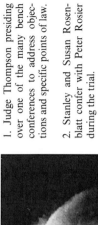

1. Judge Thompson presiding over one of the many bench conferences to address objections and specific points of law.

2. Stanley and Susan Rosenblatt confer with Peter Rosier during the trial.

3. Peter Rosier loses his composure during testimony.

4. Derek Humphry, former president of The Hemlock Society, confers with a fellow spectator during the trial.

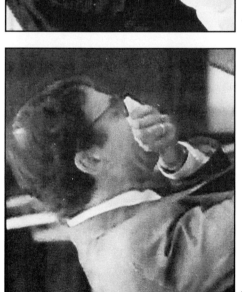

Peter Rosier and Stanley M. Rosenblatt stroll outside the courthouse during a brief recess.

The front page of the Fort Myers *News Press* announces that Peter Rosier's fate is now in the jury's hands.

Through Fitzpatrick I could establish that I was not the belligerent menace that Drs. Carlino and Harwin had tried to present. I fully expected Fitzpatrick to be truthful about the relationship we had developed during months of pretrial preparation.

> Q: Isn't it true that unlike Dr. Carlino, who said he doesn't like me, and unlike Dr. Harwin, who acts as though there is something fundamentally wrong with my personality, you and I have always had a cordial relationship—haven't we?
>
> A: Yes, sir, we have.
>
> Q: There have never been any nasty words exchanged between you and I, correct?
>
> A: Yes, sir.
>
> Q: To this day we have the kind of relationship where when we see each other out in the courtroom corridor during a recess, we are cordial to each other and capable of having a normal conversation, correct?
>
> A: Absolutely.

I wanted the jury to remember that Fitzpatrick was a representative of the great state of Florida and that I was merely a private attorney. As Peter was an underdog, so was I. I made the point that doctors as well as other witnesses had to play by the State's rules. Fitzpatrick acknowledged this but foolishly added something.

> A: And it's the same for defense witnesses. You have the same options, counselor.
>
> Q: Mr. Fitzpatrick, don't insult my intelligence please. You represent the State of Florida and you can put people in prison. How do you equate your power with my power in terms of forcing witnesses to be cooperative?
>
> A: You certainly have the right to bring the witnesses to the trial when you want them to testify as a defense attorney representing a client. You have that power, as we do.
>
> Q: Look, you have the power of subpoena. A witness could hate your guts, yet a witness does not have the option of refusing to talk to you privately, unless they are willing to go to jail for that refusal.
>
> A: Well, that's right.
>
> Q: Look at all the great power I had over Carlino and Harwin and Cantor: to this day they have never spoken to me privately.

Another small difference between my power and the State's power is that you had the authority to give the Delmans immunity and I didn't, right?

A: No, you do not.

Q: Every witness the State has had who has been on the stand at a lunch break, that witness was always kept with you people down in room 306? You never let that witness out of your sight. Isn't that right?

A: They were free to go to lunch. They chose to eat their lunch in that room.

Q: One hell of a coincidence, or maybe they just enjoyed your company so much. (*About half of the jurors were giggling; I withdrew the nonquestion before an objection could be verbalized and before the inevitable. Objection sustained.*)

I returned briefly to the theme of the utter absurdity of pouring tax dollars into this private tragedy.

Q: You and Mr. Russell and Mr. Volz and Mr. Sorenson (*another full-time State investigator*) have thousands of hours in this case, don't you—a few thousand hours, don't you?

A: It's a lengthy investigation, absolutely.

Q: [A] lengthy, complicated investigation where all of you have put in thousands of hours collectively, correct?

A: I'd say yes.

Fitzpatrick was called by the State in large part to demonstrate the purity of the State's actions and to justify the granting of immunity to the Delmans. When Susan and I would be outraged over some of the State's actions, such as repeatedly subpoenaing Peter's young secretary to give statement after statement, they wanted the jury to believe that they were simply functioning in a business-as-usual mode. They were professionals and it was I who was making this thing personal. To them Peter Rosier was just another criminal defendant. This was total crap; they were out to get Peter.

Situations like this always become personal and it is ludicrous to pretend there are clean lines of demarcation between that which is professional and that which is personal. If you (lawyer or judge) dump on me today, don't expect me to blot out the memory tomorrow. Everything is interrelated. Even gangsters get caught up in this lawyer mythology: as Michael Corleone set out to murder his enemies in *The God-*

father, he went to some pains to explain that it was all "business," not personal.

Poor, inexperienced Stanley Rosenblatt just didn't understand how the State operated (in murder cases). What was I getting so excited about? After all, they were just doing their job, according to Fitzpatrick. Whenever a lawyer says that to me—and many often do to try and justify petty, bureaucratic, and vicious conduct—I usually respond by saying that's what Adolf Eichmann said. This is just another one of my many devices to win friends and influence people.

Stephen Russell asked Fitzpatrick:

Q: Has Mr. Rosenblatt, to your knowledge, ever been a criminal defense attorney in a homicide case other than this one?
A: Not to my knowledge.

I responded on cross examination:

[MR. ROSENBLATT]: Since you have no knowledge of my ever representing a defendant in a murder case, you must therefore conclude that I, unlike Dr. Forney, am not a hired gun but rather that I am here representing Dr. Rosier because I believe that it is wrong for him to be prosecuted. (*Russell's objection was of course sustained.*)
Q: You are well aware from our discussions that I would never represent a drunk driver who killed someone? (*We all knew there was a juror who had a loved one killed by a drunk driver.*)
A: No. I don't think we have ever discussed it. I know again of your reputation.
Q: Well, based upon what you know about me and my law practice, do you think I would ever represent a drunk driver who killed someone?
A: I don't know, sir.
Q: Well I wouldn't, and I've never done it. (*This was absolutely true and likewise it was absolutely irrelevant. But that applied to about 75 percent of the trial.*)

What compromises nearly all lawyers is an adage of the profession, which says: "Clients come and go, relationships with lawyers and judges endure. The system goes on and you must work all your professional life with the same lawyers and judges. Therefore, don't burn any bridges;

don't make enemies just to win a case. Your opponent today may very well be a judge tomorrow. If you want to settle civil cases and plea bargain successfully in criminal cases, you've got to play the game. You must be part of the network of deals, posturing, and counterfeit camaraderie."

It infuriated D'Alessandro's soldiers that I could be independent of this network. I was a civil trial specialist; I disliked Fort Myers and had no intention of ever trying a criminal case there irrespective of whether we won or lost the Rosier trial. My sole objective was to gain an acquittal for Peter.

Was I ego-involved? Of course. If we lost then every half-baked, armchair, Monday-morning so-called lawyer quarterback, knowing about 2 percent of the total facts, would take pleasure in blaming me. The rap would be that I was on an extended ego trip; my confrontational, aggressive style was a turnoff to the laid-back St. Petersburg jury; my lack of understanding of the intricacies of the criminal law game, etc., etc.—all combined to doom my client.

Not only did I have zero illusions about my colleagues, I had no illusions about Peter. If we lost, Peter would hook up with any one of dozens of lawyers who would crawl out of the woodwork to proclaim incompetence of counsel or any other battle cry hoping to obtain a new trial and an appearance on some network talk show. Susan and I knew that Peter would play any angle in looking out for number one.

The truth is I found the legal, medical, ethical, and psychological (family) issues to be fascinating. I always felt my dramatic, emotional style was best suited to the criminal arena but I never wanted to represent actual criminals. What satisfaction could I derive from getting some low-life off who was a threat to others?

The great tragic playwright Eugene O'Neill just knew he could write a superb comedy and he did, *Ah! Wilderness*. I always believed I could try successfully a great first degree murder case. If we lost, that mistaken belief would be shoved down my throat.

Peter was getting 150 percent from Susan and me, and if that turned out not to be good enough, we would simply have to weather the storm.

15

Mary Rose Linden: A True-Blue Secretary

Aside from Gertrude Ahlbrecht, there was another Fort Myers resident who still had a very high opinion of Peter Rosier: his secretary, Mary Rose Linden. The State knew perfectly well that Mary Rose remained loyal to Peter, thought the Rosiers had a wonderful marriage, and was very hostile to the prosecution. Yet they felt they needed her as a witness because, on a purely factual basis, she could confirm some of the State's theories.

For example, it was Mary Rose who picked up the morphine suppositories on the day of Patricia's death and delivered them to Peter. The State believed it could introduce through her testimony the fact that Peter was a heavy dater, both during his separation from Patricia years earlier and in the period following her death. The debate over the admissibility of this evidence led to one of the angriest and longest bench conferences of the entire trial.

Through the secretary's testimony we would be doing the bad-guy, good-guy routine again. Was this any way to run a murder trial? Susan and I didn't think so. This absurd process was taking its toll on us; it was becoming more and more difficult for me to contain my fury. One hopeful fact remained: the State was just about finished and soon it would be our turn.

While still in high school, Mary Rose had first been hired by Patricia to stuff envelopes and do other mundane things. She worked for Peter from October 1980 until September 1, 1985, when Peter sold his practice. Mary Rose continued working for the doctor who bought the practice. But on the very day that Patricia died, Peter asked Mary Rose to come back to work for him. Yet another example of Peter's incredible insensitivity.

Mary Rose felt obliged to give the new owner of Laboratory Medicine Associates two weeks notice, so she actually returned to work full-time for Peter on January 27, 1986. The State would make much of Peter rehiring Mary Rose so quickly. In spite of his supposed inconsolable grief, according to the State, Peter's devious mind was clicking away as always in his own self-interest. The State contended that Peter was writing feverishly during the last weeks of Pat's life and he needed someone he could trust to begin typing what he hoped would become a best seller. One of the State's thrusts was that Peter was captivated by the image of being a successful author and yearned to say goodbye forever to the boring world of autopsies, morgues, and tissue specimens. Dr. Peter Rosier had found a unique way to resolve his midlife crisis, according to the prosecution.

Mary Rose was my kind of girl because she truly disliked Edward Volz, Stephen Russell, and James Fitzpatrick. They were unable either to charm her or to intimidate her. I appreciate witnesses who have no difficulty distinguishing between friends and enemies in a lawsuit, and most particularly in a criminal case where everything is on the line. I can't tolerate witnesses who want to be liked by their adversaries; that is wishful thinking in any event because lawyers never like a witness who hurts their position or whom they can't control.

When Peter telephoned Mary Rose on January 15 to offer her a job, he also asked her to go to the Star Pharmacy to pick up the morphine suppositories that had been prescribed by Dr. Harwin. Mary Rose testified that she handed the suppositories to Peter in his driveway; she was positive she did not enter the home. One of the Delmans had testified that she transferred the suppositories to Peter in the kitchen. A trivial conflict perhaps, but a trial lawyer seldom knows whether conflict number three or number eighteen will have the greatest impact on certain jurors, or when a collection of minor conflicts will assume some major significance.

Dr. Harwin admitted prescribing morphine suppositories on January 15. Russell and Farrell Delman were eyewitnesses to Peter inserting them. The State produced the pharmacist who filled the prescription. Was Mary Rose's testimony on this subject even necessary? I thought not.

Susan and I became livid when Stephen Russell fired out this question, particularly because it came from out of the blue:

Q: Were you aware they [Peter and Patricia] were separated for a period of time?

MRS. ROSENBLATT: We object. Your Honor, we move for a mistrial. You have already ruled that if the State thought it was going to bring up that topic he should have advised all of us as he had promised he would do and come to the bench privately, as we are doing now, rather than blurting out that prejudicial question in front of the jury. It puts us at a tremendous disadvantage because your psyche is going to be: "Well, if I sustain the objection then I have to entertain a motion for mistrial," which we all know you are not interested in doing. So now you're going to lean in their direction because of the fact that the jury has already heard it.

MR. ROSENBLATT: He should be held in contempt for that. That is real substantive misconduct. At every bench conference there was a clear understanding that before the subject of any separation was mentioned, we would approach the bench first. Your rulings have been consistent that unless the State could show you something specific on how that would be relevant, that subject would not be coming in. So Mr. Russell, in a very devious way, will argue to you falsely that we opened the door. Well, we haven't opened any damn door. What he has done is egregious, and we move for a mistrial very strongly.

MR. RUSSELL: Judge, I said I would not go into the affair without approaching the bench first. They never moved in limine* about the separation. The Court cannot continue to protect them to let the defense paint Rosier as a person who is totally dedicated every day of his life to his wife.

MRS. ROSENBLATT: Your Honor, this man is being charged with first degree murder. This is incredibly prejudicial and it has zero probative value. The State has talked about absurd and irrelevant things such as Peter smoking marijuana, perhaps engaging in phony estate planning, how he felt about Leisa Zigman, etc. . . . It has truly reached the point where it is beyond the pale; this is totally improper and it has hurt us with the jury, which is just what he intended to accomplish, and we move for a mistrial.

THE COURT: All right, I understand everybody's position on this thing. I think the lawyers have got to have a great deal of latitude. I'm not happy that you brought that up without bringing it to me privately, but I think that's just trying to shave a frog's hair, in making that distinction. I think at this point I'm going to go ahead and allow it.

MR. RUSSELL: I want to ask her: Was he depressed? Was he

---

*A motion in limine is a pretrial motion to prohibit the mentioning of certain matters.

crying all the time? My point is, I want to ask her about her awareness that he was dating during that period of time.

MR. ROSENBLATT: This is just unbelievable. The issue in this murder trial has become: Was Peter Rosier a swinger? And to make the whole subject even more ludicrous, the question is: Was he a swinger when he was separated years before his wife became ill? Judge, in the words of Dr. Delman, enough is enough.

MRS. ROSENBLATT: Could you excuse the jury, Judge? This is going to be a lengthy argument. (*The judge complies.*) This man is being tried for murder; he's not being tried for dating after his wife's death, and he's not being tried for not being husband of the year. This is very critical, Your Honor. I don't want this to be done haphazardly at a side-bar conference simply because the prosecution blurted something out about the separation. As I have repeatedly pointed out there is a weighing test that every U.S. Supreme Court case talks about. You've got to weigh the probative value of evidence versus the prejudice that evidence creates, and if the probative value is nonexistent or minuscule, it is truly outrageous to allow in inflammatory evidence.

THE COURT: The problem is, at least in part, that the jury shouldn't acquit him because he was a loving, devoted husband. That would be legally irrelevant as to whether he's done this crime. And of course they shouldn't convict him because he might not be. But we've gotten one aspect already injected into it.

MRS. ROSENBLATT: If Stanley has gotten into it at all, it has been only through cross examination, where we have the broadest kind of latitude. It's not as though we have put on a witness to affirmatively say that Peter was a marvelous husband.

MR. RUSSELL: I do intend to go into the fact that he dated a number of women between the time of his wife's death and the television interview he gave. This is very relevant. This is an issue that's central to the case. . . . It would rebut what they have been trying to paint, and that is that all he did was grieve and mourn.

MRS. ROSENBLATT: There isn't a single witness in this case who will state under oath that Peter did not love his wife and was not depressed and did not grieve over her death. They couldn't find a single person in all of Fort Myers to say that this man didn't care about Pat, that he didn't love her and that he couldn't wait until she died because he wanted to chase around. . . . The State went to the woman he had an affair with five or six years before and even she substantiated that fact. Even back then while talking to another woman he would be constantly talking about his great love for Pat. Strange behavior, sure, but what does it have to do with anything?

MR. ROSENBLATT: I said in my opening statement that this was not a perfect marriage and that's been our position all along. The State wants to give the jury the erroneous and irrelevant impression that Rosier always had girlfriends on the side.

THE COURT: It's a close question but I think all that is certainly a feature of this thing, and I don't see any way you can keep that out, although technically from a strictly legalistic point of view, it's probably not relevant, whether he was loving and devoted or whether he wasn't. You know I've got to do some balancing. It's a close question. I'm going to allow the evidence in.

MR. ROSENBLATT: (*To Stephen Russell and Edward Volz, but within the judge's hearing*) Okay, you got your way on this but let me tell you right now that if you blurt out anything about an affair, I guarantee you there's going to be a mistrial. I'm telling you guys, there is going to be a mistrial, because I'm going to carry on like a lunatic.

MR. RUSSELL: You have already done that.

MR. ROSENBLATT: No, you haven't seen anything yet. You may have seen what you thought was a Fort Myers or St. Petersburg lunatic, but I'm going to give you a New York/Miami lunatic the likes of which you've never seen.

Russell, Volz, and Fitzpatrick knew me well enough by now to believe me. They knew I was not aiming for the most courteous lawyer award or for the Mr. Congeniality prize. I was determined not to allow the prosecution to pull stunts that could result in my client's conviction.

If I did indeed carry on like a lunatic, the judge had the power to punish me in a variety of ways, including jail for contempt of court. But I held the ultimate card and the prosecutors fully understood that: I could say and do things in the presence of the jury that would mandate a mistrial be declared. Because of the time and great expense involved, that would have been a disaster for D'Alessandro's office and for the Fort Myers court system as well. It would have been a disaster for us, too; the idea of starting from scratch before a different jury was unthinkable. My other

clients and commitments had been on hold far too long already. Peter
wanted to get on with his life.

> MR. RUSSELL: Mrs. Linden, did you know that the defendant
> and his wife had a period of separation after you commenced
> employment with them in the early 1980s?
> A: I'm aware through office gossip that there was a separation.
> I don't know exactly when it was.
> Q: Were you aware that the defendant moved out of the marital
> residence and lived somewhere else for a period of time?
> A: Again, through office gossip. (*"Nothing like solid evidence on
> a totally collateral matter,"* I whispered to Susan. *Mary Rose
> knew nothing firsthand.*)
> Q: Now during the several-month period after Pat Rosier's death,
> were you aware the defendant had dated several women?
> A: I am aware that he's dated people. I don't know when.

I was furiously making entries in my final argument notebook. I was
going to pull out all the stops in asserting that if the State had a real
case they would not be wasting their time on such utter crap. I was even
weighing whether I would ridicule the judge for allowing this kind of evidence
to become the focus of the trial. This was soap opera garbage designed
to titillate, not inform.

I made it very clear through Mary Rose that the separation had occurred
years earlier and that the Rosiers were inseparable during the nine months
of Patricia's illness. The State had any number of other subjects to cover
in its relentless desire to denigrate Dr. Rosier.

Peter's submission letter sent to numerous agents and publishers (typed
by Mary Rose) was allowed in evidence over our objections. Stephen Russell
exulted in letting the jury know that all Peter received for his literary
efforts was one rejection after another.

Peter flew to Hollywood to hook up with a screenwriter, and after
much mutual hyping they convinced each other that Peter's undying love
for Patricia and the poignant circumstances of her death would make
a great movie. Peter paid the screenwriter $40,000 and a script was actually
completed; like the manuscript, it went nowhere. How would the jury
react to this irrelevant testimony?

The repeated point of the prosecution was that all this greatly depressed
Peter and motivated him to give Leisa Zigman an interview in the hope
of creating great national interest and controversy about his manuscript.
Peter didn't give a damn about the many compelling ethical and medical

issues embedded in the topic of euthanasia; as always (from the State's perspective) he was interested only in self-aggrandizement. Peter was acutely aware that until then no physician had ever publicly admitted assisting someone to end their life, let alone the physician's own wife. He believed that "60 Minutes," "20/20," and "The Today Show" would have their tongues hanging out, according to the State.

So naturally Leisa Zigman became a topic for Mary Rose Linden. Now we would revisit the burning issue of whether Peter was infatuated with this small-town reporter. Did Peter Rosier have the hots for Leisa Zigman? It was really great to be back in the seventh grade.

MR. RUSSELL: Were you aware that Dr. Rosier was infatuated with Leisa Zigman around the time of the interview? (*That is the kind of improper question which is a favorite of mine. What's good for the goose is good for the gander, I suppose.*)

A: No, I wasn't.

MRS. ROSENBLATT: (*After rushing to the bench for a side-bar conference*) That was a totally improper question: Was she aware of it? He states it as though it were a fact. There is not a shred of evidence that our client was infatuated with this woman.

MR. RUSSELL: Judge, that's the exact words in the statement of Jules Cantor, and there will be lots of shreds of evidence. This is an issue as to why he went on television, so that he could greatly enhance Leisa's standing among other things. . . .

THE COURT: I agree, the question was objectionable although the testimony of Cantor raised this. The defense has certainly assumed a lot of facts not in evidence.

MR. RUSSELL: Like every question.

THE COURT: I would require you to rephrase the question. I'm going to let the subject matter in evidence.

Q: Did you have a perception about how he felt about Leisa at that time?

A: I know he really trusted her and thought she was different from other reporters and he felt that she was a caring person, but he learned that was all a delusion.

Beautiful answer! From Mary Rose's perception Zigman was far more interested in manipulating Peter for her own selfish purposes than vice versa. Of course, Mary Rose maintained her excellent relationship with the Rosier family, and I had the opportunity to prepare her both for my questions and the State's. I asked Mary Rose:

Q: Mary Rose, as far as you know, why did Dr. Rosier agree to be interviewed on television by Leisa Zigman?

A: His intent was to try to do something about mercy killing and that was the essence of the interview. But the book being published was not the reason for him giving an interview. I mean if he wanted to do that he would have taken it directly to national television. (*She just took the words out of my mouth.*)

Q: Isn't it true that in terms of your discussions with Leisa Zigman, that she was very anxious to interview Dr. Rosier?

A: Yes.

Q: Was she pursuing him and bugging you and doing everything within her power to arrange for these interviews?

A: You know she kept calling and calling and calling. So at that point you know, I didn't know if she was so much interested in a story as she was interested in him.

Q: You mean you thought there was a personal interest on her part in Dr. Rosier as a man?

A: That's basically how I felt, yes.

Q: At any time, either before or after the Leisa Zigman interview, had Dr. Rosier ever asked you to arrange for a press conference or publicity about the book in any way, shape, or form?

A: No, he did not.

Q: Did Dr. Rosier ever ask you to write or call programs like "The Today Show" or "60 Minutes"?

A: No.

Q: When the interview was actually aired on Channel 20 and excerpts from the book were shown on the screen, did Dr. Rosier know in advance that [that] was going to be done?

A: No, he did not.

Q: Was he upset about it?

A: Yes, he was.

Q: What did he say?

A: He said that he was very upset and that Zigman had no right to use it, and that was not the purpose of the interview.

Q: What was the purpose of the interview?

A: To discuss euthanasia.

Q: When Leisa Zigman called after the first interview, [which] was never aired, and asked you about Dr. Rosier's mental state, did you tell her that he was crying all the time and that he was under the care of a psychiatrist and that he seemed emotionally unstable. Did you mention all that to her?

A: That's to the best of my knowledge.

Q: But that didn't stop her from going ahead with the second interview, the one that was actually shown to the public. Is that correct?

A: No. It didn't stop her.

Q: Did Leisa Zigman tell you that her news director thought Dr. Rosier appeared unstable in that first interview and that was the reason it wasn't aired?

A: No.

The State set up a conflict between Mrs. Linden and Carl Sousa on the issue of whether Peter was working as a pathologist during his wife's struggle with cancer. This related to the State's contention that Peter was improperly collecting huge increased disability benefits. On this point Mary Rose hurt us considerably because she backed up the prosecution.

MR. RUSSELL: Now within a month or two before the time he sold the business, all I am trying to do is get a general idea of the nature of the activities Dr. Rosier was engaged in when he was working.

A: He didn't work any more. The only time when I would see him is when he would come into the office to tell me who to send Pat's slide specimens to. That's all he dealt with once Pat became ill; he was trying to find out what her tumor was in the hope of getting her cured.

Q: My understanding was that after April of 1985 he no longer worked in terms of his surgical pathology practice. Is that correct? (*This is known in the trade as a set-up question since Russell knew that Sousa had testified otherwise and he knew from Mary Rose's statements that she would contradict Sousa.*)

A: That's right.

Q: Why was that?

A: Because he couldn't. He couldn't work; his wife was very ill and all he could do was cry. (*According to this testimony Peter was disabled when he applied for substantially increased disability benefits.*)

The jury was advised that in September 1985 Peter applied to increase his disability benefits from $7,800 a month to $15,000 per month. Peter started collecting the monthly $15,000 payment two days after his wife's death. I knew this ate away at the prosecutors because they were convinced that Peter was no more disabled than they were.

Yes, it was personal. They could not comprehend how a sophisticated, multimillion-dollar insurance company could pay benefits. Volz and Russell argued that it was wrong for a disabled person to hide his disability and apply for increased benefits. Carl Sousa had testified that he saw Peter functioning as a pathologist in September 1985 and later as well. This issue worried the hell out of us because Susan and I did not underestimate the potential for juror resentment and jealousy. The irony was that this evidence should not have been admitted by Judge Thompson.

I believed that Peter was disabled from examining tissue slides under a microscope, and I didn't think he could sell that to the jury. Peter's disability carrier accepted his disability but the State sought to try this nonissue to enrage the jury. This issue, like so many others, had nothing to do with the criminal charges, but it could have a great deal to do with whether the jury voted to convict or not. I tried to reconcile the conflict between Sousa and Linden by asking this question:

Q: In order for Dr. Rosier to send out Patricia's slides and in order for him to communicate intelligently with these various specialists all over the country, he had to prepare the slides and he had to analyze them under a microscope. Is that correct?
A: Yes he did.
Q: You recall from the correspondence with these cancer specialists at places like Yale, Johns Hopkins, and Sloan Kettering that Mrs. Rosier's lung tumor was very rare, and even they had great difficulty figuring out precisely the type of tumor it was?
A: Yes.

These answers would enable me to argue that what Sousa thought was Peter working, was in fact Peter dealing with his single and exclusive patient. This issue, along with several others, was put in a special category of my final argument notebook with the title: "Problems that need to be discussed and resolved with Susan."

To these seasoned prosecutors, Peter always delegated unpleasant tasks. He had no guts and, although he talked tough, he was Jell-o when it came to direct personal confrontations. As but one of a host of examples, he had Mary Rose call Vincent Delman to return the cigarette lighter that his daughter had given him. Mary Rose thought she was helping Peter in describing his reasoning behind this directive, but it actually constituted further documentation of Peter's pettiness. Peter was upset with Vincent because neither he nor his sons had bothered to acknowledge Jacob's birthday.

Peter had Mary Rose call the Delmans when all hell broke loose after his confession was aired on television. Amazingly, she never spoke directly to Farrell or Russell, but left messages with one of their wives and on the answering machine of another (she wasn't sure which). The message, guaranteed to create both panic and suspicion, was that Peter gave an interview on television and his criminal lawyer said they should seek counsel.

In addition to genuinely liking the Rosiers, Mary Rose had good reason to be very angry at the treatment she received at the hands of the State. The prosecution simply overdid it with her, requiring her to submit on four separate occasions to giving them private statements. She was subpoenaed for each one.

I knew the State's plan. Set up a load of nit-picking conflicts between the various statements so that her credibility would be damaged and her loyalty used as a weapon against her. There will always be some inconsistencies when a person is asked to describe the same events on different occasions. That is simply how the human mind functions; a detail will be omitted or added, the sequence of events will change.

I used to say to Fitzpatrick: "You guys are confusing Mary Rose with Nixon's secretary, Rosemary Woods. Mary Rose is loyal, but she ain't that loyal." Ms. Woods became famous, fairly or unfairly, for a missing eighteen minutes on a critical Watergate tape (the infamous "gap").

My instructions to Mary Rose would be condemned by the great majority of trial lawyers. I told her not to reread her statements, not to study them in any way, and to be very forthright with the jury about her refusal to do so. I told Mary Rose that if I were her I would tell the jury that I was sick and tired of being subpoenaed, sick of spending hours at the State Attorney's Office, and sick of studying the earlier statements each time I was called upon to give a new one. I told her to tell the truth to the best of her ability and to forget about her statements.

For this failure Steve Russell lectured Mary Rose as a teacher would lecture a student for ignoring a homework assignment. How could she not refresh her memory so that she would be in the best position to give accurate answers?

> A: I think it probably would have confused me, so that's really the reason why I didn't read the statements, you know. I didn't want to go over them because I'd be caught between what

I was remembering simply because it was in my memory, or
what I was trying to remember from an earlier statement.

There is a good deal of logic to that answer. I pointed out that, in
addition to the four statements, there were two other occasions when Mary
Rose was required to meet with Volz, Russell, and Fitzpatrick. These
interrogations took place during the trial itself, on two separate evenings;
Susan and I insisted on being present but we were not permitted to say
anything.

I called them shake-up meetings. The prosecution team of four (Investigator Sorenson included) had spread out in front of them on a long table,
reminiscent of a U.S. Senate confirmation hearing, all of Mary Rose's previous
statements. They were reminding her of what she said, with the strong
implication being that she would be in big trouble if she changed her story
at all. From a trial technique standpoint, the prosecution was terrific—
bouncing around from subject to subject and from statement to statement,
hardly allowing the witness to pause for air. It was easy to understand how
anyone lacking real mental toughness would fold under this relentless barrage.

During the course of this prosecutorial demonstration I tipped Mary
Rose off by saying things like "It is a real treat to watch seasoned
professionals like you guys conduct this inquiry; you've got it down to
an art form," or "This reminds me of every great cops-and-robbers movie,
where the criminal confesses under the pounding of two or three detectives
asking leading questions with machine-gun quickness. And you guys are
doing it without the bright lights." These kinds of comments, which resulted
in abuse being heaped upon me, gained Mary Rose a respite and put
the whole exercise in perspective for her.

Mary Rose began her testimony on a Friday but she was unable
to finish and had to return Monday morning. On both occasions she brought
her infant to the courthouse. During breaks the jurors could see mother
and baby. Of course, the suspicious prosecutors thought I arranged this
for theatrics and to intimidate them into not being overly tough in their
questioning of this twenty-four-year-old mother of two. They were of course
partially correct, but there was a more fundamental reason.

MR. ROSENBLATT: Your youngest baby is how old?
A: Six months.
Q: And you nurse the baby, correct?
A: Yes.
Q: So, in terms of your scheduling [of] various meetings with
the State, that's been a constant problem?

A: Yes. (*This was the groundwork for having the baby with her, and also I wanted to blunt the State's contention that Mary Rose had been uncooperative with them in terms of her availability for statements.*)

Q: The baby's back there in the audience seated on your father's lap? (*Volz and Russell despised me for such questions.*)

A: I haven't been able to express milk.

MR. RUSSELL: I don't know what the reason is for pointing out where the witness's baby is.

MR. ROSENBLATT: I don't know the reasons for a lot of things that you do.

Stephen Russell pursued the baby on redirect examination:

MR. RUSSELL: Now you had your baby in here the other day and your baby is in here again today. Any particular reason you had your baby in the courtroom rather than sitting outside?

A: He's not disturbing the courtroom. I don't see any reason not to have him in here, and I feel a lot more secure knowing that he is not upset. (*Another beautiful answer, one that any mother would understand and an area where the jury would, hopefully, resent Russell for probing.*)

Q: How old is your son?

A: Six months.

I could not believe that Russell was persisting in this line of questioning. I thought it was crazy to mess with a young mother and her nursing infant. Then all of a sudden the baby started to cry for some unknown reason. Perhaps Mary Rose's father took me seriously when I kiddingly said that if things got tough simply pinch your grandson on his upper thigh; based on personal experience that always gets the desired reaction. I would have paid big money to have the baby cry at precisely that moment. Russell looked back at the crying baby, looked at the mother and then over to the jury, and had that "Oh, shit, what did I do?" look on his face. In my usual mode of offering assistance to an adversary in trouble, I said,

MR. ROSENBLATT: He knows you're talking about him Mr. Russell.

MR. RUSSELL: The timing is great.

To Stephen Russell's credit, he handled the situation with some degree of humor and quickly dropped a subject that had very little likelihood of getting him anywhere in the first place.

I asked Mary Rose additional questions about "The Lady."

Q: Did Dr. Rosier write "The Lady" in order to make money?

A: No, he did not.

Q: Why did he write the book?

A: Since 1980, I was able to observe them. Pat was his life and he thought she was the most special person in the world. He felt that people could learn from the way she was. She was a very courageous person; she cared about other people, and he wanted to share her with the world.

Q: Do you think that the book was his means of keeping her alive?

A: Definitely.

Q: When you first came back to work for him on January 27, is the first thing you began to type poetry rather than the manuscript?

A: Yes. When I got there, there was a stack of poetry. He had been writing poems to her throughout her illness.

Q: What was the subject of the poetry?

A: His eternal love for Pat.

Q: Isn't it true that Peter never made a dime on his manuscript or the screenplay? In fact they both cost him a great deal of time and money. Isn't that correct?

A: He was building a monument to Pat. I don't believe he cared how much it cost him to accomplish that.

Q: Let's talk about the time frame from Patricia's death in January 1986 up until the time that Dr. Rosier went on television in November. Did you consider him—I'm certainly not asking you this as a professional person, but from your standpoint as a lay person—did you consider him to be suicidal?

A: Yes.

Q: Did he talk about it a lot?

A: Yes.

Q: Was he depressed?

A: Yes.

Q: Crying all the time?

A: Yes.

Q: Acting like a fool a lot of the time?

A: (*After a pause*) Yes.

Q: You can say it.

A: Yes.

Q: How did Dr. Rosier deal with the fact that the world was going about its business as though Pat had never lived?

A: He couldn't understand how people who knew her could just live their lives without feeling the day-to-day sorrow that he was feeling.

In his redirect examination Stephen Russell was very sarcastic about the book being "a monument to Patricia." From his standpoint the book contained foul language, spoke crudely of Peter's affair, trashed Peter's own parents and sisters as well as the Delmans, and hung out to dry enough dirty linen to smother all of Fort Myers.

Russell portrayed Peter as being too cheap to publish the book with his own money. To the State this was evidence of Peter's opportunistic interest in the subject of euthanasia. Russell attempted to demonstrate that Peter's interview with Fort Myers's Channel 20 was successful in creating a media frenzy. I countered by pointing out that if Joseph D'Alessandro had not called a press conference talking about a first degree murder investigation, Peter's fifteen minutes of fame would have vanished. What fed and sustained the flames of the Patricia and Peter Rosier saga was the fact that it became a major criminal trial involving an issue with the potential to affect anyone. In any event, Peter's manuscript had not been published and there had been no movie.

I had to remind the jury that there was another side to Peter Rosier, and in this effort I had a willing accomplice in Mary Rose. Peter and Patricia were generous employers; they did not stand on ceremony with their employees either at home or in the office. In that sense they were not snobbish at all and they maintained very natural relationships with the people who worked for them.

The Rosiers happily attended Mary Rose's wedding and gave the new couple a generous gift. Mary Rose felt free to discuss with them any personal problem that might arise.

Peter and Patricia were very direct in their charitable undertakings. Mary Rose was an eyewitness to their open-house policy during Thanksgiving and Christmas, when forlorn and homeless people would be invited into their home to partake fully in the food, drink, and festivities.

As a lawyer, I love cross examination because through leading questions it allows me to in effect testify. Mary Rose was a witness who obviously wanted to help and I think she did. (As I often say about experts, even if the jury understands little of the technical testimony, as long as they like my expert, believe he or she is a person of integrity who truly possesses expertise and who feels strongly about the justice of my cause, I am more than satisfied. The marvelous experts we had lined up for Peter certainly fell in that category.)

Certainly the jury knew that Mary Rose was trying to help Peter. I wanted them to recognize that she was a lovely, hard-working, decent young woman who was fundamentally honest. If she thought the world of Peter, he could not be the despicable monster that the State was persecuting.

The flip side of Mary Rose Linden was the State's next witness, Landis McMahon. A lifelong resident of Fort Myers who had been a close friend of Pat's, she disliked Peter with a passion and wanted him to burn.

16

Landis McMahon: Hell Hath No Fury . . .

The State was just about ready to rest its case and they sought to end on a high note that would shatter whatever was left of Peter Rosier's credibility. If a juror's skin crawls when they look at a defendant, that juror is likely to vote for conviction. The evidence the State sought to introduce through Landis McMahon would make their skin crawl, of that I had no doubt.

All the legal battles up until now were in the nature of guerilla warfare. The State had Mrs. McMahon primed to detonate a nuclear warhead. To be sure, the warhead was irrelevant, but the entire trial had focused on irrelevancies.

The issue was, would Mrs. McMahon be allowed to tell the jury that at her husband's lavish birthday celebration, which took place only six days after Patricia's death, she heard Peter say: "Here I am, the most eligible bachelor in Fort Myers, and I can't even get a nigger to fuck me."

I was confident that if a poll were taken of law school professors, five hundred out of five hundred and five would tell us there was no way in the world that that comment could be admissible. The problem was that Judge Thompson had the power to buy the five over the five hundred. He had the power to let Landis give this testimony even if the vote of the law professors was five hundred and five to zero in favor of excluding it.

If Landis gave that testimony and if the jury believed it, my client was going to be convicted period. Seconal, morphine, Peter's confessions, the testimony of the Delmans—all of that would become mere window dressing. Peter would be convicted because the jury would believe he was

245

a selfish, arrogant, racist slime ball. Susan and I were convinced Landis's testimony had the potential to cause the jury to buy the State's thesis hook, line, and sinker. If character is destiny, Peter's alleged lack of character would doom him. The jury would be only too happy to follow Judge Thompson's instructions on the law. Peter denied to us that he had used the racial epithet. We knew Peter was not a racist; we believed him.

This testimony was clearly inadmissible because it proved absolutely nothing about the crimes with which Peter was charged. Even if some off-the-wall jurist decided that the testimony had any probative value whatsoever, it was clearly outweighed by its highly prejudicial and inflammatory nature. Complicating matters was the fact that there were two blacks on the jury, one being an alternate.

We had little doubt but that, as usual, we would lose the legal argument. Thompson did not figure to veer from his kitchen-sink philosophy of letting it all hang out. The prosecutors made their argument that this testimony would show Peter's state of mind: that he was not in deep mourning and that our great marriage presentation was largely a myth. Susan had repeatedly made the very valid point that grief does not necessarily follow a formula course; some surviving spouses go off the deep end and behave badly, but that is hardly proof that they did not love their husband or wife.

Susan argued that the prejudice of Peter's supposed comment would be overwhelming and uncorrectable; she let the judge know that the entire trial would be for naught since, as an appellate specialist, she was confident that any appellate court would overturn any conviction on this ground alone. She reminded Judge Thompson that he himself had said it would be wrong for Peter to be convicted because the jury concluded he was not a loving and devoted husband.

The judge ruled that Peter's entire statement was admissible, including the word "nigger." Susan and I ignored the ruling and continued talking because we sensed the judge was uncomfortable with his decision. We were now dealing with the intangibles of Judge Thompson's innermost thoughts and emotions.

The only approach left open to us was the psychological one. Judge Thompson was intelligent enough to know that if this testimony came in, I would be ruthless in my cross examination. At that point I would have nothing to lose. Unless I could destroy Landis, Peter would be convicted. Judge Thompson was a courteous southern gentlemen who became squeamish with direct, eyeball-to-eyeball, assault-type confrontations.

Landis was a loquacious, extremely attractive southern belle who had lived in Fort Myers all her life; her father and other family members were well-known figures in the area. If I were casting a movie, Landis would be the archetypical former high school cheerleader. Knowing the nature of Fort Myers, I assumed that Judge Thompson and the McMahon's had attended some of the same social functions. Perhaps Judge Thompson or a member of his family had done business with Landis's father's auto dealership.

Judge Thompson knew that in her deposition Landis had said, in explaining away the difficulty of being 100 percent certain of a particular identification, "You know, this is like when the niggers all line up and they all look alike. . . ."

Judge Thompson knew that on cross examination I would portray Landis as a vindictive person who had falsely placed in Peter's mouth an egregious insult that would be second nature to her. I knew the judge would squirm when I would make it obvious to the national media that, yes, members of the establishment in Fort Myers still described black people as "niggers." Judge Thompson was very protective of the image of his community, and he did not want that message to get out. He tried to solve his dilemma in Solomon-like fashion.

He revised his original ruling and decided Peter's statement could be admitted absent any reference to race. This was acceptable to the State because the prosecution thought it would greatly restrict my cross examination. Susan and I shocked everyone when we said, "No deal."

It was ironic but true that we felt very strongly that the comment without the epithet was much more believable. We wanted the entire comment to be excluded, but if it was going to come in we insisted that it include the word "nigger."

We argued that the jury would understand that this very liberal New Yorker whose family had voted for Jesse Jackson in the most recent presidential election was very unlikely to have used such an insulting term. We said that absent the offending word, Peter's comment dovetailed with the testimony of Jules Cantor and others about him being on the prowl for women very soon after Patricia's death. It would be very easy for the jury to hate the man who was writing love poems and slobbering all over the place and talking incessantly about his great love, and yet who was capable of participating in a crowded birthday celebration a mere few days after his wife's death.

We were bluffing. If the judge remained consistent on this ruling we would have to go along. It would be embarrassing to reverse our position, but that was of small consequence in this context. The "nigger" reference was too volatile and dangerous; it could be such a turn-off to the jury that we simply could not risk it. We were hoping Judge Thompson would throw up his hands and say to himself that he and Fort Myers didn't need this aggravation, and therefore he would exclude the specific comment.

The back-and-forth debate extended over a two-day period. The jurors must have wondered what was going on. Jurors always speculate about long delays since the only explanation they ever get from judges is vague and ambiguous, along the line of "Certain legal matters have come up which we are considering and which really don't concern you at this point, so just relax. I will have the bailiff get you some coffee."

What follows is a basic sampling of the positions of both sides:

MR. RUSSELL: We have to know before we question her Judge, as to whether or not you will permit Mr. Rosenblatt to cross examine her on her use of the epithet from her deposition. If that comes in, I mean we may as well go into his commentary that he would even "fuck a nigger." That's a quote. We're willing to keep away from that.

MR. VOLZ: We'll have her testifying as to his comments concerning the fact that he is rich, he is the most eligible bachelor in town, and he couldn't get anyone to screw him. We will delete any reference to nigger.

THE COURT: If I had known y'all were going to put her on, I think I would have taken early retirement. (*That was perhaps the funniest thing Thompson said during the entire trial. Judge Thompson apparently knew Landis.*)

MR. VOLZ: According to the defense he was crying all the time, depressed all the time, moping around all the time. This is an event that took place within six days of his wife's death. I think it's very relevant.

MR. ROSENBLATT: No one has testified that Rosier was crying or depressed or moping around twenty-four hours a day. Besides, these are all your witnesses, witnesses the State has put on. In case you've forgotten, the State hasn't rested yet.

THE COURT: I'm going to allow the statement in without the offending word.

MRS. ROSENBLATT: But that changes the whole impact of the statement. It is far less likely that in 1986 a well-educated, liberal, board-certified physician who grew up among blacks would say anything like that. Judge, I think basically you figure the State's got us in some kind of a corner and you're forcing us to delete something to change the meaning and import of the statement attributed to our client. And I don't think it's fair, I really don't. Just to clarify this 100 percent on the record for appellate purposes, Your Honor's ruling is that the probative impact of this testimony outweighs the prejudice to the defendant. (*This is a classic example of preserving the trial record for appellate purposes.*)

THE COURT: That's correct. And it generally is relevant, coming that soon after Mrs. Rosier's death. (*Just as that was a very significant item to the judge, we felt positive the jury would view it in the same light.*)

MR. ROSENBLATT: Relevant to what? Did he kill his wife? Isn't that what this case is all about? Judge, this is becoming absurd. This case is not about shitting on Fort Myers, running around with women, buying Rolls Royces, looking to save on taxes, or wanting to write a best seller. The State thinks it's a murder trial. Their position would be arguable if Rosier had a girlfriend while his wife was alive and somehow he had an incentive for her to be dead quicker. The comment if made is made by a guy who is out to lunch who makes a very stupid and immature statement. I think you should take judicial notice of the fact that a rich man in Fort Myers who is a successful doctor with fancy cars and a big house, [a man] who is looking for a woman in this town—such a guy is a lead-pipe cinch to score in the very first lounge he walks into. You see, that's what's being missed here entirely, even if it was said it was just chitchat, it was nothing serious.

MR. RUSSELL: The Court has ruled.

MR. ROSENBLATT: This is so crazy. It's a word that is an everyday part of her vocabulary, not his. You don't live to adulthood in New York if the word "nigger" is part of your everyday parlance.

THE COURT: Well, I'm ruling all over the place on this one . . . the whole business is motive.

MR. RUSSELL: What's good for the goose is good for the gander. . . . (*What took him so long to make that brilliant observation for the umpteenth time?*) But it certainly is an issue surrounding motivation, and we have a right to rebut that.

THE COURT: I've jumped all over this one (*truer words were never spoken*). I probably will continue to jump all over it. I decided it fourteen different ways last night. It is inflammatory, it is prejudicial, it is of only marginal relevancy. Well, this has got to be decided sometime before I retire, I guess.

(This argument was transforming the judge into a stand-up comedian.)

My decision still boils down to a matter of discretion and judgment. I believe the prejudicial value outweighs any probative value. I am going to exclude the exact words in the statement. *(Susan's relentless use of the concept of prejudice outweighing probative value had obviously made an impact.)* I will let you develop the idea that the defendant was dating in some degree. I'll exclude any cross examination of Mrs. McMahon relative to her feelings about Ohio people, the specifics of her brother's suicide, and any use of the slang term for Negro.

Our bluff worked. We had correctly predicted the judge's psychological reaction. Academicians and theorists could argue whether such bluffing was improper; we did not have that luxury. A trial lawyer works with the facts as they exist and must play the cards he or she is dealt, and among those cards are the emotional underpinnings of the judge as well as one's opponent.

As decent a man as Judge Thompson was, he could not divorce himself from his roots. He was upset at the use of the epithet. To think that this term was still in common usage in the late 1980s in Fort Myers was simply scary.

Judge Thompson was man enough to admit that he had "jumped all over this" issue. He initially ruled that Peter's alleged statement could be entered in its entirety; he next ruled that the jury could hear the statement minus the reference to race; and he finally ruled that the statement was inadmissible in any form.

The law had not changed during the course of these very lengthy arguments. What changed was the chemistry, dynamics, and perceptions of the presiding judge. Rarely is the issue this dramatic and inflammable, but a similar process goes on all the time.

There is a myth that has been greatly encouraged by the legal profession and which I think is believed by most Americans: namely, that "the law is the law." The belief seems to be that a judge can in a complicated factual scenario go to a statute or appellate decision that will give him or her a definitive answer, which will tell that judge how to rule. It just doesn't work that way; it never has and it never will.

As but one of a legion of examples showing why the axiomatic and simplistic assertion that the law is the law is often false, one need only contemplate the recent Florida furor surrounding 2 Live Crew's *As Nasty As They Wanna Be* album.

Broward County (Fort Lauderdale) Sheriff Nick Navarro vowed to arrest anyone who sold the rap group's album. United States District Court Judge Jose Gonzalez ruled the album to be obscene and that police could arrest people who were selling it. Gonzalez is a well-respected judge who has been on the federal bench since 1978; before that he was a state circuit court judge for some fourteen years. He certainly knew the law.

Yet in May 1992 a three-judge panel of the Eleventh Circuit Court of Appeals overruled Gonzalez, finding the album not to be obscene. The law is the law in the sense that murder is illegal and active euthanasia is illegal. The confusion arises over the manner in which the law is applied to specific factual scenarios. Ultimately the law is what a given judge or panel of judges say it is on a given day, and it remains so until other judges on a higher court say the earlier judges were wrong.

During the Senate confirmation hearings for Judge Clarence Thomas in the fall of 1991, the senators on the Judiciary Committee kept repeating the obvious, that they were not a court of law. This was done primarily to explain away many inept and groping questions that were usually prefaced by self-serving political speeches. Yet these comments perpetuated the myth that a court of law is necessarily an orderly forum with precise rules of conduct and formulas for rigorous interrogation. The truth is that every individual judge is a law unto himself, and proceedings in a court of law are just as much of a crap shoot as countless other forums. That is the nature of the decision-making process, particularly under great pressure, when legalities must be related to very specific facts and personalities.

The way Judge Thompson functioned in the case at hand is the way judges operate in the real world: vacillation, unsure of themselves, weighing the likelihood of reversal by a higher court, not wanting to look bad to the bench and bar. This is particularly true in high-visibility cases. Unlike federal judges, state judges do not automatically get the job for life; in Florida such judges must submit themselves to the electorate periodically, although in practice it is rare for an incumbent judge to be defeated.

To his credit Judge Thompson did not suffer from what I call "the punk syndrome," an incurable malady that afflicts about 20 percent of all judges. This syndrome is manifested by an adolescent kind of false macho equivalent to the schoolyard scenario of "If you don't play by my rules, I'll just pick up my ball and go home."

These insecure judges (nearly always the possessors of very undistinguished records as private lawyers) must constantly demonstrate that they are the boss; it is their courtroom and they are in control. They perceive vigorous advocacy and a demand for a fair trial, unencumbered by constant bowing and scraping, as a direct threat to their unfettered authority.

The myth of "the law is the law" is right up there with the myth "we are a government of laws and not of men." Herbert Hoover and Franklin Delano Roosevelt functioned as president under the very same Constitution and Bill of Rights, yet the manner in which they interpreted and utilized their powers to deal with the Great Depression differed dramatically.

Even when the law seems clear it can be easily manipulated to achieve the agenda of the judge who is doing the interpreting. When President Dwight Eisenhower appointed Earl Warren to the U.S. Supreme Court in 1953, he had every reason to believe that the country was getting a very solid and safe conservative chief justice. After all, as governor of California Warren had countenanced the imprisonment of thousands of law-abiding Japanese Americans during World War II. Yet in the sixteen years Warren served as chief justice, he turned out to be one of the liberal icons of the century.

Hugo Black, who had been a United States senator from Alabama, had an affiliation with the Ku Klux Klan, and was an associate justice both before and after Warren's tenure, was even more liberal than Warren. Franklin Roosevelt expected that Felix Frankfurter, who had taught law at Harvard University for a quarter of a century, would become one of the all-time great liberals when he appointed him to the Supreme Court. Yet Frankfurter turned very conservative and construed the language of our Constitution very strictly and narrowly.

Another great fallacy is that since one is engaged in a trial in which the jury will make the ultimate decision, the identity and personality of the trial judge doesn't mean very much. Here's a bottom-line truth: evidence is the key to what causes a jury to reach a decision one way or the other, and what evidence the jury will hear and see is determined by a judge. And that decision is based more on temperament, background, specific facts, outlook, and emotions than on pure law.

If a judge is corrupt and evil, he or she can undermine either side even with a jury in the box, and this misconduct will never appear in the official record. It is very easy for experienced judges to ingratiate themselves with members of the jury. The jurors look to the judge for guidance and leadership and generally make the assumption that the judge presides because of professional merit, an assumption that in many instances is totally without justification.

All a judge has to do is act spellbound when prosecution witnesses are testifying and appear skeptical or disgusted when defense witnesses are on the stand. I have seen judges walk out of the courtroom, talk to other lawyers, or read a newspaper while critical witnesses were testifying. Jurors pick up very quickly on a grimace, an arched eyebrow, or a frown. Without saying an offending word a judge can make it perfectly clear as to which side he or she prefers. And that is why most lawyers spend a good part of their professional lives currying favor with judges.

After Judge Thompson's about-face, it was the State's turn to shock us, but it was a welcome shock. The prosecution announced that it was not calling Landis McMahon at all. Edward Volz had stated during the course of the legal argument,

> We have twenty people who can come in and testify to this statement by Rosier . . . we have this defendant making this comment on numerous occasions in front of numerous people at numerous locations . . . a whole group of people heard this comment. We want to rebut this rosy picture of this man who has been crying and so desperate. . . .

If that were true, why even consider putting on Landis since she would be so peculiarly vulnerable to cross examination? We never learned the answer to that question.

More amazing still was the fact that the State never called a witness to testify to Peter's behavior at the McMahon party. Turning to Susan, I said, "I guess it's a great advantage to Peter that I have a reputation for nasty and aggressive questioning. Maybe the other partygoers were not anxious to make my acquaintance."

"We should just count our blessings," Susan replied. "It would have been terribly damaging to Peter to have anyone say he was at this party so soon after his wife's death, a party where he was drinking, socializing, and apparently having a good time."

"It's a mystery," I confided, "but I never look a gift horse in the mouth. We know Peter was at the party, and even though we knew he didn't use that awful word—with his penchant for self-inflicted wounds—he undoubtedly would have said some things that would have played into the State's hands."

Another important item the State gave up in not calling Landis

McMahon was her deposition testimony to the effect that Patricia allegedly told her that the greatest hurt in her life was not the cancer, but Peter leaving her for another woman years earlier. There would have been another battle royale over the admissibility of this evidence, and I'm confident we would have lost again.

In an hour or so the State would be done. The Thanksgiving recess was coming up and southwest Florida was being threatened by a hurricane. The trial began on October 31, 1988; it was now November 22. The defense had yet to put on a single witness.

The tropical depression off the coast of St. Petersburg went along with our mood. Susan and I would return to Miami and then be faced with our most difficult decision of the entire trial. Would our client testify?

Actually it was not that simple. It was Peter's ultimate decision and he could ignore our recommendation. It was his freedom on the line. Susan and I had mixed emotions about putting on a defense; we felt our medical experts could do a marvelous job in making the jurors understand the many nuances involved in the whole area of euthanasia. Through them we would elevate the trial to a more scientific plane. It would be an uphill battle to convince Judge Thompson to admit all of their opinions though.

Yet we were in agreement that if Peter did not testify, we would put on no defense whatsoever. That would allow me to have the final rebuttal argument during summation. That strategy seemed risky. The State had put on a very strong case and had repeatedly exposed every blemish in the lives of Patricia and Peter Rosier.

The Thanksgiving recess would give us a respite, but time was running out.

17

Mopping Up: The State Rests

The State wasn't quite through; it wanted to pile on with two more witnesses, Patricia Jungle and Dr. Harry Lowell. Patricia Murphy Jungle and her husband were the owners of the private Park Meadow Tennis Club.

> MR. VOLZ: Do you recall a time when Dr. and Mrs. Rosier were not living together? (*Occasionally the prosecutors would simply refuse to refer to Peter as Dr. Rosier.*)
> MRS. JUNGLE: Yes. I don't know any of the details, but I do know there was a period when they were not living together.
> Q: Where was Dr. Rosier living during that period of time?
> A: He was living at "The Landings," in a condominium there.
> Q: Can you tell us what "The Landings" are?
> A: They are condominiums with tennis courts and swimming pools and I think a nine-hole golf course. (*The State was conveying the image of Peter as a swinging bachelor, the implication being that he would be having affairs in these posh surroundings.*)

Consistent as ever the State wanted the jury to believe that Peter deserved the "Callous Ass of the Year" award. Edward Volz established that at the very moment Patricia was undergoing surgery for removal of her lung tumor, Peter was at Park Meadow with his children, playing tennis. Bad enough, but Peter allowed the Delmans and Patricia's Aunt Marcia to remain at the hospital basically in the dark as to the developments in her condition. Peter had immediate access to all the doctors

255

and nurses involved with his wife's case, and could have kept Patricia's closest relatives duly advised had he been a bit more unselfish.

On the very day of Patricia's funeral Peter told Mrs. Jungle that he was writing a book about his wife and their relationship. Peter told her that Patricia's "terrible childhood" would be included and further volunteered: "I'm going to expose her family."

Q: Did you have any further discussion on that day, with Dr. Rosier, concerning the book?

A: I went into the kitchen and Peter came in behind me and he said, "I can write, I am a good writer and this book is going to be a best seller. I'm going to write about the medical community in Fort Myers. There are some doctors who have done terrible things. I'll change their names because I could get sued. They could lose their licenses for the things they've done." (*Pat Jungle was hardly Peter's closest friend but she possessed the threshold qualification of two good ears, and that's all Peter needed to unload his innermost thoughts.*)

Q: Did you have any conversation with him later?

A: One day he came into the club and I asked him how his book was doing, and he said that he had sent it to a few publishers and they had rejected it. And I said, "Well, that's too bad." He said, "Well, I'll get it published one way or the other. It will get published." (*This testimony was of course supportive of the State's theme that Peter went on television to promote his manuscript.*)

Q: How soon was this after Patricia's death?

A: Oh, maybe two or three weeks after. He was busy right after her death working on that book. (*This is how Volz ended his direct examination, and it was very effective since it demonstrated that Peter, as always, was looking out for himself.*)

Early in my cross examination, I had the witness agree with me that her testimony was not at all germane to the murder charges against Peter. I reminded the jury as often as I could of the irrelevancy and petty meanness of the State's approach.

MR. ROSENBLATT: He's very much disliked, not only in the medical community but throughout Fort Myers, isn't that correct?

A: Mr. Rosenblatt, he was disliked before he went on television. (*That answer was nasty and gratuitous, and it surprised me.*)

Q: Did you dislike him before? (*As with so many other questions I asked, I had no idea how the witness would respond to this one.*)

A: No. I thought we were like family. He was at the club every day. My husband used to hit balls with him any time he wanted. We thought he cared for us; we cared for him and for his family. And then, all of a sudden, he just quit the club.

Q: Okay. (*Was she telling me that she hated Peter because he decided to quit the club? Was pettiness scaling new heights?*)

A: My husband hit with him at no charge. They even have videos of where Jake and Liz and Peter were out for a weekend working with my husband, who was helping them with their strokes.

Q: Why are you telling us all this?

A: Because you asked me.

Q: I asked you if your husband was hitting balls? I asked you whether your husband did free things for Peter?

A: No, you didn't ask me that.

Q: I sure didn't. You're telling us all this because you want to show in some way [that] Peter was unappreciative of all the things you and your husband did for him, correct?

A: That's correct.

Q: Although you say he was disliked even before his wife died, you apparently liked him?

A: Yes.

Q: Because you and your husband considered him family?

A: Yes.

Q: And then he did this terrible thing; he dropped out of your club?

A: Well, that wasn't a terrible thing. That was his choice.

Q: It certainly was. (*Volz and Russell would climb the walls when I began a question with a statement agreeing with or emphasizing a positive point a witness had made. In final argument they would refer to this technique as one of my many "tricks of the trade."*) Other than dropping out of your club, has he done any other terrible thing to you?

A: No.

I knew that Patricia had given Mrs. Jungle several gourmet cookbooks the day before she died. Patricia also gave Mr. Jungle a book containing the inscription "Please look after my boys." Psychologically, I always attempted to convey the idea that convicting Peter would be the equivalent of convicting Patricia in absentia. As Peter repeatedly asserted in his manuscript, he and Patricia functioned as a unit; I hoped the jury would buy that.

Q: Based on your contact with Patricia Rosier over the years, you would agree that she was very intelligent and very strong. Is that correct?

A: I would say that she was very, very intelligent yes. She was very strong.

Q: Mrs. Jungle, in your lifetime you have actually seen several people die from cancer, haven't you?

A: Yes, I have.

Q: You worked at a hospital, I believe in Ohio?

A: Yes, I did. (*I learned this from having taken her deposition. Sometimes Judge Thompson's kitchen-sink philosophy worked to our advantage.*)

Q: And you have seen situations where people died a pretty horrible death from cancer, correct?

A: Not a very pleasant death.

Q: Not a very pleasant disease?

A: No. (*The State did not dream that I would attempt to make this point through a lay witness. Was it technically beyond the scope of direct examination and therefore a no-no? Of course, but it was helpful.*)

Q: Do you remember Patricia telling you that she was not simply going to let her hair fall out, but rather she would take charge and do it all at once?

A: That's correct. (*Just like she took charge of the circumstances of her death.*)

Q: Mr. Volz asked you about a separation during the twenty-two-year marriage of Dr. and Mrs. Rosier. They got back together and were living together years before she ever got the cancer. Isn't that correct?

A: As far as I know.

Q: And as far as you know, during the period of time that Patricia had cancer—from April of 1985 until her death in January of 1986—Dr. Rosier was a totally devoted husband?

A: As far as I know, yes.

The State's last witness was a neurosurgeon named Harry Lowell. Lowell was not called as an expert witness to discuss Patricia's brain tumors or anything else of a medical nature. Believe it or not, he was called to give a critique of "The Lady."

MR. RUSSELL: What was the nature of your relationship or contact with the defendant prior to the time his wife's lung cancer was diagnosed?

A: I knew him professionally. He ran the pathology service at Lee Memorial Hospital, where much of my practice was based.

Q: Did you become aware after Pat Rosier's death that the defendant was writing a book?

A: Yes.

Q: How did you become aware of that?

A: I first heard about it in the operating room at Lee Memorial and subsequently in the operating room at Southwest Regional. (*Hardly a closely guarded secret.*)

Q: And did you have occasion to come into contact with Dr. Rosier, in reference to getting a copy of the book to read?

A: Yes, I did.

Q: Would you explain how that occurred?

A: I told one of the girls in the OR to give me Pete's number, that I wanted to talk to him about that. I guess curiosity killed the cat. Subsequently, I talked with Pete and the book was delivered to my office at my request.

Q: Now, did you have occasion sometime in late September of 1986 to have dinner with the defendant to discuss the book and your critique of it?

A: Yes.

Q: What did you talk about, what areas?

A: Primarily that I thought the book was too negative. There was nothing good about his family, her family, Dartmouth, Duke, Fort Myers, or anything else. I thought he needed to find something good about somebody some place. I encouraged him to clean the book up as far as some sexually explicit stuff that I didn't think needed to be in. I told him that I would put her obituary on the last page and end the book with the idea of her going out in a simple white gown with no pockets, indicating you come in with nothing, [and] leave with nothing.

Q: Did you ever talk to him about how it might be published?

A: I told him that I thought he should publish the book himself. He adamantly refused such.

Q: Why did you tell him you thought he ought to publish it himself?

A: I thought if he wanted to espouse his cause of euthanasia that he ought to do it himself. (*Lowell's bottom-line opinion was that the book was not publishable in its present form.*)

Q: Did the defendant ever talk to you during those three hours at dinner about giving the proceeds of the book, if it [were] published, to charity?

A: No. (*Mary Rose Linden had testified that that was Peter's intention.*)

Q: During this dinner was there any discussion about the defendant's potential criminal liability in terms of what he said in the book?

A: That was basically the first part of our discussion; I told Pete immediately that I thought there may be some criminal liability along with some civil liability.

Q: What was his response?

A: He was rather cavalier, glib, or nonchalant about it. He didn't think it was of any concern. He said, "I wasn't a player, the book could be fiction or nonfiction, and basically the evidence was cremated."

Q: The words you just used—"the evidence was cremated"—are those your words or are those the words he used?

A: Those were his words.

Q: Did part of your dinner discussion allude to his thoughts about his future as a writer?

A: Well, I think it was evident that he was seeking a new career. I think most men in their forties want to. He had been to Harvard, was taking some creative writing classes, and I think he truly wanted to become an author.

Q: Did he tell you where he might be an author in terms of location?

A: Not really. I was aware, and we had discussed the fact, that he had purchased a residence in New York.

On cross examination I attempted to humanize Peter's actions:

Q: When you made the point that a lot of men in their forties think about new careers and think about doing some writing, that's not uncommon is it?

A: It's not uncommon that you want to do something different.

I don't think most people necessarily want to write. But I think there is something that happens in your forties that makes you want to do something different before it's too late. I have personally discussed with Peter going to law school or his going to law school, and I told him that I thought about that as well.

I turned to Susan and said, "Just your typical, garden-variety cross examination in a first degree murder trial." I had never taken the deposition of Dr. Lowell or even met him, so what was I going to ask him? The irrelevance of his testimony was pretty unbearable, yet I had played this game for a month; I could hardly quit now.

I have always been amazed at the number of doctors who harbor a strong desire to become lawyers. Operating on brains and spinal cords was not enough for Dr. Lowell; he also had a burning desire to learn about torts and contracts. What these surgeons don't recognize is that in the operating room they are kings; they ask for something and they get it. No one argues with them. In the courtroom the judge is in charge; your case can be gutted by evidentiary rulings from the bench. The judge or the strangers on the jury make critical decisions that control success or failure, and all the while you have some nit-picking opponent who is always taking potshots. Why would anyone in their right mind exchange almost total control for being at the mercy of perverse personalities who are oftentimes bolstered by only marginal competence?

I'm convinced that doctors acquire a romantic view of the law from their contact with lawyers who never tire of exaggerating and glamorizing nonexistent war stories. There are many lawyers who have totally undeserved reputations as courtroom warriors, when in fact they almost never try a case.

MR. ROSENBLATT: In reading over those chapters dealing with Patricia's death, you were very surprised that a board-certified pathologist was incapable of ending his wife's life?

A: Yes. I kind of chided him about his lack of any clinical expertise.

Q: You would agree, would you not, Dr. Lowell, that if a qualified physician was interested in finding out about the lethal dose of morphine, there are many books readily available where he could look up that information, correct?

A: I would think so.

Q: You would agree that someone like Patricia, who had subcutaneous metastases, is certainly prone to die at any time, and seldom lives more than two weeks? (*Peter told me I might get a great answer to this question and he was right.*)

A: That's basically a fair statement. That was one of the things we discussed at dinner that night. Peter described the sub-cutaneous metastases that he saw growing; I was convinced that she was terminal and would not live probably more than a few days to two weeks, I mean on the outside. (*Not only was this great testimony on the issue of life expectancy, but we had managed indirectly to get in Peter's testimony about the subcutaneous cancers that were readily observable on Patricia's skin.*)

Stephen Russell made some damaging points on his redirect examination. Dr. Lowell had seen many of his patients die from cancer, yet he thought a scenario of Patricia experiencing a gruesome death where she could conceivably vomit up all her blood was "extremely unlikely." Lowell hurt Peter by saying Peter's goal was that his book become a best seller. That tied in perfectly with Peter being bitterly disappointed by all the publishers' rejections and going on television to accomplish that goal.

As Dr. Lowell left the huge courtrooom in St. Petersburg, Susan and I said goodbye silently to the State's very last witness. The day had arrived at last; the State of Florida was ready to rest its case against Dr. Peter Rosier. The prosecution was finished, at least until its time came for rebuttal. But it could only call rebuttal witnesses if we presented a defense.

Before the State rested, Stephen Russell took one more shot at introducing Peter's entire manuscript.

MR. RUSSELL: Your Honor, in light of Dr. Lowell's testimony, the State would ask the Court again to admit into evidence the entire book, "The Lady," exhibit 5.

THE COURT: I'm not inclined to do that, so my ruling will remain where it is.

MR. VOLZ: Your Honor, at this time the State will rest as to its case in chief.

Nothing was simple or normal about this trial. It would have been normal now to discuss the length of the Thanksgiving recess and other mundane matters, such as the number of witnesses the defense might call. Instead there was the matter of hurricane-force winds striking the west coast of Florida.

THE COURT (*to the jury*): The information I have from the Court administrator's office is that the storm may make landfall between midnight and 7:00 A.M. It could hit Tampa or Sarasota. I feel like I should be conservative with the jurors' safety. Basically I'm going to let you all go until Monday morning at 8:30 A.M. (*The State rested on Tuesday, November 22, 1988, the anniversary of President Kennedy's assassination, and we were to return on November 28.*)

The jury was free to leave but the lawyers had to stick around. Another problem had arisen, one that had the potential to affect the outcome of the trial. The issue was possible juror misconduct.

The husband of one of the jurors was retired, as was the juror herself; he would show up every day and sit in the audience. Probably the most fundamental instruction that jurors receive from the presiding judge is, "Do not discuss the case or the evidence or your feelings about the evidence at any time before you retire to deliberate your verdict."

I am convinced that jurors violate this instruction very often. Jurors develop a camaraderie, and this is especially so during a long and controversial trial. During recesses, lunches, and long breaks (when the lawyers are engaged in private bench conferences), jurors will make their reactions known regarding witnesses, exhibits, and the lawyers. These non-verbal communications are almost never provable.

In this case there was independent evidence that this juror had violated the judge's instruction. This is the kind of thing that can lead to a mistrial since a basic premise of the jury system is that jurors will decide the case only on the basis of what they see and hear in the courtroom. That of course is why jurors are told not to expose themselves to any media accounts of the trial.

We certainly did not want a mistrial, and I could not imagine Judge Thompson granting one. He would find a way out; all of us had invested too much time and effort to let anything happen now. A member of the courtroom audience will frequently see and hear things that are excluded from evidence: for example, legal arguments conducted outside the jury's presence. If that audience member describes such events to a juror, that is considered a gross error, which may require a new trial (depending, of course, upon the philosophy and temperament of the trial judge).

Jurors as a rule are instructed to be very poker faced; they hide their emotions and their reactions. The juror in question could scarcely contain herself at times; she would nearly slide off her chair when she heard a particularly shocking piece of testimony. It was obvious to Susan, Peter, and me that she was communicating with her husband in terms of eyes rolling and gestures. The State had to be aware of this as well. Each side apparently interpreted the gestures as being favorable to them, so neither of us raised the issue with the judge. Besides, knowing Judge Thompson as we all did, there was no likelihood whatever of him taking action unless we were able to give him something concrete.

Something concrete was on its way. The reporter covering the trial for *People* magazine from beginning to end, told the judge that she heard the juror's husband speaking to her about the testimony. This was something that was properly brought to the court's attention.

The reporter's story led to a mini-trial on the ability of this juror to continue to serve. It was very clear to the reporter that the lady and her husband were discussing the case, specifically the testimony of one or more witnesses. The reporter was particularly sensitive to this problem because it became a significant issue in a recent trial she had covered in Seattle.

I was even put under oath and I knew that Stephen Russell relished the opportunity to cross examine me. I said,

> The reporter came over to me agitated and said, "Didn't the judge instruct these jurors they are not supposed to talk about it?" I said absolutely. She was 100 percent sure that the juror was talking to her husband about the case. They were discussing the testimony of various witnesses and it was very specific.
>
> THE COURT: My inclination is to do absolutely nothing until forced into it. But having been forced into it, my inclination is this. That is, to go ahead and call her into chambers and ask her some questions. (*That comment demonstrates that with a more activist judge, there would have been a totally different trial.*)
>
> JUROR: I haven't said anything to my husband about the facts of this case at all.
>
> THE COURT: Has he said anything to you or in your presence about the case?
>
> JUROR: Not that I remember. I don't think so. (*This answer was equivocal.*)

The juror was excused from the judge's chambers. Her interview was handled in such a way so as not to cause the other jurors to become suspicious. Susan and I made an on-the-spot decision that we wanted this juror to be replaced by an alternate juror. We sensed that this juror attributed her discomfiture to our side.

When the juror left the judge's chambers, our secretary felt she gave her a dirty look. That coupled with the State's strongly expressed desire to keep her mandated that we take the opposite position. We had great respect for the ability of Volz, Russell, and Fitzpatrick to assess jurors on the west coast of Florida; if they wanted her, we didn't.

> MRS. ROSENBLATT (*to the court*): To us this is a very serious matter and we think the juror is not being candid. And I don't think in a first degree murder case, if there is any doubt whatsoever, and we have an alternate juror, the doubt should be resolved in favor of removing any possible prejudice.
>
> MR. ROSENBLATT: And we have three separate people who say they heard this juror violating your order, and they are talking about at the very least three separate discussions.

Susan turned to me and said, "This woman is a loose cannon. Although the judge instructed her not to say a word about the real reason she was called in here, I bet she did."

"Let's bring in the bailiff, she probably said something to him."

Susan's intuition was correct. The deputy with the Lee County Sheriff's Department testified: "She said something about the fact, do you think I ought to resign?"

It was perfectly obvious to the bailiff that this juror was being challenged by one side or the other. And this is precisely what she was told by the judge not to convey to anyone.

> MRS. ROSENBLATT: Well Your Honor, she walked right out of here and violated your order. And, of course, she violated your order in the first instance by discussing the case with her husband. She is very upset, she links it to our side, and she will take it out on the defendant.

The State continued to object very strongly to excusing this juror. The judge said: "I still don't see the evil or prejudice."

At hearing this, I said to Susan: "To satisfy Thompson, we'd have to produce a note from her saying 'The son of a bitch is guilty.' "

So be it, we would have to live with her. If I could convince the eleven other jurors, I didn't believe this lady would be ferocious enough to hang the jury for the State. Even if that crazy contingency were to occur—if the State knew the jury was deadlocked eleven-to-one in our favor—we did not believe the prosecution would retry Peter. Besides, for all we knew this juror favored us.

Susan and I would now have a few days off to catch up on how the kids were doing in school. Would I spend most of my time preparing Peter and our other witnesses, or would I be working primarily on my final argument? Susan had an enormous amount of work to do on our motion for acquittal (which would be argued Monday morning) and the jury instruction charge conference. We knew there was not a chance in the world of Judge Thompson granting our motion; we were simply protecting the record for an inevitable appeal if Peter were convicted.

Although Susan specializes in appellate matters and prides herself on being able to research most areas of the law, she was not at all familiar with criminal law and needed guidance. Peter, on his own, had retained Alan Dershowitz, the very high-profile Harvard law professor, for two purposes. Assuming a worst-case scenario, and Peter was very realistic on that subject, there would be an appeal and he wanted Dershowitz to handle it. Susan and I concurred with that decision.

During the course of the proceedings, Alan would also hold Peter's hand so to speak and explain to him the legalities of what was going on and what Peter could expect. Susan called Dershowitz on several occasions both during the pretrial portion of the case and throughout the trial, seeking advice on how to preserve the trial record correctly. Just a day before final arguments, Peter actually paid Dershowitz a substantial additional retainer for handling the bond hearing and initial appellate process, should that become necessary.

Steven Wisotsky, a distinguished professor of law since 1975 at Nova University Law School and a law school classmate of Susan's from the University of Miami, also provided valuable assistance to us during the pretrial stages of the case. Steve prepared lengthy and detailed memoranda of law in support of our several motions for judgment on the pleadings and for an immediate acquittal prior to trial. Steve also worked diligently on the legal memorandum in support of our motion to transfer venue out of Fort Myers.

Wisotsky participated in the oral argument on these motions and although, as we anticipated, all pretrial motions were denied, we did prevail on the critical motion relating to the location of the trial. Dershowitz and Wisotsky were our security blankets on the law, and they protected us from falling into technical potholes at every stage of the proceedings. Although neither of them appeared at the trial, Susan and I considered them to be very much part of the defense team.

Peter insisted on coming to Miami over the holiday recess to discuss his testimony. He wanted to answer all the charges that had been made against him. He wanted to tell the world about Patricia and their great love. Finally, he wanted redemption.

The most important decision of the trial was soon to be made.

18

The Best Defense . . .

If we decided to have Peter testify, we would put on other witnesses as well. Therefore, one of the first things we needed to do was reread the depositions of our medical experts. They were a most impressive group and Peter was enthralled with their testimony. There would be a riveting national and international stage for telling the truth about how the medical profession and family members deal with the terminally ill.

I took all the pretrial depositions, with three exceptions: Edward Volz deposed our three medical experts.

1. George B. Koelle, who is both an M.D. and Ph.D. in the field of pharmacology, has had more than a half-century relationship with the Medical School of the University of Pennsylvania in Philadelphia, having begun there as a graduate student in 1939. He was chairman of the Department of Pharmacology from 1959 to 1981.

2. Dr. Raymond Yesner, a board-certified pathologist, has been at the Yale Medical School since 1948. He is a professor of pathology and director of the Autopsy Service.

3. Dr. Lawrence S. Hurwitz is our only expert with a private practice (in Milwaukee). He is a cancer specialist practicing medical oncology and hospice.

I had never known any of these doctors before the Rosier case; they had never testified on behalf of any of my clients. This was a huge plus (considering the cynicism which exists toward "hired gun" experts). They were head and shoulders above the State's one expert—the nonmedical doctor toxicologist, Robert Forney.

I liked and respected our medical experts, but Susan and I were particularly fond of Dr. Koelle. He functioned at a very commonsense, right-and-wrong level. He was personally outraged at criminal charges being brought under these circumstances, and he was not reluctant to say so. Unique in my career of dealing with experts, he never talked about money for his professional services, and he never sent a bill. The jury would love him. Susan, Peter, and I carefully evaluated and discussed the deposition testimony of our three medical experts as we considered whether the defense would put on a case.

Dr. Koelle was superb on the issue of gruesome versus peaceful death. During his earlier deposition I asked him:

Q: What kind of death do you think that Mrs. Rosier would have experienced?
A: A horrible one. She would have been in more and more acute pain and suffering, unless she were kept very heavily sedated. I hate to contemplate it because I have seen such patients and it's not very pleasant to watch.
Q: Could you be a little more specific or graphic?
A: She could have had vomiting. She could have vomited blood. The whole thing would have been a mess.

Dr. Koelle was vulnerable in expressing this opinion because he had never treated patients in private practice. But Koelle was a fighter and would not cave in. He elaborated on the basis for his opinion that Patricia would have experienced a gruesome death.

"When I was in medical school I saw lots of cancer patients and I had occasion to see how they die. Although I haven't had direct care of patients since I have been out of medical school, I have written a lot on the subject. I have kept in touch with cancer and cancer treatment, very definitely. I used to lecture on it here and in France and in other various places."

Dr. Koelle would educate the jurors about Seconal and morphine, as he did in his deposition:

Q: When one takes Seconal, what part of the body is affected?
A: Essentially every part, and it's a strange thing, although the barbiturates have been on the scene for over a hundred years, we still don't know their exact mechanism. They cause depression of all tissues, but the central nervous system is the one that's most affected. Death usually results from depression to the cardiovascular center and respiratory center.

He explained the difference between morphine and the barbiturates:

A: The big difference between morphine and the barbiturates is that the barbiturates are sedative hypnotic drugs with practically no effect on pain. Painful stimuli are just as painful up until the time they fall asleep. On the other hand, morphine acts predominantly as an analgesic to block the response to pain.

The tolerance to morphine is something that has never been explained. It's a fantastic thing. Some studies on morphine addicts showed that they could take as much as four and a half grams of heroin per day, which is several thousand times the therapeutic dose, and you couldn't even detect it except for the fact they had pinpoint pupils.

Dr. Koelle was very helpful on the issue of Peter lacking criminal intent:

A: A dose of six or eight milligrams of morphine added to the Seconal she took would be acting like adding a teaspoon to a bathtub for its contribution, a teaspoon full of water to a bathtub full of water. And of course the suppositories were of no consequence either.

As to whether the twenty Seconal would have killed Patricia, he said in his deposition: "I can't say for sure one way or the other. She very well could have died; she very well could have survived." Dr. Forney had been certain that the twenty Seconal would not have killed her.

Then Dr. Koelle volunteered, out of the blue, "You know, thinking this whole thing over, if I were in this situation, or, heaven forbid, if my wife had been in this situation, I think this is precisely what I would do or what I would want done to me."

Edward Volz seemed obsessed with Peter's supposedly sinister motive in talking about the death rattle. Dr. Koelle's explanation during his deposition was very interesting:

Q: Could you describe for me what the term "death rattle" means?
A: It's when, just before a patient dies, there's a relaxation of the larynx. And when the larynx is totally relaxed, the epiglottis will tend to rattle. There is an interesting story about one of the old physicians, I can't remember who it was, a fairly well known guy. He had such a degree of intellectual curiosity

that when he was dying he gave a death rattle but he was still able to say a few words. And he said to the guy next to him "Is that the death rattle?" It's just like the guy who was guillotined during the French Revolution. And a physician had gotten him to agree to wink his left eye after his head was cut off, and he did. So, just for that fraction of a second, consciousness is still around on a decapitated head. That takes extreme intellectual curiosity. I don't think everybody has a death rattle, I think sometimes it occurs and sometimes it doesn't.

Dr. Koelle was entitled to tell all the anecdotes he wished to tell. Undoubtedly the State would file a motion to exclude both the anecdotes and personal opinions, but Dr. Koelle would be a very hard man to stop on the witness stand.

Dr. Raymond Yesner of the Yale Medical School had actually studied Patricia's lung tumor while she was alive. When Peter and Patricia were traveling all over the country searching for the best possible diagnosis and treatment, they met with Dr. Juan Rosai, director of anatomic pathology at the primary Yale Medical School hospital. Patricia's tumor was very rare, so Dr. Rosai called in Dr. Yesner as a consultant.

In describing the tumor, Dr. Yesner offered the following testimony at his deposition: "The original pathologist in Florida had called it, I think, an intermediate type of small-cell carcinoma. Dr. Rosai thought that it was probably an aggressive malignant carcinoid. It turned out to be a tumor that was at least in part an adenocarcinoma, which was a mucin-feeding tumor . . . a kind of tumor that was resistant to both radiation and chemotherapy, unfortunately, and I advised the Rosiers that I did not think chemotherapy would be of much value. I thought the chemotherapy would depress the immune system and have very little if any effect on the tumor itself."

I was in the middle of a civil jury trial when arrangements were being made to depose Drs. Yesner, Koelle, and Hurwitz, in three different cities in October 1988. I begged the civil trial judge for a continuance because I needed the full month of October to complete my preparations for the Rosier trial (beginning October 31) where a man's freedom was at stake. That judge unreasonably forced me to trial anyway.

Since Dr. Yesner had had previous contact with Peter, and since they were fellow pathologists, I let Peter firm up the arrangements for a predeposition conference and told him to get a feeling for Dr. Yesner's current attitudes on the subject of euthanasia. That was a very stupid move on my part. It was always stupid to allow Peter to have unguarded conversations with anyone. That's why we assiduously kept him away from the press.

The predictable happened: Peter said more than he should have to Dr. Yesner. He admitted giving Pat a sedative. This was certainly no big deal to us, but the State was off and running claiming that the defendant had confessed yet again.

Dr. Yesner was very helpful on the issues of life expectancy and the type of death Pat could be expected to experience. The jury would have to be impressed that heavyweight academic experts like Drs. Yesner and Koelle had lined up with the defense. Dr. Yesner would also educate the jurors about the cancer process itself.

About a third of the thousands of autopsies performed by Dr. Yesner have been on individuals who have suffered from cancer. He explained that metastases to the brain and the adrenals are extremely common in lung cancer. During deposition I asked him to elaborate:

Q: And based upon the rapid growth of the adrenal tumors, what would be your prognosis for successful treatment?

A: Zero.

Q: What would be the danger of a violent death?

A: Well, a certain percentage of patients with lung cancer bleed to death, a certain number—those who have brain metastases—have probably the worst deaths because brain metastases are pretty horrible and patients can have convulsions, can have projectile vomiting, and there is always the possibility that this tumor might erode into an adjacent large blood vessel. A lung tumor could erode into a large blood vessel where the patient literally drowns in his or her own blood. (*Of course, that particular sequence would not occur here, because Patricia's lung tumor had been removed.*)

Q: Doctor, what is it about the disease or process of cancer that makes it so very painful?

A: It involves pain nerves. The tumor or the cancer cells actually invade the pain nerves. Tumor cells will grow into the nerve sheath and into the pain fibres.

Dr. Yesner made these other points: In order for a tumor to be visualized on a CAT-scan it has to be at least one centimeter, and when it is one centimeter we are talking about a billion cells. Dr. Yesner felt absolutely certain that at the time Patricia's lung tumor was removed, the cancer had already metastasized to her brain and to other parts of her body, but back then the tumors were so small they could not be detected.

In his deposition, Dr. Yesner told us that lung cancer is the most prevalent cause of cancer deaths among males in this country and rapidly becoming the most prevalent cause of death among females. It constitutes about one-quarter of all the cancer deaths that he and his colleagues were seeing at Yale.

A so-called peaceful death occurs where patients are very heavily se-dated on a morphine drip. Absent the sedation, cancer deaths can be gruesome. Patricia did not want to be placed on a morphine drip.

Dr. Yesner tesitified that as of January 10 Patricia only had days to live. I felt confident that an intelligent jury would give far more credence to Yesner than to Harwin. That was one strong reason for presenting a defense.

Observing people in the process of dying was an everyday part of the practice of Dr. Lawrence S. Hurwitz, the medical director of two hospice programs in Milwaukee. He received his bachelor of science degree from the University of Wisconsin, attended medical school at Stanford University, and also did a fellowship at Stanford in neuropathology. He served as the chief resident at the University of Toronto.

Dr. Hurwitz was very helpful to the defense on the issues of terrible pain, the likelihood of a catastrophic death, and Peter's lack of criminal in-tent. His greatest value for us was that he was in a position to explain how morphine drips work in the real world. If he were called to testify, the jury would understand that I was not just blowing smoke in my assertion that assisted death is an everyday fact of life in dealing with the terminally ill.

Most of Dr. Hurwitz's hospice work was actually home hospice. Whether the patient was in a hospital or at home he gave both the nurses and family members much discretion in terms of when and how much to increase the morphine drip. During his deposition, Dr. Hurwitz explained.

MR. ROSENBLATT: It may not be the intent of the doctor or nurse to hasten the patient's death, but isn't that the practical consequence of pain control?

A: Yes it is.

Q: And everyone knows that?

A: Everyone knows that. (*That answer really says it all about how simple it is to increase the dosage and how nearly im-possible it is to know the intent of the person doing so.*)

Q: And no one really knows if a doctor or family member in that setting, who increases the morphine drip . . . what's going on in their heads?

A: No, no one knows that. If I know that a person did not want to suffer at all and wasn't concerned about two or three extra days, that in essence I have their permission to do whatever I need to do when they are helpless, even though I know that it almost certainly hastens their death, that may not be my actual intention.

Q: Has it ever occurred in the hospice program in this area where there was a suicide attempt by a patient, where the attempt was failing, and the hospice program gave additional medication?

A: Yes. (*Well, that's precisely what occurred in the Rosier case. Certainly the hospice team member who increased the medication to cause death was never prosecuted.*)

Q: And the hospice program in effect assisted in the suicide attempt?

A: The hospice assisted in the suicide. I don't think that it was active assistance. We're talking about someone who attempted suicide and still appeared to be in pain.

Q: You didn't do anything to remove the suicide attempt. Nothing was done to keep the person alive? Nothing was administered to the person to reverse the effects of whatever drug was taken?

A: No, it wasn't.

Q: And instead, to make sure there was no pain during the suicide attempt is when additional medications were given to the patient?

A: Yes.

Hurwitz does not describe the dying process as an idyllic picture of sinking slowly into oblivion. "Many of these patients, as they die, are spared no indignity like seizures, incontinence, lying in a bed that is wet and stooled."

Peter knew the media would be very interested in revelations relating to increasing the morphine drip. Is it fair that Peter spend the rest of his life in prison for doing something that so many others have done without prosecution? It is obvious that these caretakers, whether they be family or medical, really have almost total discretion over the timing of death in a terminally ill patient.

Other points were made by Dr. Hurwitz during his deposition: He didn't believe that the morphine had any effect whatsoever, either by injection or suppositories. He didn't use morphine suppositories in his hospice program simply because he didn't believe that they work. This testimony would conflict with that of Dr. Harwin, who prescribed morphine suppositories for pain.

The adrenal tumors were enormous. He didn't think he had seen more than three or four of that size in his entire career. Adrenal tumors can cause a very horrible death, and the pain they can cause is frightening.

It was quite likely that the adrenal gland would rupture and she would hemorrhage internally. Cancer patients vomiting up and choking on their own blood was not an uncommon way for them to die. In a person with cancer of the lung or cancer of the esophagus, those kinds of things were not uncommon. The cancer simply eroded into a major blood vessel in a passage that connects with the upper respiratory or upper digestive system, and they end up bleeding to death. (So Dr. Rosier is not such a fool after all.)

The State had not called as a witness Dr. Donald E. Gerson, a treating physician, though I planned to call him if we presented a defense. Dr. Gerson was unique in that as a Fort Myers doctor he had remained friendly toward Peter. Gerson was a graduate of the Harvard Medical School and he had practiced his specialty of diagnostic radiology in Fort Myers since 1976. He had seen all of Pat's CAT-scans and had firsthand knowledge of how the lung cancer spread to her brain and adrenals.

In describing the October 23, 1985, CAT-scan of Patricia's head, Dr. Gerson testified at his deposition that it was "a terrible time." He went on to say: "There was one lesion that was immediately next to the third ventricle of the brain, kind of pushing into it. We (referring to his brother who is also a radiologist) thought it was possible that she could have something happen right then. It was possible she could die in an hour."

A CAT-scan was done of Patricia's chest on November 19 and it didn't show anything. And yet by January 10 Patricia had the huge adrenal masses. Obviously there was cancer on the adrenals on November 19, but probably less than a billion cells or one centimeter.

Dr. Gerson didn't think he'd ever seen larger adrenal masses. The masses were several times larger than the adrenal glands themselves.

Gerson said that when Patricia learned of the brain tumors she was against radiotherapy. He knew Patricia had strong feelings about controlling her own self, and he thought she would try to take control of her death. This was obviously great testimony to present to the jury.

He thought she was totally sincere about why she went on television.

Patricia once said to him: "I don't have to go through with all this; the one thing I have is that I can end all this stuff when I want." (*This would help shoot down the idea that Peter had manipulated Pat into suicide.*) Dr. Gerson's deposition was extremely helpful.

> MR. ROSENBLATT: Have you ever in your career or in your reading ever heard of a doctor anywhere in America or the world who is told by a terminally ill cancer patient that they couldn't take the pain anymore, [that they were] going to go home and commit suicide? Have you ever heard of any doctor ever reporting that to the authorities?
> A: Personally I have never heard of anybody reporting it, no.

"Peter was utterly devoted to Patricia and he did everything he could to make her comfortable. And she did everything she could to not make it too terrible for him."

"We were sitting there and Patricia was vomiting and retching uncontrollably, and my recollection was that Pete said, 'She could throw up, vomit up her blood and die.' And I think I said, 'Yeah, she could.' "

We knew Judge Thompson would be restrictive on the broader issues, yet Susan and I were confident that the great majority of the favorable testimony from Drs. Koelle, Yesner, Hurwitz, and Gerson would get in. How could we pass that up? Through the testimony of these experts, the jury would appreciate that to make Peter Rosier the scapegoat for the inadequacies of the medical and legal systems would constitute a cruel injustice. Peter felt very strongly that the testimony from this very impressive contingent of doctors would vindicate him.

The motivation of all our experts was pure, which is very seldom the case. None of them had a previous relationship with Peter or myself, none of them was an idealogue on the euthanasia issue, and none of them was in the case for either money or publicity. I would argue to the jury that comparing them to Dr. Forney would be like comparing Yellowstone Park to a rest stop on an interstate highway.

Susan reminded me of a lengthy deposition I had taken of a listed State's expert—Dr. Anthony Iannone, an M.D. professor of neurology at the Medical College of Ohio (in Toledo) since 1968. Forney, a colleague at the same school, had gotten him involved and Dr. Iannone traveled to Fort Myers to examine Patricia's CAT-scans and other records. Yet he was never called to testify by the State. I considered reading some of his expert deposition testimony as part of Peter's defense.

After the first hour or so of his deposition I had the distinct feeling that Dr. Iannone was uncomfortable in his role, particularly with Peter sitting there teary eyed the whole time. It is one thing to take a strong position in the abstract on a controversial subject like euthanasia; it is quite another to realize that your testimony could help imprison a person for life. I questioned Dr. Iannone about this during his deposition:

> MR. ROSENBLATT: So that's why you agreed to be a witness? (*He didn't seem to have anything against the idea of assisting a suicide, but he held doctors to a higher standard.*)
> A: Yes.
> Q: Because Dr. Rosier didn't function as a doctor should function?
> A: Yes.
> Q: If we had the same exact facts but Peter Rosier was an electrician or a carpenter, then you wouldn't be testifying?
> A: (*After a very long pause*) That's probably correct, yes.
> Q: You're basically doing Dr. Forney a favor? You don't need this aggravation, do you?
> A: Yeah, that is correct.
> Q: The reason you're sitting in that chair, is because a colleague at your medical school asked you to help him and the State of Florida in this case, correct?
> A: Yes.

Because Dr. Iannone is an honest man, he gave some great testimony for us. If we put on a defense, Susan had the assignment of figuring out a method whereby we could read some of his deposition testimony to the jury without calling him as our witness and being bound by any unfavorable testimony.

> Q: If a long-time patient of yours comes in to tell you that they can't take it anymore, they want to say goodbye, and they tell you they are going to end it—when that patient leaves your office, you're not calling the police, are you?
> A: No.
> Q: You would respect that patient's freedom of choice, wouldn't you?
> A: Yes.
> Q: That goes on all the time in medicine, doesn't it?

A: To some extent yes. I believe that certainly patients have the right to make such decisions for themselves.

Q: Would you not agree that in many American hospitals today that frequently what happens with terminally ill patients is that doctors secretly increase morphine drips or take such other steps as may be necessary to hasten the patient's demise?

A: I would agree with that; yes, it certainly has happened.

Q: It goes on all the time, doesn't it?

A: Yes.

Q: It does, doesn't it?

A: Yes. (*What an incredible breath of fresh air. When I would ask a Fort Myers doctor that question, they would look at me as if I was from Mars.*)

Q: Do you think that any of the doctors who very quietly increase morphine drips to end a life and put someone out of their misery . . . should be punished?

A: I don't believe so, no.

Q: My guess would be that what would make most doctors angry would be another doctor who talks straight and in the open about what goes on in the real world with terminally ill patients. That would be very upsetting to the medical community, wouldn't it?

A: Yes, I believe that would be correct.

Ironically, some of the strongest testimony came from Dr. Iannone. On the purely technical medical areas such as the differences between being asleep, in a stupor, or in a coma he would have been helpful to the State; but they could not gamble on my cross. Dr. Iannone agreed with me that it is very common for doctors to hear from patients that they intend to take matters into their own hands and end their lives.

Okay, back to the bottom-line question: Could we risk allowing Peter to testify?

Susan and I spent hours coming up with a list of all those subjects that Volz and Russell were salivating over in anticipation of their cross. Our comments reminded us and Peter where the State would be coming from and its areas of proof. Susan's title for the list was "Vulnerable Areas on Cross Examination."

The affair and separation: In his manuscript Peter had provided the

State with great material. If Peter fudged on anything the State would parade in his former girlfriend as rebuttal evidence.

The speed with which Peter began dating after Patricia's death: Peter would say that he had been terribly lonely; he was not interested in sex but, rather, companionship. Peter probably could not sell this, and his incessant sobbing would in time become a turn-off.

The Cantor garbage: Peter would be asked about prostitutes and his desire to buy a fleet of Rolls Royces and shit on all his enemies in Fort Myers. The State would set up opportunities so they could bring in the whores as rebuttal witnesses. Their appearance would not jive with Peter carrying the torch for the love of his life.

The fact that Peter was capable of attending a crowded, lavish birthday celebration less than one week after Patricia's death: Knowing Peter for several years there was no doubt in my mind of his everlasting love for and devotion to Patricia; but would we be able to convince a jury with so much damaging evidence?

The conspiracy to commit murder: In his manuscript Peter described a discussion among Patricia's brothers and father about suffocating "the love of my life." Just moments before Patricia died, according to "The Lady," Vincent said, "If someone would put his hands over her mouth, she'd die quickly, or maybe a pillow. We could put a pillow over her face." How could Peter testify that he never heard the patio discussion leading to the smothering, when he wrote about it in chapter 34, which was in evidence? How could Peter distance himself from the conspiracy when it was described in "The Lady"? Wasn't it an interesting coincidence that Vincent "put his hands over her mouth," exactly as Peter described in his manuscript?

Elizabeth's phone call with the Delmans: Peter's daughter was anxious to testify in her father's behalf. There had been testimony about a telephone conversation between Elizabeth and Farrell Delman that was very incriminating to Peter. Elizabeth had angrily chastised Farrell for not calling her brother, Jacob, on his birthday. She was angry at her uncles and grandfather for forgetting Jacob so soon after his mother's death. In this conversation, many months before Peter's television confession and any thought of a criminal prosecution, Elizabeth blurted out words to this effect: "After smothering my mother, the least you could do is call Jacob on his birthday!" Elizabeth would have great difficulty explaining her comment when cross examined by the State. The State would be able to argue forcefully that Peter knew of the smothering and had confided in his children.

PETER THE GREAT MANIPULATOR:

(A) He lied about or grossly exaggerated the likelihood of Patricia suffering a gruesome death as a means of causing her to commit suicide.
(B) He lied about her life expectancy for the same reason.
(C) He lied about his own suicide intentions for the same reason.
(D) He wanted Patricia to commit suicide sooner rather than later in order to end his own suffering, and so he could get on with his life as a best-selling author.
(E) Peter cleverly manipulated the Delmans into doing his dirty work by pretending to be out of control so that they would take action. He accomplished this by repeatedly talking about a gruesome death, the death rattle, Pat awakening as a vegetable, the coma going on for a long time, etc.
(F) He sought to minimize estate taxes (assuming a double suicide).
(G) The method by which Peter substantially increased his disability payments while, according to his loyal secretary, he was ostensibly disabled. He was getting fifteen thousand dollars per month for doing nothing; he had successfully bridged the gap between being a doctor and being an author; and his early retirement scheme had worked.

REASONS FOR THE JURY TO DISLIKE PETER:

(A) Several reasons enumerated above apply here as well.
(B) His arrogance in announcing on the TV interview and in his manuscript that he was above the law and would seek to change the law.
(C) His arrogance in thinking he could confess in his manuscript and on television and not suffer any consequences because the evidence (i.e., the body) had been burned. He was so sure of himself that he sent his manuscript to many publishers and agents.
(D) His desire for fame and fortune in wanting to be a best-selling author, the subject of a movie, and the guru of the euthanasia movement.
(E) Peter's substantial wealth coupled with his disability income, owning an expensive apartment on Park Avenue in Manhattan, and his fancy cars.
(F) The nude photos of him and Patricia hanging in their home for their two children and everyone else to see.
(G) Explicit sex scenes in the book both with Patricia and his paramour

during the separation. Detailed descriptions of sexual movie making with Patricia as her cancer was progressing.

(H) Having sex with his cancer-ravaged wife an hour or so before she gulped down the Seconal. The skins of conservative jurors would crawl.

(I) The medical malpractice case on behalf of Patricia against his own hospital and Patricia's doctor for causing her death.

THE BIGGEST POTENTIAL DANGER AREA:

Peter was in love again and had been for quite some time, and he planned to remarry in the very near future if acquitted. His future wife, a lovely woman, had lived with him in Fort Myers (although they almost never went out together in public) and lived with him in a condominium in St. Petersburg during the trial. To our astonishment the press had never mentioned this relationship. Volz, Russell, and Fitzpatrick never said a word about her during the trial but they knew of her existence. They would undoubtedly spring a surprise, out-of-the-blue question to Peter on cross examination about the girlfriend. I would object in a flash, and my objection would be sustained, but the damage would already have been done.

Susan had spoken at great length to Alan Dershowitz about how to protect the appellate record by attempting to pin down the judge as to how loose or tight he would be in terms of restricting the danger areas. As appellate specialists, Alan and Susan spoke the same language and they both possessed the extra added ingredient of having a very practical streak; their heads were not in the clouds, mesmerized by case citations and arcane principles of law. They have the ability to relate quickly both statutory and case law to practical consequences. Since Alan would be handling any appeal in the case of a conviction, he had a particular interest in a well-preserved court record.

Susan protected the record in a very lengthy hearing outside the presence of the jury by raising all these issues, but, predictably, Judge Thompson could not be pinned down to say such and such an area would be 100 percent off limits. There were always qualifiers.

The judge said things like: "It's almost impossible to rule on some of these things in advance. . . . I can conceive of circumstances where drugs would become relevant. I think draft and military service are appropriate questions to ask a witness as far as their background."

We knew it would be open season, and Volz or Russell (probably both because the cross examination would extend over days) would have a field day with Peter. The judge made it clear that there would be broad latitude in the areas of attempts to get the book published, Peter's wealth, the insurance disability circumstances, Peter's attendance at the big party very soon after his wife's death, dating, and the like. Inevitably the judge's kitchen-sink philosophy would prevail.

I would be in the very uncomfortable and unusual position of objecting constantly (again to protect and preserve the record for appellate purposes); the judge would invariably overrule my objections, and it would look to the jury that we had much to hide—which, of course, we did. I hadn't attempted to count up all the objections made by both sides, but my best guesstimate was that the State objected ten times more often than we did. I liked that because it played to my style of coming across as a nontechnical straight shooter in contrast to the prosecution whose attorneys were a bunch of nit-pickers constantly interfering with the flow of testimony.

After studying the list for a long time, Susan and I just looked at each other. Words were unnecessary. The conclusion both of us had been subconsciously avoiding was inescapable. We would strongly recommend that Peter Rosier not testify; he should not testify. If he disagreed and insisted, he would be convicted. Of that I had no doubt. Peter simply had too much baggage; he would not wear well. If he was hell-bent on testifying, he would be adding to his earlier mistakes.

In many ways Peter was a great client, but he was very hard to take on a personal level. He had opinions about every topic under the sun. At times Peter could be very honest about his own faults. At the time Loren Granoff and Alan Goldman of my office were gathering affidavits in the hope of getting the trial moved out of Fort Myers, they stayed at Peter's house. They were working feverishly and producing excellent results; yet they told me that Peter not only failed to ever show any real appreciation for their efforts, but he was constantly goading and criticizing them.

I believed that Peter would be an excellent witness on my direct examination, but he would fall apart on cross. In terms of intelligence, overall sharpness, and his general fund of knowledge, I felt he was superior to Volz and Russell. But this was their turf; they had twenty-eight years of experience between them in prosecuting thousands of criminal cases and they both had very impressive track records. They would know how to bait Peter, and they would eat him alive. Peter was terrific at repartee, making intellectual points, and clever sound bites, but that was not the game in the courtroom.

Peter knew that if he testified, much of the nation and the world would be listening. It was his one opportunity to tell everyone about his love for Patricia and speak openly about euthanasia. It was a once-in-a-lifetime chance and a very difficult decision for Peter. The Rosier personal story, the feud with the Delmans, and the broader euthanasia issues were naturals for media appeal, and that's why the courtroom was filled everyday. A significant part of our defense strategy was psychological: The way Susan and I had functioned as a team and the way we interacted with Peter and his kids would, I hoped, make the jury feel that by convicting Peter it would be the equivalent of convicting us. A married couple was defending a married couple.

Peter; his daughter, Elizabeth; his son, Jacob; and Peter's fiancée came to Miami the day before Thanksgiving to discuss with us whether Peter should testify. It was, after all, his life. He had been married to a great lady and he had a story to tell. He could not allow that story to be told by the Fort Myers News-Press or even by the New York Times, Newsweek, People, or the Associated Press.

Peter was not the selfish, Machiavellian schemer that the State was painting him to be. He wanted other loving family members to be spared his anguish in similar circumstances. He wanted to enlighten the world, and he wanted Patricia's life and death to have meaning, to be remembered.

Peter made the very telling point that jurors (in spite of what they say about accepting the premise that a defendant is not obliged to testify in a criminal trial) draw unfavorable inferences from a defendant's failure to look them in the eye and tell his story. An example: "Are you a Communist?" Answer: "I prefer not to answer that question." Most people would conclude that the guy is or was a Communist. I agreed with him.

He felt that he had sat so patiently through the whole ordeal: he reminded me of the months and months of hell, beginning with the grand jury indictment, the several days he was a prisoner at the Lee County Jail, the numerous depositions, the terrible publicity, being rejected by his former colleagues and friends, and so much more. The one thing that had sustained him was knowing that his turn would come and he would vindicate himself.

And now I was telling him in brutal terms that I believed he would fold under withering cross examination, and be convicted for his unwillingness to surrender his desire to educate the world on euthanasia and speak of his love for Patricia. Peter also truly wanted the jury and the public to be told the truth by the likes of Drs. Koelle, Yesner, Hurwitz, Gerson, and Iannone. So did Susan and I.

I told Peter it boiled down to this: "Do you want to help humankind in prison and get a ton of fan mail, or do you want to be a lot less famous and, we hope, free?" I knew Peter would never forgive me if he did not testify and was convicted anyway.

We spent hours together at my office in downtown Miami directly across the street from the huge Dade County Courthouse where turkey buzzards dry their outstretched wings on the very top spires some twenty-five floors above Flagler Street. Susan, Peter, and I went over the list slowly and meticulously. Peter debated most impressively his responses to the charges that would be hurled against him.

I reminded Peter that Volz, Russell, and Fitzpatrick had read his manuscript of over six hundred pages several times; with the exception of his immediate family and us, they knew him better than anyone.

"Your manuscript is the equivalent of voluntarily handing over to them the most intimate records of your psychiatrist. Those six hundred pages are a lawyer's dream in terms of material for cross examination. They will bombard you with questions, questions from left field, questions from off the wall in deep right, questions from anywhere and everywhere. The State will set you up so they will be able to impeach you with your own words from your manuscript. How about these questions Peter?"

- Love, love, love! You loved your wife as much as any man has ever loved a woman. Please explain to the jury why you were at a party a week after she was cremated, complaining that you couldn't get laid?

- Explain how on the one hand you were in a deep depression and under psychiatric care because of the loss of the love of your life, whereas, on the other hand, you were making it with prostitutes.

- Dr. Rosier, I have watched you during this month-long trial and I have observed that you are very quick on your feet, quick to react. Actually you look much younger than your age. Explain to the jury why you are incapable of sitting on a chair at a desk and looking at slides through a microscope, considering this is what you have been doing your entire professional life?

- Are you disabled from jogging? Are you disabled from playing tennis? Are you disabled from traveling to Europe?

- Isn't it true, Dr. Rosier, that in spite of your great love for Patricia and your obsession with her memory, you have somehow adjusted sufficiently to have established a new relationship with a woman you are living with? I guess you just have the power to put Pat out of your mind when the situation calls for that.

- You were intimately involved with every detail of what was going on from the time Patricia swallowed the Seconal until the time she died. You got morphine from Dr. Dosoretz and you got morphine from Dr. Harwin, and you injected your wife and inserted the morphine suppositories. You were receiving breathing reports from the Delman brothers, and when you went to Dr. Carlino's house you called to find out the status of your wife. It seems the only time you managed to be uninvolved was during the final act. Isn't that correct?

- Dr. Rosier, are you telling this jury that the first time you learned about the smothering was after your indictment? Then please explain how you managed to describe in exquisite detail in your manuscript—chapter 34, now in evidence—the precise mechanism of death?

- Isn't it true that you heard Vincent, Farrell, and Russell discussing the suffocation, while you were with them on the patio? How can you deny this when you wrote it in chapter 34, which has been read to the jury?

- Dr. Rosier, you never told Vincent, "Don't you dare suffocate Patricia!" or otherwise expressly disagree with the suffocation. Isn't that correct? Vincent was assisting you and completing your dirty work, correct? Isn't it true that you never wrote in chapter 34, "I told the Delmans they were not to smother my love"?

- Dr. Rosier, isn't it true that you were initially angry at Farrell when he emerged from Patricia's room, because you knew the Delmans had just suffocated your wife? Then why did you write in chapter 34 of your manuscript: "I was now outside my bedroom door and Farrell emerged. I found myself in his arms and sobbing. When he approached me, I had hated him and did not wish to touch him; but I was now in his arms and sobbing and looking up and begging Pat for forgiveness. A moment later, Russell emerge from the bedroom and told me that Pat was dead."

- You were begging Pat for forgiveness for having schemed to have her father smother her. Isn't that correct?

- Isn't it true that you told your daughter, Elizabeth, about the actual suffocation and that explains her conversation with Farrell Delman in which she accused the Delmans of smothering her mother?

- You recoil at the mention of Vincent smothering your wife; do you consider shoving suppositories up her rectum a more pleasant means of death? You certainly intended to end Patricia's life when you injected her with morphine and inserted morphine suppositories. Isn't that true? You confessed to Patricia's murder in chapter 34 but said you would fight the law, correct?

- You had the argument with Dr. Dosoretz because you wanted to get more medication from him to accomplish your goal of killing Patricia. Isn't that true?

- In your chapter 34, in your very own words, you have the Delman's talking about smothering Patricia. And you want us to believe that you, a board-certified medical doctor with a very high IQ, couldn't figure out why the three Delmans went into the bedroom? Come on!

Peter reacted as if I had belted him with right crosses. The list was the clincher to Peter as it had been to Susan and myself. There was simply too much to combat. Peter realized that he would constantly be on the defensive, and although he was confident of winning most of the skirmishes, the State would have too much firepower for him to win the war. It wasn't worth the gamble; the State's case was relatively weak on the collateral "character assassination" issues and Peter decided not to give the prosecution a second chance to strengthen its case. By not putting on a defense, we had the opportunity to rebut the State's closing argument. The last voice the jury would hear would be mine.

Susan and I appreciated very much the fact that a decision could be made that day, and Peter never revisited it. Now I could devote all my energies to preparing my final argument, and Susan could devote all of hers to the jury instructions and our various motions. Of course our decision was not conveyed to our opponents. I wanted them to dissipate their efforts in the direction of cross examining Peter and our doctors. We hoped they would put days in on that and have substantially less time to prepare for their final arguments.

I would pretend that I was going to put on a vigorous defense until five minutes before I walked into open court to announce to the jury, "Surprise Your Honor, the defense rests."

Certainly Peter had his own private doubts about how he would withstand a long, tough, probing cross examination of every facet of both his exterior and interior lives. Although he initially debated vigorously and effectively in favor of taking the stand, I think he was relieved once the decision was reached. Almost without missing a beat he started asking me questions about my strategy during final argument.

Judge Thompson was going to be generous in the time allotted to each side for closing argument. We each had four hours: I had asked for more time, the State had asked for less. Four hours was plenty; if I couldn't convince the jury in four, I wouldn't be able to convince them no matter how much time I was allotted.

Final argument would consume an entire day. The jury would be sequestered for the first time during the trial; they would stay at a hotel that night. The following morning Judge Thompson would instruct them on the law and thereafter they would begin their deliberations.

This was a new experience for me. Before this case the longest final argument I ever had was two hours, whereas the great majority of my summations were in the neighborhood of one hour. This was my very first final argument in a criminal case. I had never before been in a situation where the jury heard final argument one day and were given the law on the next. Susan would kid me that in my notes I frequently referred to Peter as the Plaintiff (the person filing suit) rather than the Defendant. (In civil cases I always represented the plaintiff.) Another first: this was the first trial during which Susan made objections in the presence of the jury.

Judge Thompson recognized and respected the need for advocacy and creativity in final argument. I am amazed by the number of lawyers with big reputations who do little more in summation than recapitulate the testimony and evidence. The bureaucrats who preside have so infected and intimidated the trial bar that many lawyers sheepishly accept the unreasonable restrictions imposed on them. Emotion, drama, and passion are looked upon askance by those who worship at the altar of the ticking clock and the speedy assembly-line movement of cases at all cost.

It is always difficult to decide how much time to reserve for rebuttal argument. The State's four hours would be sandwiched between the opening part of my final argument and my rebuttal, and it would be divided between Volz and Russell. I was inclined to leave about an hour for rebuttal. By that time it would probably be after 5:00 P.M. and the jury would be spent after listening to three lawyers argue for seven hours.

Peter agreed that my approach during final argument had to be very high risk. It is usually acceptable to attack one or two targets, but I was going after several and I would be highly insulting and sarcastic because that's how I felt, and that's what I thought would be most effective. That approach can make conservative jurors very uncomfortable. I didn't think I had a choice.

I would be coming down hard on the Delmans; blasting D'Alessandro and the State of Florida for bringing these charges and for being suckered into the immunity deal; socking it to the personnel at Channel 20; as well as the hypocrisy of the legal and medical systems in dealing with euthanasia-related issues.

One of the arguments I used that dissuaded Peter from testifying was that I would get the jury to hate the Delmans more than him. By not taking the stand the State would not have nearly as clear a target as I had with the Delmans. Peter loved it when I told him I would say to the jury: "You can't put this productive doctor away for life on the testimony of Farrell the tobacco lobbyist; Russell the body awareness teacher; and Vincent, New York's Medicaid King."

The area I would need to spend the most time on was my "Piss on the Law" theme. Whenever I came close to being direct on that subject the State would object, and their objections would always be sustained. I had to figure a way to tell the jury in a subtle way that they should disregard the law.

Volz and Russell did as good a job as I have ever seen from jury selection onward relative to the jury's absolute duty to follow the law. Before accepting the jury they got a commitment from each member to follow the law even if they disagreed with it, even if doing so led to a result with which they were unhappy. I reminded Peter that they excused any prospective juror who equivocated even in the slightest on that subject.

The prosecution was able to get all the jurors to agree that, "We are a government of laws and not of men." They repeated again and again and the jury agreed that, "We are in a court of law; this is not the legislature." The State conditioned the jury so effectively that the jurors agreed in principle with the concept that when the law is not followed, the result is a miscarriage of justice. The judge actually said as much in his formal instructions and that would be a killer. I assured Peter that I would get out my words about Martin Luther King and the unjust laws he fought against. That guaranteed that the prosecutors would be on their feet in a flash, but the black juror, the black male alternate, and the white jurors would know exactly where I was coming from.

During final argument Volz and Russell would remind the jurors of their promise to follow the law. They would act as though a binding contract had been entered into between the State and the individual jurors. They obtained the same promise on the immunity issue: "Even if you don't like the fact that the Delmans have immunity, you understand that is legally irrelevant here and this defendant must be held individually accountable on the basis of his own criminal conduct."

It's simply scary to see how easily people can be brainwashed. Ninety percent of Americans would probably agree reflexively with the statement "We are a government of laws and not of men," but that is simply bunk. Former Chief Justice Earl Warren and present Chief Justice William Rehnquist, because of their beliefs and personalities, interpreted the Constitution and federal statutes in vastly different ways, resulting in profoundly different practical consequences. The words of the laws and Constitution didn't change, only the justices did. Governors, senators, and presidents, depending on their political agendas, use the same laws to effect totally different results.

During World War II the American government legally put loyal, decent Japanese Americans in internment camps without ever charging them with crimes. In many states after World War II, it was illegal for Asians to marry Americans. Articles and books have been written about moronic, unjust, and unenforced laws that still exist.

Blacks certainly understand how the law was historically used as an instrument of repression. When I was a kid growing up in Miami Beach (after we left Brooklyn), it was illegal for an employed black domestic or any black to remain within the city limits after nightfall. Entertainers such as Sammy Davis, Jr., and Lena Horne could perform at Miami Beach's nightclubs but they couldn't sleep on Miami Beach. Sure, that was the law and we must follow the law—just like a bunch of gutless zombies.

I always said that the best thing Peter had going for him was Gertrude. The jury had never seen her but they sure as hell would, with her walker, sitting between Jacob and Elizabeth during my final argument. In spite of all the crap that had been dumped on Peter, if Gertrude and Pat and his kids have loved him so much, he can't be all that bad. He is not a guy who deserves to be sitting in a cell with drug dealers and armed robbers.

I only hoped the prosecution objects when I mention Gertrude and point to her in the audience; that will only draw more attention to her. She looks so vulnerable: she kind of reminds me of Ethel Barrymore at her frailest. Gertrude is not in some nursing home but rather in Peter's home where she's always lived. Yes, actions speak louder than words.

I didn't intend to object a single time during the State's four hours of blasting Peter and his defense team, all the while waving the flag. When they sit down they are through, but I have an hour of rebuttal. They will, of course, object during my rebuttal and I can point out to the jury very self-righteously: "I let them have their say without interrupting once. Why can't they do the same for me?"

I intended to capitalize on a serious mistake the prosecutors made in opening the door too wide during their opening statement. Very uncharacteristically for them, they said Peter was at that big party a week after Patricia's death and said something like: "Here I am, the most eligible bachelor in town and I can't get laid." But they never produced a witness to back that up. And this statement was allegedly made in the presence of many witnesses. Volz and Russell must know that during the opening part of my summation I will call this their lowest blow in an avalanche of cheap shots—these holier-than-thou prosecutors who insist that evidence comes only in witnesses' answers and not in Stanley Rosenblatt's tricky questions. Where is their evidence that Peter Rosier made that vulgar remark? Yeah, I'll sure dump some filth on them.

They can't tell the jury they had Landis McMahon ready to say that, and they can't explain why they finally decided against calling her. And if they ignore my accusation, I will repeat it during my rebuttal argument.

In the context of a law school seminar this would be a very interesting philosophical and jurisprudential point. In one sense their representation was made in good faith; in another sense it was highly prejudicial and irrelevant. It's not as though I manipulated or maneuvered them into that position; it was their choice to come on that strong during opening statements and it backfired on them. In spite of what I knew, I had no qualms whatsoever about employing this strategy.

Our instructions to Peter as to his demeanor during final argument were simple and to the point:

Believe me, the jury will be looking at you constantly. All they have to do is look straight ahead. They have been here a month and have heard all this fascinating testimony because of you. It is your life they hold in their hands and they know it. The State is going to portray you as tricky and deceitful, and I want you to come across as straightforward and decent.

Do your best to control your sobbing. Don't sit there blowing your nose or dabbing your eyes. We know it's sincere but one or more jurors could think you were acting.

Under no circumstances smirk. Sit there with a poker face, looking very sad. When they say something that gets you crazy, let the pain show; convey a sense of controlled rage and tragedy.

Look at the jury, but don't stare at them. Keep your direct eye contact to a minimum since I don't want any of them to get the impression that you are trying to intimidate them in any way.

Don't write notes. Don't whisper to me or Susan. Every now and then look over at your son and your daughter and Gertrude; it's okay if some communication passes such as a nod or a raised eyebrow or a gentle smile.

Be yourself, be natural.

I emphasized to Peter that months of meticulous preparation and profound legal analysis can amount to nothing if a lawyer and/or his client do something stupid. I told him a true story about a great lawyer (Edward Bennett Williams) and his multimillionaire industrialist client (Victor Posner) who was on trial a few years ago in federal court in Miami for income tax evasion.

The case was being tried during the oppressive Miami summer. At that time of year the sun doesn't set until about 8:00 P.M. So when the jurors would be excused at about 5:30 or 6:00 P.M., they would face the still broiling sun and go to their hotbox automobiles, which were parked outdoors. When Williams and Posner left the courthouse they stepped into an air-conditioned, luxurious limousine. The jury got even; they found Posner guilty!

The State will accuse me of trying to stir up anger and sympathy. I know myself. I will get very wrapped up in my final argument. The State will accuse me of being excessively dramatic. I could care less so long as the jury doesn't buy it.

Susan and I had the luxury of some additional time to talk about the makeup of our jury. I can remember having terrible arguments with lawyers who would ask "Why did you keep juror A? Why did you get rid of juror B?" If I had made a mistake in jury selection, I was stuck with it; it served no constructive purpose to second-guess myself while the trial was still continuing.

Although we were "stuck" with these twelve people, it was nonetheless useful to review their histories and how they had answered key questions. This knowledge could affect my approach in final argument, analogies I might choose to use, and even my choice of words.

The State had ten preemptory challenges and the defense had the same number. The State used all ten of its challenges, although at one point they accepted the jury after exercising only four. I excused several from that group, so a new batch was seated and the chemistry changed. The defense used a total of nine challenges.

The whole process of *voir dire* (jury selection) only took a little over three days, which was extremely brief in a case of this magnitude and complexity. Yet for me personally, it was by far the longest time I ever spent questioning prospective jurors. Most judges are very unrealistic and arbitrary in constricting time limits within which to question jurors. Their credo is: gotta move them cases. Judge Thompson recognized the need that lawyers have for creativity and latitude in this important phase of the trial.

Selecting fair and impartial jurors is a very tricky business. If you ask general, abstract questions that are unrelated to the facts of your particular case, jurors will not be candid with you. In order for the purpose of *voir dire* to be served, you need to be able to ask preliminary as well as follow-up questions. For example:

"Are you prejudiced against my client because he is rich or black or Jewish or whatever?" People will invariably deny both prejudice and hatred in a public setting.

"Do you have the courage of your convictions?" If a juror is for me, I don't want them to cave in simply because the majority is pressuring them. Nearly everyone will say they have the courage of their convictions; in reality few do.

"Are you intimidated by authority?" This is a very important area because obviously the prosecution is symbolically representing both the people of Florida and the great state of Florida. It is very easy to be intimidated by a grand jury indictment, an information filed directly by the State Attorney's Office, a judge telling you of your duty to follow the law, etc. Nearly everyone will say they are not intimidated by authority, when the reality is that nearly everyone is to a certain extent. And the only way to get past the pat answers is by digging.

Many nasty and unimaginative judges who subscribe to the theory that lawyers should function as robots, restrict counsel to generalized, vague questions that reveal next to nothing. Sure, you can ask questions about background, work, children, parents, and hobbies, but these are not the areas that will direct you to deeply rooted attitudes.

I am in a minority among trial lawyers, but I don't believe in the value of psychologist or sociologist jury-selection people. I think, by and large, this is a highly subjective area wherein they have attempted to create a pseudoscience. They keenly understand the insecurities of nearly all trial lawyers. I am very interested in anyone who can supply me with facts about prospective jurors, but in the final analysis it was up to Susan and me to draw conclusions from these facts.

On the other hand, I know excellent lawyers who swear by the services of some of the top jury-selection people. Many lawyers and others believe that those services were the key to success in the William Kennedy Smith rape trial.

You have to have the opportunity to draw people out of their shells, to engage them in conversation. I love to ask this question: "Do you consider yourself a detail person or a big-picture person?" In giving an example I describe Jimmy Carter as a hands-on, detail person in terms of how he functioned as president, whereas Ronald Reagan was definitely a big-picture guy who delegated much authority.

Most people will hedge somewhat initially but that's the kind of question that gets them to talk. As a follow-up question I usually ask: "If I went to your home or office and looked at your desk and closet, would I find everything neatly organized or would they be a mess?"

Anyone who was proud of the fact that he or she was a technical, detail person with a very neat desk and closet, I did not want on this jury. That kind of person would be only too happy to follow the law even though the result would be unjust. It wasn't only the substance of a given answer, but also the force and energy behind the answer. I was looking for people who could rise above the law, who were compassionate, and who could look at the big picture in terms of Peter Rosier's relationship to the criminal justice system. I wanted people who would conclude that Peter Rosier was no criminal.

I think I am also in the minority in not trying very hard to figure out beforehand who will be the foreperson of the jury. I agree completely with the idea that it is better to convince two or three strong persons rather than a bunch of weaklings. I don't believe in making my final argument to the one or two jurors I speculate are the strongest. I try to get something going with all of them in terms of eye contact and communication.

I developed one question for this trial that I had never used before. The way this question was answered with the accompanying body language and facial expressions became our litmus test. If someone answered this question the wrong way, they were gone, even if we liked the objective criteria, such as the right occupation and a seemingly liberal philosophy.

"Let's say a man parks his car at a meter that takes quarters. He goes into his pocket and finds a quarter. Suddenly he hears a scream and sees an elderly woman fall on the sidewalk; she is lying there in great pain with a broken hip. He quickly puts the quarter back in his pocket, and he goes and assists the lady. A policeman sees all this. Obviously, from a technical standpoint the man has violated the law: his car is parked and he didn't put in the quarter. I'd like to know who believes that the policeman, assuming he knows the reason why the man didn't put in the quarter, is correct in issuing a ticket? Should the policeman give him a ticket?"

Anyone who said the cop was right to give the ticket or had a duty to give the ticket, or he was only doing his job, or even if the juror felt it was totally within the discretion of the cop to make that judgment and whatever he decided was fine with them, that person was gone.

It was frightening to us that so many people felt the cop was correct. We sure as hell were in a conservative, law-and-order town. Such a person could not relate to me, my style, or my arguments. As far as I was concerned, they were assassins and would be in the State's hip pocket.

To me the cop was a moron who displayed indefensible poor judgment and smallness of mind. To me there was no gray in this decision: it was 100 percent wrong to give a ticket under these circumstances. The hell with the lousy quarter; help the elderly woman laying on the sidewalk in great pain.

Of course I hit most of the traditional areas as well:

"Do you have any connection with the medical or legal fields or do you have any legal or medical background?" I did not want anyone with a legal background or anyone who had ever worked for an attorney, because such people tend to want to run the show, and frequently other jurors will defer to them.

I asked them about any contact they might have had with the City of Fort Myers, whether they had friends or relatives there, if they ever visited, etc.

I asked the prospective jurors about their chief news source. Was it television or newspapers? I wanted to know if they had any connections to or background in the fields of media or law enforcement.

I wanted to know if they owned animals and what kind.

A particularly important question was: "Have you or any member of your family ever been the victim of a crime?" The more important follow-up question was: "Was the criminal caught?"

The great majority of the prospective jurors had been the victims of crimes and in nearly every instance the criminal was not apprehended. A real slice of Americana. This was extremely important to me in terms of making a point: "Why are we expending these tremendous resources on Peter Rosier when there are real criminals out there?"

I got rid of anyone who said that suicide was always wrong in any circumstance. I prefer people with no prior jury experience and we had a jury of mostly virgins. Repeat jurors quickly become know-it-alls. I wanted jurors who were reachable, who had open minds and could be persuaded. I explained to Peter that in a criminal case, unlike a civil case, we only needed one juror who would say: "Come hell or high water I'm not convicting this guy." A hung jury would be a great victory.

I learned a lot about these jurors by asking them if they had a favorite movie, author, or sport and to explain why. Whether someone answers boxing or golf tells me a lot. Ordinarily I will want the boxing fan, especially if he is covered with tattoos. Guys with tattoos don't cotton to orders like "You must follow the law." I did not get such a juror in St. Petersburg. If someone loves an insipid musical but never saw *Citizen Kane* or didn't like *Casablanca,* that speaks volumes to me.

One of the jurors who would have knighted the hypothetical cop for bravery told me he didn't like the classic film *Gone With the Wind.* Knowing that this guy was going to be my first challenge, and not caring whether I offended him, I said: "Millions of people consider *Gone With the Wind* the greatest movie ever made, and it would be on the top-ten list of nearly everyone. What didn't you like about it?" His priceless answer: "It dragged."

When focusing on a particular juror, our policy is that Susan studies the reaction of the others. Then, when the State is questioning jurors, I concentrate on the juror being probed, and Susan studies the others. It is amazing that most people give themselves away eventually in the sense of revealing their true selves. And that's why ample time is critical during *voir dire.*

It has frequently happened that we love a juror based on his or her answers, yet we gain a totally different perspective in terms of how that juror relates to the prosecutors or how he or she reacts to answers of fellow jurors. If your opponent is making unfunny, inane remarks and a juror is hysterical, that's someone to reject. Likewise to those who are sitting on the edge of their seat as the State explains the law of conspiracy.

Many times a juror will sucker a lawyer, giving the answer the attorney wants to hear. Some jurors are on a mission: they want to serve so they can zap one side or the other. They are unreachable. I knew that some jurors gave insincere answers to the parking meter question because they did not want me to bounce them.

This was another hypothetical question I asked, the answers to which told me a lot: "Let's say a doctor has had a physician/patient relationship with a man for twenty years. The man develops cancer, which spreads quickly; the doctor tries every possible treatment but nothing works. The patient tells his doctor that his wife is a nervous wreck, his kids are climbing the walls, and nothing is being accomplished by his hanging around in excruciating pain. His life is horrible, and he just wants to let the doctor know that he's going to end it. He doesn't want to be talked out of it; his mind is made up. My question is: Under these circumstances, and assuming the patient to be rational and intelligent, who among you believes that the doctor should pick up the telephone and call the police or Mr. D'Alessandro?"

I wanted jurors who believed that this was a personal decision and the doctor had no right to violate this confidence. I wanted jurors who believed that this was a matter of privacy, a freedom-of-choice issue. I did not want jurors who believed that government should intertwine itself in personal, family decisions. When you get a dialogue going on that kind of a question you get a feel for who your jurors are; they become flesh-and-blood people rather than ciphers.

We were playing to a very particular audience: seven women and five men. Theirs were the only opinions that mattered. Peter Rosier's fate would be decided by these twelve people.

1. Mrs. Blaney. Two children, several grandchildren. She was a retired hairdresser from Passaic, New Jersey. Her husband was an A&P warehouse supervisor for some forty-three years in New Jersey. Her parents were from eastern Europe. She had been living in the St. Petersburg area since 1981.

2. Mrs. Shumway, a surgical nurse at All Children's Hospital for the past eleven years, had lived in California and West Virginia. Her husband was an optical lens designer. She has two children, one a daughter in the Air Force. Mrs. Shumway has been a registered nurse since 1957. Would she hold Peter to a higher standard? Would she regard him as an embarrassment to the profession? In the abstract I did not want nurses on this jury, but Mrs. Shumway seemed like a sweet intelligent woman, and Susan and I felt comfortable with her.

3. Mr. Koenig was originally from Pennsylvania, but had lived in Florida since 1979. The father of four kids, he did programming for IBM, where he designed systems for the past twenty-four years. He had been smoking two packs of cigarettes a day for twenty years, and certainly he recognizes that they cause cancer. I could not relate to those jurors who said they had no idea whether there was a relationship between smoking and cancer. I didn't like his job; it seemed very technical and he had been with the same company for a long time. He had a bumper sticker on his car that said "LA Lakers." Little things mean a lot.

4. Ms. Williams was an attractive black woman, divorced, with two kids. She worked as a customer service supervisor for J.C. Penney. Her ex-husband was a mechanic. She was born in Clearwater, a small town on the west coast of Florida. Her father worked most of his career at the Ford Motor Company. Her mother worked for an insurance company some fifteen years.

Susan had made the argument that out of fifty jurors brought down, only three were black. The State excused another black woman, and Susan argued that under the law the judge had a responsibility to inquire into the basis for that preemptory challenge.

If the judge is satisfied that the true reason for the challenge is racial, the lawyer will not be permitted to have that challenge. As jurors do not admit to prejudice, neither do lawyers. They create nonracial reasons. They will look a judge in the eye and lie through their teeth. Another one of the profession's great legal fictions.

We were convinced that the State preferred a lily-white jury. Susan pointed out that the excused juror, absent her color, would have been ideal for the State in terms of her substantive answers and because she even had a close friend who worked for the state attorney. The judge refused to even inquire into the State's reasons for excusing this particular juror, so the challenge held.

5. Mr. Balagna was born in Michigan, but he had lived in St. Petersburg since 1984, when he retired as a designer for the Ford Motor Company. He held degrees in mechanical and industrial engineering. His wife was the secretary to the director of nurses at Garden City Hospital for twenty-two years. An engineer and a wife closely connected to the medical field—two strikes from my standpoint. But on the next pitch Mr. Balagna hit a double.

We discussed a movie about a man named Tucker who designed a car, called the "Arrow." He said, "I firmly believe the Big Three didn't want another car on the market and they manipulated the supplies and finances so he couldn't make a go of it." He had a mind of his own.

I said to Mr. Balagna, "Lawyers sit around and when they discuss jury selection they say you should be wary of engineers with a technical background. The conventional wisdom is that they tend to be scientific and very much downplay the human element. If you were me, would you be worried about you?"

"In our livelihood we use logic," he said. "Everything has to be logical. Based on that I would probably treat the evidence the same way." (I did not like that answer, but we liked him.)

6. Mrs. Venezia grew up and went to high school in Camden, New Jersey. She had two kids, and had been living in Florida for nine years. As a medical technologist and the assistant chemistry supervisor in a laboratory, her boss is a pathologist. How would that cut here? The odds were that her boss didn't like Rosier. Her work was technical and detailed. Her husband was the manager of a meat market.

7. Mr. Simon was from Long Island, as is Peter. He is Jewish. Mr. Simon, the retired father of four children, owned a retail store in New York. One of his daughters is doing research at Duke University, where Peter had gone to school. Mr. Simon's other daughter was a respiratory therapist, and one son was a truck driver. Another son was killed by

a drunk driver. Mr. Simon should not like Dr. Forney. Without apology Mr. Simon considered himself to be a detail-oriented, technical person. And he was the kind of person who liked to avoid arguments, which means that if he were in a minority he might very well cave in.

8. Mrs. Howard was also Jewish. She had resided in this area for twenty years. Born in Philadelphia, she lived in West Virginia and spent most of her working life in Washington, D.C. She retired from the President's Committee on Employment of the Handicapped. Before that she had been with the Women's Bureau of the Department of Labor, where her job was technical. She had no children. She said that when she was ten years old she was on her way from Charleston, West Virginia, to Philadelphia and she was out on the train platform when they got to Washington. It was nighttime and the Capitol was all lit up and very impressive. She decided on the spot that she wanted to work there someday. She accomplished that goal.

9. Mr. Melke, another retiree, had been in St. Petersburg two and a half years, although he visited the area for sixteen years every winter. He had been in heavy construction in Chicago for a general industrial contractor where he managed the piping for forty years. He was married with two children. His son was a pipe fitter, his daughter an auditor for a hotel in downtown Chicago. His wife was a legal secretary for a patent attorney. He was a fan of Mayor Daley, who he said ran Chicago with an iron hand. Would he be overly impressed with the authority of the judge and prosecutors?

He smoked one and a half to two packs a day for forty-eight years. I asked him, "What do you say to people who tell you you shouldn't smoke?" He replied, "You're right." He had a down-to-earth quality that we liked, and coming from Chicago he knew about real crime.

10. Ms. Palmer, originally from Puerto Rico, lived mainly in New York and Puerto Rico. She had been in Florida thirteen years. She worked in data communication for the U.S. Army. She was a school bus driver before she went to work for the Army. Her father was in construction and her mother worked as a clerk in a drugstore.

11. Mrs. Gaullin was originally from Jacksonville, Florida, but had lived for a while in Montana. She had lived in St. Petersburg for ten years and was married with no kids. She attended junior college and studied banking and finance. I would have preferred sociology or government. Her husband was an engineer for a company that installed and repaired telephone systems. Her mother was a receptionist for a pediatrician.

12. Mr. Lyons, another Long Islander, lived there his first sixteen years. A nineteen-year resident of St. Petersburg, he was married with

one child. A project manager for a marine equipment company, he loved to hunt and knew a lot about guns. He had a cousin with the county police department who is also on the **SWAT** team.

Five of our jurors were in their middle or late sixties and were retired. For years St. Petersburg was referred to as the retirement capitol of the United States. Three jurors were in their forties, another three were in their thirties, and only one was under thirty. Several were from New York and New Jersey; there were two native Floridians.

Did we have a good jury? I never know the answer to that question until I hear the verdict. As always we were worried about a few. We would play the cards that had been dealt us and pray for an acquittal.

19

Final Argument, Final Chance

Susan and I were refreshed by the long recess. On Friday night and Saturday we did not discuss the case; that is one of the many beauties of being a practicing Jew. The Sabbath is for Synagogue and family; dinner Friday night and lunch Saturday afternoon are the only two meals of the week when the entire family is together, and while always hectic the experience is uplifting.

We worked all day Sunday, November 27, and that evening we flew back to St. Petersburg. As predicted, the storm struck near the city, and although it did considerable property damage it was by no means a major hurricane. On Monday we were back in court. The lengthy arguments on the motion for acquittal were made as well as arguments on other defense motions (outside the presence of the jury). Judge Thompson denied them all. We had preserved the record for appellate purposes.

A silent current was underlying everything that transpired: Would Dr. Rosier take the witness stand? Would we mount a defense? No one asked us these questions directly until after our motions were denied. When asked directly I answered directly: the defense would rest without presenting the defendant or a single witness or exhibit.

Of course, we had to go through the one-minute formality of announcing this decision in the presence of the jury. Some of the jurors looked stunned; two or three seemed to smile knowingly; gasps and murmurs were heard from the audience. There was great disappointment from many members of the media upon learning that they would miss what promised to be dramatic and passionate testimony. This was followed by the letdown of the jury being excused until Wednesday, November 30. We needed

301

the rest of Monday and all day Tuesday to debate with the judge the instructions on the law that he would give to the jury.

If the law was simply the law, why did experienced lawyers need all that time to argue over what the judge should tell the jury? Again personality, temperament, and philosophy entered the equation. Different judges give different instructions. Certainly there are standard instructions, but the fight is usually over whether they apply to these particular facts and whether additional or modified charges should be given.

Trial judges are oftentimes reversed for failing to give an appropriate instruction or for giving an inappropriate one. It was prudent for Judge Thompson to be careful and deliberate. There were complicating features here in that there was both a grand jury indictment and an information (a written accusation) filed directly by the state attorney. The jury had the right to find the defendant guilty or not guilty of ten separate criminal charges.

Jury charge conferences can be terribly important. Based on my civil law background, I found them to be incredibly boring, irritating, and draining. Other cases are cited and quoted to demonstrate that particular instructions were or were not given; the lawyers debate whether the facts in those cases are distinguishable from the case at hand. Well, the Rosier case was distinguishable from every other criminal case in American history, as far as I was concerned.

Here we had a confession on television plus a confession in a 641-page manuscript written by the defendant (two chapters of which were in evidence). Russell Delman's cassette was in evidence—something created by an immunized witness well over a year after the so-called murder. And then there was the evidence that truly took the cake: a short story authored by Farrell Delman in the middle of his testimony. This evidence was unique in the annals of criminal law. What would the jury make of all this?

On Tuesday, November 29, while Susan was in "the lion's den" battling over the charges, I was in a small empty courtroom on the same floor of the Pinellas County Courthouse trying to pull together the tangled threads of this trial into a cohesive whole. Initially I would be speaking for three hours; I had to be at least somewhat organized. What to stress? What to downplay? What to exclude? There is always the danger of ignoring a subject that is of vital importance to one or more jurors.

Susan would come out occasionally and give me updates on the grim news. We were getting clobbered. At one point things got so bad she accused the judge of being an advocate and acting as the State's cocounsel, encouraging charges to the jury that would almost guarantee conviction, charges that had not been requested by the State. Everytime I went into the judge's chambers I would leave quickly because the whole process was so depressing. If the jury followed the law literally, Peter would be leaving St. Petersburg in handcuffs.

Among the instructions the judge had agreed to give were the following:

(*On the charge of conspiracy to murder in the first degree:*) It is not necessary that the agreement or conspiracy or combination or confederation to commit first degree murder be expressed in any particular words or that words pass between the coconspirators. It is not necessary that the defendant do any act in furtherance of the offense conspired. (*He could be eating a pizza across the street and still be guilty.*)

If two or more persons help each other commit or attempt to commit a crime and the defendant is one of them, the defendant must be treated as if he had done all of the things the other person or persons did . . . to be a principal, the defendant does not have to be present when the crime is committed or attempted. Every act or statement of each member of a conspiracy made in furtherance of the common purpose of the conspiracy should be considered as an act or statement of every other member of the conspiracy.

The general rule is that a conspirator is criminally responsible for a crime committed in pursuance of a common purpose or which results as a natural and probable consequence of the conspiracy. This is so even if the criminal act was not intended as part of the original design or the coconspirator did not participate in the act. (*Legally it meant nothing that Peter was not in the bedroom at the time of the smothering.*)

(*Reasonable doubt:*) Whenever the words, "reasonable doubt," are used, you must consider the following: A reasonable doubt is not a possible doubt, a speculative, imaginary, or forced doubt. Such a doubt must not influence you to return a verdict of not guilty if you have an abiding conviction of guilt.

(*Lesser included crimes:*) If you decide that the main accusation has not been proved beyond a reasonable doubt, you will next need to decide if the defendant is guilty of any lesser included crimes. The lesser crimes indicated in the definition of first degree murder are second degree murder and manslaughter. If you return a verdict of guilty, it should be for the highest offense that has been proved beyond a reasonable doubt.

This was one of several areas where the judge was giving the State a stronger instruction than the one contained in the standard jury charges. Susan had argued vigorously that the rule as to standard charges is, absent some unique facts, that the standards should be given without modification. To apply in a quasi-mercy-killing case tougher charges than a judge in Lee County would be applying for a vicious, premeditated serial killer is really outrageous. She argued that the judge in effect was commanding the jury that they must convict for the highest offense that has been proved, when the standard instructions do not require it.

Then came the closing instructions, which the State dearly loved:

You must follow the law as set out in these instructions. If you fail to follow the law, your verdict will be a miscarriage of justice. There is no reason for failing to follow the law in this case. All of us are depending upon you to make a wise and legal decision in this matter.

You should disregard any statement by the attorneys in this case [that] asserts personal knowledge of facts and issues [or] that states a personal opinion as to the justness of the cause, the credibility of the witness, or the guilt or innocence of the accused. This case must not be decided for or against anyone because you feel sorry for anyone or are angry at anyone.

Feelings of prejudice or sympathy are not legally reasonable doubts and they should not be discussed by any of you in any way. Your verdict must be based on your views of the evidence and on the law contained in these instructions. The penalty for the crime of first degree murder is life imprisonment without the possibility of parole for twenty-five years. (*If that did not invoke sympathy and anger under these circumstances, then I would be wasting four hours talking to a bunch of zombies.*)

In closing, let me remind you that it is important that you follow the law as spelled out in these instructions in deciding your verdict. There are no other laws that apply to this case. Even if you do not like the laws that must be applied, you must use them. For two centuries we have agreed to a Constitution and to live by the law. No one of us has the right to violate the rules that we all share.

That would be the last official word the jury would hear before retiring to consider its verdict. Where the hell were all of the liberal, bleeding-heart instructions that supposedly favored defendants? Susan was actually successful in getting the judge to give a few excellent instructions for us. But I had no intention of mentioning even the helpful ones in the opening part of my final argument; that was the State's turf and I would not make it easy for them to hammer me on the law. I would talk about these favorable instructions during my final rebuttal argument. Judge Thompson continued:

> The defendant has entered a plea of not guilty. This means that you must presume or believe the defendant is innocent. The presumption stays with the defendant as to each material allegation in the indictment and the information through each stage of the trial until it is overcome by the evidence to the exclusion of and beyond a reasonable doubt.
>
> The Constitution requires the State to prove its accusations against the defendant. It is not necessary for the defendant to disprove anything nor is the defendant required to prove his innocence. It is up to the State to prove the defendant's guilt by evidence.
>
> The defendant exercised a fundamental right by choosing not to be a witness in this case. You must not view this as an admission of guilt or be influenced in any way by his decision. No juror should ever be concerned that the defendant did or did not take the witness stand to give testimony in the case.

By late afternoon the charge conference was over. My summation notes were becoming jumbled; enough was enough. I do not write out or dictate my argument. Rather, I arrange key words and phrases as reminders; my notes are a checklist not a script. I start talking, I do my thing and let nature take its course. I frequently say things I had no idea I was going to say. What the jury sees is what it gets from me.

I was determined to get a good night's sleep. I was not about to review my notes again. The day arrived: Wednesday, November 30, 1988. We had begun selecting a jury on October 31 and the jury would not begin their deliberations until December 1.

I was as ready as I could get.

> THE COURT: I need to address the spectators on one point. That is this: I imagine that some of you have some rather strong feelings about this matter. Even though you may have that, you cannot express them here in any fashion. (*To the jury:*) At this time, you've heard all the evidence in the case. The

attorneys will now present their final arguments. Please remember that what the attorneys say is not evidence. However, do listen closely to them.

THE DEFENSE'S FINAL ARGUMENT*

[MR. ROSENBLATT]: I've always felt there is a necessary artificiality about surroundings such as this (*pointing to the physical trappings of the courtroom*); we hear words like cancer, tumors, chemotherapy, radiotherapy, and, in a sense, they are just words. What I would like to do is try to put the facts of this case into a more realistic setting. I'd like to begin by putting the nine months of Patricia Rosier's battle with cancer into perspective. Here we had a woman who, at age forty-two, was pretty much living the American dream.

She had had her problems as a child: her parents were divorced, her mother had mental and emotional problems. Fortunately she met a mate that she was happy with, and compatible with. He became a doctor; he became financially successful. They had two children; they were active in community life; they were able to go on long vacations.

Let's step back for a moment and think what it must have been like in late April of 1985 when Patricia Rosier learned that she had cancer, that dread word in our society. She had a lung tumor, and surgery to remove it, followed by chemotherapy. There was hope that she could be cured. And then came the horrible news at the end of October 1985 that she had brain tumors. Not one, but four! Then she had radiotherapy for those tumors. Chemo- and radiotherapy are themselves horrible and debilitating and tragic. So when we look at Dr. Rosier's behavior during Pat's struggle, let's put that behavior into a framework of reality. Don't judge him without walking in his moccasins, as the Indians say so tellingly.

And then, of course, came the biggest disaster of all. On January 10 she gets the irretrievably certain, 100 percent death sentence. Mrs. Rosier, you have two enormous masses on both of your adrenal glands. You will never see your children grow to adulthood; you will never become a grandmother;

---

*What follows are excerpts from the final arguments heard by the jury.

you will never celebrate a twenty-fifth wedding anniversary. Your life is over.

Was suicide the appropriate reaction? Who can really say? It is one thing to discuss these issues in the abstract and quite another to be faced with their reality—with the reality of unbearable pain and violent retching. Suicide is not a crime in the State of Florida. And viewed philosophically, this may be the ultimate civil liberty that people have. It's not for us to judge after the fact and without the pain whether Patricia Rosier should have made that decision—that was her decision—she made that choice. From everything you have heard in this courtroom about this wife and mother, she dealt with her situation heroically. There was never a complaint or a word about "Why me? I'm in the prime of life. I have a happy life. I have a good life. I have a loving husband. I have loving children. Why? Why? Why?" From whatever source Patricia Rosier derived her strength, she dealt with it.

A woman who would go on television to shave her head is an unusual lady. And what she did with regard to her suicide decision was one thousand percent consistent with that, not out of any sense of arrogance but with the idea: "I'm not going to lay in a bed and go on an IV drip and be semi-conscious and die in a week or two weeks anyway. I'm going to take charge." Just like she took charge of her hair. "And even bald-headed, I'm not going to hide in my house. I'm still a person, I'm going to dress well. And I will tell the television audience that if this awful disease strikes you or a loved one, you need not crawl in a hole."

Peter and Patricia were sweethearts from the age of thirteen. This is a thirty-year relationship, a twenty-two-year marriage. But the State really gives you some dynamite evidence. They give you great reasons to imprison this man for life. There was a separation years before Patricia contracted cancer. Weigh that against the evidence of Peter Rosier during Pat's illness being a super-devoted, loving, caring husband traveling all over the country trying to find a cure.

Pain is a word that can lose its meaning in the artificiality of these surroundings. A good friend of mine several years ago told me about his problem with a kidney stone. He told me the pain was simply unbelievable. I didn't doubt him, and I gave it about four seconds worth of thought until I got my own kidney stone about eight months ago. And I couldn't walk, and I couldn't sit, and I couldn't find a position that was bearable. I was going wild. Demerol didn't help. I was acting like the biggest sissy imaginable. I was awful to my kids. The pain was not to be believed. Yet it is just a word until a person experiences it.

My wife was very comforting though. She said, "Now you know what labor feels like."

What is this case all about? Patricia Rosier decides to commit suicide and her father ends her life. Those facts are not in dispute. So what are we doing here? We are here because State Attorney Joseph D'Alessandro foolishly gave the Delmans immunity. We are here because of false pride. The mistake that Peter Rosier made by going on television and writing a manuscript is equalled by the mistake Joseph D'Alessandro made by going for first degree murder in a case where he knows that we are not dealing with a criminal; we are not dealing with a crime; we're dealing with a personal family tragedy.

I want you to know that I don't take the position that the Delmans should be charged with anything. I can see that under the crazy circumstances of those twelve hours after Pat ingested the Seconal, people can do strange things. But as between the loving husband of twenty-two years and the man who doesn't see his grandchildren for thirteen years, if anyone committed a wrong it was Vincent Delman and his two sons. But they have immunity and they walk, and you're supposed to swallow that, and you are supposed to function as sheep. After all, who are you to question the authority and discretion of the great State Attorney?

Let's assume there is intelligent life on Mars and you're explaining this case to a Martian. The loving husband is charged with first degree murder and the man who ended his daughter's life after not having seen her for thirteen years, he and his sons have total immunity. Dr. Rosier is a threat to no one. We have a criminal justice system with limited resources where serious crimes go unsolved every day, and they have all this time and money to go after this public enemy number one (*pointing to the State's table, and then walking slowly to our table and gesturing at Peter*).

The Martian would want to know: "Is there intelligent

life on earth? Because this is just crazy. It is lunacy. To be talking about first degree murder of a terminal cancer patient with days to live who decides to commit suicide, whose father ends her life and gets immunity—but put this great danger behind bars."

The State's case is a patchwork of conjecture, speculation, surmise, and wishful thinking. As a prime example of the State's desperation let's analyze their conspiracy theory. Peter had a conspiracy with a man, Vincent Delman, who basically hates his guts and who admits that they have not had a real conversation since they met almost thirty years ago. They never interrelated—and two men like this are supposed to have formed a conspiracy. Shamir and Arafat don't enter into conspiracies. Vincent didn't even have a conspiracy with his sons. He didn't care whether they agreed or disagreed with what he was doing, he didn't ask for their permission. His decision was made on the spur of the moment in the bedroom, and Dr. Rosier was not in the bedroom.

And in terms of any statements that were supposedly made on the patio—"If I had the guts I would use a pillow" or "I was thinking the same thing," or "Enough is enough"— if you believe those statements were made, the testimony of all three Delmans is 100 percent crystal clear that Dr. Rosier never said a word in response. Not a word, not a gesture, nothing. And this is probably the most talkative man in America. The secrecy deal between the three Delmans was deliberately made outside the presence of Peter. If Peter knew about the suffocation, he could not have contained himself; he would have told people.

Oh, there was a conspiracy all right, and that conspiracy worked perfectly: the conspiracy to trick the State of Florida into granting total immunity to all three Delmans. It's embarrassing that they gave immunity to these three people without knowing that the smothering had taken place.

And there is also a conspiracy to get Peter, to grind Peter into the dust. To get even for real and imagined petty grievances. This sick, twisted family thing. If they believed for one minute that Peter knew what they were doing in the bedroom, then Peter's got to be part of the deal to keep it secret.

You and I were not in that house on January 15, 1986, and that's why there is a law of common sense, a law of the way people behave, a law of naturalness. To me these are more meaningful laws than those passed by politicians. The Delmans never said a single word to Peter about the circumstances of the suffocation, because they knew he knew nothing about it. In Russell Delman's cassette he said that's the most important thing to the State. Did Peter know? It's incongruous to them and it's incongruous to me.

If Peter knew that his wife's life was ended by the three Delmans and he's writing a book, what a great way to get back at them. "These vile relatives of mine. They hadn't seen her for thirteen years, and the three of them dared to kill her." You'd read that and you'd hate the Delmans. Would he give up that sledgehammer against them when in the book he is implicating himself time and time again with morphine injections, with suppositories? Why in the world wouldn't he mention it? It gives the story even greater drama.

Vincent Delman caused Patricia's death. Patricia made a rational decision to commit suicide. And 100 percent out of the mouths of the Delmans, Patricia did not want to awaken. There was nothing to rediscuss with her if for any reason the Seconal did not work. The Delmans were carrying out Patricia's wishes, not Peter's wishes.

I don't think you're going to convict this board-certified pathologist of any crime on the testimony of Vincent, Russell, and Farrell Delman. And without them the State has no case. They put on their star witness, Farrell Delman, who says: "Yeah, I lied, I committed perjury. I lied about the cassette." Something that was meaningless—who cares about that lousy cassette?

What does Farrell Delman take you for? This New York sharpie thinks he's going to come to St. Petersburg and tell the hicks anything, and you'll buy it. He thinks we're all a bunch of hicks. He's got the answer to everything. Arrogant—that's Farrell Delman. He's the guy who played the "what if" game with Deveney in New York so that Deveney could give a false proffer to Fitzpatrick.

And yet what Farrell Delman wrote over the weekend in his hotel room at the Hilton was marvelous for Dr. Rosier. Even though he says that Peter is a gutless, immoral wimp. He becomes the doctor of psychiatry—wonderful! Let him berate and insult and besmirch this man who gave his sister a happy life for twenty-two years.

But on the only thing that mattered, Farrell Delman was terrific. Farrell says Peter didn't want to kill his wife. So Peter acted legally. But me and my brother and my father, we acted illegally but we acted morally. Our intent was to kill her.

To find Peter Rosier guilty of anything, you would have to believe that this man is a moron beyond belief; that he is the most incompetent, stupid doctor who ever walked the face of the earth; because 8 mgs of morphine is nothing. Four morphine suppositories are nothing. Then the State puts on their one expert, Dr. Forney, the expert on alcohol, the guy who gets off drunk drivers. They don't put on a cancer specialist or some prestigious physician from a major institution or even an ordinary M.D.; they put on Dr. Forney. Their case has a foundation of tissue paper.

Dr. Forney said that twenty Seconal would not kill any adult. You give twenty Seconal to 100 adults, and you will still have 100 living adults. So what happens, Dr. Forney, if we add the injection of morphine and four morphine suppositories? Forney says that, absent the smothering, Patricia would have awakened and been in the same shape she was in before she ever took the Seconal.

You've got to be very skeptical of witnesses like the Delmans. They lie when there is no reason to lie. Vincent Delman tells you: "I'm asleep in the den and what finally wakes me up is an argument between Dr. Rosier and Dr. Dosoretz." We got to use our street smarts, our instincts, our common sense in figuring out who is telling the truth.

Dr. Carlino testifies that he got to the house before Dr. Dosoretz. The way Carlino proves that Vincent Delman is a liar is when Carlino says: "Yeah, I was with Peter about 15 minutes and we were in the den the whole time." Did you see a guy sleeping on the couch? Did you hear any snoring? Did you hear any breathing? Anything? And Carlino says no.

Vincent Delman was 100 percent sure the argument between his son-in-law and Dr. Dosoretz occurred in the kitchen. Dosoretz, after he finally admitted that there was an argument, said it took place at the pool outside. Vincent said Peter motioned him to leave, yet Dosoretz never saw that. As a matter of fact, Dosoretz never saw Vincent that morning, period. On such testimony you do not send a man to prison for life.

Farrell Delman conned the State of Florida and now

he is trying to con you. Don't allow yourselves to become his instrument for retribution against Dr. Rosier.

Russell Delman gave two lengthy statements wherein he never remembered Farrell saying: "I was thinking the same thing." And in both those statements he never heard Vincent say: "Enough is enough." Farrell wasn't sure if he heard those words or he merely presumed them from Vincent's body language. What was there to be confused about? Three tiny comments, then the smothering. Why the need for eight-hour predeposition conferences? The prosecutors already had detailed statements from the Delmans.

All these inconsistencies and contradictions formed the backdrop for the meeting in Fort Myers a couple of weeks ago when the Delmans met with Mr. Volz, Mr. Russell, and Mr. Fitzpatrick. At that meeting the message was: get on board, get your stories straight. It was a get-comfortable session, a reunion between old friends.

Yes, the Delmans and the home team had become buddies; after all they had the same goal—convict Peter! That's the only conspiracy in this case.

All the boys were on a first-name basis. Russell told his brother and father on the cassette: "I know you will be terrific and can support each other. Ask Ed and Jim plenty of questions and they will do their best to prepare you for your depositions. Really, it's just our job to keep ourselves emotionally and psychologically strong and protected."

Strong and protected from what? They were in no danger. They had total, blanket immunity from prosecution. They were going back to the good life in New York City and San Francisco.

Then a really amazing thing happens. There was a lot of stress and a lot of craziness during those twelve hours when Patricia remained unconscious, but then finally there is one remark which is different because that remark directly leads to action—that remark leads to the suffocation of Patricia Rosier. "If I had the guts I would use a pillow."

Yet when they take Vincent Delman's statement in March of 1987, Vincent Delman says: "I never heard that. I never heard my son Russell say: 'If I had the guts I would use a pillow.' " This is just beyond belief. They are asking you to believe that somehow Peter heard that, although Vincent didn't.

The Delman boys came up with this wonderful expression

about something triggering a memory, where they suddenly remembered something that had never happened. That's how they dealt with their inconsistencies and lies. Something triggered a memory, and now I magically remember. What do they take you for? It was coaching and rehearsing that triggered their memories.

I want you to know that when you begin your deliberations you have the right to go back in the jury room and say, "These Delmans are a joke. I don't believe anything they said. Let's go home. I'm not going to convict this board-certified M.D. pathologist on the testimony of these three guys."

Oh, you're going to hear so much about the law, the majesty of the law, when Mr. Volz and Mr. Russell get up here. Your duty to follow the law. These instructions did not come from Mount Sinai. One of the biggest events in America in the last thirty years has been the Civil Rights Movement. How did Martin Luther King, Jr., become a national figure?

MR. RUSSELL: Your Honor, we have an objection; like to approach the bench. (*Outside the jury's hearing*) Now what he is trying to do is say that Martin Luther King disobeyed the law and he's trying to imply that this jury has a right to disobey the law. That's absolutely improper. (*I smiled over at Peter, who knew this objection would be made.*)

THE COURT: I don't think he can make any argument that implies or suggests the jury can disobey the law.

MRS. ROSENBLATT: Under the jury pardon power a jury can enter a not-guilty verdict which is contrary to the law and the evidence, and the jury can simply refuse to enforce a law of which it disapproves.

MR. ROSENBLATT: The Civil Rights Movement began when Rosa Parks refused to give up her seat on a bus to a white person. Under the law she was sitting in a section of the bus which was reserved for whites. I have the right to say to this jury— was that a good law or a bad law? Was she a criminal because she violated that law?

MRS. ROSENBLATT: Judge, I'm handing you a case from the Supreme Court of Florida, which says: "The ultimate exercise of the jury pardon power is a not-guilty verdict rendered contrary to the law and evidence, a refusal by the jury to enforce a law of which it disapproves. Such verdicts are significant in a democracy as a barometer of public opinion,

as an auger of the future." Judge, there is no case that exists
in Florida which says the jury's power to pardon cannot be
mentioned.

THE COURT: I don't believe there is a case in my experience
that would allow an attorney in final argument to argue that
they [the jury] can pardon the defendant or disregard the law
and the evidence, and come in with any verdict they choose.

MRS. ROSENBLATT: In a first degree murder case the jury has
the right to find the defendant guilty of battery, which is just
about the same thing. (*This is the kind of argument that went
on for a day and a half in the charge conference.*)

THE COURT: I don't think you have a right to attack the law
and suggest that they [the jury] can disregard it. These people
have taken an oath to enter a verdict according to the law
and the evidence. You cannot make an argument that suggests
that they violate that oath.

MR. ROSENBLATT: You can make an argument which tells them
the truth and that is, they can reach any verdict they wish,
they can reach any verdict that they subjectively feel is
compatible with their concept of justice and fairness. That is
the simple truth of the matter.

THE COURT: You can't suggest to them that they can abandon
the law in this case. I won't permit that argument.

I hated to have the mood and tempo of my final argument interrupted
by this long bench conference. What did these guys have against Martin
Luther King, Jr.? That's what I hoped the shrug of my shoulders conveyed
to the jury. I tap-danced to another subject.

There is so much psychology in this case: like family
relationships and the hatred in Fort Myers against Dr. Rosier.
Peter Rosier's fellow doctors refused to speak with me. Do
these doctors have the right to be angry at Peter for opening
up his big mouth and going on television? Yes, absolutely.
But come on, let's see a sense of balance, a sense of perspective.
They are still doctors, they are still all making a ton of money;
and their former friend is charged with first degree murder.
The children have lost their mother, the State is now trying
to put their father away. Please, give me a break. Get over
your anger and be fair. The only rule he broke was the medical code of silence. Everything Peter has done has been the

opposite of clever or devious, and everything he's done has wound up hurting himself far more than anyone else.

Let's talk about the great Channel 20. They send in a twenty-three-year-old girl who is hoping to ride Peter Rosier's back to become the new Jane Pauley. In her dreams she'll become another Jane Pauley. Even she knew that Patricia Rosier shaving her head and Peter Rosier confessing [were] dynamite television, and maybe this ambitious little twit of a girl could get some national airtime and become a bigshot. Did she, maybe, lead this vulnerable silly man with his fragile ego to think she liked him, so she could manipulate him into giving this interview?

Peter Rosier knows that had he never gone on television Jacob and Elizabeth and his surrogate mother, Gertrude Ahlbrecht, would not have been put through the hell of what they've been put through; and he's going to have to live with that all of his life. I used to love "The Honeymooners," where Jackie Gleason would say to Alice something about his big mouth always getting him into big trouble. Peter Rosier had a big mouth, but that's not a crime and he feels guilty enough for what he's put his family through. Talk about self inflicted wounds, talk about being self-destructive.

This was a personal, private intimate decision and it should have been kept that way, just like the hundreds of suicides that Dr. Graves has seen and that nothing has been done about. Peter Rosier should not be made the sacrificial lamb for the sins of the system. Highly intelligent people in one field can be very dumb in other areas. A streetwise tenth-grade girl would have known what Leisa Zigman was up to. She just wanted the story. Peter thought she was his friend; Peter thought she cared. Now ambitious Leisa is the 11:00 P.M. anchor with her picture on highway billboards.

But to show you that Peter Rosier is hardly unique, let's look at some mistakes in recent American history—colossal mistakes by intelligent people. Like the Watergate taping system, which caused a president's resignation; the brilliant Robert McNamara, secretary of defense, believed that America could do the job in Vietnam quickly; the disaster of the Bay of Pigs, which allowed Castro to remain in power for thirty years.

Look how desperate the State is to have you hate Peter Rosier. Why did the State put on Jules Cantor? To say that

Peter wanted to date and crap on Fort Myers. If true, what does that have to do with a murder trial?

Mr. Volz has the audacity to get up here and say to this jury in opening statement that Peter Rosier was at a party and said: "I'm the most eligible bachelor in Fort Myers and I can't even get laid." And then not to have a shred of evidence. Did you hear from anyone at that party? That was lower than low. That was their worst cheap shot, the worst out of a hundred. There was zero evidence of any such statement made by Peter Rosier at any time.

(*Pointing my fist right into the camera lens*) You should be ashamed, whoever owns that station. You should be ashamed that this case is here because you showed that interview without saying: "Hey, let's talk to this guy's lawyer. Let's talk to his psychiatrist. What are we getting into? Is this fair?" Freedom of the press, my left foot. You wanted a hot, exclusive story!

And then they have the nerve to lie to you. Hopefully, no one on this jury believes that any part of a confession by a prominent physician to so-called murder would simply disappear. This television station is an affiliate of the National Broadcasting Company. That's "NBC Nightly News," "The Today Show," a big-deal national network. They dare to show you a snippet of this interview.

Everyone's so clever; everyone's looking out for number one, except the guy who is on trial for first degree murder. Maybe Leisa was wearing a tight dress and making goo-goo eyes at Peter. He signs a release for one dollar absolving Channel 20 of all liability whatsoever. Channel 20 got immunity just like the Delmans. Leisa comes in here with her Miami lawyer objecting on constitutional grounds.

Cover, cover—you know the expression. We're vulnerable; get a lawyer in here; object so we don't have to deal with the truth. The second interview also disappears according to them. That's an insult to your intelligence. They got rid of it. Mr. Cromwell lost it? Then bring in Mr. Cromwell.

This is a successful, well-known doctor, head of the department of pathology at Lee Memorial Hospital. They have his wife on tape. He confesses to a big-league crime. They know the whole subject of euthanasia is of national interest, he's saying these incredibly controversial things, and they lose the tapes. It ain't believable. Those tapes were destroyed.

I say the State of Florida bought a pig in a poke; they were suckered; they were defrauded by the super-slick Farrell. All three Delmans walk with no responsibility whatsoever, and a loving husband of twenty-two years is put on trial for first degree murder. Does that make sense? Is it fair? But sure, you're supposed to follow the law like a bunch of zombies.

Look at Dr. Harwin's prescription of January 10: fifty Seconal and fifty morphine tablets—all the medication in the world necessary to end her life if that's what Dr. Rosier had intended to do. If your intent is to kill someone, you give them more drugs, not less.

And talk about babies. Farrell's upset with Peter's book because he feels the Delmans don't get enough credit for Pat's death. I mean talk about sick, twisted thinking. He let her linger because he didn't have the guts to do it, to kill her, to end her life. And I asked Farrell flat out: "You now realize, after having figured all this out that Peter did not have the requisite intent to kill Pat because he didn't have the guts?" Farrell agreed.

Farrell concluded that Peter did not intend to end his wife's life because he is a gutless, immature wimp frozen emotionally at the age of eight. Well, he's not on trial for being a gutless wimp.

My wife and I live on Miami Beach and I would just like to have a dollar for every elderly widowed mother living alone in one of those hotels [who] has a successful son or daughter in New York or Los Angeles who sees them maybe once a year. And that's a mother, that's blood! So when you evaluate what Peter Rosier is all about, Gertrude Ahlbrecht is very important because that was and is an everyday thing. She is a member of the Rosier family; she is an integral part of their lives. Actions speak louder than words.

I pointed to Gertrude in the packed audience sitting between her "grandchildren," and I paused in order to make certain that the jury followed my finger. Gertrude looked like Mother Teresa after an especially trying day.

MR. VOLZ: Objection.
MR. ROSENBLATT: Oh, I shouldn't mention her?
THE COURT: Sustain the objection. Nobody should refer to people who were not witnesses.

I walked very close to the jury, saying nothing, breathing heavily in short bursts through my nose, hoping to transmit my utter disgust at the objection. During the next few minutes I noticed several jurors giving furtive glances in Gertrude's direction. They could object but I could pause for as long as I damn well pleased. When I finally spoke again I talked about the Delmans. I liked the contrast between them and Mrs. Ahlbrecht.

> Russell Delman teaches people how to sit, shows that there are alternative ways of sitting. That's what the man does for a living in California. And what Farrell does for a living is to tell people that smoking is really good for you. You smoke only a pack of Camel's a day, two is better. The Delman boys—real contributions to society. And on their immunized testimony you are supposed to put away a productive doctor for life!
>
> The defense does not have to prove anything. I believe you will hear in the State's argument a convoluted, technical twisting of common sense with abstract legalisms to somehow equate this circumstance with the robbery of a supermarket where a clerk is killed—and the two situations have nothing in common. This is a personal family tragedy; admittedly it was handled very badly for all kinds of reasons, none of which consti-tute[s] a crime. You all know the difference between murder and trying one's best to comply with a loving spouse's last wish. Peter Rosier is not a murderer, and you all know that.

Final Argument of the State of Florida

> Mr. Volz: Thank you, Your Honor. Good afternoon Ladies and Gentlemen. At this time, on behalf of the State of Florida, the people of the State of Florida, people from the State Attorney's Office and the Twentieth Judicial Circuit, I'd like to thank the members of this jury for their kind attention, for all your efforts in this case. (*I'll thank them for their efforts if they acquit.*)
>
> I want you to know that we are aware of how this trial has inconvenienced you and we appreciate the effort that you've put forth in your own personal inconvenience and sacrifice in being a member of this jury. A jury is something that we have had in this country for some two hundred years. This is the manner in which our judicial system works. It is incumbent

upon the jury to make decisions, findings of fact, and apply [them] to the law.

Even at the close of the day, after you have heard all of the arguments, you still have to keep an open mind because you won't have one of the most important tools that you will need in reaching your verdict, and that is the law. What lawyers say is not evidence; what lawyers think is not evidence; the opinions of lawyers is not evidence. (*Could he be speaking of me?*) The opinions of witnesses are not evidence, and the Court will instruct you on that. It's not what a lawyer thinks and it's not what a witness thinks, it's what the jury thinks.

Mr. Rosenblatt has just addressed you on his opinions, on his speculation, on what's happening in other places, what happened at other times, what happens with other people. It's time now that we return to the evidence: the facts and law in this case. Your verdict must be based on the evidence you heard from that witness stand and on the law that you will be charged by Judge Thompson. That is the oath you all took. (*Civics 101, but it's very effective. Jurors can become so mesmerized by their formal surroundings that even mavericks are transformed into conformists.*)

We have heard from the defense that Patricia Rosier made a rational decision to commit suicide. A rational decision is based upon proper information. One of the factors that Patricia Rosier used in making a determination to end her own life was to avoid this horrible death of vomiting up her own blood and choking on it. Yet all of the doctors that have testified in this case, all the treating physicians, said: "No, that's not going to happen."

You saw a videotape of Patricia Rosier as to how she handled herself, how she spoke. That videotape is evidence. You can take it back into that jury room. You saw how she spoke on January 14, 1986, the day before she died. There was no suicide in this case. The Seconal did not end her life. You must die, under the law, by your own hand for it to be a suicide. That is not the case here. She did not die of her cancer. The defendant and the Delmans terminated her life. Those individuals agreed, conspired, combined, and confederated with each other.

During the trial the Court gave you an instruction on *corpus delicti,* and the law is clear. A criminal case cannot go forward based upon the confession of a defendant alone. We couldn't find the cause of death. The body was burned. Without the Delmans the truth as to the circumstances surrounding Patricia Rosier's death never would have been discovered, and no one would have been held accountable for these criminal actions. You may not like the Delmans. You may think them tricky, conniving. You may think them killers. They are. (*I never called them that.*)

You may think them the scum of the earth, the lowest form of humanity. I'm not going to say anything in their defense, but I will tell you one thing. On January 15, 1986, in an effort to terminate the life of his wife, those are the people that man associated with.

Yes, they got immunity. But they didn't write a book, they didn't have that book copyrighted. They didn't go on TV in an effort to publish that book. They didn't have that book made into a screenplay. They didn't try to profit from the events of January 15. They didn't want to make a billion dollars and buy a fleet of Rolls Royces, and drive all over dumping on Fort Myers.

Dr. Rosier chose them; he was one of them, and the facts have established to you that he was their leader. The defendant had the ability to obtain the drugs; the defendant was the one [who] wanted to monitor the condition of Patricia Rosier, and he had the Delman brothers giving him breathing reports. They went to him. He was the doctor. He was the one who was making decisions as to who to call, what drugs to get, and how to administer them. He was the one saying: "This can go on for a long time," "That's the death rattle," "She will be a vegetable."

The issue before you is not whether or not the Delmans got immunity. The issue is: did the Delmans come in here and tell the truth. Were there contradictions? Sure. We all know we were in this courtroom back on October 31 and November 1 as this jury was being selected. Do we know what color suit I was wearing, what color tie I was wearing? Do you remember what you were wearing? The important thing is we were here.

Why would the Delmans come in here and lie? They have nothing to gain by lying. If they didn't tell the truth they could lose their immunity. Why would they lie and risk that? The fact that they got immunity in no way lessens this defendant's criminal responsibility for his own actions under the law.

In his opening remarks, Mr. Rosenblatt stayed away from the law. He did not go through the elements of the law, because, if you take the facts in this case, you can apply them and show how they comply with the elements and the necessary proof, and the law. I want to remind you of the oath you took as jurors, which was to follow the law; and all of us are counting on you to follow the law. If you fail to follow the law, your verdict will be a miscarriage of justice. There is no reason for failing to follow the law in this case. All of us are depending upon you to make a wise and legal decision in this matter.

Feelings of prejudice, bias, or sympathy are not legally reasonable doubts, and they should not be discussed by any of you in any way. You must follow the law. Throughout this case the defense has attempted to get you angry at the Delmans. He's attempted to get you angry at the State. He's attempted to get you angry at the State's witnesses because they wouldn't talk to him. (*I plead guilty.*) But anger is not to be considered by you in your deliberations. He's tried to get you to feel sorry for silly, dumb, poor, defendant, board-certified pathologist Robert Peter Rosier. Anger and sympathy shall not be considered by you.

The indictment contains two counts. One is conspiracy to commit murder in the first degree. Count two is premeditated murder in the first degree, and the one count contained in the Information is attempted murder in the first degree.

This defendant said on television: "I administered something to her to terminate her life." That shows intent. Why did he give her the drugs? He gave the drugs to terminate her life. When she was given the drugs, she was unconscious. She wasn't in any position to consent. The judge will instruct you that consent is not a defense. You can't consent to have someone go out and kill you. In chapter 34 [of his manuscript] the defendant is not talking about easing pain, but getting the drugs to terminate her life.

The book and the TV interview are the defendant's confessions. In his book he says: "I fully understood the implications of what I was doing. I understood the legalities, but I did not care." He knew it was murder, but he didn't care.

Why did he go on television and give Leisa Zigman the book? This Dartmouth graduate, this board-certified pathologist, this man who ran a laboratory for twelve years, this businessman, this physician? He did this right after he had gotten over twenty rejections from various publishing houses around the country. He did this after he told Patsy Jungle he would do anything to get his book published. You heard from Dr. Lowell what the contents of that book is. Far from a monument to his wife.

As he told Dr. Lowell, he was not concerned about the legalities. He had beaten the system because the evidence was burned and he's the pathologist, and he knows the value of human remains in a homicide prosecution. He knows the value of an autopsy to determine the cause of death. But that evidence wasn't around. That evidence was burned. (*By this time the yellow legal pad on which Peter doodled was drenched in tears. Would the jury think he was performing? I knew he was not.*)

He did not have to conspire with all three Delmans. He could conspire with any one of those three with the intent and the ability to commit first degree murder, and he would be guilty of conspiracy to commit first degree murder.

Legally, the agreement or conspiracy need not be expressed in any particular words, and it's not even necessary that words pass between the coconspirators. It's not necessary that the defendant do any act in furtherance of the offense. The key is a common purpose or goal. And once a conspiracy is established, each and every member of the conspiracy (*the coconspirator rule*) is responsible for the actions of each and every other member of the conspiracy in furtherance of the common purpose.

Peter was not interested in a hospice or a visiting nurse; he didn't want to control pain. He wanted to terminate a life; that was his intent. Someone else was making the decisions for Patty now, and that was this defendant. Patty wasn't making any decisions about any more drugs, this defendant was. (*Peter would literally shake like a hyperactive five-year-old whenever Volz invoked the name, Patty.*)

There's the conspiracy. The intent of all three of them was to terminate her life. That's their common purpose. When Farrell tells Vincent something it's as though Peter did, because, under the coconspirator rule, what any one of them does or says in furtherance of the common purpose of the conspiracy is attributed to each and every other member of the conspiracy. Peter is as responsible as if he was in the room with the three of them; he is as responsible as if he suffocated her.

Dr. Forney's testimony showed that there was no suicide; she did not die as a result of her own hand. There were other medications available: Methadon, Tylox, morphine. We don't know what the level was, because there was no opportunity to check the human remains to see what the level of various drugs were in her body. What quantity of drugs did Patty consume in the last week of her life? The defendant was telling everyone: "Don't let her be a vegetable; end it now." That was his message.

The defendant tells Farrell: "Whatever happened in there, don't tell me about it. I don't want to know." He may not have known all the details, but he knew when they got up from that patio table they were going to end it. He knew that.

He did nothing to get out of the conspiracy; he did nothing to stop the actions of Vincent. The common scheme of the conspiracy was to terminate her life. He was responsible for her state where she could not resist. Even if you were to find that Vincent was not part of the conspiracy and he acted on the spur of the moment, there is still a conspiracy to commit murder in the first degree based upon the actions of Farrell, Russell, and the defendant. It was the defendant who injected the morphine and the suppositories in his unconscious wife.

He was right outside that bedroom door. They don't have to like each other, they don't even have to talk to each other under the law. They were pursuing a common purpose. It was the defendant who was creating the atmosphere of panic. Because of Peter's actions and words Vincent was prompted into action.

This defendant is responsible for his own actions under the law. We are a nation of law[s], not of men. No one is above the law. We all must follow the law. That is your obligation and oath.

Again, all of us are counting on you to use your best collective effort in applying the facts to the law, and Judge Thompson will instruct you that you must follow the law as it is set out in these instructions. Your failure to do so would be a miscarriage of justice.

FINAL ARGUMENT FOR THE STATE OF FLORIDA (CONT.)

MR. RUSSELL: You only have half of what you need to decide this case. You do not have the law officially, although we are indicating to you what we anticipate those instructions will be, and you will have those in your hands as the Court reads them. That is the official law in this case. During jury selection we asked extensive questions about any personal or philosophical disagreements you might have with the law. We asked: "If the Court instructed you to follow the law and the evidence, could you do that?" And you all indicated you could. You then took an oath and your oath was to return a true verdict based only on the law and the evidence, and we expect, of course, that that oath will be followed. It's not a discretionary thing. You must follow the law. This is a court of law, this is not the legislature. (*This is why my question—"Are you intimidated by authority?"—was so critical. To acquit would be like breaking a promise extracted during* voir dire.)

The Court will tell you this case must be decided only on the evidence that you have heard from the answers of the witnesses. If there was a question asked and you got a negative answer, it doesn't matter how many times the question was repeated. That does not create evidence. If the evidence convinces you beyond a reasonable doubt of the guilt of the defendant, you should find him guilty, even though you may believe one or more other persons are also guilty. Certainly you have every reason to believe the Delmans are also guilty.

Immunity, as you all agreed in jury selection, does not lessen the guilt of another person who did not get immunity if it is shown that that person is also guilty of the crime. The Court will tell you that the witnesses' opinions on legality or illegality are certainly not to be taken as the law.

On September 8, according to Mr. Sousa, the defendant reapplied for disability at a time [when] he was not working, at a time when he was already disabled. He reapplied to increase his benefits from $7,800 a month to $15,000 per month. You have to be working in order to upgrade the policy, but he wasn't working. He couldn't look at slides. Sure. And he talks about greed in medicine. Apparently he has a lot of firsthand knowledge.

What have you gotten from the defense in this case?

Ridicule and sarcasm. You've got a whole series of clouds and issues that don't bear on the question "Did the defendant commit first degree murder or conspiracy to commit first degree murder?" We got smoke screens that don't bear on that issue. What is the purpose? The purpose is to raise anger, emotion, sympathy. Don't decide this case on the law and the evidence. (*The purpose is to get the jury to show some vision and guts and do the right thing: answer to a higher purpose and authority.*)

How are the questions couched? Mr. Rosenblatt is a highly skilled trial attorney. He repeatedly asks lengthy questions, which end with, isn't that correct? He gives you his argument in his questions.

The case was presented to eighteen members of the Lee County Grand Jury. They issued the indictment in this case. The idea is: let's try the State; we don't have a defense on the law. You haven't heard anything from the defendant on the law. I don't expect you will hear much on it, because it's so clear. Let's try the State; get the jury thinking about other things; get them to sympathize for the victim. (*Without anger or sympathy, I might just as well be at the airport.*)

Answers are evidence, not questions. Law and the evidence, that's what your oath says. You['ve] got every right to dislike immunity; it's distasteful. And those three people are not likable characters, absolutely. Did Mr. Fitzpatrick allow misconception? Certainly. It enhanced the truth.

So what's the purpose of talking so much about immunity? So you should get angry at the State. [The] State['s] trying to smear the defendant. There's another cloud. We're trying to just character-assassinate him. The State had to respond to show that this was not the love relationship of the century. The defendant has gone to California, New York, Nassau, casinos. Sympathy, emotion—let's decide this case on emotion.

Character assassination. What did he ask Farrell Delman? Didn't serve in the Army, did you? He didn't fight for America fifteen years ago. Does that help you resolve whether on January 15, 1986, this defendant committed the crimes with which he is charged?

Why does the defendant increase the disability after the lung cancer? In September he's doubling the disability when he's already disabled. Now it's not the fraud on the insurance

company, but what is he contemplating? He's already rationally
thinking about future possibilities; he had other motives in
manipulating the suicide.

Peter is an astute businessman: he understands the disability policy. If you can't do pathology, you're fully disabled
and you get the money. You're not required to go work as
some other kind of doctor. These things bear on the surrep-
titiousness and the manipulation and thinking in rational terms
about his future. How do we bridge the gap from a substantial
income to set myself up, [to] write a best seller, [to] get it
made into a movie. We've got a disability policy.

Even though you don't have all the book, there is ample
evidence to show from what Dr. Lowell said, and others have
said, that the book is very negative about everybody: family,
the Delmans, Duke University, everybody's bad except the
defendant. Some monument. If Peter was sincere about his
cause and [about] the world learning from Pat, he would have
published the book himself. He could certainly afford to do
that. He wanted to portray himself as a hero, a martyr, and
to bridge the gap. His life was going on. Mr. Rosenblatt goes
for sympathy through Gertrude and having Mary Linden bring
her baby into the courtroom. Tricks of the trade. (*Russell
pointed at me more often than he did at Peter.*)

(*Referring to Zigman*) This isn't some twenty-four-year-
old novice who is manipulating a board-certified pathologist,
head of the pathology department at Lee Memorial Hospital.
He's going to writing courses at Harvard, going to New York,
going to California—he's not being manipulated. And Mr.
Rosenblatt even sees fit to talk about my ex-wife. Anything
to get you sidetracked.

Mr. Rosenblatt goes into one of his emotional questions
about Vincent Delman and the suffocation as if it is somehow
vastly worse than the act of inserting suppositories. I would
assert to you that it's six of one, half-dozen of the other. Why
Vincent Delman's act is any more dastardly than inserting
suppositories is hard to understand. Vegetable, coma, death
rattle were motivating words to Vincent Delman, and the
defendant knew that.

Mr. Rosenblatt is the one who has indulged in character
assassination. He knocks Dr. Delman's Medicaid practice in
a low-income area of New York. Do you honestly believe

that Vincent Delman would have walked into that room with his sons and committed the suffocation, but for hearing all these things from the defendant? The defendant manipulated the Delmans into doing his bidding as he had manipulated his wife.

The defendant said: "I will challenge the law, stand up and change the law." What's that tell you? It's a recognition that he violated the law. We may not like the law, but we know we have to follow it. Farrell Delman is no expert. He gave an off-the-cuff opinion. Who knows what his opinion would be if he read the rest of the book?

Mr. Rosenblatt's questions may be dramatic—they may be entertaining questions, Perry Mason and all that—but they do not create evidence. Like him asking Farrell Delman: "Didn't the defendant tell you that he would never have anything to do with smothering?" He tries to create evidence by implication. You can see through that technique: Mr. Rosenblatt gives you style in place of substance. (*I was beginning to feel like a codefendant.*)

After I am done Mr. Rosenblatt is going to have an opportunity to come up here again. I expect that he's going to be dramatic; he is going to try to get you mad, try to get you sympathetic. What the State is asking you to do is decide this case as the law requires and your oath requires, and that is on the law and the evidence. As much as he may scream and yell and accuse, it's not going to change the law and the evidence. You will deliberate in a calm, dispassionate, and objective manner. He can scream and yell about politics, immunity, persecution, prosecution. As much as he raves and rants, saying you should believe him, there is no basis in evidence to believe him.

Motive is not required to be proven. The defendant had the intent to kill. He started his manipulations way back in October when he got the Delmans involved. This was not a mercy killing. This killing was not to end the pain and suffering of Patricia Rosier; it was to end the pain and suffering of Dr. Rosier. He was the one [who] was having the problems. Forty-four years old, going to go on to a new writing career. Her death becomes a vehicle for this. It was his suffering that was being eliminated by her death. He was the one having a problem with the dying process.

Afterward he was depressed and had a lot of guilt. He

had bungled it; it was not an elegant death. That's why he's depressed. They tried to portray this as pure love like no one had ever heard of; and, yes, we did rebut that, not just to scum up the defendant, but to put this in some perspective. Greed, self-centeredness, yes.

Your oath was to render a true verdict based only on the law and the evidence. If you fail to follow the law, your verdict will be a miscarriage of justice. All of us are depending upon you to make a wise and legal decision. The State, after you hear the law, will have proven this case far beyond any reasonable doubt. The criminal justice system is based on the expectation that each jury will reach that verdict which is based solely on the law and the evidence, and the State of Florida has every confidence that you will do that.

THE DEFENSE'S REBUTTAL ARGUMENT

Yes, Mr. Russell, I may rant and rave. You see, I never took the course that so many lawyers seem to have taken, which teaches professionalism above all—which basically means act phony, act dignified, never show your true feelings. I'm going to be true to myself and give you my true reactions to things that have been said regarding the evidence and the law, and then what you make of that is your business. But I'm not going to be intimidated; there is plenty to rant and rave about. I implore you not to be cowered either.

If the summations of Mr. Volz and Mr. Russell were to have a title it would be "You Must Follow the Law, You Have No Other Choice." It was quite a duet; their arguments were interchangeable.

When you walk into any law library anywhere in this country, there are shelves filled with books, and whether they are from the U.S. Supreme Court or the Florida Supreme Court there are opinions written by appellate judges. In probably 50 percent of those decisions the appellate judges are saying to a trial judge: "You didn't follow the law, and therefore we are reversing the trial result."

How could this be? How could a judge not understand the law that often? They are not saying to you: "Follow the law." They are saying: "Bring back the verdict that will make us and our boss look good."

And before anyone gets all teary eyed about the majesty of the law, let's step back and look at the law. The law in this country was "separate but equal" for many years. If you had a black skin, you got to sit separately at a lunch counter and go to a separate school. You had separate drinking fountains. Are we proud of those laws?

Every time there is a hearing before Judge Thompson and hundreds of other trial judges throughout this state, you have a lawyer on one side and a lawyer on the other side trying to convince the judge to rule a particular way. And each lawyer is saying that the law favors their side. I just want to get across to you the very important point that following the law is a super-difficult concept, even for people who are trained in the law.

Of course some legal concepts are very simple and fundamental, such as, the State has the burden of proving every element of a crime beyond and to the exclusion of every reasonable doubt. A defendant is presumed to be innocent and he is under no obligation to testify. That they didn't want to talk about. Why did they talk about the law so much? Because they are dead in the water on these facts. They know they ain't got a case, and they hope you will be hypnotized by legal jargon.

And what the facts are is one thousand percent up to you. It doesn't matter what Judge Thompson believes about the witnesses, doesn't matter what I believe or what they believe; the facts are up to you. You can listen to a witness, and even though there is no evidence contradicting what that witness says, you can go back there and say: "I don't believe this guy. It doesn't make sense to me, I don't buy it." You have that right!

That's why we have juries. According to their theory, there wouldn't be twelve of you here; instead there would be a big fancy computer, where you throw the facts in and then take the jury instructions and, boom, you come out with a result. What do we need the human element for? They would have you believe that you are nothing more than robots.

Well you ain't robots; you're people with common sense and native intelligence. You came here with a lifetime of experiences and interactions. And that's what will cause you to say: "I'm not convicting this physician on the testimony of their three superstars—Farrell, Vincent, and Russell." I say throw the Delmans where they belong—in the trash. Don't dignify them by sifting and weighing. That would be a demeaning process here.

They tell you that the State took its time and was careful in investigating this case for ten months before any indictment. *Mazel Tov!* Congratulations! Tell some mother whose son was killed in a hold-up: "We haven't caught the guy. I'm sorry, but we've been busy trying to put Peter Rosier in prison. We want to save society from this vicious criminal." The prosecution should be embarrassed. These men should put their skills and talents into the war against real criminals, they should go after the guy [who] beat up an old woman, the guy who raped a child. Our poor conviction rates are a national disgrace. We don't have the luxury for this self-indulgence.

This case is about the ravages of that disgusting, vile disease called cancer. It is a case about human weakness. This is not a case about murder. This is not a case about following the law and putting a doctor and family man in prison.

Murderer, [de]fraud[er], liar, manipulator, hypocrite! The State would have you believe Peter Rosier is public enemy number one. You've watched him for a month now; somehow I think none of you would be afraid to meet him in a dark alley.

They are trying to equate my cross examination of the Delmans with their truly underhanded besmirching of Peter Rosier. They are hardly on a par [with one another]. The Delmans are walking around now back in New York and California; Rosier is sitting here with his freedom on the line. Just a slightly different situation, wouldn't you say?

Oh, yes, Peter, you've been a genius. Have you been clever. Look at the fun you've had this past month. They are giving you this bull about the independence of a grand jury. A grand jury is a totally one-sided procedure; it's a rubber stamp for whatever a strong prosecutor wants. There is no defense lawyer standing up to give them the other side of the story.

This is a case built on soap bubbles. He vacillated about suicide. So what? The disability policy was the policy with the same benefits whether Patricia died on January 15 or three weeks later.

They tell you that Pat looked good on January 14. That's

just crazy when you consider the lung, the brain, the adrenals, and the tumors popping out on her skin. Two of the largest abdominal tumors anyone has ever seen, but she looked great. Please! Look at chapter 33 where Peter says the last days of her life were marred by violent vomiting. I quote from chapter 34: "It was perhaps 6:45 A.M. and I entered my bedroom with great fear in my heart, for I could not bear it. I could not bear to see my love unconscious and about to die." That's exactly what Farrell said in his analysis. Her death was inevitable, but for Peter it was also unthinkable. How could he function without his rock, without his beloved Patricia?

When the legislature of the State of Florida wrote these statutes they were thinking of people like Charles Manson and Ted Bundy and armed robbers; they were not thinking of Peter Rosier trying to fulfill his dying wife's last wish.

Once you reach a decision, not Judge Thompson, not the Supreme Court of Florida or the Supreme Court of the United States or the President of the United States can do anything about your verdict. The power and authority of a jury in a criminal case is absolute. When you return a verdict of not guilty, that can't be disturbed and it can't be appealed.

The presumption of innocence stays with the defendant throughout until it has been overcome to the exclusion of all reasonable doubt. That never happened, and that's why I chose not to put on any evidence. The defendant is not required to prove anything. That is the fundamental bedrock of our system. Before you take away someone's life or liberty, you've got to prove every element of the crime beyond and to the exclusion of every reasonable doubt.

Volz in his opening statement talked about a party for a friend about a week after [Peter's] wife died, and Peter complained that he was the most eligible bachelor in town and he couldn't get laid. Oh yes, but I'm here to get you angry and emotional. He gives us this filthy garbage. That a man who loved his wife, twenty-two years of marriage, a relationship begun at age thirteen—you're being told he's making that statement at a festive party. Where is the evidence? Zero, nothing. They ignore that in their final argument. I feel sorry for them. They are doing their best to get Joseph D'Alessandro out of his horrible mistake in granting blanket immunity to Delman 1, Delman 2, and Delman 3. What a lineup.

During jury selection I asked each of you: "Are you intimidated by authority?" Now, you are the final authority. No one can tell you how to apply the law or whether it applies.

The purpose of the criminal law is not to vindicate technicalities or to conduct abstract seminars on conspiracy theories; it should be to protect society from dangerous criminals. Spending a great deal of time and money prosecuting a doctor who allegedly attempted unsuccessfully to complete the voluntary suicide of a wife ravaged by cancer with only days to live is a crazy reason for all of us to be here.

If Peter really wanted to promote his book, he could have given CBS News or *People* magazine an exclusive. If he really intended to kill Pat, he could have injected her with an air bubble; he could have given her all the drugs he had from Dr. Harwin.

If Peter Rosier were the devious, scheming manipulator portrayed by the State, it would have been a breeze for him to accumulate massive amounts of drugs. He is, after all, a doctor, he had the power to write prescriptions or he could have obtained whatever he wanted from the pharmacy at Lee Memorial Hospital.

The medical examiner, Dr. Graves, testified that he has seen hundreds of these kinds of suicides among the terminally ill, but not once was there a prosecution of any family member. And that's where judgment and common sense and common decency and a sense of balance come into play, because these people who assist their loved ones are not criminals.

People who know they are going to die want to die in their own bed, in their own pajamas, surrounded by people who love them, not by strangers. And that's why this kind of thing goes on all the time, and no purpose is served by pretending otherwise. People may have strong abstract feelings on principle that suicide under any circumstances is wrong, but when a loved one who is in agony asks for help in assisting them to end their lives, that is a very tough call. And if someone goes along with that decision, does that make them a criminal? Of course not.

I walked over to Susan to get her input. My sixth sense told me the jury had had it; it was close to 7:00 P.M. The jurors had not had dinner, and they had been sitting there since 8:30 A.M., with the exception of a few short breaks. Had I neglected anything of real significance? The only time I ever saw Susan look so exhausted was after one of her seven C-sections. She said, "Do what you think best." That was the clincher for me. She had had it, too; she had a glazed look. I would cut short my rebuttal by about twenty-five minutes. That was a first for me, I am always begging judges for more time.

> What this case is about is an attempt by a woman to control, or at least shape, the terms of her death, perhaps an attempt to win some perverse victory over the cancer. It was a private thing that became public through the fault of Dr. Rosier. Foolish, self-destructive, yes. But a crime? No!
>
> Suicide is legal in Florida and Dr. Rosier has not been charged with assisting a suicide. There is zero independent evidence from any witness of any interaction between Dr. Rosier and the Delmans during the hours between the time Patricia took the Seconal and the time she died. So you are being asked to convict exclusively on the testimony of the Delmans. You don't imprison someone based on such testimony, which is riddled with contradictions.
>
> The thing that motivated Vincent was that this had gone on long enough: Peter was an incompetent, Pat wanted to die, and he had to pick up his wife at the airport. Peter orchestrated nothing other than a series of misfortunes to himself and to his family from that ill-fated, ill-advised, self-destructive television appearance because he trusted Leisa Zigman and because he was in a very vulnerable state.
>
> Patricia made a decision not to wake up. Vincent Delman says: "I'm not a conspirator with anyone, not even with my sons. I acted on my own and my decision was spur of the moment."
>
> Peter Rosier is a menace to no one. No one could possibly dream that he is a threat to commit a crime in the future. I wonder how many unsolved crimes have been committed in Lee County during this trial. If you are interviewed after returning a not-guilty verdict, you can say: "We don't like Dr. Rosier; we think he did bad things; we think he never should have gone on television; we're against euthanasia." Say whatever you like.
>
> One of the bottom lines here is that Peter Rosier did not begin this death, and he didn't end this death. He did some muddled things in the middle. In no way did Peter Rosier

murder or attempt to murder his childhood sweetheart, his wife of twenty-two years, the mother of his children, the love of his life. We are here because of the overreaction by Mr. D'Alessandro in charging Dr. Rosier with first degree murder, and because of his embarrassing decision to grant immunity to the three Delmans.

To contend that Dr. Rosier is a murderer is a perversion of language, of reality, of justice, and truth. Let the message from your verdict be: "It's a dangerous society out there. Don't waste your time or ours on private tragedies like this." On behalf of Peter I say to you, restore him to his family. Let him go home with Jacob and Elizabeth and Gertrude, who are here and who are supporting him. He is not a criminal; he has committed no crime. You know that. I beseech you to see that justice is done. Don't get caught up in a lot of technical nonsense and details and lesser charges. Don't throw Mr. D'Alessandro a bone by finding Dr. Rosier guilty of some lesser charge. Don't find him guilty of anything.

If there's a meaning and a dimension to all of the lawyering and judging and the law books, hopefully it's to do justice. I ask you, ladies and gentlemen, to do justice; to do the right thing and to find Dr. Rosier not guilty of any and all crimes. Thank you.

The jurors were excused. For the first time during the trial they would all be transported together to a hotel where they would have dinner and spend the night. Judge Thompson would instruct them on the law the following morning. I am not very good at reading jurors and I tend to be suspicious when they seem favorable to me. During final argument I got some bad vibes at times, and I certainly did not like it when a few of the jurors seemed overly interested in the presentations of Volz and Russell.

The hardest part of the final argument for me was having to sit there for the four hours of the State's arguments. I hate waiting. I frequently disappear (much to Susan's consternation) when juries are deliberating. I hate the second-guessing and the inane comments, the questions that have no answers, and the endless speculation: "How long do you think the jury will deliberate before they reach a verdict?" "How long do you want them to be out?"

In several highly publicized criminal cases in New York within the past year or so, juries have actually deliberated for weeks. That would drive me nuts; I am not the kind of person who can work on other cases when a jury is deliberating in a case of this magnitude. That night was a blur and I have very little recollection of it.

We were all there Thursday morning December 1, 1988. The judge read the jury the instructions and they followed along with their individual copies. The jury also had the grand jury indictment and the information and the verdict form.

The caption of the verdict form was: "State of Florida v. Robert Peter Rosier." The verdict form contained ten possibilities:

> First degree murder
>
> Conspiracy to murder in the first degree
>
> Second degree murder
>
> Manslaughter
>
> Attempted first degree murder
>
> Attempted second degree murder
>
> Attempted manslaughter
>
> Aggravated battery
>
> Attempted aggravated battery
>
> Battery

The jury retired to deliberate their verdict at 9:55 A.M. Soon thereafter they asked for all the pertinent exhibits, including Peter's television confession, Pat's television appearance, the two chapters from Peter's manuscript, Russell Delman's cassette, a diagram of the Rosier home, etc.

The jurors had their lunch delivered a little after noon. Peter and I were not hungry. We walked around the lovely lake just across the street from the courthouse. Would the jury have a verdict today or tomorrow or next week? Would we have to remain in St. Petersburg over the weekend? There was no way we could risk returning to Miami without having a result.

At five minutes before 1:00 P.M. there was a bombshell! THE JURY HAD ARRIVED AT A VERDICT. What? How could they have a verdict so soon? What did this mean? If they found Peter guilty of first degree murder, this would mean every one of my instincts and calculations had been absolutely wrong.

The court reporter could not be located. Like everyone else, she did not dream there could be a verdict so fast. After about twenty minutes of scurrying and searching she was found.

The delay allowed the courtroom to become totally packed again with reporters, photographers, television people, interested parties, and spectators. My jacket was drenched with sweat, as was Peter's.

> THE COURT: (*at 1:20 P.M.*) I'm advised that the jury has a verdict. Do we have anything to come to the Court's attention before the verdict is returned? (*No lawyer moved a muscle.*) There being nothing, let me caution the spectators that I understand there are some strong feelings about this matter, but whatever your feelings are you'll have to keep them to yourself if you want to remain in here when the verdict's returned. If you feel you cannot do that, you should step outside now. Return the jury.

The jurors returned to the courtroom. I saw no happy faces. They were as stoic as ever.

> THE COURT: Ladies and gentlemen, I understand you have reached a verdict. Is that correct?
> THE FOREMAN (*Juror Koenig*): Yes, we have, Your Honor.
> THE COURT: Hand it to the clerk.

The clerk immediately handed the verdict to the judge. He spent a long time reading it. Thompson gave no hint of a reaction. He handed the verdict back to the clerk.

> THE COURT: Madam clerk, would you publish the verdict please?
> THE CLERK: State of Florida vs. Robert Peter Rosier, verdict: We, the Jury, find as follows as to Count One of the Indictment: the Defendant is not guilty.
>> We, the Jury, find as follows as to Count Two of the Indictment: the Defendant is not guilty.
>> We, the Jury, find as follows as to the charge in the Information: the Defendant is not guilty.
>> (Bedlam.)

That word is actually contained in the court transcript and it is a perfectly accurate description of the chaos and pandemonium that ensued.

With the third not guilty, the fat lady had truly sung. It was over! The State could not appeal.

> THE COURT: Order in this court. All right. I warned you all before the outset of this, and I'm not going to tolerate that again. (*I have never seen Judge Thompson louder or angrier. On hearing the third "not guilty" Peter and I both jumped out of our seats and pounded on our table several times, and that reaction was aired that night by all the major networks.*) I recognize emotions are very strong. I'm not going to hold anybody in contempt, but if you cannot remain silent, get out of this courtroom.
>
> Ladies and gentlemen, I need to poll you to verify that for each of you this is your verdict. Mrs. Blaney, is that your verdict?
>
> JUROR BLANEY: Yes, sir.
>
> THE COURT: Mrs. Shumway, is that your verdict?
>
> JUROR SHUMWAY: Yes, sir.
>
> THE COURT: Mr. Koenig, is that your verdict?
>
> JUROR KOENIG: Yes.
>
> THE COURT: Ms. Williams, is that your verdict?
>
> JUROR WILLIAMS: Yes, sir.
>
> THE COURT: Mr. Balagna, is this your verdict?
>
> JUROR BALAGNA: Yes.
>
> THE COURT: Ms. Venezia, is this your verdict?
>
> JUROR VENEZIA: Yes, sir.
>
> THE COURT: Mr. Simon, is this your verdict?
>
> JUROR SIMON: Yes.
>
> THE COURT: Mrs. Howard, is this your verdict?
>
> JUROR HOWARD: Yes.
>
> THE COURT: Ms. Gaullin, is this your verdict?
>
> JUROR GAULLIN: Yes.

THE COURT: Mr. Lyons, is this your verdict?

JUROR LYONS: Yes, sir.

THE COURT: Mr. Melke, is this your verdict?

JUROR MELKE: Yes, sir.

THE COURT: And, Mrs. Palmer, is this your verdict?

JUROR PALMER: Yes.

THE COURT: Ladies and gentlemen, I can tell you that you will probably be accosted immediately by the press when you leave here. So I need to read you this instruction. No juror can ever be required to talk about the discussions that take place in the jury room, except by court order. We have recognized for hundreds of years that a jury's deliberations, discussions, and vote should remain their private affair as long as they wish it. Therefore, the law gives you a unique privilege to speak about the jury's work. Although you are at liberty to speak with anyone about your deliberations, you are also at liberty to refuse to speak to anyone. A request may come from those who are simply curious or from those who might seek to find fault with you. It would be up to you to decide whether to preserve your privacy as a juror. . . . We will recess at this time.

I loved the jury; they were terrific. They pardoned Peter, ignored the law and the Delmans, and did what was right. They were courageous enough not to throw the State a bone by convicting Peter of something less than first degree murder. They did not prolong their deliberations to pretend that they were sifting and weighing and measuring everything.

They went with their gut, and they realized the criminal law should be invoked against real criminals and real crimes. They were not taken in by the State's authority, rigidity, or flag waving. They did not buy the proposition that it would be a dereliction of their duty to society to find the defendant not guilty.

Peter was ecstatic and grateful. His embraces with his children, Gertrude, Patricia's Aunt Marcia, and his fiancée's mother were moving and long-lasting. His fiancée had remained at the condominium; she had never set foot in the courthouse, but his fiancée's mother, a charming and compassionate woman, attended the entire trial.

Robin drove Susan and I back to the hotel. Boxes and boxes of files and depositions would need to be packed in our Silverado truck, which Robin would drive to Miami in a few days. Susan and I flew home the morning after the verdict (Friday). We would join our brood for Shabbos. They were as unruly as ever, but they never looked better. There is truly no place like home.

20

Closing Thoughts

Peter Rosier helped his cancer-stricken wife commit suicide. Derek Humphry helped his cancer-stricken first wife commit suicide. Betty Rollin, the former NBC television newswoman, helped her cancer-stricken mother commit suicide. All three of them wrote books about their experiences. The books by Humphry and Rollin were published and sold well. The Rosier manuscript has never been published.

Peter Rosier was indicted for first degree murder; no charges were ever brought against Humphry or Rollin. Why? In part because Humphry and Rollin were likeable, and Rosier was not. Rosier was perceived as an arrogant violator of the law, whereas they were not.

Mike Tyson was convicted of rape; William Kennedy Smith was acquitted of rape. The different results were primarily due to public relations, external appearances, and strategy rather than the facts or the law. Should euthanasia prosecutions be decided by the whims of political prosecutors? Certainly not.

Our legal system has not been creative enough to treat assisted suicides by family members or physicians differently from a murder that occurs during an armed robbery. The practical solution to this problem has been for prosecutors to look the other way. The situation is not terribly dissimilar to what existed when abortions were illegal; prosecutions were extremely rare and almost unheard of against middle- and upper-class women who were terminated by a physician who was not an "abortionist."

Prosecutors go after unpopular and controversial people who have broken the euthanasia code of silence, like Peter Rosier and Jack Kevorkian (the Michigan pathologist of "suicide machine" fame). No attempt has

341

been made to identify the doctor who anonymously wrote the "Dear Debbie" article for the *Journal of the American Medical Association,* wherein he admitted "killing" a patient who was a total stranger to him. No public official came under attack for failing to prosecute Betty Rollin, Derek Humphry, Dr. Anonymous, or Dr. Timothy Quill.

Dr. Quill, a Rochester, New York, internist, authored an article in the March 1991 edition of *The New England Journal of Medicine* wherein he admitted prescribing enough barbiturates to enable a forty-five-year-old female patient with leukemia to kill herself. In spite of the fact that in New York aiding a suicide can result in a prison sentence of from five to fifteen years, a grand jury in Rochester declined on July 26, 1991, to indict Dr. Quill.

The Quill situation demonstrates just how quirky euthanasia cases can become when they got entangled in the legal morass. After Dr. Quill's article appeared, the district attorney in Rochester made a reasoned decision to do nothing. However, an anonymous tip to the prosecutor's office identified the patient and led them to her body, which was being stored for future dissection. An autopsy established the presence of a fatal dose of barbiturates, which in turn led to proceedings before the grand jury, which ultimately decided not to indict.

Consistent with the experiences of Dr. Rosier and several physicians who were prepared to testify for the defense, Dr. Quill said he had learned from scores of accounts that his story was merely the tip of the iceberg in that many doctors told him they had done similar things in secret. Dr. Quill decided to go public partly to represent an alternative to Dr. Jack Kevorkian's approach.

Dr. Kevorkian, a retired Michigan pathologist, became a national figure when it was disclosed that Janet Adkins used his "suicide machine" to kill herself on a cot in Kevorkian's 1968 van. A lethal overdose is one thing, a suicide machine quite another. I believe this difference in methods —one being seen as dignified and the other as flamboyant—explains in large part the very different ways Quill and Kevorkian have been treated by the American crimnal justice system.

As a result of the Adkins case, Dr. Kevorkian was charged with murder. However, on December 13, 1990, at a preliminary hearing, a Michigan trial judge dismissed the murder charges, ruling that Mrs. Adkins had caused her own death. The judge agreed with the medical examiner, who had previously ruled her death to be a suicide. Michigan at that time had no law making it a crime to assist a suicide.

However, a judicial order was entered prohibiting Dr. Kevorkian from using his machine again. In spite of that order, on October 23, 1991, Dr.

Kevorkian assisted two other women in their "suicides." The medical examiner in those cases concluded that the deaths were homicides. On February 5, 1992, Dr. Kevorkian was again charged with murder by a grand jury.

Dr. Kevorkian is a man not easily deterred. Fifty-two-year-old Susan Williams, long disabled by multiple sclerosis, took her life with Dr. Kevorkian's help on May 15, 1992. On June 6, 1992, the chief deputy medical examiner of Oakland County found that Ms. Williams was too weak to connect a cannister of carbon monoxide to her bed, thereby concluding that her death was a homicide and not a suicide. A primary basis for this conclusion was the videotape evidence of the death provided by Dr. Kevorkian himself.

On July 21, 1992, a circuit court judge dismissed the murder charges involving the "double suicide," because he was not convinced that Dr. Kevorkian had himself activated the suicide machine. The Oakland County prosecutor condemned the decision and said he would appeal it. He asserted that if the ruling went unchallenged, Michigan would be the only state in the nation to legalize active euthanasia.

No criminal charges were brought in the Williams case, as the authorities awaited the outcome of the earlier prosecution. The uncertainty persists. I expect that Dr. Kevorkian will one day be a defendant in a highly publicized murder trial.

Derek Humphry vigorously disagrees with Dr. Kevorkian's approach, particularly because Humphry's focus is entirely on the terminally ill whereas Kevorkian is willing to assist in the suicide of individuals who are not yet in that category. Humphry believes that Kevorkian has hurt the cause of the Hemlock Society and seems to hold Kevorkian at least partly responsible for the narrow defeat of the Washington state initiative, which was voted upon only days after the widely publicized "double suicide" in October 1991.

A revolutionary proposal was submitted to the voters in Washington on November 5, 1991. If it had passed, this initiative would have legalized active euthanasia. Active euthanasia has not been legalized in any nation or state to date. It is not even legal in the Netherlands, where since 1984 euthanasia has been tolerated by an understanding between prosecutors and physicians. If certain criteria are met doctors may give or inject lethal doses of drugs to their patients without fear of prosecution. The Supreme Court of the Netherlands (Dutch) has approved this arrangement.

The question in Washington was framed as follows: "Shall adult patients who are in a medically terminal condition be permitted to request and receive aid in dying?"

In a vote that would have been unthinkable a few short years ago, 701,818 citizens of the State of Washington voted in favor of the initiative; this represented 46 percent of the vote. That number is even more amazing in the context of jury selection during the Rosier trial, where every single prospective juror said they did not believe in active euthanasia. Through the determined efforts of Derek Humphry and the National Hemlock Society as well as other organizations, a similar proposal will probably appear on the ballot in California in November, 1992. This act would make it lawful for a physician to assist a suicide either by giving a prescription for a legal overdose or by administering a lethal injection. Win or lose in California (and I tend to think it will win), such laws are clearly the wave of the future.

The public's deep interest in this subject was vividly demonstrated by the phenomenal sales of Derek Humphry's book *Final Exit* (subtitled "The Practicalities of Self-Deliverance and Assisted Suicide for the Dying"). Without a plot, without characters, without sex or violence, this suicide manual became a runaway best seller.

Derek Humphry has announced his retirement from the Hemlock Society effective August 1, 1992. Derek sat through the Rosier trial from beginning to end and has done the same in other euthanasia trials. He understood perfectly the dynamics and risk of our "repudiate the law" strategy. Derek was fond of saying that, "A jury of twelve lawyers would have convicted Peter Rosier over a cup of coffee," and he was correct. He knew that in order for us to gain an acquittal, we would need to reach above the dry law to the hearts and minds of the jury.

In the newsletter of the Hemlock Society, which appeared following the verdict, Derek said: "After ten years of struggle to get public understanding of the legal dilemma of those who must help a dying loved one commit suicide, I think we can claim the acquittal of Dr. Peter Rosier on charges of murdering his wife as a significant victory, perhaps a turning point."

Obviously, a new day is dawning in public attitudes toward the issue of euthanasia. Many people are convinced that the right to die and the right to control the timing and circumstances of one's death will be one of the two or three paramount domestic issues of the 1990s. I agree with that view.

Americans have a "there oughta be a law" mentality. If there is a problem, pass a law to solve it. We are the ever-hopeful Charlie Browns; we keep trying to kick that football but it is always pulled away at the last second. It had been my intention in this final chapter to provide a glossary of state laws dealing with euthanasia-related subjects, such as living wills and when life support technology may be suspended. I concluded that this is such a fluid area that many of these laws will be obsolete or substantially modified by the time *Murder of Mercy* appears in bookstores.

Even the United States Supreme Court, for the first time, has entered the euthanasia debate. They did so in the tragic case of Nancy Cruzan, a resident of the State of Missouri. Ms. Cruzan had been in a vegetative state for seven years following an automobile accident. Her parents decided in total good faith to remove their daughter's feeding tube. The State of Missouri refused to honor this request, taking the position that all human life is worthy of protection regardless of its quality.

The U.S. Supreme Court in effect recognized Nancy Cruzan's right to die. The justices concluded that there was a constitutional right to refuse medical care, including feeding tubes. There was a slight catch in that the Court also said a state could require "clear and convincing evidence" that removal of the tube is what the patient would have wanted. Without that level of proof, life-sustaining equipment would remain in place. There will undoubtedly be lengthy trials in diverse jurisdictions to determine whether the "clear and convincing" standard has been met. Mr. and Mrs. Cruzan met the standard to the satisfaction of a particular trial judge, the feeding tube was removed, and their daughter died.

Sue Ann Lawrance had been unconscious since she fell from her wheelchair in 1987. Her parents, like the Cruzans, wanted to remove her feeding tube. This case was particularly memorable since it represented the first time in which a federally financed law center with ties to the National Right to Life Committee was granted legal standing to appeal a lower court decision allowing removal of the feeding tube. The patient's parents were incensed by this interference, as the parents of Nancy Cruzan were incensed that the State of Missouri refused to abide by their wishes.

On September 16, 1991, the Indiana Supreme Court ruled that the parents did have the right to end the tube feeding of their daughter, who was deemed to be in a persistent vegetative state. A persistent vegetative state is usually defined as one in which personality, memory, social interaction, thought, and emotional states are lost. Advocates for the disabled and handicapped fear that the clear lines of distinction between their charges and those in a persistent vegetative state could become blurred.

A very far-reaching federal law took effect on December 1, 1991. Titled "The Patient Self-Determination Act," it requires that every patient admitted to any hospital for any reason be asked if they want to plan for their death by filling out a Living Will. That's going to scare the hell out of someone being hospitalized overnight for a bunionectomy, hernia surgery, or merely for tests.

Living Wills and other advance directives where people write down their intentions about turning off life-support systems, if they are ever incapacitated, are the wave of the immediate future. Such advance planning makes great sense and can avoid all kinds of problems.

Every state, with the exception of Nebraska and Pennsylvania, has laws saying they will honor at least one form of advance directive. Patients have been given the right to reject aggressive medical care, whether it be in the form of a respirator, cardiac resuscitation, or nasogastric tubes. These laws are very new.

In 1991, doctors in Minnesota filed suit so that they could be permitted to disconnect the respirator of an eighty-seven-year-old woman whose family was insisting that she be maintained on life-support systems. The doctors demonstrated that she was in an irreversible coma and that her care was costing nearly one million dollars a year. They lost. Does a patient have the right to demand unceasing medical treatment in a hopeless case? Minnesota says yes.

In March 1992, a state senator in Iowa introduced a bill that would amend that state's Living Will to permit physician-assisted suicide. Michigan, Maine, and New Hampshire have similar physician-aid-in-dying bills in the works; each bill would require an advance directive authorizing such actions.

As of May 1992, twenty-eight states had surrogate or proxy laws allowing family members to base their decision on what they believe the patient would have wanted were the patient ever to become incapacitated. Many of the laws provide that if the surrogate (family member, physician, or friend) does not know the patient's wishes, the surrogate is then empowered to make that decision in the patient's best interest. The specific provisions vary from statute to statute, and nearly every state is considering similar laws.

All of these statutes and court decisions are depressingly indicative of the hit-and-miss, nudging-in-tiny-increments way in which American society so often operates in the legal realm. It reminds me in a way of our approach to the tobacco problem. For well over thirty years it has been known that cigarettes cause cancer, other terrible diseases, and death. The scientific evidence is so overwhelming that no reasonable person will argue against the causal relationship between tobacco and cancer.

Millions of cancer deaths later, do we even dream of ridding our society of tobacco? Of course not. The cowboys from the early Marlboro ads are dead from lung cancer. We ban tobacco advertising on television; we require health warnings on cigarette packages; we ban smoking in a zillion places including airplanes (because we have learned that second-hand smoke can kill nonsmokers); and we debate and pass ordinance after ordinance, statute after statute, and regulation after regulation. Millions of Americans continue to smoke.

In July 1991, the General Assembly of the Church of Christ became the first major religious denomination to accept suicide for the hopelessly ill. The Roman Catholic Church, the Southern Baptist Convention, and Orthodox Judaism are opposed to all forms of euthanasia or suicide.

In the last few years prominent Catholic theologians, individual bishops, and even some state conferences of bishops have issued contrasting opinions on the propriety of withdrawing food and fluids from the permanently comatose. On April 2, 1992, a committee of the nation's Roman Catholic bishops issued a warning against the increasingly widespread practice of withdrawing food and liquid even from irreversibly unconscious patients. These issues will be around for many years to come and can never be entirely solved even by the best intentions and the most artful drafting of statutory language.

I am personally comfortable with the position of my religion, but that does not blind me to the wrenching realities and soul-searching involved in euthanasia decisions. It is possible to be opposed to abortion and at the same time believe that women who choose that option should not be punished in any way.

If a terminally ill patient in great pain makes an informed choice to die and asks for the assistance of a loved one or a long-time personal physician, I do not view that as a problem for the American criminal justice system. Certainly not one that calls for punishment. It is easy to philosophize in the abstract and to pontificate about absolute rights and absolute wrongs, but it is quite another thing for a person to be in a situation calling for a heavy, practical decision. The Rosier jury appreciated that distinction.

Few of us will escape any involvement. Some years back my very best friend was scheduled to undergo hemorrhoid surgery, a very minor-league operation. As a result of blatant malpractice, involving anesthetic agents and egregious judgment by the physicians, my friend, age thirty-nine and in perfect health, sustained a cardiac and respiratory arrest that caused him to become comatose. The surgery had never even begun.

He remained in a coma for twenty-six days, totally nonresponsive and going progressively downhill. My friend expired naturally on the twenty-sixth day. I spent hours with him, his wife, and their two children every one of those twenty-six days. If his coma had lasted much longer, with no hope of recovery, it would have been very difficult to rule out arguments in favor of terminating heroic measures. Waiting and watching is terribly debilitating.

Our secretary, Robin Berger, who was with us throughout the Rosier trial in St. Petersburg, has become a very strong believer in euthanasia because of a harrowing experience with her grandmother, with whom she had always been extremely close.

Robin's grandmother drove herself to the hospital and walked in to be admitted for open heart surgery and a valve replacement. Following the surgery she suffered a stroke, was placed on a respirator, and remained in intensive care for some four months. Intermittently Robin's grandmother was capable of communicating; it was a horrible ordeal.

Toward the end the patient was experiencing continual seizures, which could not be quelled. Robin and her mother decided to put their beloved mother and grandmother in a hospice program; in three days she passed away. These events occurred over two years after the conclusion of Peter's trial.

On April 10, 1992, there was a seminar on "The Right to Die" held at the Sheraton Brickell Point Hotel in Miami. This program was put on by "Continuing Legal Education International." The seminar was described in their literature as "a comprehensive seminar for lawyers and health care professionals exploring current and emerging issues involved in the decision to withhold or withdraw life-sustaining medical treatment (approved by the Florida State Bar for eight hours of CLE credit and one hour of ethics credit)."

Among the faculty members were the Chaplain of the Pastoral Care Department at St. Mary's Hospital in West Palm Beach, the State Attorney for the Fifteenth Judicial Circuit of Florida in West Palm Beach, a professor of medicine and medical director of the medical intensive care unit/coronary care unit at Shands Hospital at the University of Florida in Gainesville, a professor of law at the University of Pittsburgh in the schools of law and medicine, the president of the Hemlock Society of Washington State, and the associate executive director of the Miami Jewish Home and Hospital for the Aged.

Such seminars are becoming extremely commonplace. Some of the euthanasia organizations mirror those involved in the abortion controversy: among them are the National Right to Life Committee and, of course, the flipside of that coin—the Society for the Right to Die.

Semantics and definitions are discussed in depth at these seminars. If someone has an incurable disease but they may live for a year or longer, are they "terminally ill"? Each state can establish its own criteria. Some other words and phrases, the precise definition of which can have profound practical consequences include: "brain dead," "gravely ill," "severely ill," "totally disabled," "incurable," "aid in dying," "irreversible," "persistent vegetative state," and "intractable suffering."

One frightening thing I learned during my defense of Dr. Rosier was how very easy it is to cause death to someone who is on a morphine drip. The patient has cancer or some other dread disease, and death is expected at any time so there is no reason for suspicion and no reason to perform an autopsy.

In the United States hospices generally provide home care services, but they do not provide twenty-four-hour nursing care; therefore, the burden of hour-to-hour care generally falls on family members. And if a family member, friend, or employee is so disposed, the opportunity is there to hasten death at any time.

Dr. Graves and every other medical examiner in the United States has seen many suicides among the terminally ill. I presume that the majority of these suicides are assisted in some manner, or at the very least friends and relatives know about the act. Dr. Dosoretz testified that he hears from patients all the time that they intend to take their own lives; he never reported any such confession to the authorities. Drs. Gerson and Iannone said that they never heard of any physician reporting such a conversation.

Of course, absent bizarre circumstances, no one is ever prosecuted for helping someone commit suicide. If no one is in the forest to hear the tree fall, did it really make a noise? If a criminal law is on the books, but no one is ever prosecuted under it, is it really a law?

Dr. Iannone and Dr. Hurwitz readily admitted that morphine drips are frequently increased to deliberately cause death. Dr. Iannone further agreed that doctors hasten death intentionally and that this goes on all the time. How could it be otherwise, considering the realities? Without a religious basis or some other strong belief system in opposition to suicide, there are many rational and appealing arguments to be made in favor of sparing loved ones grief, cutting short pointless agony, and saving untold millions of dollars annually on supportive care for the terminally ill.

The theoreticians and professors opposed to euthanasia can construct logical arguments about the detriment to the individual, families, and society that may ensue from deliberately hastening death. But they are not in that room minute by minute watching a once powerful and articulate individual waste away. They are not the family members or health care providers who have to deal with the vomit, the stool, pain, the drooling, and the spasms. These caretakers are hardly in the mood for a lecture.

Because of the catastrophe of AIDS these life-and-death decisions are being made many times every day all over America and all over the world.

There are few easy answers. The particular facts, the makeup of the patient, and the nature of his or her family relationships would have to be known in great detail for me to be able to express an opinion on the appropriateness of given conduct.

Had I been on the Roswell Gilbert jury, I may have found him guilty of some crime, certainly not first degree murder. His wife was not terminally ill; she had no thoughts of suicide or death; and Mr. Gilbert, without her permission or knowledge, shot her in the head. A society cannot tolerate a condition where people (no matter how well-intentioned) subjectively decide that someone else has a very poor quality of life and would be better off dead.

In spite of all the mistakes Peter Rosier made in involving the three Delmans, Drs. Carlino, Dosoretz, and Harwin; as well as his secretary and others, he was still home free had he never confessed on television. His manuscript was all over Fort Myers and no one said a word to the police or to the State Attorney's Office. The hypocrisy that exists in this country in the area of euthanasia is unbearable. How can people be told in a very self-righteous manner to follow the law when the law makes no sense and when it is invoked capriciously, randomly, and selectively?

Active euthanasia goes on all the time, as do assisted suicides. That is reality. Little will change regardless of the words and phrases that are contained in dusty statute books. Women will continue to have abortions regardless of what the U.S. Supreme Court does or doesn't do concerning *Roe* v. *Wade*. We need understanding and straight talk on this subject.

The debate should center on safeguards to protect the most vulnerable members of our society—poor people and/or those without relatives or friends and those without insurance. There must be a simple mechanism in place, unburdened by layers of bureaucracy, to see that the safeguards are effective. I don't see the best solutions in the political, legislative, or legal realms. The ultimate solutions or accommodations lie in decent values where the rights of the lonely, the elderly, and the unfortunate are respected.

If a person is truly interested in alleviating the anguish of loved ones should a tragic illness or accident occur, there is a responsibility to write out a Living Will making one's intentions known. Before a person can do that intelligently, he or she should go into a private room, close the door, and think about it. Many people have never honestly examined their own feelings and thoughts about death.

A Living Will can be a very short and simple document. It should be signed, witnessed, and notarized. The laws vary from state to state so the language of your particular statute should be checked out. What I am proposing here would be acceptable in nearly all jurisdictions. The

Living Will could say something like: "If I am ever incapacitated to the extent that I am incapable of making my wishes known, I would like to set forth herein my strong convictions on the subject of prolonging or not prolonging my life.

"If my condition is medically hopeless (meaning I will never recover my faculties of memory and intellect), I would not want to be kept alive by a respirator or a feeding tube or by any other artificial means."

You could appoint one or two people to make that decision for you if the situation is less than clear-cut. You could be more specific in discussing disabilities, such as inability to walk or talk, what you would want to occur if you were minimally responsive or barely conscious. You would probably want to give a copy of your Living Will to your closest relative, your best friend, your personal physician if you have one, and your attorney.

When we left the courthouse after the verdict, Peter received his second greatest gift. He could now talk to his heart's content, and he had lots of ears. *People* magazine did a spread on the trial, and there is one picture in particular that sums up Peter's glory: he is surrounded and squished by an army of reporters and photographers from publications all over the country and world.

Susan and I watched that scene for several minutes at a distance before we returned to the Hilton. As we were getting out of our truck in the parking lot, we ran into Edward Volz, Stephen Russell, and James Fitzpatrick. They were truly professional in their reaction in that they were friendly, charitable in their comments, and open. They were bitterly disappointed but they nonetheless displayed humor and an admirable sense of balance. They were among the worthiest opponents I have ever had.

On our way to the airport the next day we saw newsstands containing the *St. Petersburg Times* and the *Tampa Tribune*. Each newspaper had a blazing headline about the trial and Peter's large color photograph on the front page surrounded by eager listeners. After all, these people had heard about Peter Rosier in great detail for well over a month but they had not heard him utter a word in the courtroom.

Susan and I took the children (Miriam, Joshua, Rachel, Rebecca, David, and Jaclyn) on vacation to the Concord Hotel in the Catskills during the winter school recess. We saw Joan Rivers, Jackie Mason, and lots of snow. On the very first day, there I tried ice skating; after all I was a terrific skater in Brooklyn when I was seven or eight. I nearly broke my ankle, visited the emergency room of a hospital, and was on crutches for the entire "vacation." Peter and his fiancée had drive up for a few days and Peter insisted that my ankle be X-rayed.

A few days after we returned from New York, we had to leave for Houston (early January 1989). Susan and I flew but Robin was on the road again with all our files, depositions, and exhibits. That girl just loves to drive.

We had a trial scheduled in federal court before a superb judge, Chief Federal District Court Judge James DeAnda. We were convinced the case would get settled after a couple of days of trial. It turned out we were very wrong on that subject and we remained in Houston for seven weeks, never being able to return home because of the trial schedule and the length of the trip.

That was by far the longest time we had ever been away from the children. We vowed, never again. Fortunately we had Susan's mother, Shirley Goldman, and my brother and sisters plus a wonderful nanny, Catherine, to look after the kids. Shirley moved in and that gave us peace of mind.

The case in Houston was against the Arabian American Oil Company—Aramco. My client was an engineer, who had been employed by Aramco in Saudi Arabia, and his wife. They were the parents of an infant who had been improperly treated for seizures by a physician employed by Aramco. Tragically the child suffered permanent brain damage. Although the Houston law firm never offered us a dime in the way of settlement, the jury returned an excellent verdict in favor of our clients.

The Houston trial was the longest of my career; for the second time ever, Susan sat with me at counsel table and made legal objections in the presence of the jury. Another great dividend from Houston: Susan became pregnant with Rina, our Texas Tornado. We intend to stay put in Miami for quite some time. Peter got married in Boston. We were in Houston and did not attend.

Edward Volz became a county court judge; Stephen Russell and James Fitzpatrick remain with the State Attorney's Office, which has jurisdiction over Lee, Charlotte, Collier, Glades, and Hendry counties. Joseph D'Alessandro remains the number-one man with about sixty assistant state attorneys working under him.

Between raising eight children—from eleven months to eleven years of age—and a busy law practice, Susan and I have little time for socializing. Our Saturday night routine: I take "The Big Guys" to the movies and Susan catches up on her general reading. Of course, if the "Little Guys" refuse to go to sleep, Susan makes popcorn and pops in a video for them.

A dull life to some, but considering the excitement and aggravation in the cases we handle, that's the way we like it.